ALBERTA
AND THE ROCKIES

©Travel Alberta

D1419989

Editorial Director   Cynthia Clayton Ochterbeck

THE GREEN GUIDE ALBERTA AND THE ROCKIES

Editor   Gwen Cannon
Contributing Writers   Margaret Lemay, Susan Mate
Researcher   Susan Scott
Production Manager   Natasha G. George
Cartography   Mapmobility Corp., Peter Wrenn
Photo Editor   Yoshimi Kanazawa
Proofreader   Claiborne Linvill
Layout & Design   Nicole D. Jordan
Cover Design   Laurent Muller, Ute Weber

Contact Us: The Green Guide
                                    Michelin Maps and Guides
                                    One Parkway South
                                    Greenville, SC 29615
                                    USA
                                    www.michelintravel.com
                                    michelin.guides@us.michelin.com

                                    Michelin Maps and Guides
                                    Hannay House
                                    39 Clarendon Road
                                    Watford, Herts WD17 1JA
                                    UK
                                    ☎ (01923) 205 240
                                    www.ViaMichelin.com
                                    travelpubsales@uk.michelin.com

Special Sales: For information regarding bulk sales,
                                    customized editions and premium sales,
                                    please contact our Customer Service
                                    Departments:
                                    USA   1-800-432-6277
                                    UK   (01923) 205 240
                                    Canada 1-800-361-8236

One Team...
A Commitment to Quality

There's just one reason our team is dedicated to producing quality travel publications—you, our reader.

Throughout our guides we offer **practical information**, **touring tips** and **suggestions** for finding the best places for a break.

Michelin driving tours help you hit the highlights and quickly absorb the best of the region. Our descriptive **walking tours** make you your own guide, armed with directions, maps and expert information.

We scout out the attractions, classify them with **star ratings**, and describe in detail what you will find when you visit them.

Michelin maps featured throughout the guide offer vibrant, detailed and easy-to-follow outlines of everything from close-up museum plans to international maps.

Places to stay and eat are always a big part of travel, so we research **hotels and restaurants** that we think convey the essence of the destination and arrange them by geographic area and price. We walk you through the best shopping districts and point you towards the host of entertainment and recreation possibilities available.

We **test**, **retest**, **check and recheck** to make sure that our guidebooks are truly just that: a personalized guide to help you make the most of your visit. And if you still want a speaking guide, we list local tour guides who will lead you on all the boat, bus, guided, historical, culinary, and other tours you shouldn't miss.

In short, we remove the guesswork involved with travel. After all, we want you to enjoy exploring with Michelin as much as we do.

The Michelin Green Guide Team

PLANNING YOUR TRIP

INTRODUCTION TO ALBERTA AND THE ROCKIES

©Travel Alberta

©Travel Alberta

CONTENTS

DISCOVERING ALBERTA AND THE ROCKIES

©Travel Alberta

HOW TO USE THIS GUIDE

PLANNING YOUR TRIP

The blue-tabbed PLANNING YOUR TRIP section at the front of the guide gives you **ideas for your trip** and **practical information** to help you organize it. You'll find tours, ideas for recreation in the great outdoors, a calendar of events, information on shopping, sightseeing, kids' activities and more.

INTRODUCTION

The orange-tabbed INTRODUCTION section explores **Nature** from the plains to the mountains. The **History** section spans from early settlement up to the present. The **Art and Culture** section covers art, literature, music and dance and cinema, while the **Alberta Today** delves into modern Alberta.

DISCOVERING

The green-tabbed DISCOVERING section features Alberta's Principal Sights, arranged geographically and by region, featuring the most interesting local **Sights**, **Walking Tours**, nearby **Excursions**, and detailed **Driving Tours**.

🖹Contact information, ⬧admission charges, 🕐hours of operation, and a host of other **visitor information** are given wherever possible. Admission prices shown are normally for a single adult.

STAR RATINGS★★★

Michelin has given star ratings for more than 100 years. If you're pressed for time, we recommend you visit the ★★★ or ★★ sights first:

★★★	Highly recommended
★★	Recommended
★	Interesting

Sidebars

Throughout the guide you will find peach-colored text boxes (like this one), with lively anecdotes, detailed history and background information.

Address Books - Where to Stay, Eat and more...

WHERE TO STAY

We've made a selection of lodgings and arranged them within the towns by price category to fit all budgets (*see the Legend on the cover flap for an explanation of the price categories*). For the most part, we've selected accommodations based on their unique regional quality, their regional feel, as it were. So, unless the individual lodging embodies local ambience, it's rare that we include chain properties, which typically have their own imprint.
See the back of the guide for an index to the accommodations featured throughout the guide.

WHERE TO EAT

We thought you'd like to know the popular eating spots in Alberta. So, we selected restaurants that capture the regional experience—those that have a unique regional flavor (*see the Legend on the cover flap for an explanation of the price categories*). We're not rating the quality of the food per se; as we did with the hotels, we selected restaurants for many towns and villages, categorized by price to appeal to all wallets.
See the back of the guide for an index to the restaurants featured throughout the guide.

MAPS

- Regional **Driving Tours** maps.
- Alberta map with the **Principal Sights** highlighted.
- Maps for major **cities** and **villages**.
- **Local tour** maps.

All maps in this guide are oriented north, unless otherwise indicated by a directional arrow. The term "Local Map" refers to a map within the chapter or Tourism Region. A complete list of the maps found in the guide appears at the back of this book, as well as a comprehensive index and list of restaurants and accommodations.

See the map Legend at the back of the guide for an explanation of map symbols.

A Bit of Advice

Green advice boxes found in this guide contain practical tips and handy information relevant to the sight in the Discovering section.

ORIENT PANELS

Vital statistics are given for each principal sight in the DISCOVERING section:

- **Information**: Tourist Office/Sight contact details.
- ▶ **Orient Yourself:** Geographic location of the sight with reference to the downtown core as well as surrounding towns and roads.
- P **Parking:** Where to park.
- **Don't Miss:** Unmissable things to do.
- **Organizing Your Time:** Tips on organizing your stay; what to see first, how long to spend, crowd avoidance, market days and more.
- **Especially for Kids:** Sights of particular interest to children.
- **Also See:** Nearby PRINCIPAL SIGHTS featured elsewhere in the guide.

SYMBOLS

Spa	**Spa Facilities**		**Tours**
Kids	**Interesting for Children**	P	**On-site Parking**
	Also See	▶	**Directions**
	Tourist Information	✕	**On-site Eating Facilities**
⊕	**Hours of Operation**		**Swimming Pool**
⊘	**Periods of Closure**	⚠	**Camping Facilities**
⊶	**Closed to the Public**		**Beaches**
⊜	**Entry Fees**		**Breakfast Included**
	Credit Cards not Accepted		**A Bit of Advice**
♿	**Wheelchair Accessible**		**Warning**

Contact - Addresses, phone numbers, opening hours and prices published in this guide are accurate at the time of press. We welcome corrections and suggestions that may assist us in preparing the next edition. Please send your comments to:

UK
Michelin Maps and Guides
Hannay House
39 Clarendon Road
Watford, Herts WD17 1JA
travelpubsales@uk.michelin.com
www.michelin.co.uk

USA
Michelin Maps and Guides
Editorial Department
P.O. Box 19001
Greenville, SC 29602-9001
michelin.guides@us.michelin.com
www.michelintravel.com

Writing-on-Stone Provincial Park,
Southern Alberta
©Randy Mayes/iStockphoto.com

PLANNING YOUR TRIP

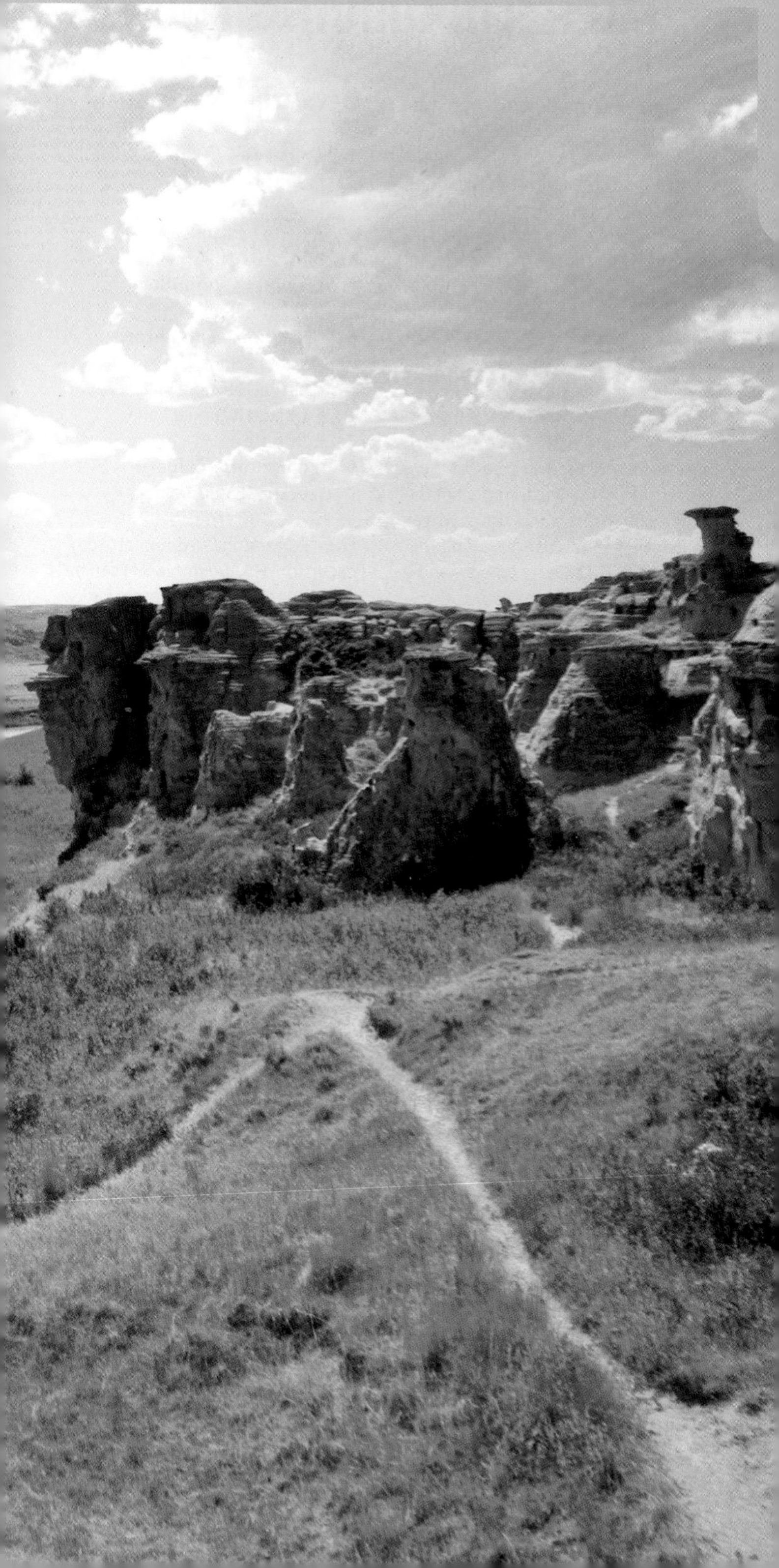

MICHELIN DRIVING TOURS

Driving allows travellers to appreciate the vastness of this province, where distances between cities and towns can be great. The following two fast-paced tours, in duration 9 days and 12 days, respectively, are intended as planning tools, not as fixed routes.

1 Calgary-Edmonton Loop

Round-trip of 1,361km/844mi from Calgary. Time: 9 days. This tour enables visitors to discover some of the fascination of the westernmost of the Prairie provinces: grand vistas, wheat fields, ranches and cowboys. The oil-rich Alberta cities of Calgary and Edmonton are visited as well as the Alberta Badlands.

DAYS/ ITINERARY/ SIGHTS

1–2 **Calgary**★★
3   **Calgary – Elkwater** (432km/268mi); Alberta Badlands★★★
4   **Elkwater** Cypress Hills★★
5   **Elkwater – Vermilion** (478km/296mi)
6   **Vermilion – Edmonton** (154km/95mi); Ukrainian Cultural Heritage Village★; Elk Island National Park★
7–8 **Edmonton**★★
9   **Edmonton – Calgary** (297km/185mi); Calgary★★

From Edmonton, an optional 5-day excursion of 1,106km/686mi can be made to the Rocky Mountain Parks: Edmonton–Jasper 339km/210mi; Jasper–Lake Louise; Lake Louise–Calgary 214km/133mi.

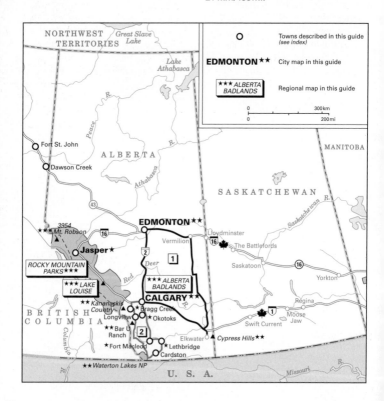

2 Southern Alberta

Round-trip of 642km/400mi from
Calgary. Time: 12 days. This tour treats
visitors to a variety of natural and
manmade attractions situated in the
southern portion of the province. Bar
U Ranch, Waterton National Park and
Head-Smashed-In Buffalo Jump are
highlights.

DAYS/ ITINERARY/ SIGHTS

1–2 **Calgary**★★

3-4 **Calgary – Bragg Creek**
(45km/28mi); Kananaskis Area★★
5 **Bragg Creek – Waterton**
(251km/155mi); Bar U Ranch★★
6–7 **Waterton;** Waterton
National Park★★
8 **Waterton – Lethbridge**
(123km/76mi); Cardston
9–10 **Lethbridge**★
11 **Lethbridge – Fort McLeod**
(50km/30mi); Head-Smashed-In
Buffalo Jump★★
12 **Fort McLeod – Calgary**
(173km/107mi); Okotoks

WHEN AND WHERE TO GO

When to Go

CLIMATE

Climatic conditions vary across
Alberta. Winter is generally long and
cold; summer is short and hot. Precipitation is low (380-500mm/15-20in a
year), sometimes arriving in the form
of blizzards in winter and thunder-
storms in summer. July is the driest
and hottest month: mean maximum
for Calgary is 24°C/76°F. Daily weather
reports by Environment Canada are
available on television and radio,
in newspapers and on the Internet
(www.weatheroffice.gc.ca). Other
online weather services are
www.theweathernetwork.com
and www.weather.com.

SEASONS

Alberta's main **tourist season**
extends from the last Monday on or
before May 24 (Victoria Day) to the
first Monday in September (Labour
Day). Many attractions lengthen the
season to the Thanksgiving weekend
(second Monday in October). In mid-
size to large cities, sights are usually
open year-round, though often at
reduced hours.
From mid-April to mid-May, visitors
can enjoy comfortable daytime
temperature but chilly nights in

spring; in some mountain parks,
spring skiing is still possible well into
May or even June.
Most visitors go to Alberta during the
summer season, extending from the
last weekend in May to early September. July and August are considered
peak season and are ideal for outdoor
activities such as kayaking, cycling,
canoeing and hiking. Hot but rarely
humid days will see temperatures
ranging from 20°-33°C/68°-90°F
across most of the province. May and
September are pleasant months with
warm days but cool evenings. The
southern regions along the Canada/
US border as well as the forests of the
mountain parks exhibit brilliant **fall**
colours from mid-September until
early October.
For the sports enthusiast, the Alberta
winter, generally from mid-November to mid-March, offers excellent
opportunities to enjoy an array of
winter activities such as downhill
skiing, cross-country skiing, snowshoeing and snowmobiling.
Most areas of Alberta experience
moderate to heavy snowfall, but each
winter can be vastly different.
Main highways are snowploughed,
but vehicles should be winterized and
snow tires are recommended.
The far northern regions of Alberta are
accessible year-round except sections
of the Athabasca River delta north of

Fort McMurray. Communities such as Fort Chipewyan can be reached only by winter ice road, usually December to early February and otherwise by boat or small airplane.

WHAT TO PACK

In summer, it is advisable to have a raincoat or hooded coat, and an umbrella. Warmer wear, including a hat, neck scarf and gloves, is necessary in early spring, late autumn and of course, winter, when heavy top coats and layers of clothing are essential. In summer it can be cool in the evenings in many places, so taking some warmer clothes is recommended. As there will be times when walking is the ideal means of transport in both the cities and the countryside, comfortable and warm footwear is essential, especially for sightseeing.

If you are an outdoor enthusiast, pack your hiking boots as well. It's a good idea to take along an extra tote bag or day-use backpack for shopping at outdoor markets, carrying a picnic and bringing your purchases home.

Themed Tours

From Stettler, **Alberta Prairie Railway Excursions** take riders on 5hr to 6hr round-trip train trips through the countryside of Central Alberta. En route the train might be set upon by an outlaw gang on horseback who "rob" passengers at gunpoint. All excursions include a home-cooked roast beef supper at Big Valley's community hall; some also take in live theatre or a murder mystery. There are special excursions for children and families. Trains run late May–mid-Oct; call for winter excursions. Fares from $85 up (children $35 up). For schedules and reservations: ☎403-742-2811 or 800-282-3994; www.absteamtrain.com.

Rocky Mountain Vacations, based in the neighbouring province of British Columbia, offers popular multiday luxury rail tours mid-Apr through mid-Oct, including trips through the Rocky Mountains, with departures from Calgary, Banff and Jasper. For details ☎877-460-3200 Canada & US or www.rockymountaineer.com.

Take a 2- or 3-day **covered-wagon trek** through Central Alberta, sponsored by Alberta Prairie Wagon Trains. Trip includes 3 meals/day, overnighting on the trail, visits to historic sites and learning how to steer a horse-drawn wagon. Treks offered Jul & Aug from $275/person. Children under 7 years of age not permitted. For dates and reservations: ☎403-740-2796; www.absteamtrain.com.

KNOW BEFORE YOU GO

Useful Websites

Travel Alberta
www.travelalberta.com
(The official Travel Alberta website)

Tourism Calgary
www.tourismcalgary.com

Tourism Edmonton
www.edmonton.com/tourism

Tourism Red Deer
www.tourismreddeer.net

Fort McMurray Tourism
www.fortmcmurraytourism.com

Banff/Lake Louise Tourism
www.bannflakelouise.com

Jasper Tourism
www.jaspercanadianrockies.com

Drumheller Tourism
www.traveldrumheller.com

Alberta government
www.gov.ab.ca

Alberta Tourism, Parks, Recreation and Culture (official government site)
www.tprc.alberta.ca

Current information:
www.calgaryherald.com
www.calgarysun.com
www.ffwdweekly.com
www.businessedge.ca
www.cbc.ca/calgary
www.lethbridgeherald.com
www.reddeeradvocate.com
www.edmontonjournal.com
www.fortmcmurraytoday.com
www.cbc.ca/edmonton

Tourist Offices

Official government tourist offices operated by provincial, municipal and regional agencies distribute road maps and brochures that provide information on points of interest, seasonal events, accommodations and recreational activities. All publications are available free of charge. Telephone numbers and websites for local tourist offices are listed in this guide under each entry heading in *Discovering Alberta*. These offices provide additional information on accommodations, shopping, entertainment, festivals and recreation. On the maps in this guide, information centres are indicated by the symbol 🅸.

International Visitors

In addition to tourism centres, visitors from outside Alberta may obtain information from the nearest Canadian embassy or consulate in their country of residence. Many foreign countries maintain consulates in Edmonton or Calgary also. For further information and a complete list of Canadian embassies and consulates abroad, go online to www.voyage.gc.ca.

SELECTED CANADIAN CONSULATES AND EMBASSIES

US
1175 Peachtree St. NE, 100 Colony Square, Suite 1700, Atlanta, GA 30361-6205, ☎404-532-2000. www.atlanta.gc.ca
1251 Avenue of the Americas, Concourse Level; New York, NY 10020-1175, ☎212-596-1628. www.newyork.gc.ca
550 South Hope St., 9th floor, Los Angeles, CA 90071-2627, ☎213-346-2700. www.losangeles.gc.ca

Australia
Level 5, Quay West Bldg., 111 Harrington St., Sydney, NSW 2000, ☎9-364-3000. www.international.gc.ca/australia

Germany
Leipziger Platz 17, 10117 Berlin, ☎30-203120. www.berlin.gc.ca

United Kingdom
38 Grosvenor St., Macdonald House, London W1K 4AA, ☎020 7258 6506. www.london.gc.ca or www.canada.org.uk

ENTRY REQUIREMENTS

As of January 2008, citizens of the US need a valid passport or Air NEXUS card to visit Canada and return by air. Canadian and US citizens must present a passport, or both a driver's licence and a birth certificate together. All other visitors to Canada must have a valid **passport** and, in some cases, a visa *(see list of countries at www.cic. gc.ca/english/visit/visas.asp)*.
Parents taking children under 18 years of age into the US, or returning to the US after visiting Canada, must present a birth certificate for them.
To bring children into Canada, single parents (divorced, or simply unaccompanied by their spouse) must present a notarized permission letter from the other parent; in addition bringing a birth certificate for each child is strongly advised.

As of June 2009, or earlier, only a passport or other appropriate secure document will be accepted for anyone, including US citizens, to enter the US. Check the websites www.canada.travel or www.travel.state.gov (US government site) for the most recent updates. No vaccinations are necessary. Most airlines, even smaller domestic carriers, require valid government-issued photo ID. Persons who have been convicted of a crime—or, in some cases, arrested—should be aware that they may be denied entry to Canada. If you have any doubt, check with Canadian border authorities before heading to Canada.

CUSTOMS REGULATIONS

Non-residents may import personal baggage temporarily without payment of duties. You must be at least 18 years old to bring **alcoholic beverages** into Alberta, limited to 1.14 litres (40 imperial ounces) of wine or spirits, or 24 bottles (355ml or 12 ounces) of beer or ale, duty-free. You may bring into Canada duty-free 200 cigarettes, 50 cigars and some other forms of **tobacco.** All **prescription drugs** should be clearly labelled and for personal use only; it is recommended that visitors carry a copy of the prescription. For more information, call **Border Information Service** ☎800-461-9999 (within Canada) or ☎204-983-3500; or visit **Canada Border Services Agency online** at www.cbsa-asfc.gc.ca.

Canada has stringent legislation on **firearms**. A firearm cannot be brought into the country for personal protection while travelling. Only long guns may be imported by visitors 18 years or older for hunting or sporting purposes. Certain **firearms** are prohibited entry; restricted firearms, which include handguns, may only be imported with a permit by a person attending an approved shooting competition. For further information on entry of firearms, contact the **Canadian Centre for Firearms** (284

Wellington St., Ottawa, ON K1A 1M6; ☎800-731-4000; www.cfc-cafc.gc.ca). Most animals, except domesticated dogs and cats, must be issued a Canadian import permit prior to entry into Canada. **Pets** must be accompanied by an official certificate of vaccination against rabies from the country of origin. Payment of an inspection fee may be necessary. For details, contact **Canadian Border Service Agency** (2588 28 St. Calgary, AB T1Y 7G1; ☎800-461-9999 within Canada, ☎204-983-3500 outside Canada; www.cbsa-asfc.gc.ca).

CURRENCY EXCHANGE

♿See Money in Basic Information.

HEALTH

Alberta has an extensive health-care system, but offers no free health care to out-of-province guests. Several major insurance companies such as Manulife Financial offer reimbursement for expenses as a result of emergencies under their Visitors to Canada Plan. The plan must be purchased before arrival, or within five days of arrival, in Canada. For details contact **Manulife Financial** (2 Queen St. East, Toronto, ON, M5W 4Z2; ☎800-268-3763; www.coverme.com). You may also be able to arrange travel insurance through your national automobile association, such as the American Automobile Association.

Accessibility

Full wheelchair access to sights described in this guide is indicated in admission information by the symbol ♿. Most public buildings and many attractions, restaurants and hotels provide wheelchair access. Disabled parking is provided and the law is strictly enforced. For details contact the provincial tourist office online www.travelalberta.com. Many national and provincial parks have restrooms and other facilities for the disabled (such as wheelchair-accessible nature trails or tour buses). For details about a specific national park, call ☎888-773-8888 or visit *www. pc.gc.ca.* For Alberta provincial parks, go online to *http://gateway.cd.gov. ab.ca.* Additional information on accessibility is available from **Easter Seals Canada** *(90 Eglinton Ave. East, Suite 208, Toronto, ON M4P 2Y3; ☎416-932-8382; www.easterseals.ca).* Passengers who need assistance should give 24-48hrs advance notice; also contact the following transportation providers to request their informative literature for riders with disabilities:

Via Rail
☎888-842-7245
Special Needs Services:
☎800-268-9503 (TDD)
www.viarail.ca

Greyhound Canada
☎800-661-8747 (Canada)
☎800-397-7870 (TDD)
www.greyhound.ca

Red Arrow Motorcoach
☎800-232-1958
www.redarrow.pwt.ca

Reservations for hand-controlled vehicles from rental companies should be made well in advance.

GETTING THERE AND GETTING AROUND

By Plane

Canadian, American and other foreign carriers offer air service to Alberta's major airports in Calgary (www.calgaryairport.com) and Edmonton (www.edmontonairports. com). **Air Canada** *(☎888-247-2262 Canada/US; www.aircanada.com)* flies from numerous Canadian and US cities. Aside from these direct routes, connections are offered from many major US and other Canadian cities. Air Canada offers service to and from all major European cities, the Caribbean, Asia and the Pacific. Domestic air service is offered by Air Canada as well as its affiliated regional airlines and by Calgary-based **WestJet** *(☎800-538-5696 or 877-952-0100 TDD).* Air service to remote areas is provided by many charter companies. For specifics, contact the provincial tourist office for Alberta.

By Train

Amtrak offers daily **rail** service from New York City to Toronto, and connections are offered from many major US cities. For schedules in the US ☎800-872-7245 or *www.amtrak. com*. **VIA Rail,** Canada's national passenger rail network, links many cities within Canada. Edmonton and Jasper are its only Alberta stops. Amenities include dining cars and lounges, baggage handling (including bicycles), reservation of medical equipment, wheelchairs and preboarding aid with 24hr minimum notice. Unlimited train travel for 12 days within a 30-day period is available systemwide through **CANRAILPASS** *(Jun to mid-Oct, 12 days $837, 3 day extension at $71/day; off-season $523).* Special rates are offered for students with an ISIC card, youth and senior citizens. For information and schedules, contact the nearest VIA Rail office or call ☎888-842-7245 (US & Canada); *www.viarail.ca.*

By Coach/Bus

Bus travel across Canada and to and from the US is offered by **Greyhound** (☎416-367-8747 or 800-661-8747, Canada or 800-231-2222, US; www. greyhound.ca). For information and schedules, visit www.greyhound.ca or call the local US bus terminal. It is advisable to book well in advance when travelling during peak season. The major intercity bus line is also **Greyhound**. Canada Travel Passes, which are sold internationally, offer unlimited travel from 7 days up to 60 days. Peak season rates range from $329 to $750 (reduced rates available in off-season and for senior citizens). Other regional companies such as **Red Arrow Motorcoach** (☎800-232-1958, www.redarrow.pwt.ca) operate routes across Alberta. **Brewster Transportation** (☎403-221-8242; www.brewster. ca) provides transportation to Banff and Jasper National Parks, including direct service from Calgary International Airport and major hotels. (⚐ See the yellow pages of local telephone directories for more information).

By Car

Given Alberta's considerable size and sometimes rugged terrain, it is difficult to cover all of the province's attractions and two major cities in one visit. ⚐ See Driving Tours for suggested itineraries.

Along with air and limited rail access, access to Alberta from the US is possible by car at the following entry points along Montana's northern border: Aden, Carway, Del Bonita, Wild Horse, Coutts and Chief Mountain.

Alberta has an extensive system of well-maintained major roads. In the north, remote regions and mountain parks, however, many roads are gravel or even dirt.

⚐ Extreme caution should be taken when travelling these roads.

DRIVERS' LICENCES

Foreign **drivers' licences** are valid in Alberta for one year. Drivers must carry vehicle **registration** information and/or a rental contract at all times. Vehicle **insurance** is compulsory (minimum liability is $200,000). US visitors should obtain a Canadian Non-Resident Inter-Province Motor Vehicle Insurance Liability Card (**yellow card**), available from US insurance companies. For additional information, contact the Insurance Bureau of Canada, (777 Bay St., Suite 2400, Toronto, ON M5G 2C8; ☎416-362-2031; www.ibc.ca).

GASOLINE AND ROAD CONDITIONS

Gasoline is sold by the litre (1 gallon = 3.78 litres); prices many vary slightly from place to place, but are higher than in the US. All distances and speed limits are posted in kilometres (1 mile = 1.6 kilometres). During winter it is advisable to check road conditions before setting out. **Snow tires** from November to April and an **emergency kit** are imperative, especially at higher altitudes such as mountain parks. The Alberta government provides road reports and conditions: visit online Alberta Infrastructure and Transportation at www.infratrans.gov.ab.ca.

ROAD REGULATIONS

Speed limits, unless otherwise posted, are 100km/h (60mph) on freeways, 90km/h (55mph) on the Trans-Canada routes, and 80km/h (50mph) on most highways and rural roads. Speed limits in cities and towns range from 40km/h to 60km/h (25-40mph). Service stations that are open 24 hours can be found in large cities and along major highways. The use of **seat belts** is mandatory for all drivers and passengers in Alberta. The province prohibits the use of **radar detectors** in vehicles. Traffic in both directions must stop (except on divided roads) for a yellow school bus when signals are flashing. **Right turns on red** are allowed after coming to a complete stop, unless a sign indicates otherwise.

IN CASE OF ACCIDENT

If you are involved in an accident resulting in property damage and/or personal injury, you must notify the local police (Edmonton and Calgary have their own municipal police service, while rural areas and towns are served by the Royal Canadian Mountain Police or RCMP) and remain at the scene until dismissed by investigating officers, unless otherwise advised by police. For assistance contact your insurance provider or roadside assistance organization such as the Alberta Motor Association (www.ama.ca). Hospital and emergency aid are indicated on highways signs.

CANADIAN AUTOMOBILE ASSOCIATION (CAA)

This national member-based organization *(1145 Hunt Club Rd., Ottawa, ON K1V 0Y3; ☎613-247-0117; www.caa.ca)* offers services such as travel information, maps and tour books, accommodation reservations, insurance, technical and legal advice and emergency roadside assistance. These benefits are extended to members of other international affiliated clubs (proof of membership is required). The CAA maintains for its members a **24hr emergency road service** ☎**800-222-HELP.** The Alberta arm of CAA (Alberta Motor Association) maintains for its members a 24hr emergency road service *(☎888-426-2444, www.ama.ab.ca)*.

CAR RENTAL

Most major rental car agencies have offices at airports and in major cities in Alberta. Minimum age for rental is usually 25. To avoid a large cash deposit, payment by credit card is recommended. More favourable rates can sometimes be obtained by making a reservation before arriving in Alberta, but be aware of drop-off charges. Rates are highest in moun-

tain parks or on weekends/holidays and during special events such as the annual Calgary Stampede in early July each year. Be aware of drop-off charges if picking up and leaving your car in different cities.

- **Avis:** ☎800-331-1212. www.avis.com
- **Budget:** ☎800-268-8900. www.budget.com
- **Discount:** ☎800-263-2355. www.discountcar.com
- **Dollar Rent-a-Car:** ☎800-800-3665. http://ww2.dollar.com
- **Enterprise:** ☎800-325-0087. www.enterprise.com
- **Hertz:** ☎800-654-3131. www.hertz.ca
- **National:** ☎800-227-7368. www.nationalcar.ca
- **Thrifty:** ☎800-847-4389. www.thrifty.com

ALBERTA'S MAJOR HIGHWAYS

Alberta is accessible by two designated Trans-Canada routes running east-west: Highway 1 travels through southern Alberta, while the Yellowhead portion of the Trans-Canada (Highway 16) winds through Central Alberta. The main north-south route is Highway 2, also called the Queen Elizabeth II Highway. Other key routes are Highway 93, the Icefields Parkway between Banff and Jasper; Highway 63 north to Fort McMurray; and Highway 3 between Lethbridge and Medicine Hat.

©Travel Alberta

Highway 2, approaching Dunvegan Bridge, Dunvegan

WHERE TO STAY AND EAT

Hotel and Restaurant listings fall within the Address Books in the Discovering Alberta section. For price categories, ₢see the Legend on the cover flap.

Where to Stay

₢*For a selection of accommodations, see the green boxes titled **Address Books** within the major cities and areas described in the guide. Lodgings in this guide can also be found in the Index under the heading **Where to Stay.***

Alberta offers accommodations suited to every taste, price point and comfort level. Luxury **hotels** generally are found in major cities or resort towns such as Jasper, Banff and Canmore, while **motels** normally are clustered on the outskirts of town or on designated strips such as Motel Village in north-west Calgary. **Bed-and-breakfast inns** (B&Bs) are found in residential areas of cities and towns, as well as in more secluded natural areas. Many properties offer special packages and weekend rates that may not be extended during peak summer months (late May–late Aug) and during winter holiday seasons, especially near ski resorts. Most resort properties include outdoor recreational facilities such as golf courses, tennis courts, swimming pools, spas and fitness centres. Activities—hiking, mountain biking, watersports and horseback riding—often can be arranged by contacting the hotel staff. Alberta guests will pay a four-percent hotel **occupancy tax** that is built into hotel rates. Travel Alberta *(www.travelalberta.com)* and regional visitor centres offer free publications listing accommodations by location and type. In Alberta's less populated or more remote regions, it may be difficult to find accommodations at the end of a long day's drive, so advance reservations are recommended, especially during the tourist season (Victoria Day to Labour Day) as well as during the Christmas holidays.

During the off-season, establishments outside urban centres may be closed or operating with reduced hours; it is therefore advisable to telephone ahead. Guaranteeing reservations with a credit card is recommended.

HOTELS

Rates for hotels vary greatly depending on season and location. Expect to pay higher rates during holiday and peak seasons, especially at resort towns such as Banff and Jasper, where you can easily pay $600 for a one-night stay in the historic Fairmont Banff Springs or the Fairmont Lake Louise. For deluxe Calgary hotels such as the Sheraton Eau Claire or Hyatt Regency in Calgary, plan to pay at least $300-$600/night per standard room, based on double occupancy in peak season. In Edmonton, the venerable Hotel Macdonald overlooking the Fort Saskatchewan River valley will be similarly priced. Edmonton is also home to Canada's only inn situated in a historic site : Hotel Selkirk at Fort Edmonton Park drops its price substantially in winter when the park is closed to the public. Moderate hotels or smaller boutique inns such as Calgary's Hotel Arts will usually charge $60-$300/night (prices peak in summer). When making a reservation, ask about packages including meals, passes to local attractions, etc. Typical amenities at hotels include televisions, alarm clocks, in-room phones, smoking/non-smoking rooms, restaurants and swimming pools. Suites and in-room efficiency kitchens are available at some hotels. Always advise the reservations clerk of late arrival; unless confirmed with a credit card, rooms may not be held after 6pm.

MOTELS

Along major highways or close to urban areas, motels such as **Comfort Inn**, **Quality Inn** and **Choice Hotels**

(☎800-221-2222; www.choicehotels.com), **Travelodge** (☎800-667-3529; www.travelodge.com) and **Days Inn** (☎800-325-2525; www.daysinn.com) offer accommodations at moderate prices ($60–$150), depending upon the location. Amenities include in-room television, alarm clock and telephone. Smoking and non-smoking rooms, restaurants and swimming pools are often available on-site. Some in-room efficiency kitchens may be available. Family-owned establishments and small, independent guest houses that offer basic comfort can be found all across Alberta.

Note: Travellers intending to attend the annual Calgary Exhibition and Stampede in July are advised to book up to a year in advance. The 'Greatest Outdoor Show on Earth' attracts tourists from around the world and spontaneous visitors will have difficulty finding a room. Most hotels also significantly boost their room rates during this 10-day period.

BED AND BREAKFASTS AND COUNTRY INNS

Most B&Bs and country inns are privately owned; some are located in historic structures in residential sections of cities or small towns. In rural areas lodgings can be a rustic cabin or a farmhouse. At B&Bs the room rate generally includes complimentary breakfast ranging from continental fare to a gourmet repast; some offer afternoon tea and evening sherry or light snacks. Guests are invited to use the sitting room and garden spots. More information can be found through an organization representing the province's B&Bs; go online to www.bbalberta.com.

Country inns are larger establishments, usually with more than 15 rooms and with full-service dining facilities. Private baths are not always available, and often there is no phone in individual rooms. Smoking indoors may not be permitted. Reservations should be made well in advance, especially during peak seasons and holidays. Ask about minimum stay

requirements, and cancellation and refund policies. An organization called Charming Inns of Alberta (www.charminginnsofalberta.com) represents a dozen inns in the province such as Kilmorey Lodge in Waterton Lakes National Park or the eco-friendly Aurum Lodge at Nordegg near both Jasper and Banff National Parks. Most establishments accept major credit cards, but some B&Bs may not. Rates vary seasonally ($75-$200) for a double room per night. Rates may be higher when amenities such as hot tubs, private entrances and scenic views are offered.

RESERVATION SERVICES

Numerous organizations and regional tourism boards offer reservation services for hotels, B&Bs and country inns, as does Travel Alberta, the provincial tourism organization: ☎800-ALBERTA (252-3782) or www.travelalberta.com.

Other reservation services include:

Alberta Hotel and Lodging Association (www.ahla.ca)
Alberta Bed-and-Breakfast Association (www.bbalberta.com)
Alberta Country Vacations (www.albertacountryvacation.com)
Charming Inns of Alberta (www.charminginnsofalberta.com)

For a complete listing, search the Internet using the keyword "bed and breakfast" and Alberta or ask your travel agent.

HOSTELS

Hostelling International Canada, affiliated with the International Youth Hostel Federation, offers budget accommodations in Waterton, Calgary, Edmonton, Canmore, Jasper, Banff and other locations in the Canadian Rockies. A simple, no-frills alternative to hotels and inns, hostels are inexpensive dormitory-style accommodations (blankets and pillows are provided) with separate quarters for males and females. Many have private family/couples rooms that may be reserved in advance. Amenities include fully equipped self-service kitchens, dining areas, common rooms and laundry facilities. Rates average $15–$25 per night for members (higher for non-members). Hostels often organize special programs and activities for guests. Advance booking is advisable during peak travel times, but walk-ins are welcome. Membership is $35/year, but non-members are also admitted. When booking, ask for available discounts at area attractions, rental car companies and restaurants. For information and a free directory, contact **Hostelling International Canada** (☎613-237-7884 or 800-663-5777; www.hihostels.ca).

UNIVERSITIES AND COLLEGES

Most universities make their dormitory space available to travellers during summer vacation (May–Aug). Rooms are spartan; linens are provided. Bathrooms are communal and there are no in-room telephones. Rates average $20–$35/day per person. Reservations are accepted. When booking, ask about on-campus parking and food service. For more information contact the local tourist office or the university directly.

FARM AND COUNTRY VACATIONS

Farm and ranch lodgings are rustic and especially suited for families with children. Visitors are paying guests on a working grain or livestock farm or a cattle/horse ranch, and participation in daily chores depends on the host's preference. Guests might be asked to gather eggs, feed animals or perhaps milk a cow. Wagon and sleigh rides, hiking through pasture, canoeing or fishing at an on-site pond, and even berrypicking, may be available activities. Breakfast is included. Other meals can often be requested and may be taken with the host family. Rates begin at $50-$60 for double occupancy. Inquire about deposit and refund policies and minimum stay requirements. Credit cards may not always be accepted.

GUEST RANCHES

Primarily located in the mountain regions of the Alberta Rockies or the vast tracts of ranchlands across the province, guest ranches offer a vacation that can be enjoyed by singles, couples or families. Comfortable accommodations may be a room in a main lodge or in a cabin. Home-cooked meals are usually served family-style; in addition, scenic trail rides, overnight camp-outs, hiking, guided fishing trips, swimming, rafting, country dancing and campfire gatherings are often available. All equipment is provided and some ranches offer supervised youth programs. Many are working cattle and horse ranches and guests are encouraged to pitch in. Rates average $770–$1,950/week per person; some ranches may require a minimum stay. Ask about deposit and refund policies when booking a reservation. Alberta Country Vacations (www.albertacountry vacation.com) provides comprehensive information on guest ranches, working ranches, backcountry holidays and little-known countryside gems.

CAMPING AND RV PARKS

Alberta has excellent campgrounds that are operated privately or by the federal and provincial governments. Government sites are located in the many national and provincial parks. Fees are nominal. These campgrounds are well equipped and fill up quickly. Most park campgrounds are open mid-May through Labour Day, and usually operate on a first-come, first-served basis though some offer limited pre-booking. Dates are subject to change: visitors should check with park visitor centres for rates and maximum length of stay. Some parks offer reservation services; some offer winter camping. Campsites often include a level tent pad, picnic table, fireplace or fire grill with firewood, and parking space near a potable water source.

Most have toilet buildings and kitchen shelters. Some campgrounds are for tents only; others allow recreational vehicles; most do not have trailer hook-ups, although many have sewage disposal stations.

Many accommodate persons with disabilities.

Rustic campgrounds, located near hiking trails in the backcountry, can be reached only on foot. Some parks offer hut-to-hut cross-country skiing with rustic overnight accommodations or even winter tent sites. For a list of campgrounds, contact Travel Alberta. Advance reservations are recommended, especially during summer and holidays.

NATIONAL AND PROVINCIAL PARKS

Campgrounds are relatively inexpensive but fill rapidly, especially during school holidays. Facilities range from simple tent sites to full RV hook-ups (reserve 60 days in advance) or rustic cabins, tepees or trapper's tents (reserve one year in advance). Fees vary according to season and available facilities (picnic tables,water/electric hook-ups, used-water disposal, recreational equipment, showers, restrooms): camping & RV sites $15–20/day; cabins $40–$140/day. For all national park reservations, contact the park you are visiting or **Parks Canada** (☎888-773-8888; www.pc.gc. ca). For provincial parks, contact the provincial or local tourism office for information (👍 See Provincial Parks in the index). As well as five national parks, there are hundreds of provincial parks and protected areas.

PRIVATE CAMPGROUNDS

Commercial campgrounds offer facilities ranging from simple tent sites to full RV hook-ups. They are slightly more expensive ($20–$60/day for tent sites, $30–$35/day for RVs) but offer amenities such as hot showers, laundry facilities, convenience stores, children's playgrounds, pools and hot tubs, airconditioned cabins and outdoor recreational facilities. Most accept daily, weekly or monthly occupancy.During the winter months (Nov–Apr), campgrounds in northern Alberta may be closed. Reservations are recommended, especially for longer stays and in popular recreational areas such as Kananaskis Country.

FISHING CAMPS, FLY-IN LODGES AND WILDERNESS CAMPS

Alberta offers the experienced angler or the outdoor enthusiast a variety of fishing lodges and camps, some of which are so remote they can only be reached on foot or by private boat, helicopter or float plane. Cabins, backcountry huts, main lodge and dormitory-style buildings are typical accommodations. Summer tent camping may also be offered. Outfitters offer packages that include transportation, accommodations, meals, supplies, equipment and expeditions led by experienced guides. Activities can include trail riding, lake and stream fishing, boating, birding, wildlife tracking, nature walks and rock climbing. Some camps have hot tubs or saunas. Wilderness camps located in Alberta's northern regions offer all-inclusive hunting/fishing packages. In many cases, non-residents of Alberta must be accompanied by licensed guides and have obtained appropriate hunting/fishing permits.

Where to Eat

👍For a selection of restaurants, see the green boxes titled **Address Books** within the major cities and other areas in the Discovering Alberta section of the guide. Restaurants in this guide can also be found in the Index under the heading **Where to Eat**.

From Calgary's 1969 invention of the Bloody Caesar beverage (tomato and clam juice with vodka) to "Cowboy Cuisine" that pays homage to Alberta's status as a world-class cattle producer, regional fare encompasses traditional comfort foods, as well as unique creations. Alberta's traditional dishes, supplemented by those of its diverse ethnic population—especially Chinese, East Indian, Vietnamese and Japanese—have resulted in a richly varied cuisine. Local specialties include top-grade Alberta beef and the famous Prairie Oysters, a.k.a. bull testicles; during the Calgary Stampede, you can visit a ranch and watch calves being neutered in the annual spring Testicle Festival. Alberta's agricultural backbone also dishes out prime lamb, pork and game (buffalo, venison, elk), which are featured as Rocky Mountain cuisine in legendary eateries such as the River Café at Calgary's Princess Island Park or the revolving Panorama Dining Room atop the Calgary Tower. In Edmonton, it's the Asian fusion of Wild Tangerine that captures the city's modern multicultural side, while the long-running Red Ox Inn is famous for its beef tenderloin, duck and Arctic char. In recent years, many Alberta farmers have bowed to health pressures to incorporate more grain-fed and organically raised animals; vegetarian restaurants (like The Coupe in Calgary) are becoming increasingly abundant in a province based on oil and agriculture.

Although Alberta is a landlocked province, its proximity to its West Coast neighbour affords a fresh supply of fish and other seafood; excellent seafood can be found at Catch or Buchanan's in Calgary, Murrietta's (Calgary, Edmonton, Canmore) and Normand's in Edmonton.

WHAT TO SEE AND DO

Outdoor Fun

WATER SPORTS

From jet-boating, circuit canoe trips, white-water rafting and kayaking to scenic floats and paddles, Alberta is a water baby's paradise. The province features more than 600 lakes, 245 rivers and 315 creeks. Inexperienced paddlers are advised to book a guide or consult with locals before taking to the water (consider checking with the Alberta Professional Outfitters Society at www.apos.ab.ca). Lifejackets are mandatory in urban areas of Alberta and when outside city limits on flat water, they must be within easy access on the boat. It is illegal to drink and boat: some major waterways such as the Bow River near Calgary or the Red Deer River in the Alberta Bandlands

Kayaking on Lesser Slave Lake

near Drumheller are patrolled by government enforcement officers. For trip planning and more information, visit www.paddlingcanada.com, www. canoekayakcanada.ca , and for leaving no trace travel, go to http://lnt.org.

FISHING

Alberta is a fisherman's paradise, especially in the north, where many fly-in lodges arrange expeditions. The Bow River that runs east from the Continental Divide in the Rockies through Calgary and farther south is rated one of the world's Top 10 **fly-fishing** rivers due to its abundant and large brown and rainbow trout. Don't be surprised to see men and women fly-fishing among the glittering glass and steel skyscrapers of downtown on their lunch break. Northern Alberta is home to countless fly-in fishing lodges and many sections of fish-filled waterways. Non-residents must obtain a license, available from a sporting goods store. For information on seasons, catch and possession limits, contact the Public Information, Education and Outreach *(Main Floor, Great West Life Building, 9920 108 St., Edmonton AB T5K 2M4; ☎780-944-0313; www.mywildalberta. com)*. Some parks offer boat and canoe rentals.

The province is also a world-class **fishing** destination, boasting opportunities from independent outings on streams, creeks and brooks to guided fly-fishing expeditions on glacier-fed rivers or at remote fly-in lodges in the North. Anglers can choose from among six different zones of Alberta: Central (pike, walleye, perch and lake whitefish); North (pike, walleye, perch, lake trout and Arctic grayling); South (rainbow, brown, brook, cutthroat and bull trout); Calgary and area (brown and rainbow trout; the Bow River lures anglers from around the world); Canadian Rockies (trout, mostly catch-and-release) and Edmonton and area (walleye, northern pike, goldeye, sturgeon). In the winter, **ice fishing** is also popular on most lakes and streams in the province.

HIKING

The question is not where you can hike in Alberta—it's where you *can't* hike. The Rocky Mountain parks offer hundreds of trails for novice hikers and experts. Famous treks include the Plain of Six Glaciers from Lake Louise (watch avalanches roar in the distance as you circuit the lake) and the alpine flora-strewn Sunshine Meadows west of Banff, where you can wander along the Continental Divide. Jasper National Park northwest of Edmonton also affords countless journeys on foot, like the trails in the vicinity of Lake Miette and Pyramid Lake. There are numerous lesser-known but equally memorable jaunts such as Jumping Pound Mountain and Moose Mountain in Kananaskis Recreation Area; these trails are even more popular with mountain bikers (rentals are available at Kananaskis Village or Bragg Creek). Check out challenging Turtle Mountain in Crowsnest Pass near the British Columbia border, or fossil beds and mushroom-shaped hoodoos in the Badlands at Dinosaur Provincial Park. The rigorous Crypt Lake hike in Waterton Lakes National Park is rated as one of Canada's most scenic (this is grizzly country; be bear aware), but the less adventurous can circle the park's Cameron Lake or head for the crimson cliffs of Red Rock Canyon. In national and provincial parks, hikers should ask park officials about trail conditions, weather forecasts and safety precautions. Overnight **hikers** in backcountry areas are required to register at the park office before setting out and to deregister upon completion of the trip. Trail distances are given from trailhead to destination, not round-trip, unless otherwise posted. Topographic maps and a compass are indispensable for backcountry hiking; Gem Trek Publishing *(☎250-380-0100 or 877-921-6277; www.gemtrek.com)* and Federal Maps, Inc. *(☎416-607-6250 or 888-545-8111; www.fedmaps.com)* are two sources for obtaining detailed topographic maps. Maptown (www. maptown.com) in downtown Calgary offers a huge range of maps including digital and topographic.

RIDING

Horseback riding opportunities in Alberta range from hour-long trail rides to week-or-more expeditions deep into the Rocky Mountain backcountry along with dude ranch experiences where you can round up cattle, shear sheep or even clean out the horse barn. ⚓*See Guest Ranches under Where to Stay above.* The Spruce Meadows Equestrian Centre *(☎403-974-4200, www.sprucemeadows.com)* at Calgary's southwestern limits hosts regular national and international show-jumping events each year. For more information on equestrian events, contact Equine Canada *(☎866-282-8395; www.canadaequine.com).*

SKIING AND BOARDING

Alberta's downhill/cross-country and snowboarding opportunities lure thousands of snow lovers to the Rocky Mountains each winter. Enjoy spectacular mountain and snow conditions for alpine as well as nordic (cross-country) skiing and snowboarding. Telemark (free-heel skiing, a cross between downhill and nordic) is also a popular pastime at ski resorts and in the backcountry, as are one-day or multi-day heli-ski trips. Key ski resorts include Naskiska at Mount Allan southwest of the city, Mount Norquay and Sunshine Village near Banff, Lake Louise farther west and Marmot Basin in Jasper 300km/200mi north along the scenic Icefields Parkway (Hwy 93). Check *www.skicanada.org* for packages, resorts, ski and snowboard organizations across Canada; for snowboarding: *www.out-there.com.* Travel Alberta also offers information on www.skicanadianrockies.com.

WILDLIFE WATCHING

Canada is renowned for its wildlife, whether it's viewing grizzly or black bears, admiring herds of bighorn mountain sheep, or observing birds such as bald eagles and warblers. For information about Canadian wildlife, visit the Canadian Wildlife Federation's website: www.hww.ca. Wildlife is best observed in Canada's provincial and national parks, particularly more remote areas such as Wood Buffalo National Park in the far north of Alberta or Waterton Lakes National Park near the Alberta/US border. When watching or photographing wildlife, keeping a respectful distance is crucial. Stiff fines are given in parks for feeding and otherwise habituating wildlife: so never feed, pet or disturb wild creatures of any kind. Though carrying pepper spray in case of an unlikely encounter with an aggressive bear is common among hikers, ☺please note that the use of pepper spray is prohibited in Alberta.

Spas

Wellness and spas go hand in hand, particularly when married to spectacular scenery. In Alberta, you can soak in a hot tub overlooking the Rocky Mountains at Banff's Buffalo Mountain Lodge, or bathe in Hungarian mineral salts at the ultra-lavish Willow Stream Spa at the Fairmont Banff Springs Hotel. The hustle of city life is left behind at the peaceful Stillwater Spa at the Hyatt Regency in downtown Calgary. In Edmonton the modern Pink Lime and The Board Room offer a respite; the latter is Alberta's first men-only spa. There are spas galore in the alpine towns of Canmore, Banff, Lake Louise and Jasper, ranging from destination spas where meals and lodging are included to day spas that don't house overnight guests. The Inn and Spa at Heartwood in Drumheller offers a full range of spa and aesthetic services in three heritage buildings, along with golf lessons, Badlands helicopter tours, and package trips to the nearby theatre town of Rosebud. For more information about spas, go online to *www.leadingspasofcanada. com* or *www.spacanadianrockies.com.*

Activities for Children Kids

In this guide, sights of particular interest to children are indicated with a Kids symbol. Many of these attractions offer discounted admission to visitors under 12 years of age as well as special children's programs designed for all ages. Alberta's national parks usually offer discount fees for children. In addition, many hotels and resorts feature special family discount packages, and most restaurants offer children's menus. Kids can do a sleepover with the dinosaurs or take part in an archaeological dig at the Royal Tyrrell Museum in Drumheller, or ride a zipline at speeds up to 140 km/h-86 mi/hr off a 90metre ski jump tower at Canada Olympic Park in Calgary. Calaway Park on the Trans Canada Highway en route to Banff is a big hit with kids, as is Fort Edmonton Park in Edmonton and Heritage Park in Calgary. The amusement park, themed hotel rooms and sea-lion performances at West Edmonton Mall are huge draws for children.

Calendar of Events

Throughout the province, Alberta offers annual fairs, festivals and celebrations, many of them cultural or ethnic or based on historical events. Edmonton is known as Alberta's Festival City, staging nearly 30 major festivals through the summer months alone. Here is a sampling:

SPRING

May **Calgary International Children's Festival,** Calgary *www.calgarychildfest.org*

May-Sept **Banff Summer Arts Festival**, Banff, *www.banffcentre.ca*

SUMMER

Jun **Spock Days/Galaxyfest**, Vulcan, *www.town.vulcan.ab.ca*
Waterton Wild Flower Festival, Waterton, *www.watertonwild flowers.com*

Jul **Canadian Badlands Passion Play,** Drumheller, *www.canadianpassionplay.com*
Calgary Stampede, Calgary, *http://calgarystampede.com*
Calgary Folk Music Festival, Calgary, *www.calgaryfolkfest.com*
Capital EX, Edmonton, *www.capitalex.ca*

July-Aug **Big Valley Jamboree,** Camrose, *www.bigvalley jamboree.com*
Vegreville Pysanka Folk Festival, Vegreville, *www.vegre villefestival.ca*

Aug **Canmore Highland Games,** Canmore, *www.canmorehigh landgames.ca*

Chuckwagon Racing, Calgary Stampede, Calgary

©Travel Alberta

The Edmonton Fringe, Edmonton, *www.fringetheatreadventures.ca*
Whoop-up Days and Rodeo, Lethbridge, *www.exhibitionpark.ca*
Sept **Barbeque on the Bow,** Calgary, *www.bbqonthebow.com*

FALL

Oct **Word Fest,** Calgary-Banff, *www.wordfest.com*
Oct-Nov **Banff Mountain Festivals,** Banff, *www.banffcentre.ca*
Rodeo Royal, Calgary, *http://event.calgarystampede.com/rodeo_royal*

WINTER

Nov **Canadian Finals Rodeo,** Edmonton, *www.canadianfinalsrodeo.ca*
Dec **Heritage Park: 12 Days of Christmas,** Calgary, *www.heritagepark.ca*
Jan **Ice Magic Festival,** Lake Louise, *www.banfflakelouise.com*
Feb **Calgary Winter Fest,** Calgary, *www.calgarywinterfest.com*

Shopping

BUSINESS HOURS

Business hours in Alberta are, for the most part, Monday to Friday 9am–5pm. In general, retail stores are open Monday to Friday 9am–6pm (until 9pm Thursday and Friday), Saturday 9am–5pm. In most cities, shops are usually open on Sunday afternoon; many small convenience stores in gas stations may be open much longer hours. ☞*For banking hours, see Money in the Basic Information section.*

GENERAL MERCHANDISE

Downtown areas provide opportunities for shopping at department stores, national chains, specialty stores, art galleries and antique shops. Major department stores in Canada include Hudson's Bay Co. (known locally as "The Bay") and Sears Canada. Revitalized historic districts, such as Old Strathcona in Edmonton, and Inglewood and Stephen Avenue in Calgary, house boutiques, art galleries, theatres, trendy cafes and restaurants. Large shopping malls—like mammoth West Edmonton Mall on the outskirts of Edmonton or Chinook Centre in Calgary —are generally located outside downtown areas. Bargain hunters will want to look for **outlet malls** that offer savings of up to 70% at brand-name factory stores. Recreational outerwear companies, such as Mountain Equipment Co-op and Coast Mountain Outfitters enable visitors to equip themselves from head to toe before setting out on hiking, hunting or fishing trips, or even to the yoga studio. As for fashionable, but probably pricey, **ski clothes,** try Edmonton, Jasper, Banff, Calgary and Canmore. Searching for a cowboy hat or colourful neckerchief? The latest in **Western gear** is available at stores such as Lammle's Western Wear, and Riley & McCormick Western Stores (www.realcowboys.com) in Calgary, while elaborate cowboy boots are tooled at the Alberta Boot Company in Calgary and Grand Saddlery in Cochrane. You can also pick up western gear in small shops, boutiques and cafes in towns along the Alberta Cowboy Trail driving tour such as Longview, Okotoks, Pincher Creek, Bragg Creek and Cochrane.

ARTS AND CRAFTS

Aboriginal arts and crafts (First Nations, Métis and Inuit) are plentiful; museums and cultural centres on tribal lands exhibit and sell baskets, carvings, jewellery and other handiwork. Native items can be found at Head-Smashed-In Buffalo Jump Interpretive Centre near Fort Macleod and the new Blackfoot Crossing Interpretive Centre east of Calgary in Gleichen. Calgary, in particular, has many shops selling art, jewellery, leatherwork, stenciled goods and metal works done in popular cowboy motifs. The Alberta Craft Council Gallery and Shop (www.albertacraft.ab.ca), located in Edmonton, showcases and offers for sale the works of many provincial artists. Edmonton is famous for its crafts and artisan goods at the weekly Strathcona Farmers' Market (⬤see Farmers' Markets below).

FARMERS' MARKETS

Edmonton is the site of the weekly Strathcona Farmers' Market, which is held every Saturday year-round near the funky Whyte Avenue strip; fresh produce, flowers, baked goods and crafts are for sale.

The bustling indoor Calgary Farmers' Market held at Currie Barracks in the city's southwest area is open weekends during the winter, but longer hours in summer.

Just northwest of Calgary, the outdoor Bearspaw Farmers' Market is open weekends during the summer and fall, while the more downscale Calgary Crossroads Market, also indoors, operates year-round on weekends as well as Fridays.

A summer market (May to Oct) in the foothills town of Millarville, southwest of Calgary, showcases everything from farm goods and fresh fruit to giant local flower bouquets, crafts, preserves, cowboy art and country wares.

Most smaller cities and towns also hold half-day or full-day weekly markets. The Saturday market (mid-May to mid-Oct 8am–12:30pm) of the Lethbridge and District Exhibition (☎403-317-3217; www.exhibitionpark.ca) on the exhibition grounds (3401 Parkside Dr.) has farm-fresh produce, meats,

crafts, jewellery and knick-knacks. For more information on markets in other communities, visit **Alberta Farmer's Market Assn.** online at www.albertamarkets.com.

Sightseeing

RIVER AND LAKE CRUISES

Cruising the many rivers and lakes of Alberta is a relaxing way to enjoy the province's natural beauty. In addition to those described below, cruises can be found under individual Sights in the *Discovering Alberta* section (⬤see *Rocky Mountain Raft Tours and Minnewanka Boat Tours in Banff National Park, Maligne Tours on Maligne Lake in Jasper National Park, and riverboat tours in Calgary and Edmonton*).

The journey by passenger cruise boat from the Canadian side of Waterton-Glacier International Peace Park to the US is remarkable in many ways. The wind is so strong through this glacial mountain gap that the trees actually grow in a distinct tilt. **Waterton Shoreline Cruises** offers a variety of boat trips along the Waterton lakeshore to Goat Haunt, Montana. An interpretive guide will point out interesting points en route such as grizzly bear haunts. Some of the tours (which last from 3hr-5hr) include a shuttle stop at Crypt Landing, and a daunting but scenic hike to an alpine lake offering breathtaking scenery and

Craft Store at Métis Crossing, Smoky Lake

wildlife-viewing opportunities. Late May to mid-October, with fares from $30. For schedules and reservations: ☎403-859-2362 or www. watertoncruise.com.

Peace Island Tours takes visitors on 60km/37mi cruises down the Peace River to Peace Island in the northern part of the province. Tours depart from the town of Peace River. For details, ☎780-624-4295 or go online to www.peaceisland.ab.ca.

TRAIL RIDES

Explore the breathtaking mountain vistas of the Kananaskis on guided horseback rides sponsored by the legendary **Boundary Ranch,** located 110km/66mi southwest of Calgary. Even the most timid greenhorn cannot resist the lure of alpine meadows, wildlife spotting (think bear, deer and bighorn sheep) and an optional barbecue steak feast. The ranch's experienced guides offer hourly trail rides, as well as half- and full-day packages through the same stunning terrain. Not enough adventure for you? The Surf and Saddle combo tour takes in a morning of white-water rafting, a BBQ steak lunch and an afternoon trail ride. Overnight and multiday trips are available upon request. Prices vary, as trips can be highly customized; for details: ☎877-591-7177 or go online to www.boundaryranch.com.

For a host of other riding adventures, from overnight packhorse trips to trail rides and even hay rides, contact **Alberta Outfitters Association:** ☎800-742-5548 or online at www.albertaoutfitters.com.

UNESCO WORLD HERITAGE SITES

Of Canada's 14 World Heritage Sites, Alberta's diverse landscape has earned the province five UNESCO designations (see additional descriptions of these sites in the Discovering Alberta section). Situated in the far south to the deep north, the United Nations sites can all be visited in 12-14 days by car or RV—a 1,890-km/1172mi journey that takes travellers through both major cities (Calgary and Edmonton) as well as remote and rugged terrain. **Wood Buffalo National Park** in northern Alberta is the world's second largest national park, and is home to the largest free-roaming herd of wood bison on earth. To the south, the Canadian Rockies deliver a UNESCO site that consists of four national parks: **Jasper National Park** northwest of Edmonton and **Banff National Park** west of Calgary (Yoho and Kootenay National Parks to the west in British Columbia). Banff and Jasper parks lure travellers from around the world year-round, with summer and winter competing as peak season. **Dinosaur Provincial Park** southeast of Calgary is the third UNESCO site, an undulating, lunar-like landscape of rock formations and some of the largest dinosaur bone fields in the world. Travel west to **Head-Smashed-In Buffalo Jump,** a site used for 5,500 years by aboriginal peoples to drive buffalo over a cliff to their deaths; the carcasses supplied food, clothing and tepee hides. It was here that nomadic Plains Indians survived for more than 10,000 years. A seven-tiered interpretive centre, staffed by First Nations guides, built into the sandstone cliffs tells the story in elaborate detail. The fifth site, bordering the US, is **Waterton Lakes National Park,** which together with Glacier National Park in Montana, became the world's first international peace park in 1932. This pocket of wilderness, surrounded by jagged cliffs, glaciers and pristine lakes, offers opportunities to spot a grizzly or black bear. Learn more about these and the world's 800plus other UNESCO sites at http://portal.unesco.org.

NATIONAL PARKS AND RESERVES

Since the creation of the first national park in Banff in 1885, the amount of protected land managed by Parks Canada has grown to 41 national parks, including five in Alberta. They are: Waterton Lakes National Park, Banff National Park, Jasper National

Park, Elk Island National Park and Wood Buffalo National Park.

General Information

Most points of interest are in the southern national parks, accessible by car. Well-marked hiking trails permit outdoor enthusiasts and novices alike to enjoy the backcountry. Parks are open year-round; however, some roads may be closed during the winter. Daily entry or use fees range from $2.50 to $6 per adult. Discounts are offered at some parks to senior citizens (25%) and children (50%). Additional fees are charged for camping, fishing and guided programs.

Visitor centres *(open daily late May–Labour Day; reduced hours the rest of the year)* are usually located at park entrances. Staff members are available to help visitors plan activities. Trail maps and literature on park facilities, hiking trails, nature programs, camping and in-park accommodations are available on-site free of charge. Interpretation programs, guided hikes, exhibits and self-guided trails introduce the visitor to each park's history, geology and habitats.

For a listing of in-park activities, see the description of specific parks in the Discovering Alberta section.

A good reference for planning a visit to Canada's national parks is Roberta Bondar's **Passionate Vision: Discovering Canada's National Parks** *(Douglas & McIntyre, Ltd., 2000).*

DISCOUNTS

For Students and Youths

Student discounts are frequently available for travel, entertainment and admissions. Age eligibility varies: child rates usually apply for up to 12 years old; youth rates from 12–17 years of age. With a valid student card, any student 12 years and older can obtain an International Student Identity Card for discounts on rail travel and more (available at many Via Rail stations, or online from www.isic.org).

One of Alberta's many RV camping sites

©Travel Alberta

For Senior Citizens

Many attractions, hotels, restaurants, entertainment venues and public transportation systems offer discounts to visitors age 62 years or older (proof of age may be required). National and provincial parks usually offer discount fees for seniors. Although Canada has no national organization for retirees or older citizens, visiting seniors should feel free to ask specific businesses if such a discount is available.

Books

Who Has Seen the Wind.
W.O. Mitchell (1947).
This Canadian classic by an award-winning Alberta novelist tells the tale of prairie boy Brian O'Connal's growing awareness of life, death, God and the spirit and power of the wind.

Green Grass, Running Water.
Thomas King (1993).
This fictional work by an award-winning First Nations writer tells the story of five Blackfoot Indians whose lives intertwine in comical yet touching ways. The novel explores revisionist history, nostalgia and myths about aboriginal people.

The Best Places for Heading Out.
Bruce Masterman (1999).
This user-friendly book is the definitive eco-adventure guide to southern Alberta, taking readers

on journeys to little-known fishing holes, mountain bike trails and rarely-seen ancient petroglyphs (rock carvings).

High Plains: The Joy of Alberta Cuisine. Cinda Chavich (2001).

While largely billed as a cookbook, this visually mouth-watering tome takes you on a culinary trip through Alberta and its regional cuisine. The award-winning book delves into the emergence of sustainable farming and food production and the singularity of Alberta's cuisine.

Nitsitapiisinni: The Story of the Blackfoot People. Glenbow Museum (2001).

Produced by The Blackfoot Gallery Committee of Calgary's acclaimed Glenbow Museum, this book chronicles the life of the Blackfoot First Nations and their important place in the history in southern Alberta.

Boondoggles, Bonanzas and Other Alberta Stories. Brian Brennan (2003).

This book enlivens the history of Alberta with people like Charles Hatfield, "the Rainmaker of Medicine Hat" and events such as the massive Frank Slide in 1903, when a town was buried by a coal-mine collapse. A provincial interpretive centre tells the tale.

Mavericks: An Incorrigible History of Alberta. Aritha Van Herk (2007).

Divided into 14 essay sections, this book explores the characters, issues and challenges that shaped southern Alberta and its Wild West persona. Van Herk's stories run the gamut from wicked weather and dinosaur graveyards to oil booms, pioneers, social reform and political antics.

Films

Days of Heaven (1978).

A Western with a little romance and a little tragedy thrown in for good measure. Richard Gere and Sam Shepard star in this film about a turn-of-the-century Chicago steel mill worker who heads for

Texas (filmed in southern Alberta) with his girlfriend.

Unforgiven (1993).

Clint Eastwood's photo is plastered on walls at practically every shop in Longview. He and Gene Hackman spent many months here filming this action Western about two retired sharp-shooters who join forces to claim a reward for capturing a killer.

Legends of the Fall (1994).

Brad Pitt and Anthony Hopkins brought Hollywood to the Cowboy Trail, filming mostly in the rolling ranchlands near Longview, southwest of Calgary. The epic tale, set in the early 1900s, showcases a father's efforts to raise three sons in the wilderness.

Shanghai Noon (2000).

Large parts of this action movie starring Jackie Chan and Owen Wilson were set among the dramatic hoodoos and coulees of the Drumheller area east of Calgary and south of Edmonton. Chan's character travels to the Wild West to save a kidnapped princess.

Brokeback Mountain (2005).

Much of this award-winning film, starring the late Heath Ledger and Michelle Williams, was filmed among the majestic peaks and lush alpine meadows of Kananaskis Valley west of Calgary. The movie, ostensibly set in Wyoming, details a bittersweet love story between two cowboys.

The Assassination of Jesse James (2007).

Brad Pitt loved Alberta so much he returned with Casey Affleck to shoot this drama, an adaptation of Ron Hansen's 1983 novel of the same name about the life and death of the notorious outlaw.

Bury My Heart at Wounded Knee (2007).

This HBO-made movie starring Aidan Quinn was filmed in the foothills and mountains west of Calgary. The drama chronicles the tragedy of Native American displacement and deprivation as the US expanded west.

BASIC INFORMATION

Electricity

120 volts, 60 cycles. Most small American appliances can be used. European appliances require an electrical transformer, available at electric supply stores.

Emergencies

Alberta's cities and many rural areas have 911 telephone service for emergency response. When 911 is dialled from any telephone in a served area, a central dispatch office sees the dialling location and can redirect the call to the appropriate emergency response agency—fire department, police or ambulance. Much of rural Alberta is not within range of cellular telephone service, and although coverage extends along most major highways, service can be unreliable in wilderness regions.

Public Safety Canada maintains extensive links to information and services on public safety: www.safecanada.ca.

Liquor Laws

The legal drinking age in Alberta is 18. Liquor can be purchased at private beverage stores but not supermarkets or grocery stores except if in a standalone building. That rule does not apply in some remote communities, where liquor can be purchased by an approved vendor in an approved outlet such as a convenience store.

Mail/Post

Post offices across Canada are generally open Monday to Friday 8am–5:30pm; extended hours are available in some locations. Sample rates for first-class mail (letter or postcard; up to 30 grams): within Canada, 52 cents; to the US, 93 cents; international mail, $1.55. Mail service for all but local deliveries is by air. Visitors can receive mail c/o "General Delivery" addressed to Main Post Office, City, Province and Postal Code. Mail will be held for 15 days and has to be picked up by the addressee. Some post offices have fax services, and all post offices offer international courier service. In addition to post offices, postal facilities are located at selected Canadian retailers, offering convenient extended and weekend hours. For information regarding postal codes or locations of facilities, ☎866-607-6301; *www.canadapost.ca.*

Metric System

Canada has adopted the International System of Units popularly known as the metric system. Weather temperatures are given in Celsius (C°), milk and wine are sold by millilitres and litres, and grocery items are measured in grams. All distances and speed limits are posted in kilometres (to obtain the equivalent in miles, multiply by 0.6). Some examples of metric conversions are:

1 kilometre (km) = 0.62 miles
1 metre (m) = 3.28 feet
1 kilogram (kg) = 2.2 pounds
1 litre (L) = 33.8 fluid ounces =
     0.26 gallons
(1 US quart = 32 fluid ounces)

Money

Canadian currency is based on the decimal system (100 cents to the dollar). Bills are issued in $5, $10, $20, $50, $100, $500 and $1,000 denominations; coins are minted in 1 cent, 5 cents, 10 cents, 25 cents, $1 and $2. Exchange money at banks for the most favourable exchange rate.

You don't need to carry much cash while visiting Canada: ATM machines are widely available, and most merchants accept debit or credit cards. Self-serve gas, parking lots and even store check-outs are common. Do carry a few "loonies" or "toonies" (the $1 and $2 coins) for parking meters, tips and snacks. Most public telephones accept calling cards at no charge, but local calls cost 25–50¢ (one or two quarters). Most ATMs dispense cash in increments of $20.

BANKS

Banking institutions are generally open Monday to Friday 9am–5pm. Some bank branches are open on Saturday morning, and some offer extended evening hours. Banks at large airports have foreign exchange counters and extended hours. Institutions generally charge a fee for cashing traveller's cheques. Most principal bank cards are honoured at affiliated Canadian banks.
Use bank branded ATM machines to avoid the higher fees charged by private operators.

CREDIT CARDS AND TRAVELLER'S CHEQUES

The following major credit cards are accepted in Canada: American Express, Carte Blanche, Discover, Diners Club, MasterCard/Eurocard and Visa. Most banks will cash traveller's cheques and process cash advances on major credit cards with proper personal identification.

CURRENCY EXCHANGE

The most favourable exchange rate can usually be obtained at branch offices of a national bank. Some banks charge a small fee for this transaction. Private exchange companies generally charge higher fees. Airports and visitor centres in large cities may have exchange outlets as do some hotels. The Canadian dollar fluctuates with international exchange rates. Exchange facilities tend to be limited in rural and remote areas. If arriving in Canada late in the day or on a weekend, visitors may wish to exchange

some funds prior to arrival (a few banks are open on Saturday mornings in major cities, however).
You can use ATMs to withdraw Canadian currency from your home account, but check with your bank first to see if it has reciprocal arrangements with a Canadian bank for a lower fee.

TAXES

Canada levies a 5% Goods and Services Tax (GST) on most goods and services. Alberta is the only Canadian province with no provincial sales tax.

Public Holidays

The following holidays are observed in Alberta. Banks, government offices and schools are closed:
New Year's Day: January 1
Family Day: Third Monday in February
Good Friday: Friday before Easter Sunday
Easter Monday: Monday after Easter Sunday
Victoria Day: Closest Monday on or before May 24
Canada Day: July 1
Civic Holiday: 1st Monday in August
Labour Day: 1st Monday in September
Thanksgiving: 2nd Monday in October
Remembrance Day: 2nd Wednesday in November
Christmas Day: December 25
Boxing Day: December 26

Smoking

Like most other Canadian provinces and territories, Alberta has enacted comprehensive smoke-free legislation. Municipal bylaws are commonplace, particularly in Calgary and Edmonton, where smoking is banned in restaurants and bars. Smoking has been banned from aircraft, buses, trains and most offices for some time, but restrictions for other public spaces vary. Only casinos operating on First

Nations lands are by law allowed to let customers smoke. Smoking in public places is increasingly unacceptable.

Telephones

To call long distance within Canada and to the US, dial 1+ area code + number. For overseas calls, refer to the country codes in most telephone directories, or dial "0" for operator assistance. Most operators speak English and French. Collect calls and credit card calls can be made from public pay phones. For local directory assistance, check the white pages of the phone directory or dial 411; outside the local area code dial 1+ area code + 555-1212. Telephone numbers that start with **800, 866, 877** or **888** are toll-free *(no charge)*. To dial a local call, dial the area code plus the number. A local call costs 25 to 50 cents. Be aware that many hotels place a surcharge on all calls.

EMERGENCY NUMBERS

911 service, operated through municipalities, is extensive in Alberta, and can be accessed from cell phones; if for

some reason 911 doesn't work, dial "0" for the operator and ask for the police.

Time

Alberta operates on Mountain Standard Time (MST), which is one hour ahead of most of British Columbia and two hours behind Ontario. Daylight Saving Time (clocks are advanced 1 hour) is in effect from the first Sunday in March until the first Sunday in November. Some parts of Alberta such as the Peace River area do not observe Daylight Saving Time.

Tips

Tips or service charges are not normally added to a bill in Alberta. However, it is customary to tip for services received from food servers, porters, hotel maids and taxi drivers. In restaurants and for taxi drivers, it is customary to tip 10-15% of the total amount of the bill (excluding taxes). At hotels, porters should be tipped $1 per bag, and maids $1 per night.

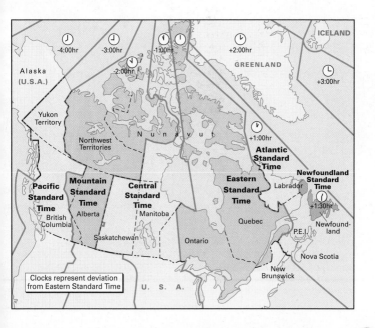

Northern Shadow Dancers
Peace River, Northern Alberta
©Travel Alberta

NATURE

Alberta is home to a diverse landscape that encompasses the granite spires of the Rocky Mountains, the fluted gullies of the Canadian badlands, the hardy conifers of the northern boreal forest and the patchwork of prairie land that spans much of the eastern portion bordering the province of Saskatchewan.

The second-most western province in Canada, Alberta covers 661,190sq km/255,285sq mi—6.6 percent of the country's landmass—and extends 1,223km/758mi from its southern boundary with Montana north to Canada's Northwest Territories. It sits between the 49th and 60th parallels. The Wild Rose province, which celebrated its centennial in 2005, was named after Princess Louise Caroline Alberta, daughter of Queen Victoria, and wife of the then governor-general of Canada, the Marquess of Lorne.

Geologic Past

THE GREAT ICE AGES

Four times during the past million years, the North American climate has become progressively colder. Snowfall became increasingly heavy in the north and was gradually compressed into ice. This ice began to flow south, reaching as far as the Saskatchewan and Missouri river systems in the US before retreating. At peak coverage, 97 percent of Canada and all of Alberta were submerged under ice up to 3km/2mi deep at the centre and 1.6km/1mi deep at the edges. The last Ice Age receded more than 10,000 years ago.

But parts of the province's geographic history stretch back millions years, particularly the badlands of central and southern Alberta. The **Red Deer River,** formed after the last Ice Age, carved a wide swath through the sculpted badlands, exposing ancient animal and plant fossils and revealing dinosaur beds that are among the most expansive and well preserved in the world.

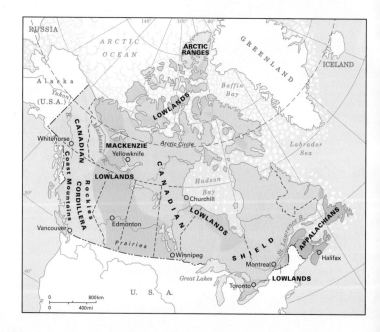

Major Natural Areas

THE CANADIAN SHIELD

Canada has at its centre a massive upland known as the Canadian Shield, which encompasses nearly half of the country's area. While widely thought to be restricted to the far northern part of the province, the shield actually plunges more than 6km/3.75mi beneath mountains and plains to create a foundation for much of the province's geology.

The Canadian Shield is formed of ancient, hard rocks of the **Precambrian** era (more than 540 million years old) known for their great rigidity and strength. Its subregions include most of the exposed shield north of **Lake Athabasca,** which is evidenced by glaciated bedrock. The **Athabasca Plain,** including northern Lake Athabasca, features glacial outwash deposits laid shallowly over bedrock.

BOREAL FORESTS

The geologic makeup of northern Alberta supports vast northern boreal forests, which exist as an almost continuous belt of coniferous trees extending across North America and Eurasia. Set upon formerly glacial areas and permafrost, the boreal forests support myriad animals and plants. They stretch from Newfoundland in eastern Canada to Alaska near the northern tundra and to the Great Lakes in southern Canada. The forests are also home to vast oil deposits, including the massive oil sands of northwest Alberta near Fort McMurray—the largest oil reserves in the world. The sands contain bitumen, a dense and sticky black oil that seeped from the banks of the Athabasca River. Aboriginal people used this sludge to waterproof their canoes; explorer Peter Pond first documented this phenomenon in his journals in the late 1770s.

Major deposits of oil-encrusted sand are spread across more than 38,500sq km/ 15,000sq mi, luring major energy companies to the region to extract what is said to be an estimated 1.7 billion barrels worth of accessible oil. The area is undergoing an economic boom as corporations line up to lay claim to or expand their oil excavation. Forestry is another major natural resource in the heavily treed, boggy terrain.

ROCKY MOUNTAINS

Part of the Canadian Cordillera, the Canadian Rockies stretch roughly 1,550km/ 900mi from the US border through western Alberta and eastern British Columbia. This massive mountain chain extends across more than half of the Alberta's western border. It is made up of a unique mix of topographic conditions that produce flora and fauna not found anywhere else in Alberta. With major valleys that parallel the mountain ranges, river systems leaving the eastern slopes of the Rockies flow to the east (compared to those on the other side of the Continental Divide, which run to the west). The mountains, composed of sedimentary rock, are underlain by upthrust and folded carbonate and quartzitic bedrock, which merges into layers of sandstone and shale composing the foothills of the eastern slopes.

The two major mountain ranges are the eastern Front Ranges and the western Main Ranges, home to many of Alberta's largest rivers, which drain into the Arctic Ocean, Hudson Bay or the Gulf of Mexico. The mountains contain three subregions—montane, subalpine and alpine—distinguished by altitude and other environmental conditions, including regionally unique flora and fauna. The highest peaks (rising more than 3,000m/10,000ft) occur in the region's central zones; lower mountains are found in the far north and south.

FOOTHILLS

Adjacent to the Rocky Mountains are the **Upper and Lower Foothill** regions of Alberta, also known as the **Eastern Slopes.** These vast, flat-topped hills, which run from northern Alberta to the south as a transitional zone between the Rocky Mountains and boreal forests, are home to a wide variety of animals, and contains the most inland habitat for grizzly bears in North America. The region features several outlying hill sections

Wild Rose, Alberta's provincial flower

including the **Swan Hills** and **Naylor Hills** in northern Alberta.

GRASSLANDS

Spread across 30 million acres in southeast Alberta, the **Alberta Grasslands** make up 14 percent of the province's landmass. They are part of the **Great Plains** that stretch south through the US and the **Gulf of Mexico;** they are made of bedrock cloaked with dense glacial till deposits. This region incorporates the Canadian badlands with their distinctive ravines, coulees and hoodoo terrain carved out by the **Red Deer River.** The grasslands, which feature dry, mixed-grass, northern fescue and foothills fes-

Mountain Goats

cue, all boast different climates and eco-systems. The least developed grasslands in Canada are considered unique: the **Canadian Forces Base Suffield** north of Medicine Hat and the **Milk River-Lost River** area of extreme southeast Alberta. Created by the advance and retreat of glaciers, the area offers terrain such as sand dunes, hewn canyons, gorges and lakes.

Geographical Features

VEGETATION

With a diverse landscape and myriad geological features, Alberta boasts an impressive range of vegetation. Yet **forests** predominate, covering nearly 60 percent of the province. The southern **grasslands** feature a mixture of grass varieties such as spear grass, wheatgrass and blue gama grass. The foothills offer a range of trees including spruce, larch, fir and pine, while mixed varieties like aspen and poplar are found in the southern and eastern regions. The major forests of the north and west boast jack pine, birch, black and white spruce, tamarack and other coniferous trees; Alberta's **prairie-parkland** region holds groves of aspen and poplar along with varieties of wheatgrass. Tiny cacti can be found in dryer areas such as Writing-On-Stone Provincial Park or the badlands. Some 2,000 blooming plant species brighten the Prairies; the wild rose, which blooms abundantly in southern Alberta, is the official provincial flower. Spring and summer displays of blooms in the **alpine meadows** of the Rocky Mountains are stunning.

WILDLIFE

Wildlife is abundant in Alberta. Tourists come from around the world to glimpse **bighorn sheep, mountain goats, deer, moose** and **bear.** Opportunities to see wildlife are greatest in the mountain parks or the foothills, where "bear jams" of cars along the highways are often an indication that an animal is nearby. While the sight of a mother sow and cubs is a highlight of any trip, caution is urged. Traffic pileups can result in chaos, as eager humans vie for limited roadside space on often narrow, winding highways, and distracted motorists fail to leave space for passing vehicles. Along with the larger mammals, Alberta is home to many other creatures including **beaver, marmot, coyotes, foxes, wolves** and **cougars** (both rarely seen by humans), **squirrels, chipmunks** and the ubiquitous **prairie gopher**—also known as the Richardson's ground squirrel. This particular squirrel is the bane of many prairie farmers, due to its voracious burrowing that can leave a wheat or barley field pockmarked by holes.

The province is also home to hundreds of species of perching **birds and waterfowl** including indigenous residents such as blue jays, whisky jacks, woodpeckers, herons, swallows, owls and chickadees. Migratory birds include pelicans, trumpeter swans and golden eagles; the prime seasons for viewing migratory birds are spring and fall. For a comprehensive list of species and viewing locations, visit www.travelalberta.com.

CLIMATE

Alberta's climate is varied, but generally manifests itself in cold winters (especially in the north, as Arctic air masses send the mercury plunging) and warm summers. Its most unusual weather anomaly, found in few other places in the world, is the **chinook**—a sudden warming pattern caused when winds warm as they sweep down the Rockies into southern Alberta (and some other parts of the province lying in the shadow of the Rockies). This eagerly awaited phenomenon, especially during a cold spell, is a welcome relief in winter since it causes a rapid climb in temperature, often leaping from bone-chilling cold to above freezing in several hours. Generally speaking, Alberta sees 1,900 hours of sunshine annually in the north, and 2,300 hours in the south near Lethbridge. Temperatures range from –8°C/17°F in the South to –24°C/–11°F in the north in January; in July temperatures range from 20°C/68°F in the south to 16°C/60°F in the north.

HISTORY

Immigration and exploration have honed Alberta's history. The door to colonization of Canada's First Nations was opened in the late 1670s when the Hudson's Bay Company was given rights to govern most of Western Canada, known at the time as Rupert's Land. By the 1700s, fur traders were establishing trading posts across the province, particularly along the Rocky Mountains and to the north. Explorers such as Peter Pond and David Thompson, as well as gold-seekers and voyageurs (French-speaking fur-traders and adventurers), soon followed.

It wasn't until the Canadian Pacific Railway reached Alberta in the early 1880s that settlers arrived en masse, along with the North West Mounted Police. Realizing the tourism potential of the Rockies, the CPR convinced the government to create nature preserves—precursors to Canada's Rocky Mountain national parks. In 1905 Alberta was admitted to Confederation as the eighth province; by then the region's wheat economy had taken hold. Just 42 years later, the discovery of oil and then natural gas changed the economic fortunes of the province forever.

Prehistory to Present

PREHISTORIC NOMADS

The first people of Alberta are thought to have migrated from what is now the US and Eastern Canada after the melting of the last ice cap in Western Canada more than 10,000 years ago. Archaeologists suggest these were nomadic hunters looking for giant mammals such as bison, which European pioneers erroneously named buffalo. The massive beasts were driven over cliffs to their deaths in highly ritualized hunts, providing almost all the raw goods their pursuers needed for food, clothing, tools and shelter.

NATIVE PEOPLES

Plains Indians, primarily the **Blackfoot** or **Assiniboine** (Stoney) in the southern part of the province and **Cree** and **Athabascan** in the north, survived for years on hunting and trapping. They relied mostly on the plentiful bison; its hide was used for clothing and shelter, its bones and sinews for tools and the meat and organs for food. The annual bison hunts were a carefully choreographed event. Nomadic clans would set up camp near an area of steep cliffs, usually along a river. An area between camp and the cliffs was designated a kill site where the animals were butchered for a year's worth of supplies; meat was usually dried and pounded into a pulp and mixed with saskatoon berries and fat to create a staple known as pemmican.

The hunt was generally preceded by ceremonies and prayers to the Creator for a bountiful harvest, and the selection of hunters—usually single males, as the hunt itself was physically demanding and could be dangerous. Hunters cloaked themselves in animal hides, and one person imitated the sound of an injured calf. The female bison, attempting to aid the calf, would be forced along rock-lined drive lanes that led to the cliffs. A stampede resulted, with so much momentum that it was too late for the beasts to stop when they reached the cliffs. Southern Alberta is home to one of the best preserved of these sites, Head-Smashed-In Buffalo Jump near Fort Macleod, where bone deposits 11m/33.5ft deep have been found. A seven-tiered interpretive centre has been built into the sandstone cliffs to tell the story of the buffalo and their ultimate demise, brought by the arrival of the settlers, horses and guns.

Settlement's Impact

The settlement of the West had a devastating affect on the life of First Nations people in other ways. The influx of fur traders and hunters to the north had, within two centuries, wreaked havoc on the traditional aboriginal lifestyle due to the dwindling supply of beaver, fox and caribou. The bird and fish populations were similarly depleted. Alcohol was introduced to a society of people who did not have a tolerance for "firewater"; the effects of the intoxicant are still seen today as a major social problem. The most significant damage was caused by the arrival of horses and guns; not

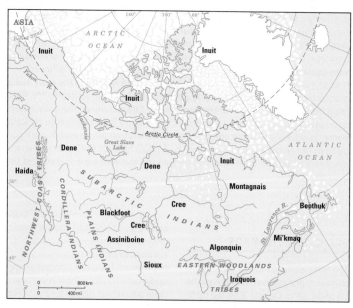

only did they lead to the buffalo's near-extinction (it was considered a sport to shoot the woolly creatures from passing rail cars), they also heightened tensions among warring tribes. The fur trade put guns into the hands of northern First Nations such as the Cree, allowing them to force the Blackfoot farther and farther south in a series of bloody territorial battles. In the mountains and foothills, where the buffalo did not thrive, previously nomadic clans that had survived on hunting and harvesting berries and plants took up grain farming.

Starting in the 1840s, missionaries opened schools for children. The notion of teaching Indian children literacy and European habits dates from the early days of colonization; French nuns ran schools for Indians in 17C Quebec. Schools for Indians became more numerous in Western Canada in the 1880s, and in 1892 the federal government launched a program to fund residential schools, with a stipend for each child enrolled. The goal became not only to teach children basic skills, but to assimilate them into the white majority. As a result of this infusion of cash, aboriginal children were removed, sometimes forcibly, from their families and enrolled in schools, often far from their homes, run by religious groups, mostly Catholic but also Anglican, Presbyterian and United Church. Although some children benefited, the experience was traumatic for many youngsters, who were separated from their families, sometimes for years, and not allowed to speak their own language. In some cases children were mistreated by their teachers. It is asserted that these schools are in part responsible for many of the social ills that afflict First Nations communities today. The last residential schools closed in the late 20C. In June 2008, Prime Minister Stephen Harper, in the House of Commons, speaking on behalf of the Canadian government, issued a formal apology to First Nations, Inuit and Métis people for the abuse suffered at residential schools.

With their traditional lifestyle eroded and starvation and social ills such as substance abuse and poverty taking hold of native peoples, First Nations chiefs signed treaties with the federal government that exchanged freedom for a land base and social assistance. Legendary Blackfoot Confederacy Chief Crowfoot signed Treaty 7 in southern Alberta in 1877; two other treaties were signed about this time with bands in central and northern Alberta. Many tribes were given land that was unsuitable for farming or other means of economic self-sufficiency; however, numerous court battles have been fought in recent years after oil, gas and other valuable natural resources were discovered on these lands. A series of Supreme Court of Canada rulings upholding aboriginal treaty rights and land title have led to a present-day era of greater consultation between First Nations and companies attempting to do business on aboriginal land.

Part of the Blackfoot Confederacy, the people of the **Blood Nation** live on Canada's largest reserve, which totals 354,490 acres in southern Alberta and stretches from the southeast, near Lethbridge, toward Cardston to the south and west. Nearly 8,000 people live on the reserve.

The Métis

In the late 18C and early 19C, the fur trade touched most indigenous people in some way, especially those in northwestern Alberta, a key part of the fur-trade corridor. Explorer-trader Peter Pond helped build Fort Chipewyan on Lake Athabasca in the late 1780s, and the good relations he and other traders fostered with local First Nations went a long way toward developing a close relationship between the two groups. Over time, families began to intermarry, creating a new ethnic group in Canada called the Métis. Formerly known by the derogatory term half-breed, the Métis are descendants of mixed-blood parents, usually European (primarily British, French and Scottish). Many of these marital unions involved an inter-change of values and customs: First Nations adopted the prevalent Roman Catholic religion of their spouses as well as their traditions and music; their European partners absorbed the lifestyle dear to First Nations, living off the land, eating aboriginal foods and learning their language.

Their past long and storied, the Métis played a significant role in Canada's—and Alberta's—history and culture. The first threat to them came with the arrival of settlers along the Red River in 1812. In 1870 the situation escalated when the new Dominion of Canada decided to take over the vast lands of the Hudson's Bay Company, an area that included Alberta. As more settlers arrived, the Métis saw their traditional life disappearing. They turned to 25-year-old **Louis Riel,** who set up his own provisional government in order to recognise Métis rights. Riel gained no sympathy from English Métis and other settlers. After foiling a plot to assassinate him, Riel executed an adventurer from Ontario, Thomas Scott, an act Riel was to regret. Nevertheless his plea on behalf of his people was heard. In July 1870, the new province of Manitoba was created.

In the decades that followed, many Métis moved to Alberta seeking a new home base after they were forced out of European settlements in Saskatchewan and Manitoba. The influx of Métis and their landless status led the Alberta government, after many on-and-off-again efforts, to put legislation in place, in 1989, to reaffirm eight Métis settlements in northcentral Alberta, making the province the only one in Canada with a Métis land base. Today these Métis settlements allow citizens to operate businesses in their communities that promote Métis culture and history, and encourage economic partnerships with companies seeking to develop natural resources such as oil and gas. In 2007 a new tourist attraction named **Métis Crossing** *(www.metiscrossing. com)* opened on 512 acres of land along the North Saskatchewan River north of Edmonton to showcase the Métis heritage through demonstrations such as erecting a trapper's tent, making fry bread and paddling a voyageur canoe.

THE TAMING OF THE WEST

During the 1860s, the Province of Canada, composed of present-day Ontario and Quebec, together with the colonies of Nova Scotia, New Brunswick and Prince Edward Island, held discussions that resulted, on July 1, 1867, in creation of the **Dominion of Canada,** (although Prince Edward Island didn't join until 1873). Alberta was not yet a province, however, and in the eyes of much of Eastern Canada was still an untamed frontier. The government purchased what is now the **Northwest Territories,** which included Alberta, from the **Hudson's Bay Company (HBC)** two years later to shore up its assets in the western colonies. It gave the fur-trading giant a cash settlement and rights to its trading posts in the north.

Frontier Alberta gained a reputation over the next few years as a lawless place. In 1857 Captain John Palliser was sent west from Winnipeg by British authorities to determine Alberta's agricultural and trade potential. His report five years later praised northern Alberta, then a fur-trade hub, but dismissed the south as "an extension of the Great American Desert." In the early 1870s trading posts were established in the **Cypress Hills** in southeastern Alberta by Americans from Montana. In exchange for furs, they illegally traded "firewater," an extremely potent brew. In the winter of 1872-73 **Assiniboine Indians,** camped near two of these posts, were joined by Canadian and American wolf-hunters whose horses had been stolen by Cree raiders. Thinking the Assiniboines were the thieves, the drunken "wolfers" attacked the Indian camp, killing 36 people. When news of this massacre reached Ottawa, Prime Minister Sir John A. Macdonald acted quickly. He created the **North West Mounted Police** (renamed the **Royal Canadian Mounted Police** in 1920), and dispatched the new police force to the Northwest to stop such border incursions and the illegal whisky trade. The perpetrators were arrested but later acquitted for lack of evidence.

In 1874 North West Mounted Police, under the guidance of Col. **James Macleod,** marched west from Toronto to bring order to the whisky trade in the lawless prairies. The mounted police established **Fort Macleod** on the Oldman River in southern Alberta.

Some 250km/160mi north, on rolling prairie grasslands west of Calgary, **Matthew Cochrane** took advantage of government-sponsored grazing leases that offered low prices for land to encourage homesteading in the area. In 1881 he bought about 190,000 acres and established a sprawling ranch that paved the way for others to set up cattle farms on prime land where the buffalo once roamed. By this point, **Fort Calgary** had existed for more than five years along the bank of the Bow and Elbow rivers. Some 50 Mounties took six weeks to erect the fort with supplies they had brought in by bull train from Montana; within seven years wind and rain had eroded the mud and clay plastered on the fort's log beams, and the fort had to be rebuilt.

Since 1821 **Edmonton House** had been the Hudson's Bay Company's most important post in the West. The **Klondike gold rush** of 1896-99 in the Yukon bolstered communities such as Edmonton and Peace River. While the majority sailed up the Pacific to reach Dawson City, a few of the 100,000 gold seekers tried an overland—nearly impassable—course from Edmonton. By late in the century, the city had secured its place as a strategic commercial centre and the most northern major metropolis in Canada.

The **Dominion Lands Act** of 1872 allowed prospective homesteaders to register for 65ha/160 acres. Title was given after three years if a homestead had been built and an amount of land cultivated. The prospect of free land attracted inhabitants of an overcrowded Europe. Under Sir **Wilfrid Laurier**, the Canadian government advertised the Prairies all over the world: "Free homes for millions." Millions indeed came, from Ontario, the Maritimes, the US, Iceland, Britain, the Ukraine and other parts of Europe. Finally a means of reaching the region and transporting produce to market was needed. To solve this problem, construction of a railroad was needed.

THE COMING OF THE RAILWAYS

To encourage British Columbia to join Confederation in 1871, the province was promised a transcontinental rail link. After a few false starts, construction of the **Canadian Pacific Railway** finally got under way in 1881. It was an immense and difficult project, the western mountain ranges alone posing a formidable barrier. The line reached **Calgary** and the town of **Banff** in 1883, though there was great debate at this point over whether the line could possibly be laid through the Rockies to the West Coast. As construction of the railway crawled over two years, the CPR built several grand hotels. The majestic **Banff Springs** went up in 1888 and became what was then the world's largest hotel; the **Chateau Lake Louise** was built two years later along a particularly beautiful alpine lake. The track was completed by 1885, when the last spike was nailed in the new province of British Columbia.

A northern line built by the **Grand Trunk Railway** marked its inauguration in 1914. Construction of GTR's subsidiary line, the Grand Trunk Pacific Railway, began in the Prairie Provinces in 1905, moving west from Saskatchewan to reach Edmonton in 1909. By 1911, the line had cut through Jasper and traversed the Continental Divide. In April 1914 the track laid through the rugged Rocky Mountains had reached its terminus at the maritime city of Prince Rupert in British Columbia.

THE 20TH CENTURY

Canada's purchase of land controlled by the HBC opened the way for settlement of the West; the building of the transcontinental rail line provided the means. Thousands of immigrants poured into the region, necessitating the creation of two new provinces in 1905: **Alberta** and its eastern neighbour **Saskatchewan**. By 1912 the remaining parts of the Northwest Territories south of the 60th parallel had been redistributed to Manitoba, Ontario and Quebec. This was a tough time for Alberta farmers, who just prior to World War I were struggling under the weight of government price restrictions. Once the war ended, the Canadian Wheat Board emerged as a voice for farmers' rights. Two decades later, an international economic depression and severe weather, including drought, forced many farmers out of business, though the demand for wheat leapt with the onset of World War II and continues unabated even today. (Agricultural products make up 2.3 percent of the nation's Gross Domestic Product).

Although agriculture was Alberta's prime domestic and export commodity, that all changed on Feb. 13, 1947—the day a huge **oil deposit** was discovered at Leduc Oil Well No. 1, just south of Edmonton. And much like the Klondike's influx, surveyors and prospectors from across North America flooded into the province to find black gold. Other major discoveries, including the Pembina oilfields of northcentral Alberta and the gargantuan Athabasca oil sands north of Fort McMurray in the remote boreal forest, made the province a major world oil producer. Calgary became the centre for most of the country's head offices of the oil and gas companies, while Edmonton used its proximity to the oil sands (more than 400km/248mi to the north) to become a key service and supply centre. Both of these cities, economically, retain these distinctive roles today.

Alberta's contribution to the **world wars** was significant, especially in WWII when thousands of men (later, women) served overseas as infantry, artillery soldiers and engineers in such regiments as the Calgary Highlands, the Calgary Regiment and the Loyal Edmonton Regiment. Internment and POW camps were established in Alberta at Wainwright and in Kananaskis Country, while many British Commonwealth training camps also operated in Alberta during the war.

Politically, the 20C witnessed much upheaval and change in Alberta. In 1927, five women led by **Emily Murphy** of Calgary banded together to contest a rule under the British North America Act that restricted a **woman's rights,** including the opportunity to enter political life. The women, the now-legendary Famous Five, fought to have women recognised as "persons" under the act, taking the case to the Supreme Court of Canada. Their first attempt was rejected, but in 1931 the Judicial Committee of the Privy Council of Great Britain, which served as the highest appeal court in the nation, ruled that the word "persons" included both men and women. Bronze statues of Murphy, along with Nellie McClung, Louise McKinney, Irene Parlby and Henrietta Muir Edwards, stand testament to their legacy in downtown Calgary.

A big moment came in 1971, when the long-ruling Social Credit Party, which had controlled the government for more than 35 years on a platform of strong farmer support, was ousted after nine consecutive election wins by Peter Lougheed's Conservative party. The Tory stronghold on Alberta has continued into the new millennium under the premierships of Don Getty (1985-1992) and Ralph Klein (1992-2006), a former Calgary mayor who resigned after 13 years as a controversial but popular provincial leader. The present premier is Ed Stelmach, a farmer who represents Fort Saskatchewan-Vegreville in the Legislative Assembly. The latter part of the 20C also saw the emergence of a new political force in Canada, the right-wing Reform Party.

THE 21ST CENTURY

Shiny SUVs, sports cars and pick-up trucks are just one sign of the economic fortunes of Calgary today. High-rise offices and condominiums are part of a construction boom that dominates the downtown skyline; and many corporations continue to establish head offices in the city. Edmonton, too, is undergoing a rapid growth spurt as northern Alberta's oil sands brace for another massive expansion. Both cities are struggling to manage their growth in a time when demand for skilled labour, as well as a worker shortage in sectors such as retail, hospitality and tourism, has far outstripped supply. Yet Calgary prospers as a tourist magnet, drawing visitors to its Western culture and serving as a departure point for the Canadian Rockies. Edmonton thrives as a government city and cultural hub. It is known as the 'Festival City' for its many theatrical and artistic events that run almost consecutively from spring to late fall.

Time Line

PRE-COLONIAL PERIOD

10,000 BC — Date of earliest evidence of human habitation in Alberta.

8,000-6,000 BC — Extensive drought causes many lakes in central and southern Alberta to dry up.

2,500 BC — First known aboriginal ceremonial sites appear; they are large architectural forms called Medicine Wheels created on high hills.

BRITISH REGIME

1670 — **Hudson's Bay Company (HBC)** is formed.

1778 — Peter Pond of the **North West Company,** HBC's rival, establishes Alberta's first trading post south of Lake Athabasca.

1793 — Alexander Mackenzie crosses British Columbia to the West Coast.

1821 — Edmonton House emerges as HBC's most important post in the west.

1835 — Deadly flu epidemic sweeps through aboriginal communities in the **Athabasca** and **Peace River** districts.

1841 — **Act of Union** creates the United Province of Canada.

1847 — **Responsible government** system is implemented in Canada.

1857 — Capt. John Palliser is sent by the British to report on Alberta.

1858-61 — British Columbia's gold rushes.

CANADIAN CONFEDERATION

1867 — British North America Act establishes Canadian Confederation.

1869-70 — Riel Rebellion occurs in Red River Valley.

1870 — Canadian Confederation buys Hudson's Bay Company land; Manitoba is created.

1872 — **Dominion Lands Act** is passed.

1873 — North West Mounted Police is established.

1877 — First Nations chiefs and the federal government sign Treaty 7.

1885 — Canadian Pacific Railway is completed. Canada's **first national park** is created in the Alberta alpine town of Banff.

1896 — Gold is discovered in the Klondike.

1905 — Alberta becomes a province; Edmonton is named as its capital city.

1912 — First Calgary Stampede— a rodeo and cowboy competition and celebration— is held.

1914-18 — World War I.

1916 — Women are granted the right to vote.

1923 — Alberta Wheat Pool opens for business.

1931 — **Statute of Westminster** grants Canada control of external affairs. Alberta's 'Famous Five' win their fight to have women included as "persons" in the British North American Act.

1939-45 — World War II. Alberta receives large numbers of European immigrants; Alberta agriculture and other industries prosper during and after the war.

1942 — Alaska Highway is completed.

CONTEMPORARY ALBERTA

1947 — "Black Gold"(oil) is discovered at Leduc, south of Edmonton. TransCanada PipeLines from Alberta to eastern Canada completed.

1960 — First Nations people get the right to vote in federal elections.

1962 — Trans-Canada Highway is completed.
Alberta gives aboriginal people the right to vote in provincial elections.

1967 — Great Canadian Oil Sands (now Suncor) launches the first large-scale Athabasca oil sands extraction operation near Fort McMurray.

1971 — Peter Lougheed's Conservative government ousts the long-ruling Social Credit Party after 36 years. Alberta Bill of Rights is introduced.

1973 — Federal government's move to restrict domestic oil prices launches a long-running feud between Premier Peter Lougheed and Prime Minister Pierre Trudeau.

1980 — Trudeau launches the controversial National Energy Program; Lougheed responds by cutting oil production in Alberta.

1981 — Alberta sinks into an economic recession that is in large part blamed on the new energy program.

1985 — Former Edmonton Oilers quarterback Don Getty is elected premier.

1988 — Fifteenth Winter Olympic Games begin in Calgary as well as in new venues such as Nakiska at Mount Allan ski hill in Kananaskis Country west of Calgary and the Canmore Nordic Centre in Canmore.

1992 — Getty resigns and is replaced by former Calgary mayor Ralph Klein.

1993 — Negotiation of **North American Free Trade Agreement** (NAFTA) among Canada, Mexico and the US.

1994 — Approved by Canada, Mexico and the US, NAFTA takes effect, giving Canada secure access to US and Mexican markets and boosting Alberta's economic footing.

1998 — Federal government issues a statement of reconciliation offering regrets for its role in forcing aboriginal people to attend the much-loathed residential schools. Klein government announces $2.5 billion government surplus.

THE NEW MILLENNIUM

2001 — A nationwide **census** confirms a population of 29.5 million in Canada, and 2.98 million in Alberta, or 10 percent of the nation's total.

2002 — Canadian troops join international peacekeeping mission in Afghanistan.

2005 — Alberta, the Wild Rose province, celebrates its centennial. Populist Alberta premier Ralph Klein resigns after 13 years; his party chooses Ed Stelmach to succeed him.

2007 — In September, the Canadian dollar closes slightly above parity with the US dollar for the first time in 31 years. Premier Ed Stelmach announces a controversial new royalty framework for energy companies that infuriates the industry.

2008 — Census of the Canadian aboriginal population reveals that 17 percent, or 188,365, live in Alberta.

2009 — Alberta is slated to host a huge, Olympic-style event, the 40th **WorldSkills Competition,** showcasing excellence in trades and technology. Held every two years, the international contest is expected to draw more than 1,000 competitors along with 5,000 experts, delegates and judges, as well as spectators from around the globe. Stampede Park in Calgary will be a host venue.

ART AND CULTURE

The culture of Canada, including Alberta, is rooted in a blend of British, French, and aboriginal traditions, and influenced by successive waves of immigration. American media and entertainment dominate, but various federal and provincial government programs and laws support Canadian cultural initiatives. The federally funded Canadian Broadcasting Corporation (CBC) provides national television and radio coverage. The Alberta Council of the Arts offers funding for Alberta-based artists and arts organizations throughout the province.

Art

NATIVE EXPRESSIONS

Over centuries, Canada's indigenous peoples have developed diverse modes of artistic expression that bear witness to their distinctive lifestyles and beliefs. Since the aboriginal peoples were generally nomadic, little remains of their prehistoric art. However, petroglyphs, or carvings on rock, found in various sites in Alberta, particularly southern Alberta, are as much as 8,000 years old. Much of the aboriginal art sold in the province hails from the Inuit people of northern Canada (Northwest Territories, Yukon and Nunavut). Some art is available from the First Nations of northern Alberta, usually birchbark baskets, beaded jewellery and clothing such as porcupine quill buckskin or leather jackets and moccasins. Locally produced paintings are also available (**Jane Ash Poitras** is a big name among aboriginal artists), as well as carvings such as antler carvings produced by Athabasca artist **Dusty Bearht.** The contemporary paintings of Cold Lake's **Alex Janvier** are bold, colourful works.

Plains Cree artist **George Littlechild** is well known for his mixed-media paintings, as is visual artist **Joanne Cardinal-Schubert** (writer, curator, poet and activist) from the Blackfoot Confederacy. She won a National Aboriginal Achievement Award for her contributions to art since the 1960s. Her *Self Portrait as an Indian Warshirt* created a national buzz in 1991; it hangs in the Glenbow Museum in Calgary. Stores in major cities, including museum shops at the Glenbow and the Provincial Museum of Alberta in Edmonton, have extensive aboriginal arts and crafts for sale, as do the pricy galleries in tourist towns such as Banff and Jasper.

PAINTING AND SCULPTURE

Alberta's fine arts are reflective of the province's cowboy culture and natural assets. Alberta-born **Paul van Ginkel,** who travels between Calgary and New Mexico, is internationally known for his elaborately detailed paintings that are primarily western-themed. Works of art in the province run the gamut from elaborate art murals and horse portraits to landscape paintings and bronze sculptures of cowhands. Many of these works can be found in major urban centres—on display in Edmonton's Art Gallery of Alberta, for example, or for sale at high-end outlets such as Webster Galleries in Calgary.

Alberta's art history does not stretch nearly as far back in time as eastern Canada's. Until the early 20C, many artists saw the province as a sparsely populated land and shied away from moving there. Its natural grandeur, however, lured famous Canadian artists to paint in Alberta, including members of the legendary Group of Seven painters from Ontario, such as **A.Y. Jackson** (1882-1974) and **Lawren Harris** (1885-1979). In the early 1920s, these two landscape artists initially trekked with guides into the Rocky Mountains backcountry, shunning the more popular sites like Lake Louise and Banff in search of unspoiled nature. They also travelled to other parts of the province, such as the Alberta Badlands near Drumheller, with their hoodoos, hewn valleys and wild rose-blanketed coulees.

Born in Calgary, **Maxwell Bates** (1906-1980) studied at the Calgary Art Club and the Provincial Institute of Technology. He favoured French post-impressionist paintings, and lived abroad for a number of years. Upon his return to Calgary, Bates, an expressionist painter, produced a number of works, mostly landscapes and figures in bold colours. His most well-known paintings are *Girl with Yellow Hair* (1956) and *Cocktail Party 1* (1965).

The arts scene was slow to advance in the province, however. In the 1930s several groups, such as the Alberta Society of Artists, banded together to change this reality. The **Banff Centre,** Calgary's **Alberta College of Art and Design** and other local training institutes soon emerged, attracting acclaimed instructors from around the world and providing outlets for area painters, sculptors and other artists.

In the early 1960s **Marion Nicoll** (1909-84) broke new ground with her dramatic abstract paintings, including one titled *The Prophet*. In the 1970s and 80s, works created by members of the University of Alberta's arts faculty helped to make Edmonton a focal point of the modernist movement. Also active were the 1920s-spawned Edmonton Art Gallery (now the Art Gallery of Alberta); Latitude 53, formed in 1973 and still promoting contemporary visual culture; and the Society of Northern Alberta Print Artists, established in 1982.

Literature

In great measure, Canadian literature resonates with a rich sense of place; Alberta's body of literary works is largely no different. Whether in the explorers' journals of the 18C-19C, the diaries and novels of 20C immigrant settlers, or the poems and short stories of the 20C and 21C, writers grapple with what it means to be Canadian. Alberta has produced its fair share of writers, including award-winning novelist **W.O. Mitchell** (1914-88) of Calgary, who devoted his writing to depicting life on the prairies. Mitchell penned such Canadian classics as *Who Has Seen the Wind* (1947), *The Kite* (1967)

and *Roses are Difficult Here* (1990). Writer **Andy Russell** (1916-2005), a conservationist, wrote some two dozen books about his life, including *Memoirs of a Mountain Man, Trails of a Wilderness Wanderer* (2000) and *The Life of a River* (2001). Alberta writers have done well in the annual **Governor General's Literary Awards;** winners have included university literature professor **E.D. Blodgett,** who authored more than 10 volumes of poetry. He won the Governor General's award for *Apostrophes: Woman at a Piano* in 1996, along with several other provincial and national honours. Legendary Alberta newspaperman **Bob Edwards** (1865-1922) turned some of his columns into books, including one titled the *Best of Bob Edwards*. Edwards himself is also the subject of books such as two written by Glenbow Museum chief curator emeritus **Hugh Dempsey,** a Calgary historian and writer.

Music and Dance

While plenty of radio stations play mainstream rock, pop, hard rock, folk and alternative tunes, country music is big in Alberta and many of its country artists have gone onto international fame. Legendary Canadian **Ian Tyson** *(Four Strong Winds)*, who ranches and owns a cafe in Longview in southern Alberta, has been heard on radio speakers for more than 30 years. Nashville (Tennessee) has Alberta to thank for such superstars as **Terri Clark, Paul Brandt** and **Carolyn Dawn Johnson,** as well as up-and-comers like **Corb Lund** of the group DFDF and **Emerson Lane** from northwest Alberta. Aside from country, rock and rollers **Nickleback,** from the town of Hanna near Drumheller, found international fame by providing music for the recent *Superman* movies. Internationally acclaimed folk singer **Joni Mitchell,** who found fame in the 1960s and 70s, hails from southern Alberta. Calgarian **Jann Arden,** who for a time owned The Arden diner on the city's trendy 17th Avenue S.W. strip, has reached international audiences with her folk/pop music. In 2008, superstar chanteuse **Feist,** who hails from Calgary, returned home to her base in Europe after taking home several Canadian Juno music awards.

Alberta offers a wealth of **classical music** at venues such as Calgary's EPCOR Centre for the Performing Arts, Edmonton's Francis Winspear Centre for Music and the Jubilee Auditorium in both cities. Even smaller cities such as Red Deer, Lethbridge, Fort McMurray, Grande Prairie and Medicine Hat have performing arts centres, though smaller in size than those in larger cities. The **Calgary Philharmonic Orchestra**, the University of Alberta Symphony Orchestra and the Edmonton Symphony Orchestra give well-attended concerts; smaller musical groups include the Calgary Youth Orchestra, Calgary Civic Symphony, Edmonton Chamber Music Society and the Edmonton Youth Orchestra. The **Calgary Opera** and the **Edmonton Opera** stage performances year-round.

Alberta's **dance** scene is equally diverse. With more than 20 years of performing under its belt, Decidedly Jazz Danceworks is a perennial Calgary favourite that has showcased around the world. Other Calgary dance companies include Springboard, Dancer's Studio West and Alberta Dance Theatre, which is aimed at youth. In Edmonton, the Alberta Dance Factory and Brian Web Dance Company feature contemporary dance along with hip-hop, highland and jazz. The renowned **Alberta Ballet** has toured the world and performs regularly in Calgary and Edmonton. Edmonton's **Metis Cultural Dance Society** is praised for its lively fiddle music and dance; and Southern Alberta's **Red Thunder Dancers** have thrilled audiences around the world with First Nations dancing and drumming.

Cinema and Theatre

Although most movies shown in Canada are imported from the US, Alberta—particularly the Rocky Mountains west of Calgary—serves as a frequent **location** for shooting US and international films. The **Alberta Film Commission** (www. albertafilm.ca), an arm of the provincial government, pitches the province to film scouts from around the world. The commission's film development division recruits out-of-country movie makers with such enticements as affordable production rates, experienced film crews, lower food and supply costs, and lack of a provincial sales tax.

One of the earliest major Hollywood movies filmed in Alberta was a western called *Days of Heaven* (1991), starring Richard Gere and Sam Shepard, wherein the foothills of southern Alberta stood in for the grasslands of Texas. The **Unforgiven** (1993) was a major blockbuster film starring Clint Eastwood and Gene Hackman; it was filmed in the Longview area on the Cowboy Trail. Brad Pitt and Anthony Hopkins came to this neck of the woods to film *Legends of the*

©Laszlo Uhrik/Alberta Film

Filming in Slave Lake during winter

Fall (1994); and *Shanghai Noon* (2000) brought Jackie Chan and Owen Wilson to the Drumheller area and other parts of the province. *Brokeback Mountain* (2005), shot largely in the Kananaskis area west of Calgary, earned accolades for its cinematography; the lush alpine scenery was directly linked to a leap in interest from tourists outside the province and country. The movie starred actors Jake Gyllenhaal, Michelle Williams and the late Heath Ledger. Brad Pitt returned to the areas south and west of Calgary to film *The Assassination of Jesse James* (2007), a western about the notorious outlaw, which also stars Casey Affleck.

Canadians factor significantly in a surprising number of major films—as actors, directors, film-crew members and animators. For more information about Canada's contribution to film, visit northernstars.ca.

The hamlet of Rosebud, 110km/80mi east of Calgary, attracts more than 60,000 visitors each year to its professional **theatre** offerings held at the Rosebud Opera House. At Edmonton's annual Fringe Theatre Festival each summer, the L'uni Theatre stages French-speaking productions only, while the Northern Light Theatre performs provocative works. Other venues include the Citadel Theatre, Princess Theatre, Varscona Theatre, Workshop West Playwright's Theatre, John L. Haar Theatre and Jubilations Dinner Theatre. In Calgary, shows are mounted by Theatre Calgary, Alberta Theatre Projects, the offbeat Loose Moose Theatre Company and Theatre Junction. Venues include the EPCOR Centre for the Performing Arts, Pumphouse Theatre, historic Grand Theatre, Vertigo Theatre, and Lunchbox Theatre, which offers shorter productions for the office lunch crowd downtown.

ALBERTA TODAY

Alberta is one of Canada's wealthiest provinces. Its ample oil and gas reserves are helping to satisfy the increasing international hunger for fuel. In turn, these natural resources are fuelling population growth within the province. Record high oil prices have spurred an economic boom that is attracting industry workers and their families, entrepreneurs, investors, adventurers and others to the province. Growth in such industries as manufacturing, research, cattle and grain has further bolstered the economy. Alberta is experiencing a population spurt of more than two percent a year (Canada's growth averages one percent annually). Residents in Alberta's two main cities of Calgary and Edmonton number over one million people each; Fort McMurray—which is witnessing a huge oil-sands expansion—and other pockets of the province are seeing an influx of new residents. After erasing its debt early in the new millennium, the provincial government is operating with a sizable surplus today, despite the fact that Alberta is the only province that does not levy a provincial sales tax.

The Economy

Statistics Canada provides electronic publications for readers seeking detailed information (fees may apply): www.statcan.ca. Another source is the Canadian government's website www.canada.gc.ca, which provides links to all government publications.

DIVERSIFICATION

While traditionally reliant on agriculture and natural resources, Alberta's economy has seen recent growth from other sectors such as manufacturing; between 1995 and 2005 shipments of products increased 108 percent to $59 billion or nine percent of the province's Gross Domestic Product (GDP). Information technology is another booming industry in Alberta: IT firms and telecom companies generated revenues of $8.7 billion and exports of $1.8 billion in 2004. Sponsored research to universities reached more than $650 million in 2005; the provincial government kicks in almost $200 million a year for research. Also strong are architectural, engineering and construction services, which produce more than $27 billion in revenues annually. The cattle industry continues to support a strong food-processing industry.

ENERGY

Major deposits of oil-encrusted sand are spread across northeastern Alberta within dense and isolated boreal forests. Oil and gas account for one-quarter of Alberta's GDP, almost 70 percent of exports and 35 percent of Alberta government revenues—a major reason that dropping oil prices inject fear into the financial sector. In 2006-2007 Alberta oil and gas royalty revenues amounted to $12.75 billion—more than 30 percent of the provincial government's total revenue. The energy industry accounts for 275,000 direct and indirect jobs in areas such as conventional oil, oil sands, natural gas, coal and coal-bed methane (natural gas found in coal seams). Because of its rich fossil fuel deposits, Alberta is sometimes called the Texas of the North, or the land of blue-eyed sheikhs.

Canada has the world's second-largest proven crude oil reserves. Most are situated in Alberta's oil sands, which hold more than 174 billion barrels, an amount believed to be the largest oil reserves in the world. The province's proximity to the US, along with skyrocketing demand for oil, has made Alberta the largest oil supplier to the US for more than six years (the province accounts for more than half of the nation's energy production). Conventional oil is found throughout Alberta; oil sands in the north lay beneath more than 140,800sq km/54,363sq mi—an area larger than the state of Florida. Oil sands produced almost 1.1 million barrels of crude a day in 2004, one-third of Canada's total output. According to the Alberta government, about $87 billion has been committed to oil sands development until 2016; close to 70 percent of the oil sands remain open for exploration and lease.

Canada is the world's third largest natural gas producer and second largest exporter. About 55 percent of Canada's 6.4 trillion cubic feet produced in 2004 went to the US; natural gas and natural gas liquids comprised 40 percent of Alberta's exports in 2005. Also in 2005 Alberta produced about 13.8 billion cubic feet of natural gas a day, and 5 trillion cubic feet per year – accounting for 80 percent of Canada's natural gas.

MINING, PETROCHEMICALS AND ELECTRICITY

With its singular geology, Alberta boasts 70 percent of Canada's coal reserves; nine major mines in the province produce 27-30 metric tonnes of marketable coal each year. Most of the coal is low in sulphur, meaning it burns cleaner and with more efficiency than other coal sources that emit higher sulphur dioxide levels. The Genesee 3 coal-fired power plant near Edmonton is considered Canada's most technologically advanced. About half of Alberta's electricity is generated from coal, though an increasing amount is fuelled by natural gas. Generation from renewable resources—hydro, biomass (wood) and wind power—has been increased almost 50 percent since 1998, to over 1,350 megawatts a year.

Alberta is also a strong player in the petrochemical manufacturing sector, producing more than $9 billion in products and $5.3 billion in exports yearly. Products made from petrochemicals include camera film, computer keys, detergents, hard hats, skateboard wheels and chewing gum. There are four petrochemical plants in Alberta (Joffre and Fort Saskatchewan are the world's largest) with a combined annual production capacity of 8.6 billion pounds.

AGRICULTURE

If oil and gas are king in Alberta, agriculture is queen. One third of provincial land—52 million acres, an area about the size of Nebraska—is devoted to crop and livestock production. Alberta

©Travel Alberta

Canola Fields, Northern Alberta

is Canada's second largest agricultural producer, netting 22 percent of Canada's farm cash receipts. Agriculture injects about $2.8 billion into Alberta's Gross Domestic Product; agri-food trade accounts for $5 billion in exports. With so much open land, Alberta boasts nearly 6 million head of cattle, or 40 percent of Canada's total. Beef is the province's number one agri-food export, accounting for $1.4 billion in 2005.

Pork comes in second (14 percent of national total), and many farmers also raise sheep, goat, deer, elk, reindeer and bison, while poultry is also a strong market. The province is a national leader in the production of crops such as wheat, barley, canola, flax and oats. Irrigation is used in many areas, especially in the drier south; some 1.63 million acres (five percent of Alberta's cultivated land) are irrigated. One of the chief irrigated crops is sugar beets; no other province produces sugar from them.

FORESTRY

More than 60 percent of Alberta's land base is forest, an area equal to 94 million acres. Eighty-seven percent of this land is public land, overseen by the provincial government and managed for sustainable development. The forestry industry alone generates $3.8 billion in revenues and maintains 48,000 jobs. Every year, according to the provincial government, some 75 million seedlings are planted to sustain these forests. Yet forestry comprises only a miniscule fraction of the provincial GDP because most of the trees are part of slow-growth forests.

THE NEW ECONOMY

Although the Alberta economy is still dominated by the energy and agriculture sectors, the high-tech, retail, tourism and services sectors are also gaining strength. On a per capita basis, Canada is next only to the US in the number of personal computers, with 669 per 1,000 inhabitants in 2005. Long considered one of the best-wired countries, Canada boasts comprehensive and inexpensive **telecommunications services**—no doubt a contributing factor to the nation's top ranking in worldwide Internet use per capita. Canada's long-distance telephone services were deregulated in 1992. Deregulation of the local telephone market in 1998 resulted in alternative carriers and resellers entering the market with new competitive services, although downturns in the worldwide telecommunications industry in 2001 led to consolidation and layoffs within Canada. Several Alberta-based companies are world leaders in the telecommunications equipment market. Biotechnology and information and communications technologies in Alberta are concentrated in Edmonton; a high-speed broadband Internet service links 429 communities across the province through more than 11,000 km/7,500mi of fibre and wireless technology.

Government

Alberta is one of ten provinces and three territories composing Canada, which is a **federal state.** The central government in **Ottawa,** the federal capital, assumes responsibility for such matters as defence, foreign affairs, transportation, trade, commerce, money and banking, and criminal law. The system of government at both federal and provincial levels is parliamentary.

Alberta's **Legislative Assembly,** a grand sandstone building, was built in 1912 on the site of the original Fort Edmonton, overlooking the North Saskatchewan River. The leader of the provincial government is the premier, who appoints cabinet ministers to a variety of portfolios including energy, economic development, agriculture, health and social services. The Conservative Party has held power in Alberta since 1971; the Liberal Party holds official opposition status and the New Democrats represent the socialist side; all parties have elected members sitting in the Legislative Assembly, known as MLAs.

The **federal Parliament**—which sits in Ottawa, the capital of Canada—is composed of a House of Commons whose members are elected from federal ridings, or electoral districts, across the country and an appointed Senate. The Canadian head of state is the **British monarch.** Her authority is exercised by the **governor general,** who was at one time appointed by the monarch but today is chosen by the elected representatives of the Canadian people. Each province has its own **lieutenant governor,** selected by the federal government with the consent of the provincial government. Actual power lies with the Canadian **prime minister,** who is the leader of the majority party in Parliament. The prime minister rules through a cabinet drawn from elected representatives (and sometimes from members of the Senate), and must submit his or her government for re-election after a maximum of five years, or if he or she is defeated in the House of Commons.

Visitors to Alberta will notice the **Royal Canadian Mounted Police or Mounties,** who provide policing on highways and in many towns and smaller cities as well as at airports and federal installations. Calgary and Edmonton have their own municipal police forces.

Population

DEMOGRAPHICS

As of July 2007, Alberta had a population of 3.3 million people, about two million divided evenly between metropolitan Calgary and Edmonton and the rest in smaller cities and rural areas. The 65-and-older group makes up 13 percent of the total Canadian population, while the proportion of Albertans under the age of 15 is at its lowest level ever, at 17.7 percent. The working population (ages 20-44) is much larger in urban areas, as many young adults leave their homes in rural communities to go to school or find work. Immigration is also highly concentrated in urban centres.

LANGUAGE

English is the official language of Alberta: the majority of residents (2.5 million of a total 3.3 million) speak English as their mother tongue. Less than two percent (61,000) speak French, which is spoken only in small pockets, despite the fact that French language rights have been extended to the legal and educational systems across the country.

Alberta is a land of immigrants, though not to the extent of other Canadian cities such as Montreal, Toronto or Vancouver. Ethnic groups such as Sudanese, Chinese and Vietnamese are represented in the province, as well as those from Central and South America. Most immigrants live in Calgary or Edmonton, though ethnic diversity is high in some places, like Brooks in southern Alberta, where a concentration of Africans and Asians work in the meat-processing industry.

Moraine Lake, Banff National Park
©H.P. Merten/World Pictures/Photoshot

DISCOVERING ALBERTA AND THE ROCKIES

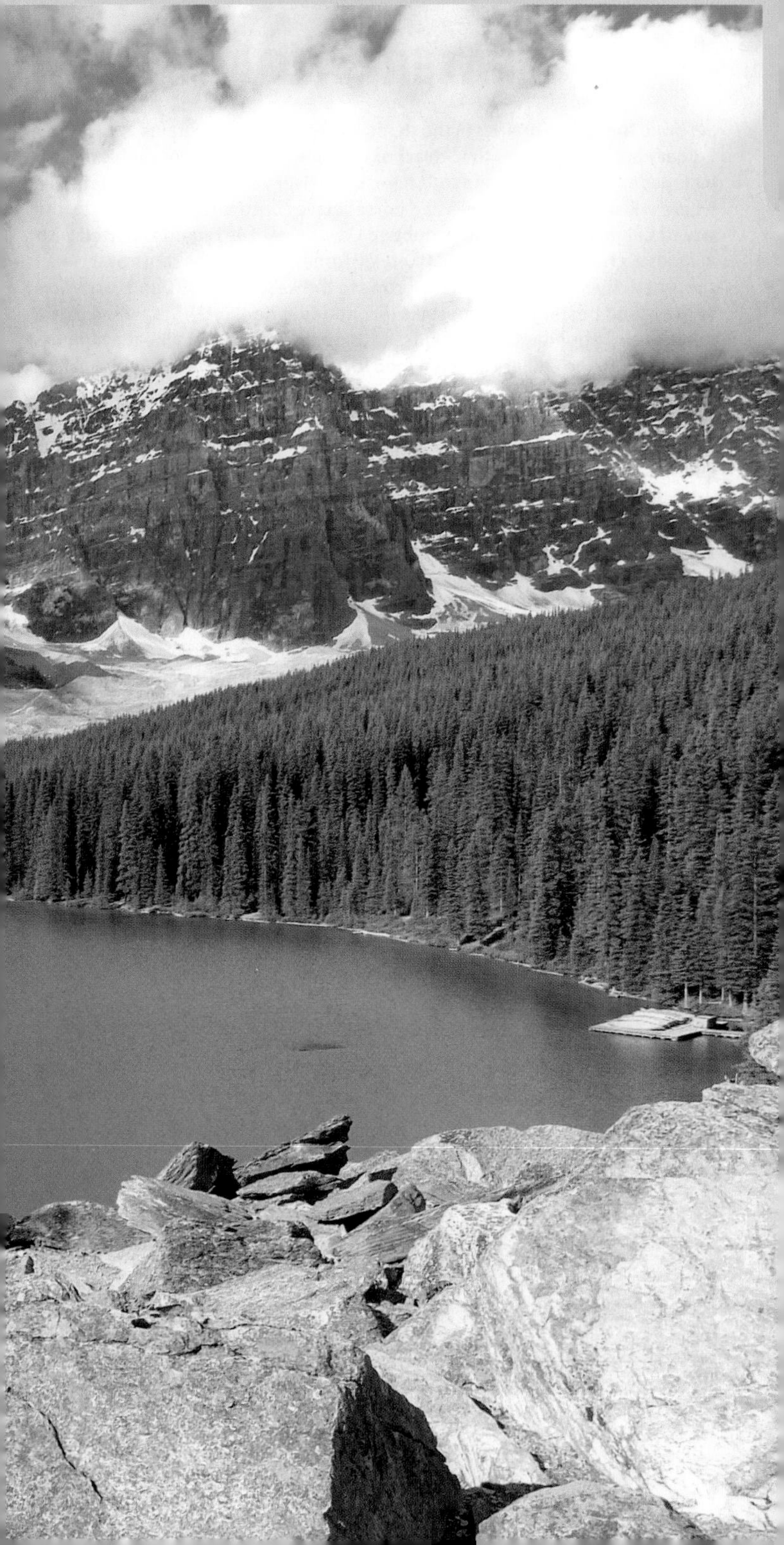

GREATER CALGARY

Set amid the rolling prairies in the shadow of the Rocky Mountains, the Greater Calgary area is known as the "Heart of the New West." Its geographic mosaic includes expansive grasslands, glacier-carved river valleys and saffron foothills where whisky traders, outlaws and horse thieves once ruled. Anchored by the city of Calgary—affectionately dubbed Cowtown—the region is dotted with villages such as Bragg Creek and Okotoks/Turner Valley to the southwest, small suburban cities like Cochrane and Airdrie to the west and north, and vast tracts of grassland hosting oil pumpjacks (or "nodding donkies"), sprawling cattle ranches and abundant wheatfields. With cattle as king and wheat running a close second, the Calgary area is a food lover's paradise, offering regional fare such as elk, bison, venison, Grade A beef and even ostrich. Many producers have turned to sustainable agriculture and organic farming; now vegetables—once a mere afterthought on menus in cowboy country—take centre stage at numerous eateries, not just at high-end vegetarian hotspots.

Winters here are generally moderate, though several deep freezes through the season can be counted on, as well as the reliable west wind called chinook, which turns warm as it blows from the mountains to the foothills in Greater Calgary. Temperatures have been known to climb 30°C/86°F in several hours; you know there's a chinook (they last 1-4 days on average) when a solid line of clouds arc across the blue sky. Summers in Calgary are generally delightful, sunny and warm.

The outdoors is a big part of life in the area: white-water rafting down the Kananaskis [Can-nah-NASS-kiss], Elbow or Upper Bow rivers to Calgary (novices should hire a guide); cycling along Calgary's excellent riverside trails, and mountain biking or hiking Bragg Creek's endless alpine paths. Big Hill Springs Provincial Park northwest of Cochrane is a little-known strolling and cookout spot, while dozens of new golf courses have sprung up in the city, the foothills and the river valleys *(the season is usually May to October)*. The Bow and Elbow rivers attract anglers from around the world, particularly the lower reaches of the Bow south of Calgary, where trout fishing is abundant and wildly popular. There are also scenic cycling and hiking trails around the tidy city of Cochrane, northwest of Calgary.

©Travel Alberta

Night skyline, Calgary

Address Book

For dollar-sign categories, see the Legend on the cover flap.

WHERE TO STAY

$ Westways B&B – *216 25th Ave. SW, Calgary.* P ⌼ ☎403-229-1758 or 866-846-7038. www.bedandbreakfast.com. *5 rooms.* Built in 1912 in the Arts and Crafts style, this pleasant inn is a 20min walk from downtown. All rooms come with a private bath and high-speed Internet connection. For couples, either of the two largest rooms—each with a king bed and gas fireplace—is more than adequate. Copious breakfast.

$$ Big Springs Estate B&B – *Hwy. 567, 35km/22mi northwest of Airdrie city limits.* P ⌼ ☎403-948-5264 or 888-948-5851. www.inntravels.com. *5 rooms.* A stay at this modern ranch house provides a taste of life under the big sky. The friendly hosts make guests feel at home on their 35-acre spread. Comfortable bedrooms have private baths, duvets and robes and slippers. Evening snacks and breakfast in a cheery dining room.

$$ High Country House B&B – *53Burney Rd., Bragg Creek.* P ⌼ ☎403-949-0933. www.highcountryhouse.com. *3 rooms.* Antique-furnished estate home on two treed acres in the eastern Rocky Mountains; an eight-minute stroll to the shops and restaurants of Bragg Creek. In-room high-speed Internet, breakfast.

$$ Inglewood B&B – *1006 8th Ave. SE, Calgary.* P ⌼ ☎403-262-6570. www. inglewoodbedandbreakfast.com. *3 rooms.* A pretty backyard alongside the Bow River and simply furnished rooms with private baths make this bed-and-breakfast a good choice for travellers looking for a simple alternative to a hotel. The management staff are particularly friendly. The property is within easy walking distance of Stampede Park and other major attractions.

$$$ Blackfoot Crossing Tepee Village – *On Siksika Reserve off Hwy. 842, 100km/62mi east of Calgary & 10km/6mi south of Trans-Can Hwy.* ✗ ⌖ P ☎888-654-6274. www.black

footcrossing.ca. *Tepees accommodate 4 or 8 people. 30-day advance reservations required.* Spend a night in the great outdoors snug within an authentic Plains Indian **tepee** (lined for warmth in cold weather). Basic packages provide air mattresses, water, wood stove and wood, but guests must bring their own sleeping bag. Higher-priced packages add sleeping bags, blankets, pillows and towels, plus an hour-long visit by a First Nations storyteller. Food is not included, but meal service is available for purchase on-site. Rates include admission to Blackfoot Crossing Historical Park and dance performances as well as other benefits.

$$$ Hotel Arts – *119 12th Ave. SW, Calgary.* ✗ ⌖ P ⌼ ☎403-266-4611 or 800-661-9378. www.hotelarts.ca. *185 rooms.* This formerly drab chain hotel just west of the Stampede exhibition grounds has been turned into a chic, high-rise hotel after a recent $10 million renovation. "Arts" is the operative word here; the style seamlessly blends retro with modern as seen in the futuristic globe chairs paired with over-sized red lampshades and slate fireplaces. Colourful, contemporary artwork adorns the walls of the public areas. Decorated by local artists and designers, guest rooms and suites come equipped with sleek furnishings and flat-screen TVs. The Raw Bar is a hip spot for sushi and martinis; the **Saint Germain ($$$$)** restaurant is known for its upscale French fare. A fitness centre and an outdoor pool complete the amenities.

$$$$ Kensington Riverside Inn – *1126 Memorial Dr. NW, Calgary.* ⌖ P ⌼ ☎403-228-4442 or 877-313-3733. www. kensingtonriversideinn.com. *19 rooms.* Located in the Kensington district across the Bow River from downtown, this cozy inn offers perks such as Egyptian cotton towels, heated towel bars and polar fleece bathrobes. Rooms feature high ceilings and some have private balconies, garden patios or gas fireplaces; the Bow River pathway runs right out the front door. Rates include evening hors d'oeuvres, free local calls, wireless Internet, a daily newspaper and a gourmet breakfast.

$$$$ Fairmont Palliser – *133 9th Ave. SW, Calgary.* ✕ ♿ 🅿 ≋ ☎*403-262-1234 or 800-257-7544. www.fairmont.com. 405 rooms.* Although not as conspicuous as its famous sister properties in the Canadian Rockies, this historic, 12-storey hotel is an elegant oasis amid Calgary's urban bustle and steps away from the sea of restaurants lining Stephen Avenue Walk pedestrian mall. The Alberta sandstone landmark (1914) sits close to the financial district, attracting business travellers as well as vacationers. Many rooms are on the small side, but each comes with plush duvets and bathrobes, as well as modern conveniences such as high-speed Internet access. The hotel no longer has a spa but offers in-room services such as massage and pedicures from reputable offsite providers. A fitness room and an indoor swimming pool are on the premises.

WHERE TO EAT

$ Diner Deluxe – *804 Edmonton Trail NE, Calgary.* ♿ ☎*403-276-5499.* **Comfort Food.** Piled-high all-day breakfasts, fun decoration and friendly staff explain why there's almost always a line outside this diner's doors. Located just north of downtown, the family-run diner offers comfort food with a twist: from omelettes and organic chicken sausages at brunch to sundried tomato, pesto and white-cheddar baked macaroni and cheese at dinner. The cornmeal-crusted pickerel with brown rice is a local specialty. All the baked goods, including desserts, come fresh-as-can-be from the adjoining Urban Baker.

$ Spolumbo's – *1308 9th Ave. SE, Calgary.* ♿ ☎*403-264-6452, www. spolumbos.com. Lunch only (til 5:30pm). Closed Sun.* **Delicatessen.** Three first-generation Italian friends, all former players with the Calgary Stampeders football team, have scored big with this Italian hotspot near the Calgary Zoo in the trendy historic Inglewood district east of downtown. At this 100-seat delicatessen, you can get a grilled sausage on a bun, heaped with roasted peppers or onions; or a panini sandwich exploding with deli meats. There's also a deli counter where fresh sausages (try apple chicken, turkey blueberry, Greek lamb or spicy Italian) are available to go.

$$ Bistro Provence – *52 North Railway St. Okotoks.* ☎*403-938-2224. www. bistro-provence.ca. Closed Sun & Mon.* **French.** French-born restaurateur Nicolas Desini has put the town's restaurant scene on the map with fresh, locally sourced cuisine in a small (seating for 20), casual setting. Traditional French fare includes frog's legs, cassoulet and escargot; also try the pheasant, duck and rack of lamb. Lunch offerings are simpler such as panini sandwiches, salads and pasta. A French market on the premises is stocked with herbs and spices, dressings, gourmet chocolates, fresh breads, pastries and other delicacies, and the bistro offers weekly cooking classes.

$$ Blue Dog Cafe – *110 3rd Ave., Cochrane.* ♿ ☎*403-932-4282. Brunch only Sun.* **International.** There's a distinct shortage of good Southern food in Alberta, though a few well-regarded Latin and Cajun restaurants have opened their doors in recent years. One such find is the Blue Dog, a pretty eatery in a restored heritage house that dishes out Louisiana-style entrées such as Creole mustard chicken, perfectly spiced with a heap of creamy mashed potatoes. The fish burger, made with perch, is served crusty and hot. Jambalaya and Cajun pasta dishes are generous. Tempting Asian, Mediterranean and Caribbean offerings are on the menu as well. If you're lucky, live blues or jazz music (usually every second weekend) will spark up your meal. If you make a reservation *(recommended)*, try to get a spot on the outdoor patio.

$$ Buzzards Cowboy Cuisine – *140 10th Ave. SW., Calgary.* ♿ ☎*403-264-6959. www.cowboycuisine.com.* **Steakhouse.** This Calgary institution sports a rustic, timber interior decorated with authentic ranching relics, saddles and barbed-wire art. A menu of western specialties and comfortable leather chairs make this eatery a popular spot. While fried prairie oysters (beef testicles) raise eyebrows, most diners stick to what the city is famous for—Alberta beef. Chicken dishes and locally raised bison are also on the menu.

$$ Clay Oven – #349, 3132 26 St. NE & #359, 3132 26 St. NE, Calgary. &☎403-250-2161. **Indian.** Some frequent travellers include a stop at this non-descript restaurant near the airport in their arrival plans. From butter chicken and Bengal bhartha (smoky, tandoori-roasted eggplant with onions and tomatoes) to the best garlic naan bread in town, the Clay Oven offers some of the city's finest Indian food. There's also a vegetarian menu.

$$ Deane House – 806 9th Ave. SE, Calgary. Lunch only (til 3pm). &☎403-269-7747. www.fortcalgary.com. **Contemporary.** Built in 1906 for the commanding officer of the North West Mounted Police, this two-storey wooden house is perfect for a light lunch or scrumptious weekend brunch after visiting adjacent Fort Calgary or the zoo. Innovative salads are a staple, but daily offerings range from quiche to pan-fried Arctic char, served indoors, or on the screened-in porch with its lovely views of the Bow and Elbow Rivers.

$$ Madrina's Ristorante – 20 Balsam Ave., Bragg Creek. &☎403-949-2750. http://madrinasristorante.com. Closed Mon. **Italian.** This rustic yet elegant eatery dishes out succulent pizzas, pasta and seafood as well as small plates such as baked camembert with roasted garlic and fig jam or smoked salmon and crab cakes. Signature dishes include scallopine piccata (veal with capers and lemon in a white-wine butter sauce) and pollo saltimbocca (breast of pros-cuitto-wrapped chicken with sage in a white-wine sauce). The outdoor deck is a favourite in summer.

$$ The Palomino Steakhouse – 109 7th Ave. SW, Calgary. &☎403-532-1911. www.thepalomino.ca. Closed Sun. **Steakhouse.** This lively restaurant/bar on the 7th Avenue downtown LRT line boasts the best BBQ in Calgary, particularly its slow-smoked Bronto-saurus Beef ribs, pork ribs and chicken. Steaks are thick and succulent; most entrées come with your choice of sides including black-eyed peas, sweet potato mash, grits loaded with cheese, and an awesome coleslaw. Big screen TVs, a substantial beer list, weekend live bands and afternoon music jams are other draws.

$$ Pulcinella – 1147 Kensington Crescent SW, Calgary. &☎403-283-1166. www.pulcinella.ca. **Italian.** This restaurant is one of the few in the city offering the distinctive Napoletana-style thin-crust pizza. Market-fresh toppings include dried meats such as pros-cuitto, fresh basil, buffalo mozzarella and grilled vegetables. Splurge on an appetizer of battered deep-fried oyster mushrooms in gorgonzola cream. The hardwood floors and giant forno oven add to the authentic Italian feel.

$$ Thai Sa-On – 351 10th Ave. SW, Calgary. ☎403-264-3526. **Thai.** The diversity and complexity of Thai cuisine make for an extensive menu, but everything at this unpretentious, fam-ily-run restaurant is authentically fresh and flavourful. Hearty eaters love the whole snapper, spiced and served with savoury vegetables and coconut rice. Vegetarians can choose from the likes of pad paq tua, a peanut-based curry.

$$$ The Ranche – Bow Bottom Trail SE, Calgary. &☎403-225-3939. www.crmr. com. No lunch Sat. **Canadian.** At this beautifully restored 1896 ranch house, set in Fish Creek Provincial Park, the imaginative menu is based on local products. Fresh and smoked game (buffalo, elk, caribou), Alberta beef, lamb and pork and a variety of seafood are creatively partnered with berries and organic vegetables. Medallions of caribou, for example, are served with blueberry sourdough bread. Sunday brunch on the veranda is a real treat.

$$$$ River Café – Prince's Island Park, 200 Barclay Parade SW, Calgary. ☎403-261-7670. www.river-cafe.com. Closed month of Jan, Remembrance Day & Dec 25. **Canadian.** With the ambience of a rustic ski lodge, this restaurant, set on an island in downtown Calgary, offers upscale seasonal cuisine focusing on Canadian ingredients such as buffalo, Alberta beef, salmon, maple syrup, cranberries, and prairie grains. Dine around the fieldstone fireplace or out-doors under wide patio umbrellas on the deck. Access is by footbridge from the Eau Claire Market parking lot.

Calgary★★

POPULATION: 1,226,443 – MAPS P 66, P 70

Known as Texas North for its shiny skyscrapers, unabashed Wild West roots and cosmopolitan lifestyle, the city of Calgary is built on agriculture and oil-patch prosperity. Covering the largest land area of any city in Canada (420sq km/162sq mi), Calgary is one of the nation's fast-growing metropolises, with more than a million residents, mainly because of Alberta's vast oil wealth and Calgary's favourable business climate (no sales tax). The city's importance as a transportation centre is also a factor, intersected as it is by several major highways, and served by a busy international airport. Year-round, it's a sprawling centre for outdoor enthusiasts, fuelled by proximity to the snow-capped mountains an hour west. Threaded by two glacier-fed rivers, the Bow and the Elbow, the city lures more than five million visitors annually with its wealth of recreational opportunities, including world-class fly fishing, skiing and golf. The famous Calgary Stampede—a 10-day celebration every July—pays homage to the city's western roots and its role as a leading cattle producer. The 1988 Winter Olympic Games focused worldwide attention on Calgary and left enduring venues as well as memories: the Nakiska Ski Area in Kananaskis Country west of Calgary; the bobsled, luge and ski jumps at Canada Olympic Park; and the Olympic Sports Hall of Fame.

- **Information:** Tourist Office, 200-238 11th Ave. SE. ☎403-263-8510, or 800-661 1678. www.tourismcalgary.com.
- ▶ **Orient Yourself:** The mountains rise to the west. The city's core sits on the south side of the Bow River, which joins the Elbow River at Fort Calgary, east of downtown. Stephen Avenue Walk (8th Ave.), at the heart of downtown between 4th St. SW and Macleod Trail, is a historic district with restaurants and shops. It runs east to west and is bounded by 7th Ave. (the downtown LRT line, which is closed to vehicle traffic except transit) and 9th Ave. Calgary is infamous for one-way streets, including Macleod Trail north (2nd St. SE, passing the Saddledome) and south (1st St. SE). Chinatown lies south of the Bow River at Centre Street (look for stone lions guarding the bridge as it crosses the river going north). From Riverfront Ave. SW, access the lower level of Centre Street Bridge to reach Memorial Drive, a major east-west thoroughfare that follows the north banks of the Bow River from Deerfoot Trail (a key north-south route that makes up part of Hwy. 2 connecting Edmonton with southern Alberta) to 16th Ave. north (a major east-west route that becomes the Trans-Canada Highway).
- **Parking:** Parking meters are valid 9am–6pm daily; rates $1–$3.50/hr. The Light Rail Transit (LRT) is free downtown; the downtown line runs along 7th Ave.
- **Don't Miss:** The Glenbow Museum, the Calgary Zoo, Prince's Island Park.
- **Organizing Your Time:** Allow one week to see the sights of Calgary: 2 or 3 days for downtown and the balance for excursions. Add another week if attending the Stampede (for which it's best to book a year in advance).
- **Especially for Kids:** Heritage Park and the Bar U Ranch are surefire winners.
- **Also See:** CANADIAN ROCKIES.

A Bit of History

Origins – In 1875 a North West Mounted Police post was built on this site. It was named Fort Calgary by Col. James Macleod, commander of the police in the Northwest, for his home in Scot-

land. The name is derived from what is most likely a Gaelic word meaning "Bay Farm." A new era of order helped curb the whisky trade that had already left a tragic footprint on the local Blackfoot population. In 1877 chiefs of the Siksika, Stoney, Tsuu T'ina, Kainaiwa and

Practical Information

AREA CODES

The City of Calgary has just one area code (403), so local calls must be dialed with the three-digit area code. Calls to Edmonton and northern Alberta require the 780 area code in advance of the number. For more information: ☎403-555-1212 or www.telus.ca.

GETTING THERE

BY AIR

Calgary International Airport **(YYC)** (☎403-735-5000; www.calgaryairport. com) 17.5km/10mi northeast of downtown. **Air Canada** (☎888-247-2262 Canada/US; www.aircanada.com) flies from numerous Canadian and US cities. Aside from these direct routes, connections are offered from many major US and other Canadian cities and from major international cities. Domestic air service is offered by Air Canada as well as its affiliated regional airlines and by Calgary-based **WestJet** (☎800-538-5696 or 877-952-0100 TDD; www.westjet.com).

Transportation to Downtown:
By **airport shuttle** $15 one-way; for schedules www.calgaryairport.com.
By **taxi:** About $40. Banff Airporter ☎403-762-1677 or 888-449-2901. www.banffairporter.com (for taxi companies, see By Taxi below).

BY CAR

From airport to downtown: The drive from Calgary International Airport to downtown takes about 30min; from airport follow Barlow Trail south about 15 km/9mi to Memorial Drive west.

Main routes to downtown
From the west: via the Trans-Canada Highway (about 20km/15mi from city limits to downtown), take Memorial Drive eastbound exit and follow the river, crossing to city centre at the 10th St. NW bridge or via the bridge (turn right) at Edmonton Trail.
From the north or south: via Highway 2 (the route becomes Deerfoot Trail), take Memorial Drive westbound exit ramp, pass the Calgary Zoo on your left until reaching the 4th Avenue flyover to downtown (about 3km/2mi) and watch for signs.

From the east: via Highway 1; continue about 20km/12mi from city limits on what has now become 16 Ave. East to Deerfoot Trail, exit off the overpass (watch for signs and stay in left lane) to Deerfoot Trail South; the next exit, to the right, will be about 5 km/2.5mi) to Memorial Drive west toward downtown. (◖See explanation earlier in this section on Memorial Drive to downtown.)

BY MOTORCOACH

Both **Greyhound Canada** (800-661-8747; www.greyhound.ca) and **Red Arrow Motorcoach** (☎403-531-0350 or 800-232-1958; www.redarrow.pwt.ca) service Calgary.

GETTING AROUND

BY PUBLIC TRANSPORTATION

Calgary Transit operates an extensive public transit system of regular buses, express buses and light-rail transit (known as the **LRT** or C-Train). Hours of operation: LRT Mon–Sat 6am–1:30am, Sun 9am–1:30am. **Buses** Mon–Fri 5am–1:30am, reduced service weekends and holidays. Exact fare required, adult $2.50; youth $1.50. Day Pass $6.75 adult, $4.50 youth. Purchase tickets & tokens at stores displaying the Calgary Transit ticket decal. Free transfers between buses & C-Train; LRT is free downtown. System maps & timetables available free of charge. Route information ☎403-262-1000 or www. calgarytransit.ca.

BY CAR

Use of public transportation or walking is encouraged within the city as streets are often congested and street parking may be difficult to find. Calgary has a strictly enforced tow-away policy. Motorists should park in designated **parking** areas which are identified by a sign with a green 'P'; there is usually a 2hr limit though some all-day parking is available; public, off-street and metered parking facilities are located throughout the city.

For a free map and information about parking fees, call ☎403-537-7000. www.calgaryparking.com.
Car rentals: Avis ☎403-269-6166 or 800-879-2847; www.avis.com. **Budget**

403-266-0550 or 800-267-0505; www.
budget.com. **Hertz Canada** ☎403-221-
1681 or 800-263-0600. www.hertz.ca.
Thrifty Car Rental ☎403-262-4400 or
800-847-4389. www.thrifty.com. Most
offer free pick-up and drop-off services
from hotels.

BY TAXI: Associated ☎403-299-1111.
Mayfair ☎403-255-6555. www.
mayfairtaxi.com.

GENERAL INFORMATION

VISITOR INFORMATION
Tourism Calgary ☎403-263-8510 or
800-661-1678 (Canada/US).
www.tourismcalgary.com.
Visitor information centres are found
in three locations: **Calgary Tower,** 101
9th Ave. SW, ☎403-850-2362; **Calgary
International Airport,** Arrivals Level,
☎403-735-1234 and at **Southcentre
Mall,** lower level near The Bay department store, ☎403-271-7670. Website
for all is www.tourismcalgary.com/
aboutus/vic.htm

ACCOMMODATIONS
For a listing of suggested hotels, 🍂 see the
Address Book. For hotels/motels contact
Tourism Calgary ☎403-263-8510 or 800-
661-1678 (Canada/US). www.tourismcal-
gary.com. Reservation services: Hotels.
com ☎800-224-6835 (Canada/US)
http://deals.hotels.com.

LOCAL PRESS
Daily: Calgary Herald, Calgary Sun,
Globe and Mail, National Post. **Weekly:**
ffwd Arts Weekly. **Monthly:** Avenue
magazine (www.avenuemagazine.ca)
and free guides to entertainment,
shopping, and restaurants: Where
(www.wherecalgary.com).

ENTERTAINMENT
Consult the arts and entertainment
supplements in local newspapers
(Thursday or Friday editions) for schedules of cultural events and addresses
of principal theatres and concert halls.
Ticketmaster (☎403-777-0000 for concerts or 416-872-1111; www.ticketmaster.
ca) sells tickets for theatre and the arts.
The Epcor Centre for the Performing
Arts lists upcoming events at www.
epcorcentre.org.

USEFUL NUMBERS ☎
♦ **Police:** 911 (emergency) or

403-266-1234 (non-emergency).
♦ **Calgary International Airport** –
403-735-1372.
♦ **Canadian Automobile Assn** –
4700 7 Ave. SW. 403-240-5300 or 800-
642-3810.
♦ **CAA Emergency Road Service**
(24hr): 403-246-0606
♦ **Shoppers Drug Mart** (24hr pharma-
cy) with many locations: 800-746-7737.
♦ **Road Conditions** – 877-262-4997.
♦ **Weather** – www.weatheroffice.gc.ca.

SHOPPING

SPECIALTY SHOPS
Callebaut Chocolate – 1313 1st St. SE,
Calgary. ☎403-265-5777 or 800-661-
8367. www.bernardcallebaut.com.
Bernard Callebaut came to Calgary from
Belgium 25 years ago and set about
creating the best chocolates in Canada,
using fresh Alberta dairy products. Now
Callebaut confections are available in
28 retail outlets in Canada, 4 in the US
and through catalog sales. Specialties include nut clusters, truffles and
nougats. Daily factory tours (call ahead)
and best of all, free samples.
Sunterra Markets – Five locations in
Calgary: head office and restaurant at
#200, 1851 Sirocco Dr. SW. ☎403-266-
2820. www.sunterramarket.com.
Owners of this family business have
ensured top-quality products by raising
and producing their own meat and
game through sustainable and often
organic practices. This is the place to
get pre-made food to go (meat, side
dishes, sandwiches, salads, soups and
desserts) along with groceries and deli
foods like olives, cheeses and baked
goods. Also a good selection of specialty items such as gluten (wheat)-free
and sugar-free products.

FARMERS' MARKET
Calgary Farmers' Market – 4421
Quesnay Wood Dr. SW, Calgary. ☎403-
244-4548. www.calgaryfarmersmarket.
ca. 🅿. You'll find plenty to keep you
busy in this former army warehouse at
Currie Barracks off Crowchild Trail. This
year-round market (Fri-Sun in winter,
extended hours in summer) overflows
with farm produce, organic foods,
hand-made sausages, baked goods and
other comestibles. The emphasis here is
always on supporting regional (Alberta

and British Columbia) vendors, usually 80 to 100 on-site at any one time. The seafood and produce are the freshest in the city; you'll also find gift items and imports, crafts, books and clothing. A food court offers every cuisine under the sun, and vendors often put out free samples (don't miss local favourite Simple Simon Pies, which specializes in savoury and sweet tarts and pies). A great kids' play area makes the market an ideal place for a family outing.

WESTERN WEAR

As you would expect, Calgary has a great selection of stores stocking Western wear and gear. Here's a sampling: **Alberta Boot** (614 10th Ave. SW; ☎403-263-4605; www.albertaboot. com) specializes in fine handmade Western boots (the Mounties' footwear of choice). With hundreds of pairs, the selection is vast; prices range from economical to astronomical. **Lammle's Western Wear** (209 8th Ave. SW; ☎403-266-5226 or 877-526 6537; www.lammles. com) is an Alberta chain offering ranch wear, boots and hats. Locations include a 1911 heritage storefront on Stephen Avenue Walk. **Chase Cattle Co.** (Willow Park Village, 10816 Macleod Trail SE #100; ☎403-269-6450) sells high-end ranch dress wear, including highly decorated shirts, skirts and jackets.

VINTAGE CLOTHES

For upscale chic and second-hand clothes, head to the boutiques of Calgary's trendy Mount Royal Village, Inglewood, Kensington or Marda Loop neighbourhoods.

SHOPPING MALLS

The city boasts numerous mega-malls including **Market Mall, Southcentre, Chinook Centre, Deerfoot Meadows** as well as downtown's interconnected **Banker's Hall/Eaton's Centre/Scotia Centre. Downtown on 8th** (between 5th St. SW and 1st St. SW). **Uptown 17** (17th Ave. SW from 2nd St. to 14th St.): over 400 shops and restaurants (www. uptown17.ca).

SPORTS AND LEISURE

SPORTS

Calgary Flames (ice hockey): season Oct–May at Pengrowth Saddledome, ☎403-777-2177. http://flames.nhl.com.

Calgary Stampeders (football): season mid-Jun–Nov at McMahon Stadium, ☎403-289-0258 tickets & schedules. www.stampeders.com.

NIGHTLIFE

Calgary is rooted in western hospitality—and not just during the Calgary Stampede. Not surprisingly, country music is king and you won't have to go far to find big hair and belt buckles, even in cosmopolitan Cowtown. **Ranchman's Cookhouse and Dance Hall, Inc.** (9615 Macleod Trail S.; open Mon–Fri 4pm, Sat from 3pm; ☎403-253-1100; www.ranchmans.com) is probably the most popular country and western music haunt in town, particularly during Stampede when big-name performers get the dance floor hopping. Dance lessons nightly at 7pm; learn the two-step, double shuffle or the West Coast swing. Check out the sea of country and western photos covering the walls, artifacts and other memorabilia. Ranchman's is usually rockin' with live and taped music any night of the week. Another Western-style favourite is **Cowboys,** a hotspot that for nearly a decade attracted massive crowds (even traffic jams) as mini-skirt-clad young women in low-cut tops and men with oversized belt buckles, skintight jeans and cowboy hats lined the pavement along 9th Avenue at 5th Street SW downtown waiting their turn to enter the packed bar. Cowboys was displaced by an office tower and now has a newly renovated and expanded home at 1088 Olympic Way SE (☎403-265-0699; www. cowboysniteclub.com). It occupies the former space of Coyote's Bar and Dance Saloon, which was previously known as Dusty's. The atmosphere here is best on weekends and during Stampede, when fair-goers walk the four blocks north to the saloon, which offers live shows and taped music.

If country music isn't your thing, there are plenty of other options along the Stephen Avenue Walk including the **James Joyce Irish Pub** (114 8th Ave. SW; ☎403-262-0708; www.jamesjoyc-epub.com) or the uber-cool urban nightclub, **Velvet at the Grand** (608 1st St. SW., open Tue-Sat from 5pm; ☎403-244-8400; www.crmr.com) a restaurant and bar in the renovated 1912 Grand Theatre building downtown, where patrons sit on, you guessed it, velvet chairs (don't miss the unisex bathroom in the stylish upstairs loft). Velvet caters especially to a professional crowd, who flock here for drinks after work.

SPAS

After a day of shopping or sightseeing, treat yourself to a trip to one of Calgary's many spas. The three cited here offer a full menu of services. **Stillwater Spa** *(Plaza Level, Hyatt Regency ; ☎403-537-4474; www. stillwaterspacalgary.com)* offers professional treatments and services within a serene, European-styled space where the hustle of downtown Calgary seems very far away. The soaker tub and funky showers alone are worth a stop, along with the pedicures. Just south of downtown in the trendy Mission district on 4th St. SW, **Sante Spa** *(☎403-228-2772; www.santespa.com)* blends traditional spa treatments with medical esthetics (Botox, chemical peels, intense pulse light treatments) under the guidance of specialized physicians and dermatologists. The spa is especially renowned for skin care such as the 90-minute Signature Anti-Aging Facial. The Egyptian-styled **Oasis Spa & Wellness Centre** *(☎403-216-2747; www.experienceoasis. ca)* in the upscale Mount Royal district is indeed an oasis of serenity; the interior is marked by lovely touches such as the stylish grand room, where tea, mineral water and fruit are available for guests to help themselves. Hot stone therapy and energy balancing treatments are very popular here. The spa also offers yoga and stretch classes on-site.

RECREATION
Parks in the City

The southwest edge of Calgary is home to **North Glenmore Park** *(7305 24th St. SW; ☉ open year-round daily 5am–11pm; ☎403-268-2489; www.calgary.ca).* You can park there and cycle, glide or stroll the 14km/9mi circle loop through the prime wetlands of the Glenmore Reservoir. **Fish Creek Provincial Park** *(access off Bow Bottom Trail SE & from 37th St. SW; ☉ open year-round daily 8am, closing hours vary; ☎403-297-5293;*

www.tprc.alberta.ca/parks/fishcreek) in Calgary's far south is a little piece of paradise along the Bow River as it journeys south. The park **visitor centre** *(15979 Bow Bottom Trail SE)* is open weekdays 8:15am–4:30pm, but closed during the lunch hour from noon to 1pm (☉ closed major holidays). **Nose Hill Park** *(parking off 14th St. NW at 56 Ave., 64th Ave. & Berkley Gate, or Shaganappi Trail at Edgemont Blvd. NW; ☉ open daily 5am–11pm; ☎403-268-2489; www.calgary.ca)* in northwest Calgary is a grassland plateau that can be walked for hours without crossing the same path again.

Spruce Meadows

Southwest of downtown via Macleod Trail, then west along Hwy. 22X. ☎403-974-4200. www.sprucemeadows.com. One of the finest show-jumping facilities on earth, Spruce Meadows is an oasis of perfect turf on the city outskirts. The 120 ha/300 acre site encompasses outdoor rings, indoor arenas, stables for 700 horses and a three-storey tournament centre. Major annual events include The Masters *(2nd weekend of Sept)*; and the world's richest show-jumping tournament in prize money ($2M), attracting some 50,000 spectators daily and a television audience of millions. Other outdoor tournaments are the National *(1st week of Jun)*; Canada One *(last weekend of Jun)*; and the North American *(early July)*, coinciding with the Calgary Stampede.

Royal Canadian Pacific Train

Luxury train travel reached its peak in the late 19C and early 20C in the railcars built specially for Canadian Pacific executives. Long retired, these cars have returned to the rails for leisurely tours through the Rockies. Departing from the Palliser Hotel, CP pavilion and train overpass in downtown Calgary, the Royal CP train is pulled by historic locomotives through spectacular mountain scenery. Four- and five-day excursions include comfortable staterooms, gourmet meals in the well-appointed dining cars, and overnight stops at such popular destinations as Banff and Lake Louise. Limited summer and fall schedule. *For information: ☎403-508-1400 or 877-665-3044 (North America, UK & Germany). www.cprtours.com.*

The Calgary Stampede

Hailed as "the Greatest Outdoor Show on Earth," the **Calgary Stampede** is a grand 10-day event held annually in Calgary beginning in early July. Almost the entire population of the city dons western garb (boots, jeans and cowboy hats) and joins the festivities. In recent years this event has attracted close to a million spectators. The exhibition kicks off with an elaborate, four-hour parade that is broadcast worldwide. There are flapjack breakfasts, street dances, concerts and a $1.6 million **rodeo** tournament that brings competitors from around the globe. Livestock shows and chuckwagon races are held in Stampede Park, as is the rodeo, where a lengthy midway features rides, games, live musical entertainment and plenty of food. Invented in Calgary, the **chuckwagon races** recall the wagon races held by cowboys after a cattle roundup; they are, without doubt, an exciting part of the stampede. Near the South Gate, the Indian Village showcases several colourful tepees, which can be entered, and First Nations arts and crafts are for sale. *Details of all events can be obtained from the Stampede office: 403-261-0101 or 800-661-1260 and online at www.calgarystampede.com.*

Piikani First Nations met with the federal government near what is now Blackfoot Crossing Historical Park to sign Treaty 7, which established reserves across southern Alberta. A small community of white settlers grew up around Fort Calgary and quickly developed in the 1880s when the Canadian Pacific Railway company decided to route its railway south through Calgary and the Kicking Horse Pass, rather than through Edmonton and the Yellowhead Pass. This momentous decision resulted in a huge influx of settlers to the lush grazing lands of the region. The Dominion Lands Act of 1872 also encouraged the movement of cattle herds northward from the US. Canadians began to form their own herds in the area, and well-to-do Englishmen arrived from overseas to establish ranches. Calgary rapidly became a marketing and meatpacking centre, gaining the nickname of Canada's Cowtown, which has stuck to this day.

"Black Gold" – The discovery of oil in 1914 at Turner Valley, south of Calgary, marked the birth of western Canada's petroleum industry. For about 30 years, this valley was the country's major oil producer. Then in 1947, a great discovery was made at Leduc, just south of Edmonton, and Calgary began a period of phenomenal growth. While agriculture such as grain farming and cattle help build Calgary's economy, the energy sector is by far the city's biggest employer today. Calgary is home to more corporate headquarters—including most major international energy firms—than any other Canadian city. The metro population has grown steadily over the past two decades, especially in the past five years, due to a thriving economy that has spurred an influx of workers from across Canada. New construction, particularly downtown but also in new residential suburbs, has created a building boom as well as a shortage of skilled tradespeople. Streets in the city's core are filled with new pickup trucks, SUVs and sports cars, while high-end clothiers, home-decor stores and art galleries stand testament to the city's wealth. The downside is a widening of the poverty gap: a decline in affordable housing and a higher cost of living have created greater homelessness. More than three multistorey homeless shelters in Calgary's downtown east side attempt to fill the growing need for shelter. Traffic is increasing throughout the city, especially on major routes such as Deerfoot Trail and 16th Avenue East, although a ring road north of the city is expected to open in the next few years to help ease traffic congestion.

Downtown

Calgary's downtown has undergone a phenomenal transformation since World War II and continues to develop. In recent years, the **Calgary Tower,** surrounded by a host of attractive, glass-fronted high rises, has been overshadowed by the brown marble headquarters of **Petro-Canada,** which dominates the city's glittering skyline. A **pedestrian mall** stretches five blocks from 3rd St. SW along 8th Avenue, east to Macleod Trail (2nd St. SE). At the western end lie the big bank blocks: the twin reflecting-glass towers of Bankers Hall, the Scotia Centre and the black towers of the Toronto Dominion (TD) Square are all connected to one another and to The Bay and Eaton's department stores by second-floor bridges. More recently, CIBC Place has added a post-Modern look to the downtown.

Most of downtown lies along a network of sky bridges (known as **Plus 15** walkways) that allow office dwellers, shoppers and visitors to travel through most of the city's core via these glass-encased, elevated walkways. The Calgary Plus 15 system is reputedly the longest interconnected indoor walkway in the world, linking many major downtown attractions such as theatres, hotels and restaurants. The easterly stretch of the 8th Avenue mall, known locally as the Stephen Avenue Walk, is the city's historic district, filled with early 1900s vintage Alberta sandstone buildings now converted to small shops and cafes. At the northeast corner of this district, the Romanesque Revival city hall building at 7th Avenue and Macleod Trail SE is a 1907 stone beauty. The tiered, blue reflecting-glass structure east of city hall is Calgary's **Municipal Building,** rising around a 12-storey atrium. Across 2nd Street Southeast (Macleod Trail) stands the **Epcor Centre for the Performing Arts,** an attractive series of brick buildings. Toronto Dominion Square harbours an indoor greenhouse (4th floor), **Devonian Gardens★**, with some 20,000 tropical plants, plus fountains and sculptures (◷ open year-round daily 9am–9pm; ♿☎403-268-2489).

☹Caution should be used when walking in downtown Calgary east of the Municipal Building—including Fort Calgary and the zoo on St. George's Island—as property crime, violence, prostitution and drug-related incidents have become rampant in an area city leaders had been trying to revitalize. Avoid the area after dark and be alert during the day.

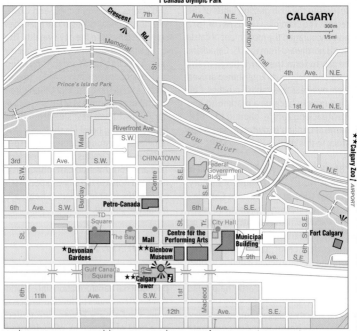

★ Rocky Mountain House NHS. ★★ Bar U Ranch NHS. ★ Heritage Park ┆ Grain Academy ★, Saddledome ★

Glenbow Museum★★

130 9th Ave. SE, across from the Calgary Tower. (The museum is connected with the Telus Convention Centre.) ◷Open year-round daily 9am–5pm (Thu 9pm). ◷Closed Dec 25. ⬮$14. ✕⚹☏403-268-4100. www.glenbow.org.

Opened in 1976, this eight-storey building houses western Canada's largest museum. It is known for its extensive historical artifacts and archives. Glenbow's founder, Eric Lafferty Harvie (1892-1975), used his oil fortunes to amass art and artifacts from North America, South America, Asia, West Africa, and the Pacific islands; in 1966 he gave his collections to Alberta. The holdings are grouped into five categories: Native North America, Community History, Military and Mounted Police, World Cultures, and Minerals. In addition the museum mounts temporary, usually themed, exhibits of art, artifacts and sculpture.

Galleries on three floors contain displays from the museum's substantial collections, with a special emphasis on Western Canadian culture. In the lobby, off the main entrance, a large acrylic and aluminum sculpture by James Houston titled **Aurora Borealis** is the focal point. To the right of the entrance, the museum cafe serves made-to-order sandwiches for weekday lunch.

In addition to temporary exhibits, the second floor houses the Asian Gallery, which showcases Buddhist and Hindu art, masks, and paintings spanning AD 1C to the 18C; and a children's discovery room for ages 4 and older.

On the third floor, the **Nitsitapiisinni Gallery** reflects the colourful history of the Blackfoot Indians, who have inhabited the northwest plains of Alberta for centuries. The Glenbow's newest exhibit, **Mavericks: An Incorrigible History of Alberta** (the title of Aritha Van Herk's recent book), is an interactive look at the past 100 years in the Calgary area. The elaborate exhibit celebrates the life and legacies of dozens of remarkable Albertans during different eras.

The fourth floor focuses on the museum's mineral collection, which includes rock crystals, fool's gold and glow-in-the-dark specimens. Also on view are exhibits on West Africa and on the history of warfare around the world.

Calgary Tower★★

In Palliser Square, 101 9th Ave. SW. Observation deck. ◷open daily 7am–11pm; hours adjusted seasonally; ◷deck sometimes closed for events. Call to confirm hours. ⬮$12.95. ✕⚹🅿☏403-266-7171. www.calgarytower.com. Self-guided audio tour available.

This tower was completed in 1968, requiring 15 months to construct at a cost of $3.5 million; renovations and upgrades have been ongoing in subsequent years. No longer the tallest structure in Calgary's skyline (surpassed by the 215m/706ft tall Petro-Canada Centre's West Tower in 1983), Calgary Tower has become a familiar landmark, nonetheless, and an iconic symbol of the city itself. The observation deck features touch-screen multimedia exhibits on the buildings seen. The enclosed **glass floor** (2005) extends 11m/36ft along the perimeter of the observation deck, enabling visitors to "walk" over traffic whizzing down 9th Ave. some 160m/525ft (190m/626ft to the top of the tower's spire) below. Jaw-dropping **views**★★ of the city, its sprawling neighbourhoods and the distant Rockies reward those who ride the elevator up the 52 floors to the deck (in just over 60 seconds). Providing a panorama of the city, the slow-revolving dining room on the top floor serves regional specialties like game, salmon and Alberta beef.

Prince's Island Park

Memorial Dr. & 3rd St. NW. ◷Open daily year-round.

The duck ponds, fountain and serene lagoon on this tree-lined island create a lush oasis within fast-paced downtown Calgary. Sun-seeking workers head to the island at noontime to stroll its red-shale paths, read, bird-watch or have lunch. Others lace up sneakers or in-line skates for a workout along the pathways that lead from the Eau Claire district into the park. Others dash from work to the Bow River, within which the island sits, to cast a line for fish or take an evening paddle. Set among the trees in the park, the upscale River Café, a pretty, rustic

©Travel Alberta

Telus World of Science

lodge is hugely popular with locals and visitors (&see Address Book).

Telus World of Science★

[Kids] *701 11th St. SW.* ◷*Open year-round Mon–Fri 9:45am–4pm (Fri 5pm), weekends 10am–5pm.* ☞*$13.50 (includes admission to Creative Kids Museum).* ✗ &☐ *($1.50/hr)* ☎*403-268-8300. www.calgaryscience.ca.*

This downtown science centre, a favourite with local and visiting families, boasts a state-of-the-art planetarium called the **Discovery Dome** *(shows 45min; $3 additional fee)* and a museum of all things scientific. In the **OneWorld** exhibit, kids learn about climate change through a remote-control camera, toy hybrid cars, and experiments with wind and solar power. In **Farm It,** children solve weather-related problems in a computer game about farming. WOWtown is designed for children 7 years and younger. An outdoor playground, Amazement Park, has such equipment as tube slides, and building blocks for bridge construction.

Connected to the science centre by an enclosed walkway, the adjacent **Creative Kids Museum** *(www.creative kidsmuseum.com),* opened in 2006, displays children's art and features hands-on activities that enhance the museum's innovative setting. Kids can crawl through simulated Alberta landscapes to explore a hoodoo, learn to pay greater attention to the world around them through interactive games in the Perceptions gallery, become an artist in Scribble Dee Dee, and dress up in costumes and take to the stage in the theatre.

A new, 12,090sq m/130,000sq ft science centre is slated to open in 2011 on a 6ha/15acre site north of the zoo.

Epcor Centre for the Performing Arts

205 8th Ave. SE. Entrances off Olympic Plaza. ◷*Open daily. Check for performance times.* ☞*Guided tours first Thu of month 5pm.* ☞*Depends on the event.* ✗& ☐ ☎*403-294-7455. www.epcorcentre.org.*

Bounded by 8th Avenue, 9th Avenue, Macleod Trail and 1st Street Southeast, Epcor Centre is housed in a sprawling, six-level redbrick building that occupies a full city block in the Olympic Plaza Cultural District. One of Canada's largest arts centres, it is home to numerous performing arts groups such as Theatre Calgary, Alberta Theatre Projects, One Yellow Rabbit and the Calgary Philharmonic. The centre boasts the 60-seat Motel Theatre, the 1,800-seat Jack Singer Concert Hall, which houses a rare pipe organ, and two other theatres. Attracting more than 400,000 guests a year, the multi-disciplinary arts facility also hosts special concerts, dance performances, poetry readings and other events.

Additional Sights

Crescent Road Viewpoint★

Rising above the Bow River and Prince's Island Park, this road offers a fine view of downtown and the snow-clad Rockies. The road is a pleasant evening walk among stately manor houses and manicured cottages, especially at night, with benches interspersed along the red shale pathway on the bluff, or on the sidewalk in front of the homes.

Fort Calgary

750 9th Ave. SE. ◑Open year-round daily 9am–5pm. ◑Closed Jan 1, Good Friday, Dec 24-26. ▤$10.50. ✕♿🅿☎403-290-1875. www.fortcalgary.ab.ca.

An **interpretive centre** on the 16ha/40acre site of the original 1875 North West Mounted Police post recounts the history of the city from 1875 to the 1940s. All structures, save the superintendent's house, were reconstructed, beginning in 1994, using tools and methods common to the era when the fort was initially built. Visitors follow a chronological pathway past museum exhibits, and may even try on a Mountie uniform, complete with accessories. In addition to the reconstructed post, the stables, blacksmith shop, carpenter shop and two-storey men's barracks are open for tours by costumed interpreters; inside the barracks are exhibits dating from 1888 to 1914 about the Mounted Police. The nearby **Deane House** (*see Address Book*), the 1906 clapboard former home of the NWMP superintendent, is now a popular restaurant, which also hosts special events such as murder-mystery nights. Paths within Fort Calgary's grounds afford **views** of the Elbow and Bow rivers, and a pedestrian bridge allows access to St. George's Island and the zoo (*caution should be taken on the trails after dark*).

Calgary Zoo★★

Kids *1300 Zoo Rd. NE. On St. George's Island. By car: North entrance access via St. George's Dr., which exits west of Deerfoot Trail from Memorial Dr. westbound. South entrance access via Memorial Dr. eastbound (watch for signs) east of Edmonton Trail. On foot: south entrance accessible*

Hippopotamus, Calgary Zoo
©Travel Alberta

by bridge over Bow River from 9th Ave. ◑Open year-round daily 9am–5pm. ◑Closed Dec 25. ▤May–Aug $18, rest of the year $16. ✕♿🅿☎403-232-9300, or 800-588-9993. www.calgaryzoo.org.

Located partly on an island in the Bow River, this attractive zoo houses a variety of animals from all over the world and a tropical greenhouse filled with exotic plants, flowers, butterflies and birds. The **prehistoric park** re-creates western Canada as it looked when dinosaurs roamed the earth between 225 million and 65 million years ago. Life-size reproductions of these giant creatures stand among mountains, volcanoes, hoodoos and swampland, along with the vegetation that might have existed in their day. The **Canadian Wilds** section, adjacent to the park, admirably reproduces the taiga (boreal forest), muskeg, tundra, aspen parkland and Rocky Mountain habitats of western Canada and is populated with moose, bears, beavers, sheep, goats, deer and other natural denizens. The diverse habitats of the **Destination Africa** exhibit include jungle, savanna and other African terrain and, of course, giraffes, hyenas, hippos, tigers and elephants. Calgary's zoo has won numerous awards for conservation work, education and authentic habitats.

Grain Academy★

17th Ave. & 2nd St. SE., in the Roundup Centre at Stampede Park, on the Plus 15 level. ◑Open year-round Mon–Fri 10am–4pm. ◑Closed major holidays. ♿🅿($11/vehicle)☎403-263-4594. www.grainacademymuseum.com.

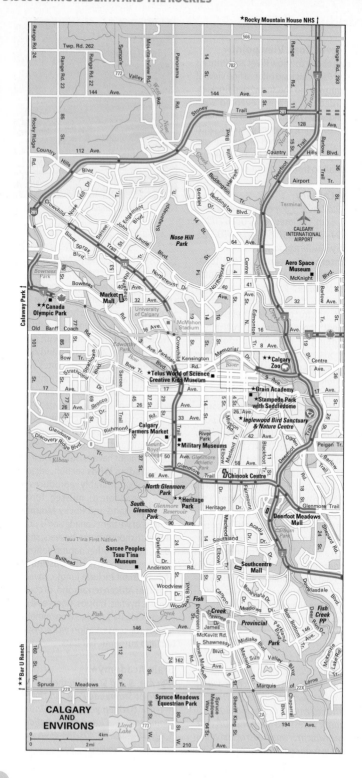

★ Rocky Mountain House NHS ↑

Range Rd. 24
Twp. Rd. 262
Range Rd. 22
Range Rd. 23
Symons
772
Valley
Mountainview Rd.
Panorama
West Rd.
144 Ave.
14 St.
782
566
Range Rd.
Range Rd. 293
2

85 St.
Rocky Ridge
112 Ave.
Nose Creek
144 Ave.
6 St.
Trail
North Branch
201
128
15 St.

Country Hills Blvd.
Crowchild
201
Nose Hill Dr.
Edgemont Blvd.
Sarcee Trail
John Laurie Blvd.
Shaganappi Tr.
Berkley Dr.
Beddington Tr.
Beddington Blvd.
14 St.
64 Ave.
Nose Hill Park
Centre St.
4 St.
40 St.
41 St.
32
Country Hills Blvd.
Deerfoot Tr.
Airport Tr.
Terminal
CALGARY INTERNATIONAL AIRPORT
Barlow Trail
36 St.

Bowness Park
Silver Sprgs Blvd.
53 St.
85 St.
1A
Northmount Dr.
Northmount Dr.
McKnight Blvd.
Aero Space Museum
Barlow Tr.
19 St.

★★ Canada Olympic Park
Bowness Rd.
40 St.
32 Ave.
Market Mall
University of Calgary
McMahon Stadium
16 Ave.
Crowchild Tr.
Parkdale Blvd.
Memorial Dr.
8 St.
Edmonton Tr.
16 Ave.
Centre St.
36 St.

Old Banff Coach Rd.
Bow Tr.
Strathcona Dr.
101
85 St.
69 St.
Sarcee Trail
Edworthy Park
Kensington Rd.
River
9 Ave.
★★ Calgary Zoo
17 Ave.
36 St.

17 Ave.
77 Ave.
26 Ave.
Richmond Rd.
37 St.
45 St.
29
17 Ave.
★ Telus World of Science
Creative Kids Museum
★ Grain Academy
14 St.
5 St.
4 St.
★ Stampede Park with Saddledome
★ Inglewood Bird Sanctuary & Nature Centre
26 Ave.
17 Ave.

Glenmore Tr.
Discovery Ridge Blvd.
8
Calgary Farmers Market
Mount Royal College
★ Military Museums
River Park
33 Ave.
Crowchild Trail
Elbow Dr.
Macleod Tr.
42 St.
58 St.
Blackfoot Tr.
11 St.
Ogden Rd.
Peigan Tr.
Barlow Tr.
18 St.

Elbow River
37 St.
50
66 Ave.
Glenmore Athletic Park
Glenmore Trail
★ Chinook Centre
Fairmount Dr.
Glenmore Trail

North Glenmore Park
South Glenmore Park
Glenmore Reservoir
★★ Heritage Park
Heritage Dr.
90 Ave.
14 St.
Macleod Tr.
Acadia Dr.
Deerfoot Meadows Mall
24 St.
Shepard Rd.

Tsuu T'ina First Nation
Bullhead
Sarcee Peoples Tsuu T'ina Museum
Oakfield Dr.
Southland Dr.
Elbow Dr.
Canyon Meadows Dr.
Southcentre Mall
Bonavista Dr.
Bow Bottom Tr.
Deer Valley Tr.
Douglasdale Blvd.
Fish Creek PP

Fish Creek
Woodview Dr.
Woodbine Blvd.
Fish Creek
Evergreen St.
Tawnee St.
James McKevitt Rd.
Fish Creek Provincial Park
Midlake Blvd.
Sun Valley Blvd.
Macleod Tr.
Deer Run Blvd.
Mckenzie Lake Blvd.

↑ ★★ Bar U Ranch
160 St. W.
112 St.
37 St. Tr.
146 Ave.
24 St.
162 Ave.
James McKevitt Rd.
Shawnessy Blvd.
6 St.
Marquis of Lorne
22X

Spruce Meadows
22X
96 St. W.
80 St. W.
210 Ave.
Spruce Meadows Equestrian Park
Sheriff King St.
Spruce Meadows Way
64 St.
194 Ave.
2A
Chaparral Blvd.

CALGARY AND ENVIRONS
Lloyd Lake
773

0 ——— 4km
0 ——— 2mi

Alberta's only grain interpretive centre, this museum focuses on one of mankind's basic food sources. It presents a working model of a prairie grain elevator, a model railway showing the movement of prairie grain through the Rocky Mountains, and a film (12min) on the history of grain production in western Canada.

The museum is located in Stampede Park near the distinctive 20,240-seat **Saddledome**★, constructed in 1983. The flowing saddle design of the stadium's roof echoes Calgary's cowboy past (*Pengrowth Saddledome, 555 Saddledome Rise;* ◷*open year-round Mon–Fri 8:30am–5pm;* ☞*1hr guided tours Jun–Aug on non-event days Mon–Fri 11am–2pm, last tour 1pm, reservations required:* ☎*403-777-1375;* ☎*403-777-4636; www. pengrowthsaddledome.com*).

Military Museums★

4520 Crowchild Trail SW, 8km/5mi southwest of downtown. Take Flanders Ave. Exit off Crowchild, head east, turn right onto Amiens Rd. and follow signs. ◷*Open year-round daily 9:30am–4pm.* ◷*Closed Dec 25 & Jan.1.* ☞*$6.* ♿🅿☎*403-974-285. www.themilitarymuseums.com.*

Situated on 13 acres west of downtown Calgary, this museum is devoted to military life in western Canada. Initially opened as the Museum of The Regiments in 1990, the original long, low-lying building housed exhibits on the four founding regiments.

Today elaborate exhibits and dioramas illustrate the history and impact of the country's armed forces, including their role in world wars, regional conflicts, peacekeeping efforts and joint operations in other countries such as Afghanistan. Highlights include a sensor-activated audio system telling of battles such as Dieppe and Vimy Ridge; a vast collection of rare war medals; and an outdoor exhibit of Sherman tanks, anti-tank guns, a CF-18 fighter jet and statues of heroes.

An ambitious renovation and expansion, expected to be completed in fall 2008, will add a new Air Force Museum, a new interactive children's discovery centre, and a new military history library affiliated with the University of Calgary Library. The Naval Museum of Alberta, the largest naval museum in Canada, will be relocated to the site; its collections include vintage aircraft, naval guns and extensive photographs documenting naval history. Renovations to the original building, slated for completion in 2010, will result in a new art gallery, temporary exhibit space and a classroom.

The Cowboy Trail

Starting at Mayerthorpe northwest of Edmonton and stretching south to Lundbreck near Crowsnest Pass, **Highway 22** has been dubbed "The Cowboy Trail," passing as it does through much of Alberta's ranchlands. Encompassing mixed forests, foothills and grasslands, the scenic 584km/434mi route crosses six rivers on its lengthy, linear journey (north to south: North Saskatchewan, Little Red Deer, Red Deer, Bow, Highwood and Oldman rivers). Southwest of Calgary, the highway traverses stunning big-sky country dotted with yellow wheat fields and large cattle ranges against the eastern slopes of the majestic Rocky Mountains. You'd recognize these rolling hills in such movies as *Unforgiven, Legends of the Fall,* and *Jesse James.* Western film producers flock to this area, and the Cowboy Trail has spawned a crop of national and international country music stars like Corb Lund, Paul Brandt, Teri Clark, and Ian Tyson, who owns a ranch in Longview. The two-lane road is a corridor of cities and small communities that welcome travellers en route, offering hospitality, food and services. Many of these businesses have banded together as members of the **Cowboy Trail Tourism Association** to promote services and activities largely expressive of the Western experience. Guest ranches and cabins, outfitters, tourist attractions, restaurants, antiques shops, bakeries and even "cowboy" churches can be accessed on the association's website. *For a map and listing of specific businesses,* ☎*403-652-7010 or 866-627-3051 or go online to www.thecowboytrail.com.*

©Travel Alberta

Prince House, Heritage Park

Heritage Park★★

Kids *1900 Heritage Dr. SW, 16km/10mi southwest of downtown. Take Macleod Trail SW to Heritage Dr.* ⊙*Open mid-May–Sept daily 9am–5pm. Rest of Sept–mid-Oct weekends only 9am–5pm. Nov 22–Dec 1 weekends only 9am–4 pm.* ✺*$15, rides $3 extra.* ✕⬧*(partial)* ⓟ☎*403-268-8500. www.heritagepark.ca.*

Occupying a pleasant site in a recreation area overlooking the Glenmore Reservoir, this 26ha/64-acre park re-creates prairie life of a bygone era with a pioneer community and a reconstructed Hudson's Bay Company post. The turn-of-the-19C town features a church, drugstore, bakery, general store, post office, newspaper office, pool hall, police post, houses and a station for a functioning **steam train** that gives tours of the site. Beside the tracks stands a working grain elevator, and on the outskirts of the town are farm buildings and a windmill. A replica of the *SS Moyie*, a three-tiered **paddle wheeler** once used on Kootenay Lake, offers boat trips on the reservoir *(every 35min),* and the antique **midway** has memorable rides. Brunch in the restored Wainwright Hotel (1907) is a classic summer outing for Calgarians, as is a visit to the park's bakery. The first phase of a $55 million expansion is slated for completion in fall 2008 and will include year-round attractions, such as an 1893 railway station and an area called Gasoline Alley, complete with antique cars and a heritage garage.

Canada Olympic Park★★

Olympic Rd. SW, 12km/7mi west of downtown by Trans-Can Hwy. 88. ⊙*Open May–Sept Mon–Fri 8am–9pm, weekends & holidays daily 8am-5:30pm. Rest of year times vary.* ⊙*Closed Dec 25.* ✺*Prices depend on activity.* ✕⬧ⓟ☎*403-247-5452. www.canadaolympicpark.ca.*

During the 1988 Winter Olympic Games, this large facility was developed to host competitive ski-jumping, luge, bobsled and freestyle-skiing events. Today, it is Alberta's second-most visited attractions after the Rocky Mountain Parks, drawing more than a million visitors a year. During the summer months, a chairlift *($12)* provides access to the ski-jump towers as well as to mountain biking and hiking trails. Another summer thrill, launched in 2007, is a ride on a zipline *($49/person)* that drops from the 90m/295ft ski jump, at speeds of up to 140kmh/100mph, to simulate the sensation of skiing down the ski jump as an athlete would. Winter visitors can hop aboard a bobsleigh (with an experienced driver onboard) and zoom down the icy 1,500m/4,920ft Olympic track at speeds of up to 120kmh/85mph for an exhilarating 60 seconds *($149/person)*. The park is also home to the Olympic Hall of Fame museum *(admission $6)*, where you can snap your photo next to the torch used during the Calgary Olympics, and see 20 other torches that have been used since the 1936 Berlin Games. The newest attraction is a virtual reality hockey shootout display that lets visitors feel as though they're playing against an on-ice opponent of Canada's Olympic hockey team. The park also hosts the Flag of Nations Concourse.

Excursions

South of Calgary

Okotoks★
Hwy. 2, 32km/20mi south of downtown Calgary.
📍*Station Cultural Centre, 53 North Railway St., ☎403-938-3204. www.okotoks.ca.*
This town of some 17,000 people sits within the foothills of the Sheep River Valley, backdropped by the snow-capped Rocky Mountains. A number of early 20C buildings remain from Okotoks' former days as a railroad town *(walking tour brochure available at the cultural centre).*

In 1998 residents adopted a municipal plan outlining growth limits based on infrastructure capacity, specifically the water-drawing capacity of the Sheep River. They identified four areas of responsibility that would ensure a sustainable community: environmental, economic, social and fiscal. Today Okotoks has been called "the greenest community in Canada" for its ecological focus and conservation efforts. The town maintains a central composting site and a waste-water treatment facility that turns sewage into compost; several solar heating installations are in place, and its recycling system, begun in 1992, has one of the highest success rates in the country.

The Big Rock
Hwy. 7, 10km/6mi southwest of Okotoks. www.tprc.alberta.ca.
A jarring sight along Highway 7, southwest of the town of Okotoks, this 16,500-ton boulder, split nearly in two, rises mysteriously out of the surrounding prairie grass. Known as the largest glacial erratic in the world, the huge quartzite rock is thought to have been deposited 18,000 years ago by an advancing glacier speckled with boulders from a landslide in the Jasper area. Indigenous peoples painted pictographs, still visible today, on the rock surface *(⚠visitors are cautioned not to climb on the rock, which*

The Big Rock, Okotoks

©Travel Alberta

might damage the pictographs). The Big Rock has been designated a provincial historic site.

Bragg Creek★

44km/27mi west of Calgary by Trans-Can Hwy., then head west on Hwy. 66. www.braggcreek.ca.

Ensconced within coniferous forests, this tiny community of artisans and commuters serves as the gateway to Kananaskis Country (☙ *see The Canadian Rockies),* a vast recreational reserve lying to its west. A small ranching community settled in the 1880s, Bragg Creek is named for early rancher Albert Warren Bragg. The hamlet is set at the confluence of the Elbow River and the namesake creek. The main street, White Avenue, edges the east side of the river. Rustic restaurants and postcard-pretty B&Bs (☙ *see Address Book),* galleries, craft shops, spas and shopping malls lure Calgarians and tourists here on weekends. The **Bragg Creek Trading Post** *(117 White Ave.; ☎403-949-3737)* stocks moccasins and aboriginal crafts along with hardware, groceries and outdoor equipment. Lined with antiques and craft shops, small malls are located in and around the village, including the Bragg Creek Market Mall, Trading Post II Mall and Bragg Creek Shopping Centre *(www. braggcreek.ca/braggcreek/malls.htm).*

Just 22km/13mi west of Bragg Creek, popular **Elbow Falls** can be found off Highway 66 *(watch for sign).* In early summer *(Jun)* melting snows and spring rains raise the Elbow River's water levels. ♿Paved paths lead to three lookouts, and a gravel pathway.

Turner Valley★

Hwy. 22, 60km/37mi southwest of Calgary. ☎403-933-4944. www.turnervalley.ca.

Several small towns straddle Highway 22, catering to the growing traffic by operating craft and gardening shops, antiques stores, cafes and B&Bs; Turner Valley is one of them. But it wasn't always so. Gas seepages along the Sheep River led to construction of a well, the Dingman #1 drilling platform. In 1914 the well's production of natural gas resulted in short-lived interest in the valley. A subsequent gusher of naphtha in 1924 and the discovery of oil here in 1936 created Alberta's oil and gas industry. Turner Valley's oil field became the largest in Canada, and the community burgeoned into a boom town. In 1942 the field peaked, and in the early 1950s the industry's focus shifted to Leduc, southwest of Edmonton, where oil had been discovered in 1947. Located on the riverbanks near town, the country's oldest gas-processing plant, dating to the1930s, has been preserved as an example of early technology. Until recently, it was possible to tour the **Turner Valley Gas Plant,** which ceased operations in 1985; visitors could view the scrubbing facilities, pipelines, engine room, Horton spheres and other areas and equipment *(currently the historic gas plant is closed, pending cleanup of contaminants found on-site).* Today tourism helps drive Turner Valley's economy. A wooden oil derrick, a replica of the Dingman #1, rises near the town bandstand. This symbol of the town's fame is ubiquitous here, as are plantings and containers of colourful flowers in summertime. Children play in the community park, spectators turn out for parades, and tourists take in the scenic surroundings of the town's setting.

Longview

Hwy. 22, 81km/50mi southwest of Calgary. ☎403-558-3922. www.village. longview.ab.ca.

Just 21km/13mi south of Turner Valley, Longview is a tiny community straddling Highway 22. It began as a service centre for area ranches. The 1914 oil strike in Turner Valley created a temporary boom town until the 1940s, when the petroleum industry's presence shrank in the area. Still a service town today, Longview is famous for its multiple flavours of beef jerky like terroualo and spiced pepper sold in stores nearly everywhere in town. It's also known for singer Ian Tyson's coffeehouse, Navajo Mug, which serves take-out lattes and cappuccino and snacks. Longview's Twin Cities Hotel, a 9-room lodging along the highway, includes a saloon where live cowboy jam sessions are held in the winter months; the cafe is popular for its beef burgers and apple

©Travel Alberta

Bar U Ranch

crisp (⏰*open daily 11:30am–8:00pm;* ☎*403-558-3787*).

Bar U Ranch★★

Kids *100km/62mi south of Calgary via Hwy.2 South (Macleod Trail) & Hwy. 22 South.* ⏰*Open late-May–early Oct daily 9am–5pm.* ⏷*$7.05.* ✕&☎*403-395-2212 or 888-773-888. www.pc.gc.ca.*

In operation from 1882 to 1950, this working ranch was once the epitome of Alberta ranching. Set among the rolling foothills south of Calgary, the National Historic Site preserves many restored ranch buildings from the early 20C. Notable features are the replica cowboy camp, complete with a chuckwagon; an ice house; the ranch post office; and several large barns, including a **saddle-horse barn** now devoted to fascinating depictions of ranch life. Guests may take rides in buckboard wagons pulled by the Bar U's signature Percheron draft horses. The site itself, nestled in a beautiful vale along Pekisko Creek with the snowy Rockies in the near distance, is memorably scenic.

Ranch life events such as stock dog demonstrations and cowboy breakfasts take place almost every weekend in the summer, to the delight of visiting greenhorns. On Sundays, there are cowboy brunches and demonstrations of ranchhand activities.

Highway 541, which intersects Route 22 north of the ranch, offers a spectacular 210km/130mi loop **drive**★ to the west

to return to Calgary. Climbing through aspen parkland foothills into the Rockies, the road becomes Route 40, also known as the Highwood Pass (⏷*Hwy. 40 is closed in winter for the lambing season for bighorn sheep*). The pass traverses Kananaskis Country, an Alberta recreational area with trailheads providing access into the high country (⏷*see The Canadian Rockies*).

Blackfoot Crossing Historical Park★★

On Siksika Reserve, 100km/62mi east of Calgary by Trans-Can Hwy., then take Hwy. 842 south 10km/6mi.
⏰*Open mid-May–Sept daily 9am-6pm. Rest of the year Mon–Fri 9am–5pm, Sat 10am–4pm.* ⏷*$10.* ✕&℗☎*403-734-5171 or 888-654-6274. www.blackfoot crossing.ca.*

Opened in 2007, this world-class aboriginal attraction was designed by Calgary architect Ron Goodfellow in consultation with tribal elders. Inspired by traditional native structures, the main building takes the form of a 5,766sq m/62,000sq ft sundance lodge, surmounted by a half-circle roof and seven tepee-shaped skylights symbolic of ancient encampments. More than an architectural marvel, the $25 million facility, overlooking the Bow River, tells the tale of Blackfoot culture, history and traditions through interactive exhibits and artifacts. The complex includes a 65-seat theatre where dancing and drumming are per-

Blackfoot Crossing Historical Park

formed, a restaurant, a museum shop, a conference centre, an archival library and tepees to accommodate overnight guests (see Address Book).

Visitors approach the building via a wall-lined walkway that narrows—buffalo-jump fashion—to the entrance, itself sited east to catch the sunrise. Embedded in the walls are bas-reliefs of Blackfoot leaders and ceremonial robes. Inside the main gallery, four 15m/50ft poles, angled tepee style, rise to support a 6m/20ft-high ceiling ringed with a central tepee skylight. Guided or self-guided interpretive tours are offered for the building *(45min guided tour)* and on ancestral lands *(1hr guided tour)* along the Bow River, where the Siksika Nations lived for many generations. Key sites include the spot where Chief Crowfoot and four other First Nations chiefs signed Treaty 7 with the federal government in 1877, as well as Crowfoot's grave.

Vulcan Tourism and Trek Station

Vulcan★

120km/74mi southeast of Calgary. Hwy. 2 south then east on Hwy. 23. ☎403-485-2417. www.town.vulcan.ab.ca.

Vulcan ears? Check. Walkie-Talkie? Check. Captain Kirk is on the deck and Spock at his side, ready for adventure. Welcome to the small agricultural town of Vulcan, named for the Roman god of fire. In the 1920s Vulcan had nine big-capacity (the largest storage capacity in Canada) grain elevators all lined up in a row along the railroad tracks; they were known far and wide as "nine in a line"—until a 1971 fire destroyed them. The **Vulcan Historical Museum** *(232 Centre St.;* open mid-Jun–Aug Tue–Sat 10am–4:30pm)* features displays on the town's past. Today, with only 3,700 residents, the town has once again captured widespread attention. A novel attraction is the town's visitor centre, **Tourism and Trek Station** *(115 Centre St.;* open mid-May–Oct daily 9am–5pm; rest of the year Mon–Fri 9am–5pm, Sat 10am–4pm; ☎403-485-2994; www.vulcantourism. com)*, built to resemble a spaceship to evoke the popular 1960s TV series *Star Trek. Star Trek* memorabilia and a virtual reality game are on hand. The town has built a replica (1995) of *Star Trek's* **Starship Enterprise** *(along Hwy. 23)* and hosts an annual Galaxyfest/Spock Days *(end of Jun)* that attracts Trekkies.

North of Calgary

Cochrane★

35km/25mi northwest of Calgary via Crowchild Trail (Hwy. 1A). ☎403-851-2500. www.cochrane.ca.

This small city of 14,000—one of Alberta's fastest-growing communities—sits on the site along the Bow River where former Senator Matthew Cochrane catapulted the ranching industry to prominence in 1881 by leasing 190,000 acres of fertile grass land. Within a few years, the Calgary area, including the then-tiny settlement of Cochrane, was scored with small farms and mega-ranches, as pioneers took advantage of generous government subsidies to encourage land development in the West. As you drive down the curving **Cochrane Hill** into town along Highway 1A *(the town is also accessible by the Trans-Can Hwy.)*, look up to the right to see if any hang gliders are catching wind from the steep bluffs overlooking the town. Cochrane's downtown has some interesting boutiques, the locally famous **Mackay's Ice Cream Shop** *(220 1st St West; ☎403-932-2455; www.mackaysicecream.com)* and several restaurants (ℹ *see Address Book).*

A quarter-mile north of downtown, one of the finest **views**★★ of the snow-capped Rockies can be seen from the steep, straw-coloured hills above **Cochrane Ranche House** *(101 Ranche House Rd., off Hwy.2;.* ⏱ *grounds open daily year-round; interpretive centre open May–Labour Day daily 9am–5pm;* ⏱ *closed major holidays;* ☎ *403-851-2565; www.cochraneranchehouse.ca).* Formerly the Western Heritage Centre, this newly refurbished facility holds the town offices and a conference centre. It occupies the site of the former Cochrane Ranche, the first big cattle ranch in Alberta. The interpretive centre features displays on the area's ranching heritage and Senator Cochrane in particular. The peaceful grounds at the base of Big Hill are popular for picnics along Big Hill Creek. On the steep bluff, a bronze statue of horse and rider titled *Men of Vision* stands amid wildflowers. A shale trail follows the creek, and it is possible to hike to Big Hill Springs Park *(15km /9 mi north)* from here.

Cowboy churches are a growing trend in the western part of the province. Every Tuesday *(7pm)* the **Cochrane Cowboy Church** *(☎403-637-2732; www.thecowboytrail.com)* holds its Western-style service at the Ranche House. Attendees in cowboy hats and boots come for Gospel music sung to the accompaniment of guitar, bass and banjo, and refreshments after the chairs are stacked.

Big Hill Springs Provincial Park

16km/10mi north of Cochrane by Hwy. 22 west, then 11km/7mi east on Highway 567.

⏱ *Open year-round; firepit and picnic facilities maintained mid-May to October.* ☎403-297-5293. www.tpr.alberta.ca.

Tucked well off the main highways north and west of Calgary, this 65-acre park is set in a small valley. The oasis is popular with families, strollers, picnickers and dog walkers *(leash required)*. A shady trail *(2 km/1.3mi round-trip)* leads up to the spring source of Big Hill Creek, where waterfalls tumble over rocky outcroppings. ⚠*This area is bounded by private land that is not open to hikers.*

Airdrie

39km/28 mi north of Calgary via Deerfoot Trail north (Hwy. 2). ☎403-948-8800. www.airdrie.ca

Airdrie has become a bedroom community for Calgary. Most of the city's residential areas lie on the west side of Highway 2. A city of 38,000 and still growing, Airdrie has an agricultural- and industrial-based economy . Founded in 1889 during construction of the cross-Canada railway, it is a recreational centre largely because of its location along Nose Creek, a waterway that runs south through Calgary and empties into the Bow River. The creek has led to the creation of nice parks, most notably **Nose Creek Park** *(borders Main St.)*, with fountains and abundant waterfowl. Nearby on Main Street sits the **Nose Creek Valley Museum** *(1701 Main St.; ☎403-948-6685)*, which has First Nations artifacts, heritage furniture and farm equipment.

CANADIAN ROCKIES

Frequently rising over 3,000m/10,000ft, the Canadian Rockies constitute the easternmost range of North America's Western Cordillera, a long mountain system covering the western quarter of the country that is part of the Canadian Cordillera (consisting of, from east to west, the Rocky Mountains, the interior basins and plateaus, the Coast Mountains, the Inside Passage along the coast and the outer islands). Beginning at the border with the US, the Canadian Rockies stretch roughly 1,550km/900mi through western Alberta and eastern British Columbia in a northwesterly direction. To the north these mountains are bounded by the broad plain of the Liard River; to the east by the Interior Plains; and to the west by the Rocky Mountain Trench, one of the longest continuous valleys in the world. The spine of the Rockies forms part of the Continental Divide—or Great Divide—which serves as the boundary between the provinces of British Columbia and Alberta, and determines the drainage of rivers into the Pacific, Atlantic or Arctic oceans. Today four contiguous national parks in the Rockies are one of Canada's most popular natural attractions.

Bookending these Rocky Mountain parks are two massive, pristine areas devoted to recreation as well as habitat preservation. Southeast of the parks, Kananaskis Country is an Alberta recreational area of steep mountains, glacier-clad peaks and snowmelt freshets that includes three provincial parks, with innumerable trailheads affording access to the high country. To the north, above Jasper National Park, sprawls Willmore Wilderness Park, a 459,671ha/1,135,872 acre reserve, also within Alberta, with no public roads but an abundance of wildlife. Waterton Lakes National Park is situated apart from the other Rocky Mountain parks, in the southwest corner of Alberta.

Paddling on Lake Louise

©Leslie Forsberg/Michelin

Address Book

*⚑For dollar-sign categories, see the
Legend on the cover flap.*

WHERE TO STAY

*⚑Almost all hotels in the national parks
area offer access to outdoor activities,
guides and outfitters. The Fairmont
hotels also offer Mountain Heritage
Guide programs.*

$ HI-Lake Louise Alpine Centre –
203 Village Rd., Lake Louise. ☎*403-670-
7580 or 866-762-4122. www.hihostels.ca.
46 rooms, including family rooms,
164 beds.* ♿ℙ. This hostel's stylish
wood-framed appearance and high
standards make budget travel a pleasant experience. Dorm-style rooms are
spotless and come with two to six beds.
Private rooms are also available. Guests
have access to a kitchen, a reading
room, laundry facilities, a café and wireless internet. Other Hostelling International facilities in the region are located
in Banff, Jasper and Yoho parks, Golden,
BC, and along the Icefields Parkway.

$$ Blue Mountain Lodge – *137
Muskrat St., Banff.* ☎*403-762-5134. www.
bluemtnlodge. com. 10 rooms. Minimum
2-night stay.* ℙ⚌. Built in 1908, this
small bed-and-breakfast offers afford-
able rooms, all with a private bath,
cable TV and wireless internet. The rate
includes an ample cold breakfast buffet.
Guests also have use of a communal
kitchen and a ski-storage area.

$$ Georgetown Inn – *1101 Bow Valley
Trail, Canmore.* ☎*403-678-3439 or
800-657-5955. www.georgetowninn.ca.
20 rooms.* ✕♿ℙ⚌. This charming,
Tudor-style inn offers a rustic getaway
with modern amenities. Most guest
suites have fireplaces and fridges, and
a continental breakfast is included in
room rate. The courtyard and English
country garden make a peaceful oasis
in summer. But at the end of the day, sit
by the cozy fireplace in the dining room
and pub, decorated in the style of a
traditional English watering hole.

$$ Kootenay Park Lodge – *Hwy.93, in
Kootenay National Park.* ☎*403-762-9196.
www.kootenayparklodge.com. 10 cabins.*
Closed Oct–Apr. ✕♿ℙ. This renovated
lodge was originally a CPR wilderness
lodge in the 1920s. Built in the 1930s,
the old-fashioned park-lodge style log
cabins offer both comfort and charac-
ter. Some cabins have fireplaces, and
one has a kitchen. The lodge's dining
room offers traditional hearty soups,
breads and salads, and entire complex
sits by itself with nothing nearby
for miles.

**$$ Mystic Springs Chalets and Hot
Pools** – *140 Kananaskis Way, Canmore.*
☎*403-609-0333. www.mysticsprings.ca.
44 suites.* ℙ⚒. It's not often a resort
property is welcoming both to high-
end business travellers and families,
but this chalet-style development is just
that. From its expansive, self-catered
suites with gourmet kitchens to the
central courtyard with family-friendly
hot pools, Mystic Springs has carved
out a niche with visitors all year round.
The resort chalets are also pet-friendly
and feature thoughtful touches such as
exterior storage for outdoor gear. The
outdoor pool is a heated salt
water pool.

$$ Spruce Grove Inn – *Banff Ave.,
Banff.* ☎*403-762- 3301 or 800-879-1991.
www.banffvoyagerinn.com. 114 rooms.*
♿ℙ. Built in 2002, this lodging is
spanking new by the venerable stand-
ards of many park hotels. It is situated
on a strip of motels that leads into
downtown Banff from the Trans-Canada
Highway. Although the inn keeps
rates relatively low by offering fewer
amenities, its rooms are spacious and
comfortable. Ski storage and heated
underground parking are included in
the rate. Many restaurants lie within a
10-minute walk.

$$$ Brewster's Mountain Lodge
– *208 Caribou St., Banff.* ☎*403-762-2900
or 888-762-2900. www.brewster-
mountainlodge.com. 60 rooms, 17 suites.*
♿ℙ. This western style hotel, with
its distinctive peeled log exterior, sits
just one block from downtown Banff.
A timber stairway leads upstairs to spacious, updated bedrooms. Continental

breakfast, included in the room rate, is served in an inviting downstairs dining room.

$$$ Icefield Chalet Hotel – *Icefields Parkway at Athabasca Glacier.* ✕ ♿ 🅿 ☎877-423-7433. www.columbia-ice field.com. 32 rooms. Closed Oct–Apr. These hotel-style rooms perch on the third floor of the Columbia Icefield Centre and offer functional housing for families. The views here are sensational, either of the glacier (slightly more pricey) across the parkway or the mountains directly behind the chalet. Guests have full access to meals at the dining room on the second floor, and can peruse the Jasper National Park Glacier Gallery on the first floor at their leisure.

$$$ Num-ti-Jah Lodge – *40km/25mi north of Lake Louise on Hwy. 9, Lake Louise.* ☎403-522-2167. www.num-ti-jah. com. 25 rooms. ✕ ♿ 🅿. The original lodge was built some 80 years ago by Jimmy Simpson, a mountain guide. Refurbished and expanded, the timber-frame inn overlooks Bow Glacier and Bow Lake from a splendid setting. The **Elkhorn Dining Room ($$$)** offers a table d'hôte of West Coast cuisine. Comfortable lounge and library. No TV or phone, although a satellite phone is available.

$$$ Paradise Lodge & Bungalows – *105 Lake Louise Dr., Lake Louise. Closed Oct–May.* ☎403-522-3595. www. paradiselodge.com. 45 cabins & suites. ♿ 🅿. The undeniable charm of this heritage property, located between the valley floor and Lake Louise, attracts the same guests year after year. Well-tended gardens surround the tidy cabins, built in the 1930s, some of which feature vaulted ceilings and claw-foot tubs. Larger than the cabins, the suites contain fireplaces and offer the best views; some have kitchens, equipped with basic amenities.

$$$ Tekarra Lodge – *1.6km/1mi south of Jasper. Hwy. 93A South, Jasper.* ☎780-852-3058 or 800-709-1827. www.tekarra lodge.com. 52 cabins. Closed Nov–Apr. ✕ ♿ 🅿. After 1913, when motor vehicles were permitted in the Rocky Mountain parks, "bungalow camps" such as this one sprang up. Tekarra dots the open forest above the Athabasca River with rustic cabins featuring com-

fortable beds, cooking facilities and wood-burning fireplaces. There is a telephone at the front desk, but no TV. The views across the Athabasca River Valley to the Rockies, from lawn chairs perched above the river, are superb. The **Tekarra Restaurant ($$)** serves a varied menu, on the hearty side.

$$$$ Baker Creek Chalets – *BowValley Pkwy., Lake Louise.* ☎403-522-3761. www.bakercreek.com. 33 cabins and suites. ✕ ♿ 🅿. Situated between Lake Louise and Banff on the Bow Valley Parkway, Baker Creek's cozy log chalets provide well-priced accommodations. The chalets all have balconies and kitchenettes. Suites in a newer building are done up in warm, earthy tones. Plan to eat at the **Baker Creek Bistro ($$$)**, an unpretentious dining room that serves up hearty Canadian-style meals.

$$$$ Buffalo Mountain Lodge – *Tunnel Mountain Dr., Banff.* ☎403-762-2400 or 800-661-1367. www.crmr.com. 108 rooms. ✕ ♿ 🅿. This sprawling lodge offers a peaceful retreat from the bustle of Banff, just a short walk away. The sizable bedrooms include a fireplace, and a balcony or patio. Some bathrooms feature claw-foot bathtubs and heated floors. The renowned **Sleeping Buffalo Restaurant ($$$$)** specializes in local produce and game raised on a ranch nearby. As well as the customary strenuous activities, the hotel offers a comfortable lounge with excellent single-malt Scotch.

$$$$ Cathedral Mountain Lodge – *Yoho Valley Rd., in Yoho National Park.* ☎250-343-6442 or 866-619-6442. www. cathedralmountain.com. 7 cabins. Closed Oct–Apr. ♿ 🅿. The peeled pine and spruce log cabins of this new resort feature wood-plank floors, river-rock fireplaces and forest green and claret colour accents. Though slightly more expensive, the river view cabins have front porches with exquisitely relaxing vistas over the Kicking Horse River to the mountains beyond. Lodge guests enjoy free canoeing on Moraine Lake.

$$$$ Emerald Lake Lodge – *Emerald Lake Rd., in Yoho National Park.* ☎250-343-6321 or 800-663-6336. www.crmr. com. 85 rooms in 24 chalets. ✕ ♿ 🅿. Set among towering evergreens, this quintessential mountain getaway overlooks one of the region's most picturesque lakes. Large comfortable rooms with fieldstone fireplaces, pine furnishings and private entrances promote a restful stay. Take your meals in the main lodge or at the casual lakeside cafe. A wide range of summer and winter activities is available nearby, and a free shuttle connects to the Lake Louise ski resort.

$$$$$ Fairmont Banff Springs – *405 Spray Ave., Banff. ☎403-762- 2211 or 800-257-7544. www.fairmont.com. 778 rooms.* ✕ ♿ 🅿 Spa. This turreted châ-teau overlooking the Bow River is one of the world's best-known mountain playgrounds. First opened in 1888 as the centrepiece of William Van Horne's plan to draw tourists to the Rockies on the Canadian Pacific Railway, "The Springs" has since been thoroughly modernized. Although on the smallish side, rooms are smartly decorated. The real attractions are the opulent ambi-ence and an abundance of facilities, including the luxurious Willow Stream Spa, a 27-hole golf course and riding stables. No less than 11 restaurants range from an intimate wine bar to the top-drawer **Banffshire Club ($$$$)**, the latter specializing in roasted Alberta lamb and beef, bison carpaccio, venison and other Canadian classics. Visitors are welcome at all hotel eateries.

$$$$$ Fairmont Chateau Lake Louise – *111 Lake Louise Dr., Lake Louise. ☎403-522-3511 or 800-257-7544. www.fairmont.com. 489 rooms.* ✕ ♿ 🅿 Spa. This famous mountain resort's stunning view of turquoise blue Lake Louise is perhaps the most renowned in the Canadian Rockies. Restaurants include the **Fairview Room ($$$)**, offering fine contemporary fare accompanied by dramatic views. Outside, colourful gardens lead to a paved walkway bor-dering the lakeshore. Activities range from canoeing the lake to rock-climbing and barn dancing.

$$$$$ Fairmont Jasper Park Lodge – *Old Lodge Rd., Jasper. ☎780-852-3301 or 800-257-7544. www.fairmont.com. 446 rooms in a complex of cabins and lodges.* ✕ ♿ 🅿 Spa. Sprawling along turquoise-coloured Beauvert Lake, this historic property boasts its own championship golf course as well as extensive sports

facilities. Accommodations range from chalet-style cottages to log cabins that have hosted royalty, including Queen Elizabeth II. Dining spots include the illustrious **Edith Cavell Dining Room ($$$$)**, named for a nearby mountain and featuring a menu of Canadian game and seafood.

$$$$$ Lake O'Hara Lodge – *Trans-Can Hwy., in Yoho National Park. ☎250-343-6418, 403-678-4110 (off-season). www. lakeohara.com. 23 cabins and rooms. (Rates include all meals and shuttle to the lodge.) Closed Oct–Jan, mid-Apr–mid-Jun.* ✕. Originally built by the Canadian Pacific Railway as a backcountry lodge, this hostelry on Lake O'Hara is one of the most splendid in Canada. The main lodge holds a restaurant and eight standard guest rooms, but the lakeside cabins are more coveted. Access to the property is by shuttle only; no private cars are allowed on the site *(parking is 15km/9mi east of Field)*. In the winter season *(early-Feb–early-Apr)*, guests ski or snowshoe 12km/7.5mi to the lodge. No TV, radio or internet connections. 🏕Parks Canada and the Alpine Club of Canada (👈*see Practical Information*) have campsites on Lake O'Hara.

$$$$$ Moraine Lake Lodge – *In Banff National Park, at Moraine Lake above Lake Louise, Lake Louise. ☎877-522-2777. www.morainelake.com. 33 rooms, 12 cabins. Closed Oct–May. No children under 8 years of age.* ✕ ♿ 🅿 ☕. This stunning, ultra-deluxe post and beam lodge was designed by famed British Columbia architect Arthur Erickson. It has an enviable site over-looking Moraine Lake. Views of the famous Valley of the Ten Peaks are the allure—Erickson even included a glass

Fairmont Banff Springs Hotel

©Travel Alberta

ceiling in the dining room—and the landscape is the lodge's focus, as rooms have no phones or internet access. Cabins and rooms feature hand-crafted log furniture, pine accents and soaking tubs. A continental breakfast is included in the rate.

$$$$$ Post Hotel and Spa – *Pipestone Rd., Lake Louise.* ☎*403-522-3989 or 800-661-1586. www.posthotel. com. 94 rooms.* ✕ ♿ 🅿 Spa . A short walk from the village, this stylish retreat, part of the ultra-luxe Relais & Châteaux group, is set along the tumbling waters of the Pipestone River. Spacious guest rooms feature polished logwork, luxurious bathrooms and balconies; many feature a hot tub and fireplace. The **dining room ($$$$)** is renowned for its Canadian cuisine.

WHERE TO EAT

$ Barpa Bill's Greek – *223 Bear St., Banff.* ☎*403-762-0377.* **Greek.** You're on the run but in desperate need of something warm and Mediterranean. Despite its not-so-appetizing name, this little takeout joint is a hit with those with families and those on a budget, serving heaping Greek fare such as chicken pita sandwiches laden with veggies and garlicky *tzatziki* sauce.

$ Grizzly Paw Brewing Company – *622 Main St., Banff.* ☎*403-678-9983. Brewery tours available. www.thegrizzly-paw.com.* **Canadian.** Sports buffs love this place, billed as the only brewing company in the Rockies. Hamburgers, quesadillas, nachos, and chicken wings are plentiful and fresh. The beer selection is heavenly, especially when quaffed during a sunny spring day on the patio. Bring a non-imbibing friend to drive so you can try the mini-samplers of the Grizzly Paws' tasty brews. And bring the kids, too: "the Paw" crafts its own soda pop using 30 percent less sugar than commercial concoctions.

$$ Becker's Gourmet Restaurant – *Hwy 93, Jasper.* ☎*780-852-3535. www. beckerschalets.com.* ♿ *Closed mid-Oct–early May. Breakfast & dinner.* **Canadian.** Diners can look across the Athabasca River to distant mountains while enjoying cuisine prepared from fresh local products such as Alberta beef, lamb, bison, venison and rainbow trout. On

colder evenings, a fire crackles in the riverstone fireplace. Repeat customers ask for a bowl of housemade ice-cream.

$$ Crazyweed Kitchen – *1600 Railway Ave., Canmore.* ☎*403-609-2530. www. crazyweed.ca. Closed major holidays.* **International.** With the freshest seafood (sustainably caught), a seasonal, innovative menu and special attention to detail, this Canmore institution dishes out a gustatory feast featuring everything from East Indian onion rings to Vietnamese pork meatballs, Thai grilled chicken and red curry seafood bowl. The wood oven pizza is particularly tasty, as are the perfectly crisp pommes frites (fried potatoes).

$$ Jack Pine Bistro & Lodge – *In Rundlestone Lodge, 537 Banff Ave., Banff.* ☎*403-762-2201 or 800-661-8630. www.rundlestone.com.* ♿ *Breakfast & dinner.* **Contemporary.** Many tourists miss this fine restaurant, located away from the town centre, but it's worth seeking out for Canadian game such as bison rib-eye, Pacific coast seafood, Atlantic lobster and Alberta beef. Knowledgeable wait staff and Canadian wines round out the pleasant experience. Try a glass of British Columbia ice wine with your dessert.

$$ Lake Louise Railway Station & Restaurant – *200 Sentinel Rd., Lake Louise.* ☎*403-522-2600. www.lakelouise station.com.* ♿ *Dinner year-round. Lunch summer only. Closed Oct–mid-Nov.* **International.** This former Canadian Pacific Railway station, built in 1910, has been furnished with Arts and Crafts pieces to serve as an offbeat setting for fine dining. Eclectic lunch and dinner menus bring the world to your table with Asian, Italian and East Indian dishes as well as Canadian. The restored 1925 CPR dining car offers seasonal service only and a more limited dinner menu, but the interior is nothing short of luxurious.

$$ Melissa's Restaurant and Bar – *218 Lynx St., Banff.* ☎*403-762-5511. www. melissasrestauant.com.* **Steakhouse.** This perennial favourite serves all-day breakfasts plus heaping burgers, nicely charbroiled steaks, and other delicious fare. Its huge popularity (plan to stand in line) comes in part from its sponsorship of the popular annual road races

(10km/6.2mi, plus a half-marathon 22km/13.5mi) that attract runners and walkers from around the world early each September. Families are welcome at this long-running eatery.

$$ St. James's Gate – *205 Wolf St., Banff.* ☎*403-762-9355. www.stjames gatebanff.com.* **Pub food.**
One of the many noted figures and celebrities who frequent Banff, Justin Trudeau, son of late Canadian prime minister Pierre Elliott Trudeau, was spotted noshing on appetizers and beer at this classy Irish pub. Highly polished wood imported from Ireland frames much of the interior of this spacious bar. An excellent beer and whisky selection, live music and a whole lot of ambiance.

$$$ Maple Leaf Grille & Lounge – *137 Banff Ave., Banff.* ☎*403-760-7680, or 866-403-7680. www.banffmapleleaf. com.* ♿. **Canadian.** This popular dining room, faced in cedar and presided over by a moose head, offers imaginative Canadian dishes such as Brome Lake duck with Saskatoon berry jus, wild BC salmon, braised lamb shank and bison tenderloin, both from Alberta. Desserts, such as ginger bread cake with pumpkin ice cream and caramel pecan sauce are equally creative. Request an upstairs table for the best views and a quieter dining experience.

$$$ Murrieta's Bar & Grill – *200 - 737 Main St., Canmore.* ☎*403-609-9500. www.murrietas.ca.* **Contemporary.**
There are three restaurants in this Alberta company's area coverage: Canmore, Calgary and Edmonton. Unlike a chain, each restaurant is individually inspired, and Canmore's offers soft lighting, dark woods and regional cuisine with a twist. Try the flatbread pizzas and stylish salads at lunch; the dinner menu features salmon, pickerel, Arctic char and other fish, game, duck, lamb and flavorful pastas worthy of a nice night out.

$$$ Quarry Bistro & Wine Bar – *718 Main St., Canmore.* ☎*403-678-6088, www.quarrybistro.com. Closed Wed. & major holidays.* **Contemporary.**
Open-beam construction gives this artful, European-style bistro a spacious look, and an open kitchen allows patrons to see what Chef David Wyse is preparing. Co-owned with sister Naomi, the bistro has wowed locals and travellers alike with fresh and flavourful food that incorporates local, organic ingredients. A traditional Italian dish like cannelloni is newly minted with elk, and that French staple, coq au vin, is brought into the 21C with an organic chicken breast, topped with wild mushrooms and double-smoked bacon. A fine wine list adds to one's dining pleasure.

$$$$ The Trough Dining Co. – *725B 9 St.,Canmore.* ☎*403-678-2820. www.thetrough.ca.* **Caribbean.**
While Canmore's dining scene consistently makes Best Restaurant lists in Alberta, this tiny hotspot is not only stylish (think wood floors, glass waterfall and slate countertops), but was recently rated as one of Canada's top eateries. Preparation and fresh ingredients are key: the Caribbean-spiced ribs are simmered for hours until the meat falls from the bone; yet despite the strong ethnic influences, the emphasis is very much on the regional dishes like lake duck confit.

Composed of sedimentary rock deposited by ancient seas some 1.5 billion years ago, the Rockies have a distinct layered appearance. They first began to uplift 120 million to 70 million years ago because of the collision of tectonic plates. During the last Ice Age (75,000 to 11,000 years ago), glaciation carved the mountains into the terrain seen today: U-shaped valleys, glacially fed lakes, canyons, bowl-shaped cirques and hanging valleys with waterfalls and glaciers. Since the end of the Little Ice Age, or Cavell Advance, in 1870, the Rockies' glaciers have begun a significant retreat.

The area contains other impressive provincial parks and reserves, notably Mount Assiniboine *(between Banff and Kootenay; not accessible by road).* Modern parkways dissect the region's wide river valleys, and hiking trails crisscross the backcountry, allowing access to an awesome landscape of soaring peaks, alpine lakes, waterfalls and glaciers.

Rocky Mountain Parks★★★

MAPS P88, P91, PP96-97, P99

Internationally known for spectacular mountain scenery, the Rocky Mountain Parks draw some 6 million sightseers a year. These terrestrial wonders, with their diverse topography, vegetation and wildlife, are the jewels of western Canada. The major parks in the Canadian Rockies are Banff, Jasper, Yoho and Kootenay national parks and Mount Robson Provincial Park. Situated next to each other in the southern part of the mountain range, they form one of the largest mountain parklands in the world, covering over 22,274sq km/8,600sq mi. Banff and Jasper national parks, as well as the Icefields Parkway, lie within the province of Alberta (AB); Kootenay and Yoho national parks fall within the boundaries of British Columbia (BC). Situated in the southwest corner of Alberta, Waterton Lakes National Park is Canada's fifth Rocky Mountain park.

- ▢ **Information:** Each park has a visitor centre. Parks Canada: www.pc.gc.ca. Alberta Tourism: www.travelalberta.com. Tourism British Columbia: www.hellobc.com.
- ▶ **Orient Yourself:** The parks are connected by excellent roadways. **Highway 93**, starting at Radium Hot Springs, BC, stretches north to link the Kootenay, Banff and Jasper parks. East-west, Highway 1, the **Trans-Canada Highway,** links Calgary to Banff, then turns north to Lake Louise, where it again turns west, crossing Yoho park to emerge at Golden, BC. In the north, Highway 16, the **Yellowhead Highway,** also runs east-west, linking Edmonton to Jasper, crossing the park and emerging at Tête Jaune Cache, BC.
- ▣ **Parking:** When hiking or skiing, park only in designated lots: police ticket cars parked on the roadside. ☺Never get out of your car to photograph or feed wildlife, an extremely dangerous and potentially ticketable offence. When you sight wild animals near the roadway, be sure to pull over to the shoulder so you do not block traffic lanes.
- ☺ **Don't Miss:** Icefields Parkway between Lake Louise and Jasper offers spectacular views of glaciers; in the autumn during elk rutting season, you can hear male elks bugle; Parks Canada promises that if you visit Yoho in May or June, you'll see a bear; at the Vermillion Pass, in Kootenay National Park, you can stand astride the Continental Divide (also called the Great Divide).
- ☾ **Also See:** THE KOOTENAYS

Flora and Fauna

Still largely wilderness, the Rocky Mountain Parks are inhabited by a variety of animal and plant life. Even along roadways black bear, coyote, elk, moose, mule deer, mountain sheep, squirrels and chipmunks are often seen. More rarely, white-coated mountain goats and bighorn sheep may be spotted, and in more remote areas, grizzly bears roam. Plant life varies greatly because of the drastic changes in elevation. Wildflowers are abundant throughout the vegetation zones. Their bloom follows the snowmelt up the mountainsides from late June through early August. Stands of Douglas fir, lodgepole pine, white spruce and trembling aspen in the valleys gradually give way to alpine fir, Lyall's larch and Engelmann spruce on the higher slopes. Just below the tree line lies a band of krummholz vegetation—trees dwarfed by the severe conditions. Above the tree line (normally 2,200m/7,200ft on south-facing slopes, lower on north facing), only the low, ground-hugging vegetation of the alpine tundra survives: mosses, lichens, wildflowers and grasses

A Bit of History

Archaeological evidence indicates nomads traversed this region 10,000

Practical Information

GETTING THERE

BY AIR – Canadian, US and international air carriers serve Calgary International Airport *(17km/11mi from downtown Calgary)*, and Edmonton International Airport *(30km/19mi from downtown Edmonton)*. Banff is 128km/79mi west of Calgary via the Trans-Canada Highway and Jasper is 366km/227mi west of Edmonton via Hwy. 16. **Air Jasper** offers charter service out of Jasper Hinton Airport *(☎780-865-3616. www. airjasper.com)*.

Banff Airporter shuttle buses operate from Calgary International Airport to Canmore and Banff with connections to Lake Louise. ☎*403-762-3330, or 888-449-2901. www.banffairporter.com.* Scheduled van and **bus services** connect Banff and Lake Louise to the Calgary airport, with frequent departures daily, as do chartered shuttle and bus services. Buses also connect the Calgary airport with Jasper, while regular bus service by **Greyhound** and **Sun Dog Tour Company** connects Edmonton with Jasper. 🍁 *See By Bus below.*

CAR RENTAL – Major car-rental agencies serve the Calgary and Edmonton airports, as well as Banff and Jasper. 🍁 Since Banff and Jasper, as well as Field, BC (Yoho), are within national parks, you will need to pay entry fees at the gate: $9 per person per day, or $18 per day for a car with 2-7 passengers.

BY BUS – Greyhound provides **bus** service between Calgary and the Banff/Lake Louise area and between Edmonton and Jasper; it has Canada's most extensive inter-city bus service. *(☎800-661-8747. www.greyhound.ca)*. Sun Dog Tour Company provides bus connections among Calgary, Banff, Lake Louise and Jasper as well as sight-seeing tours. *(☎780-852-4056 or 888-786-3641. www.sundogtours.com)*

Red Arrow Motorcoach provides service from Calgary, Red Deer Edmonton, Fort McMurray and Edmonton to Banff and Lake Louise. ☎*403-531-0350 or 800-232-1958. www.redarrow.ca.* **Brewster Inc.** connects Calgary to all the Rocky Mountain resorts as well as to Canmore and Kananaskis Country; in addition, the company organizes sight-seeing

coach tours in the area. ☎*403-221-8255 (Calgary), 403-760-6934 (Banff) or 800-760-6934. www.brewster.ca.*

BY TRAIN – **VIA Rail** runs the **Skeena** between Jasper and Prince Rupert, with an overnight stop in Prince George, year-round. The **Canadian,** running between Toronto and Vancouver, passes through Edmonton and Jasper *(☎604-669-3050 or 800-561-8630; www.viarail.ca)*. The **Snow Train** *(www. snowtraintojasper.com)* takes skiers to Jasper from Edmonton, Vancouver or Toronto, and points along the way. There is no passenger rail service to Banff. *(☎888-8422-7245. www.viarail. ca).* **Rocky Mountaineer Vacations** offers spectacular train rides on three routes that take in Vancouver and Whistler, BC; Banff; Jasper; and Calgary *(☎877-460-3200 or international toll-free 1-604-606-7245; www.rocky-mountaineer.com)*.

GENERAL INFORMATION

WHEN TO GO

The Rocky Mountain parks are open year-round. The **summer season** is June to mid-September, peak season being July and August, when daylight extends to 10pm. Visitors should be prepared for cold weather even in summer, since snowfall in August and September is not unusual. Throughout the **winter,** most park roads remain open. Parkways are regularly cleared, but snow tires are strongly recommended from November to April.

VISITOR INFORMATION

Each national park has a visitor centre, operated by Parks Canada, where schedules, pamphlets, maps and permits are available. Go to the Parks Canada website, www.pc.gc.ca, and select the specific website you wish to access. A park pass *($9 per person per day, valid until 4pm the next day)* is interchangeable among national parks (multiday passes are available) and can be obtained from park visitor centres, entrance gates or campground kiosks.

ACCOMMODATIONS

The Canadian Rockies are known for their **back-country lodges,** often accessible only on foot, skis or by helicopter. These wilderness hostelries range from rustic cabins to comfortable and even luxurious alpine chalets with fine food. Primitive cabins that rent for $25-$32 per night per person can be reserved in both national and provincial parks through The Alpine Club of Canada *(Indian Flats Rd., Canmore; ☎403-678-3200; www.alpineclubofcanada.ca).* Numerous **campgrounds** are located throughout the national parks. At least one campground in each park offers powered sites and showers. Banff, Jasper and Kootenay National parks offer **campsite reservations,** starting at various dates after March 1 (☎877-737-3783, www.pccamping.ca). Reservations are highly advisable; even though there are 10,000 campsites in Jasper valley, on many summer nights every single one is occupied. Unreserved sites are offered on a first-come, first-served basis. **Hotels,** resorts, motels, B&Bs, chalets and condominiums abound in the area. For lodging information, contact the Banff/Lake Louise Tourism Bureau *(☎403-762-8421; www.banff-lakelouise.com)* or the Jasper Chamber of Commerce *(☎780-852-3858, www.jaspercanadianrockies.com).*

RECREATION

All four national parks, as well as many provincial parks, offer **hiking, backpacking, bicycling, horseback riding, canoeing, fishing, swimming** (except Yoho) and **winter sports.** Banff and Jasper have facilities for **tennis** and **golf;** Banff has **bowling;** boat tours and canoe rentals are also available. For details contact Parks Canada (*see above).* Fairmont Banff Springs, Fairmont Lake Louise and Fairmont Jasper Lodge hotels offer **guided hikes/snowshoe/ ski excursions.** Skilled naturalist guides explain the history, ecology, and legends of the mountains: available for everyone, not just hotel guests. Reservations can be made with the hotel concierge: Fairmont Banff Springs ☎403-762-2211; Fairmont Chateau Lake Louise ☎403-522-3511; Jasper Park Lodge ☎780-852-3301. The Fairmont Banff Springs and the Jasper Park Lodge have renowned **golf courses,** while Kananaskis Country

Golf Course has two 18-hole courses (☎403-591-7272). Other popular golf courses are located at Canmore and Radium Hot Springs, BC.

Outfitters specializing in **wilderness excursions** provide equipment, guides and transportation. Flightseeing is not permitted within the national parks. Canmore-based Alpine Helicopters Ltd. offers sightseeing and heli-hiking (☎403-678-4802. www.alpinehelicopter.com). For more information, contact the Banff/Lake Louise Tourism Bureau (☎403-762-8421. www.banfflakelouise.com), the Jasper Chamber of Commerce (☎780-852-3858. www.jaspercanadianrockies.com) or Tourism Canmore (www.tourismcanmore.com).

The Canadian Rockies offer **winter sports** from mid-November to mid-May including **downhill skiing, snowboarding, ice-skating, dogsledding** and **cross-country skiing.** Three areas are near Banff: **Lake Louise (**☎403-522-3555 or 800-258-7669. www.skilouise.com); **Sunshine Village (**☎403-277-7669 or 877-542-2633.www.sunshine-village.com); **Ski Banff @ Norquay** (☎403-762-4421. www.banffnorquay.com). **Marmot Basin** is near Jasper (☎780-852-3816 or 866-952-3816 www.skimarmot.com). Amenities include restaurants, ski rentals, ski schools and day-care services. An adult lift ticket at these resorts runs $48-$80 a day, but there are many packages. The multi-day Tri-Area pass at Banff includes free transport between your hotel and the slopes. Buses shuttle skiers from lodgings to the slopes for $6–$10 one-way. For **Nordic skiers,** there are 80km/50mi of trails around Banff, while the parks, notably Kananaskis, have vast networks. **Canmore Nordic Centre Provincial Park** (☎403-678-2400, www.canmoreadventures.ca) on the site of the 1988 Olympic Nordic events, has 70km/43mi of trails for the intermediate and advanced cross-country skier. Facilities include ski rentals, lessons and a day lodge. The centre was recently extensively renovated.

USEFUL NUMBERS

Area Codes: Banff 403, Jasper 780, Yoho and Kootenay 250.
RCMP (Police): ☎403-762-2226

Park Wardens: Banff ☎ 403-762-4506; Jasper ☎780-852-615
Emergency (Banff, Jasper, Kootenay and Yoho): **911**
Park Weather Forecasts: ☎1-900-565-5555 (charged per minute), 888-292-2222 (from cell or pay phones, credit card required) or www.weatheroffice.gc.ca.

Trail Conditions: Banff:☎403-522-1264; Jasper ☎780-852-6177or 877-423-7433. Look on Parks Canada website, www.pc.gc.ca.
Avalanche Hazard (winter): Look on Parks Canada website, www.pc.gc.ca, or consult www.avalanche.ca.

years ago. The First Nations peoples living here were overwhelmed, prior to European contact, by the **Stoney tribe,** who moved into the Rockies in the early 1700s. During the mid- to late 18C, the **fur trade** burgeoned in the Rockies, and by the mid-19C, mountaineers and explorers had arrived. By 1885 the **Canadian Pacific Railway** (CPR) line had crossed the Rockies and reached the West Coast. Recognizing the mountains' tourist potential, the CPR convinced the government to establish "preserves"—the origin of the parks. During the late 18C and early 19C, the railway company built fine mountain chalets and hotels, a number of which are still in operation. By the 1920s all four Rocky Mountain national parks had been established. In 1984 the combined four parks were designated a World Heritage Site.

1 Banff National Park★★★

Canada's first and most famous national park, Banff encompasses impressive peaks, scenic river valleys and the popular resort towns of Banff and Lake Louise. This preserve lies at the southeastern end of the chain of mountain parks. One of Canada's major resort areas, Banff draws an international crowd.

A Bit of History

In the 1880s construction of the transcontinental railroad and discovery of natural hot springs on Sulphur Mountain elevated Banff to national prominence. The mineral springs were first noted by Sir **James Hector** in 1858, the first European to cross Kicking Horse Pass,

which became the rail route through the Rockies. In 1883 Siding 29 (sidings are switch tracks from the main track) was constructed near the hot springs. While prospecting for minerals, three rail workers discovered the springs and attempted to stake a claim. But the interests of the railroad magnates prevailed. Canadian Pacific president **George Stephen** felt the siding needed a romantic name, so he called it Banff after his native Banffshire, Scotland. The 26sq km/10sq mi Banff Hot Springs Reserve was established in 1885 by the government around Cave and Basin Hot Springs. In 1887 bathhouses were installed and a rail station built. The federal reserve was expanded 673sq km/260sq mi and renamed Rocky Mountain Parks Reserve. In 1888 the CPR opened what was then the world's largest hotel, the **Banff Springs Hotel.** Built at the confluence of the Bow and Spray rivers, this renowned "chateau" remains the dominant landmark. Banff gradually became a social gathering place for wealthy travellers, who arrived by train. Not until 1915, after a bitter fight, were automobiles admitted to the park—a factor that made the area more accessible to the general public. The reserve was renamed Banff National Park in 1930.

Town of Banff and Environs★★

🛈 *Banff Town Hall, 110 Bear St. ☎403-762-1200. www.banff.ca., www.banfflake louise.com.*
Situated at the southeast end of the park system, this well-known resort town on the Bow River sits at an elevation of 1,380m/4,534ft amid breathtaking

mountains. Though bustling with visitors much of the year, the community maintains the charm of a small alpine town. Tourists and residents alike celebrate artistic creations during the **Banff Arts Festival** *(Jun–Aug)*. Operated by Parks Canada, the **Banff Information Centre** *(224 Banff Ave; open late-Jun–Aug daily 8am–8pm; rest of the year times vary; closed Dec 25; ☎403-762-1550; www.pc.gc.ca)* provides information on park activities.

Whyte Museum of the Canadian Rockies★ (A)

111 Bear St. Open year-round daily 10am–5pm. Closed Jan 1, Feb 14 & Dec 25. $6. ☎403-762-2291. www.whyte.org.
Opened in 1968, this contemporary building houses a heritage gallery that traces the history of mountaineering and tourism in the Canadian Rockies. On view are historical items and Stoney Indian artifacts and clothing. An art gallery features changing exhibits by regional and international artists. The museum also gives tours of seven historical local houses and sponsors regular lectures.

Banff Park Museum★ (B)

91 Banff Ave. Open mid-May–Sept daily 10am–6pm. Rest of the year 1pm–5pm. Closed Jan 1 & Dec 25-26. Tours in summer daily 3pm; rest of year weekends 2:30pm. $3.90. ☎403-762-1558. www.pc.gc.ca.
Constructed in the trestlelike "railway pagoda" style of the turn of the 19C, this historic museum maintains its 1903 appearance both inside and out. Now a National Historic Site, the museum features glass-cases displaying minerals and preserved animals of the Rocky Mountains. Among the collections is a series of prints by renowned wildlife artist **Robert Bateman.**

Cascade Gardens★ [C]

At the south end of Banff Ave., across Bow River Bridge. Open Jun–Sept daily.
These terraced gardens, with their rock-lined pool and cascades, provide an excellent **view★** of **Cascade Mountain,** the 2,999m/9,840ft peak that towers above the north end of Banff Avenue. The stone 1935 Gothic Revival building at the centre of the grounds houses the park administration offices.

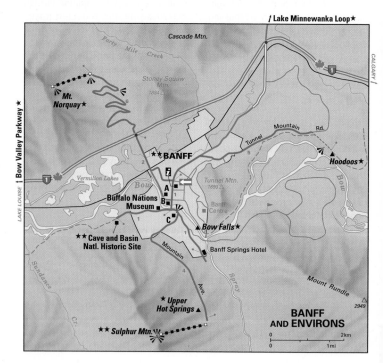

Buffalo Nations Luxton Museum★

Kids *On the south bank of the Bow River. 1 Birch Ave.* ○*Open mid-May–early Oct daily 11am–6pm. Rest of the year daily 1pm–5pm.* ☞*$8.* ♿ ☎*403-762-2388. www.buffalonationsmuseum.ca.*

A replica of a log fur-trading fort, this museum displays native artifacts and dress, quillwork, tools and life-size dioramas depicting aspects of Plains Indian life. The museum is owned by the Buffalo Nations Cultural Society.

Bow Falls★

At the foot of the Fairmont Banff Springs Hotel, the Bow River tumbles over a wide, low lip, just before its confluence with the Spray River.

Cave and Basin National Historic Site★★

○*Open mid-May–Sept daily 9am–6pm. Rest of the year Mon–Fri 11am–4pm, weekends 9:30am–5pm.* ○*Closed Jan 1, Dec 25-26.* ☞*Tours in summer 11am, 2pm & 4pm. Rest of the year weekends 11am.* ☞*$3.90.* ♿ ☎*403-762-1566. www. pc.gc.ca.*

Canada's national park system began at this site in 1885. The arched stone building, restored to its 1914 appearance, surrounds an open-air swimming pool *(not open for swimming)* of hot springs water (average temperatures 30–35°C/86–95°F). The complex includes the natural cave pool, fed by a hot spring, and a museum tracing the more than 100-year history of the Canadian parks system.

Sulphur Mountain★★

3.5km/2mi from downtown. ♿○*Access by gondola (8min ascent) year-round daily. Hours vary.* ☞*$26.* ☎*403-762-1566. www.banffgondola.com.*

The 2,285m/7,500ft summit allows a splendid 360-degree **panorama**★★★ of the Bow Valley, Banff and the turreted Banff Springs Hotel (east and north); the Spray Valley (southeast); Mt. Rundle and the more distant Fairholm Range and Lake Minnewanka (northeast); Mt. Norquay (north) and the Sundance Range (southwest). Bighorn sheep frequently graze along the trails here.

FLOATING DOWN THE RIVER

Summertime crowds in downtown Banff can be daunting, but a remarkably serene interlude begins at the base of Bow River Falls (near the Fairmont Banff Springs Hotel golf course). **Rocky Mountain Raft Tours** offers one-hour *(○mid-May–Sept;* ☞*$40)* and three-hour *(Jul–Aug; $80)* guided tours down the Bow River on oar-powered rafts *(☎403-762-3632; www.banffrafttours.com).* You can also rent a canoe and paddle yourself. A quiet two-hour trip leads up the valley along Echo Creek to the three Vermilion Lakes and back, amid hushed forests. You are likely to see elk, deer, bears and eagles.

Upper Hot Springs★

Kids *3.5km/2mi from downtown; follow Mountain Ave.* ○*Open mid- May–early Sept daily 9am–11pm. Rest of the year Sun–Thu 10am–10pm, Fri–Sat 10am–11pm.* ☞*$7.30.* ♿ ☎*403-762-1515 or 800-767-1611. www.pc.gc.ca.*

Discovered a year after the Cave and Basin hot springs, the mineral waters (average temperature 38°C/100°F) now feed a large public pool perched on the mountainside and offering a good view of Bow Valley.

Hoodoos★

These naturally sculpted pillars of cemented rock and gravel can be viewed from a scenic nature trail above Bow River *(1km/.6mi; trailhead off Tunnel Mountain Rd.).*

Lake Minnewanka Loop★

Begins 4km/2.4mi from downtown.
Along this 16km/10mi drive, three lakes serve as natural water-sports playgrounds: Johnson, Two Jack and Minnewanka, a dammed reservoir that is Banff Park's largest water body. Tour boats offer cruises down this lake to Devil's Gap *(depart mid-May–early Oct daily 10am, 12pm, 2pm, 4pm & 6pm;* ☞*$40; Lake Minnewanka Tours* ♿☎*403-762-3473; www.minnewankaboattours. com. Also charter fishing and boat rentals. Times and prices vary).* The road passes **Bankhead,** an abandoned early 20C

coal-mining operation. An interpretive trail explains the site.

Mount Norquay★

8km/5mi northwest of downtown. Access by chairlift Dec–mid-Apr daily 9am–4pm (Fri 10pm). ⊗ $49 (Fri 5pm–10pm $24). ☎403-762-4421. www.banff norquay.com.

A well-graded switchback road climbs Stoney Squaw Mountain toward Mount Norquay's chairlift, providing increasingly better **views** south and east over Bow Valley and of the townsite of Banff, backdropped by **Mount Rundle,** which is shaped like a tilted writing desk.

Bow Valley Parkway to Lake Louise★

48km/30mi. Begins 5.5km/3.5mi west of town.

An alternative to the faster-paced Trans-Canada Highway, this scenic parkway was the original 1920s road connecting Banff and Lake Louise. Sightings of elk, deer, moose and coyote are not uncommon along the road. Curving through evergreen forests along the north bank of the Bow River, the route offers **views**★ of the Sawback Range to the northeast—in particular, crenellated Castle Mountain—and of the Great Divide peaks to the southwest. Frequent lookouts feature interpretation of regional geology, flora and fauna. At **Johnston Canyon**★★ *(17km/11mi)* a paved, often

cantilevered pathway over the narrow limestone canyon leads to the **lower falls**★★ *(about 1km/.6mi)* and the **upper falls**★★ *(about 1.6km/1mi)*. The Inkpots, a collection of cold springs, are located beyond the upper falls *(6km/4mi)*.

▶ *At Castle Junction, Hwy. 93 leads west from Bow Valley Parkway to Kootenay National Park.*

Lake Louise and Area★★★

Smaller and less congested than Banff, this townsite and its environs in the park's west-central section encompass massive, glaciated peaks and pristine lakes, most notably Lake Louise. Called "lake of little fishes" by the Stoney tribe, Lake Louise was first viewed by a nonnative in 1882. Taken there by a Stoney guide, **Tom Wilson,** a packer for railway survey crews, named the water body Emerald Lake because of its brilliant blue-green colour. Two years later, the lake was renamed for Queen Victoria's daughter, **Princess Louise Carolina Alberta,** wife of a governor-general. By 1890 a small guest chalet had been built on the shore. By the early 1900s a road had been built to the lake, a large chalet had been constructed and guests were flocking there. In 1925 the CPR completed the present **Château Lake Louise,** which rises elegantly by the lake.

Bow River Valley, Banff National Park

©Travel Alberta

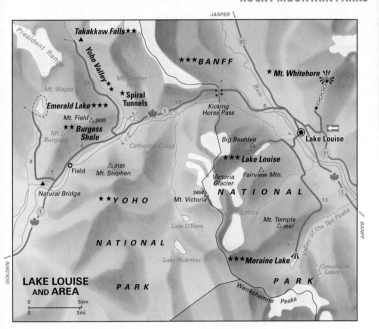

Lake Louise Village

Located just off the Trans-Canada Highway, next to Samson Mall. Visitor centre ⏱open year round late Jun–Labour Day daily 9am–8pm; rest of the year hours vary; ⏱closed Dec 25; ☎403-522-3833; www.pc.gc.ca..

A small resort crossroads with several shops, hotels and visitor facilities, the village is located just off the Trans-Canada Highway. A park **visitor centre** *(hours above)* features excellent **displays** on the natural history of the area, including the Burgess Shale *(🍂see below)*, and provides information about drives, hikes and natural attractions.

Lake Louise★★★

4km/2.5mi west of village.

Set in a hanging valley backdropped by the majestic mountains of the Continental Divide, this beautiful glacier-fed lake with the stately chateau near its shore remains one of the most visited and photographed sites in the Canadian Rockies. Visible at the far end, the **Victoria Glacier** once stretched to the site of the chateau. The 2km/1.2mi-long lake (with a width of .5km/.3mi and a maximum depth of 75m/246ft,) was created when this glacier retreated, leaving enough morainal debris to serve as a dam. The

chateau is actually built on the moraine. Fed by glacial meltwater draining off the surrounding peaks, the lake (maximum temperature 4°C/40°F) changes colour with light conditions and as the summer progresses. Known as glacial flour, fine powdery silt suspended in the water refracts the green rays of the spectrum and emits hues ranging from bluish-green to emerald.

The far end of the lake is dominated by **Mount Victoria** (3,464m/11,362ft). To the left of Victoria stands the rocky face of **Fairview Mountain** (2,744m/9,000ft), and to the right rises the dis-

LAGGAN'S MOUNTAIN BAKERY

Samson Mall, Lake Louise. ☎403-552-2017. Tucked away in Lake Louise's only shopping centre, this popular bakery provides an inexpensive option for a quick meal. Glass-fronted cabinets display breakfast croissants, pastries, muffins and cakes. Sandwiches can be ordered from the blackboard menu. Coffee is self-serve. If all the tables are full, enjoy your meal outside beside the Pipestone River, behind the adjacent alleyway.

tinctive rounded shape of **Big Beehive.** A 2km/1.2mi trail leads along the lake's north shore. Additional trails ascend into the backcountry. Two popular **day hikes** lead to teahouses: one at Lake Agnes *(3.5km/2.2mi from the lake)* and another at the Plain of Six Glaciers *(5.5km/3.3mi from the lake)*. Details on hikes are available at the chateau and at park visitor centres. Occasionally, hikers can watch or hear avalanches roar from the glaciers.

Moraine Lake★★★
13km/8mi from village.
Smaller and less visited than Lake Louise, Moraine Lake occupies a splendid **site** below the sheer walls of the Wenkchemna peaks.
Moraine Lake Road climbs above the Bow Valley, offering an impressive **view**★★, first of one of the park's highest peaks, ice-capped **Mount Temple** (3,547m/11,644ft) and then of the glaciated **Wenkchemna** or **Ten Peaks.** A short walk leads up the rock pile damming the north end of the lake, providing the best **view**★ of the surroundings. The pile is believed to be the result of a rock slide from the adjacent pinnacle of rock called the Tower of Babel. Other trails lead to the end of the lake and to nearby backcountry lakes and valleys.

Mount Whitehorn★
Access by gondola (15min ascent) May–Jun daily 9am–4pm; Jul–Aug daily 9am–5pm; Sept daily 9am–4:30pm (last ride 30 min before closing). ☎$24. ☞Guided interpretive walk $5. ✗☎403-522-3555. www.skilouise.com. Restaurant at base.*
From the top of the Friendly Giant gondola, a **panorama**★★ of Bow Valley spreads out, with the Wenkchemna peaks and Mount Temple filling the horizon. To the west Lake Louise can be seen cupped below the Victoria Glacier.

② Yoho National Park★★

Smallest and most compact of Canada's Rocky Mountain parks, Yoho (a Cree expression meaning "awe") is a place of raging rivers and waterfalls, deep wilderness valleys, and the site of the Burgess Shale, one of the most important fossil beds ever discovered. The Trans-Canada Highway cuts diagonally through the park, passing over **Kicking Horse Pass** (1,625m/5,330ft), a point on the Continental Divide, as well the boundary between Alberta and British Columbia and between Banff and Yoho national parks.

A Bit of History

The name of the pass derives from an incident here involving geologist **James Hector** of the Palliser Expedition (1857-60). He was accidentally kicked by his horse, fell unconscious and, mistaken for dead, was almost buried by his men. Situated in the centre of Yoho in the valley of the roaring Kicking Horse River, the small town of **Field** serves as the park hub. The **visitor centre** features displays on the Burgess Shale and other park attractions (♿☀open late Jun–Labour Day daily 9am–7pm; rest of the year daily 9am–4pm; ✪closed Dec 25; ☎$9 park use-fee; ☎250-343-6783; www.pc.gc.ca.) ⚠Collection of fossils anywhere in Yoho is strictly prohibited.

Sights

Spiral Tunnels★
When the Canadian Pacific Railway first crossed Kicking Horse Pass, trains descended into the Columbia Valley at a dangerous 4.5 percent grade. In the shape of an elongated figure eight, these two tunnels allowed trains to make the treacherously steep, 4.5 percent descend down "the big hill" leading into the valley at a more moderate 2.2 percent grade; long trains may actually have their locomotives passing beneath the end of the train overhead in the tunnel. The tunnels were opened in 1909. An overlook along the Trans-Canada Highway, 3.2km/2mi west of Kicking Horse Pass, affords the best **view** of the tunnels.

Yoho Valley★★
Access road of 13km/8mi with switchbacks; no trailers allowed.

Situated between Mt. Field and Mt. Ogden, lovely Yoho Valley is accessed by a climbing road that includes a look-out above the confluence of Yoho and Kicking Horse rivers. Near the road's end Yoho Peak and Glacier can be seen straight ahead, with Takakkaw Falls to the right.

Takakkaw Falls★★

One of the highest waterfalls on the continent—and second highest in BC—this torrent of meltwalter from the Daly Glacier cascades in two stages for a combined total of 254m/833ft to join the Yoho River. A short paved walk leads to the base of the falls, which are visible from the road.

Burgess Shale★★★

Visit by guided hike only, Jul–Sept Thu–Sun 8am, return 6:30pm. Hikes depart from Yoho Trading Post in Field. $100/person. Reservations required. Moderate to strenuous hikes on steep trails: 6km/3.5mi round-trip to Mt. Stephen fossil beds; 20km/12mi round-trip to Burgess Shale. Contact Burgess Shale Geoscience Foundation between Mon–Fri 9am–3pm. ☎800-343-3006. www.burgess-shale.bc.ca. Instead of hiking, visitors may choose instead to view Burgess Shale exhibits at Field or Lake Louise visitor centre.

The Burgess Shale, located on **Mount Field** (2,635m/8,6432ft) and considered the richest Cambrian site in the world, contains evidence of multicellular life in the oceans 515 million years ago. Because of its excellent fossil preservation, the Burgess Shale enjoys world renown among professional paleontologists and amateur enthusiasts; on the World Heritage List, it is considered the richest Cambrian site in the world.

In 1886, an employee of the Canadian Pacific Railway discovered rich trilobite beds on **Mount Stephen** (3,185m/10,447ft). In 1909 American palaeontologist **Charles Walcott** found unique fossils of soft-bodied animals on loose pieces of shale on Mount Field. He later discovered a rich fossil-bearing shale layer higher up the slope, and spent five summers quarrying this layer. The formation has since led to historic discoveries in palaeontology and evo-

lutionary biology. Paleogeologists have used what they learned here to alter their understanding of how evolution works, creating a modern theory of random mutation and extinction and rapid change, rather than the orderly survival of the fittest previously envisioned.

The moderately challenging trail to the Burgess Shale offers excellent **views**★★ of Emerald Lake and the President Range in particular. At the small hillside quarry, visitors can sometimes observe researchers excavating shale by hand and see recent fossil finds.

Wapta Falls★

22km/13mi west of Field.

Although it is only 30m/98ft high, this torrent of water carries the entire flow of the Kicking Horse River over a cascade. The shelf from which the blue-green water plunges is about 800m/500ft wide, leading some people to compare the overall impression with Niagara Falls.

Emerald Lake★★★

Accessible via 8km/5mi road off Trans-Can Hwy. ✕Food and lodging available.

Aptly named by Tom Wilson in 1882, this beautiful lake lies at the foot of the President Range. Glacial runoff from these mountains gives the water its striking green colour.

Shortly after leaving the highway, the road to the lake offers views, from a parking area, of a **natural bridge** of limestone cut by the turbulent Kicking Horse River. The **site** is lovely, with Mt. Stephen rising above the river to the northeast and the mountains of the Van Horne Range visible downstream. The road ends at the lake. Situated at the southeastern end of the lake, with Mt. Burgess rising behind it, Emerald Lake Lodge traces its beginnings to a 1902 CPR chalet. Mt. Wapta lies to the northeast and the peaks of the President Range to the west. A pleasant **trail** (5km/3mi) circles the lake. After the turnoff to Emerald Lake, the Trans-Canada Highway follows the scenic **lower gorge** of the Kicking Horse River to its junction with the Columbia River and the town of Golden.

3 Icefields Parkway★★★

233km/145mi (Trans-Canada Hwy. junction to Jasper).

Designed expressly to dramatize the incredible landscape, this unequalled parkway (Highway 93) runs below the highest mountains in the Canadian Rockies. Following the valleys of five rivers, the road angles northwesterly along the eastern flank of the Continental Divide, connecting Banff and Jasper parks. Glaciers, lakes and waterfalls are abundant along the route, as are interpretive lookouts that explain the natural and human history of the area. Driving the route also exposes visitors to the reality of climate change, as glaciers throughout the parkway's length are in rapid retreat.

The parkway was begun during the Great Depression as a public works project and first opened in 1940. Though it traverses some of the most spectacular mountain scenery in North America, its relatively gentle grades make it popular with bicycle riders. *Drivers must exercise caution.*

Officially, the parkway encompasses the entire distance from Banff to Jasper, a total of 288km/197mi. But it's the 232km/144mi stretch from Lake Louise north that is the most scenic and most famous. The only services available on this stretch are at Saskatchewan Crossing and the Columbia Icefield/Athabasca Glacier.

From its southern terminus, the parkway quickly climbs, providing fine views of the Waputik Range.

Sights

Hector Lake★
16km/10mi.
Named for James Hector, the lake is set below the Waputik Range (south), Mt. Hector (east) and Bow Peak (north). It's the second-largest lake in Banff National Park.

Crowfoot Glacier★★
33km/20mi.
After rounding Bow Peak, the parkway reaches a viewpoint from which this glacier spreads across the lower rock plateaus of Crowfoot Mountain. The glacier's name reflects its original shape with three terminal lobes. Glacial regression has eliminated the lobes.

Bow Lake★★
37km/23mi.
Directly by the road, this lovely lake is best seen from the lookout leading to historic, red-roofed Num-ti-Jah Lodge (*see Address Book*), visible on the north shore of the lake. The Bow Glacier hangs above the lake between Portal and St. Nicholas peaks.
Passing through a green meadowland of birch and willow, the parkway reaches Bow Summit (2,069m/6,786ft), the highest pass on the route.

Peyto Lake★★★
40km/25mi to spur road. P*Park in the lower lot;* *a short trail leads to a viewpoint.*
The striking turquoise waters of this lake are fed by Peyto Glacier. Both lake and glacier are named for late 19C guide Bill Peyto. **Mistaya Mountain** rises precipi-

---

Full Retreat

The Icefields Parkway could not have been built when the Athabasca Glacier was first observed in the late 19C—it covered the site of today's road. Since then, like virtually all glaciers worldwide, the glacier has been receding, a fact scientists attribute to climate change. The Athabasca Glacier has retreated about 1,500m/4,921ft since the turn-of-the-20C; visitors who walk to the toe of the glacier pass numerous signs marking the glacier's extent over the past century. The Illecillewaet Glacier, in Canada's Glacier National Park, has retreated 2km/1.3mi since 1887. And in the US Glacier National Park, current rates of glacial recession mean the park's entire glacial remnant—now just 27 percent of its 1850 extent—will disappear by 2030.

tously from the opposite side of the lake, with Peyto Peak on its left. The Mistaya River Valley stretches north from beyond the lake.

The road descends to the valley and passes a series of lakes. At **Lower Waterfowl Lake** lookout *(56km/35mi)*, there is a fine **view**★ of the Great Divide peaks, especially towering Howse Peak (3,290m/10,791ft) and pyramidal Mt. Chephren (3,307m/10,847ft).

Mistaya Canyon★

72km/45mi to spur road for parking; follow trail into valley for 400m/.3mi.

This narrow gorge, cut by the Mistaya River, has sculpted limestone walls. Continuing northward, the parkway passes Mt. Murchison (3,337m/10,945ft), which rises to the east, and the steep cliffs of Mt. Wilson (3,261m/10,696ft), looming above the road. Both are part of the **Castle Mountain Syncline,** a downfold stratum that runs from Castle Mountain, outside Banff, to Mt. Kerkeslin, near Jasper. After the road descends into the valley of the North Saskatchewan River, a lookout *(76km/47mi; trail through trees)* affords a **view** of the Howse River Valley. David Thompson travelled this corridor in 1807 on his way to set up the first trading post west of the mountains, near present-day Invermere.

Very quickly the parkway reaches its junction with Highway 11—the David Thompson Highway *(food, services).*

The parkway then runs below the massive cliffs of Mt. Wilson (to the east), with views of Survey Peak and Mt. Erasmus to the west and then the layer-cake facade of **Mt. Amery.**

At 105km/65mi the road hugs the base of Cirrus Mountain, whose sheer cliffs are known as the **Weeping Wall** because streams cascade down them. Soon thereafter the parkway rounds "the big bend" and climbs quickly above the valley to a lookout that allows a spectacular **view**★★ of the North Saskatchewan Valley. A second, almost adjacent lookout directly faces the filmy spray of **Bridal Veil Falls.**

Parker Ridge★★

118km/73mi.

This ridgetop affords a magnificent **view**★★★ of glaciated backcountry, particularly the **Saskatchewan Glacier,** one of the major outlet glaciers of the Columbia Icefield. A switchback trail *(2.4km/1.5mi)* ascends through dwarf, subalpine forest and then through treeless tundra, carpeted in summer with dwarf alpine flowers.

At 122km/76mi the parkway crosses Sunwapta Pass (2,035m/6,675ft) to enter Jasper National Park, with views ahead of Mt. Athabasca and other peaks surrounding the Columbia Icefield.

©Travel Alberta

Athabasca Glacier

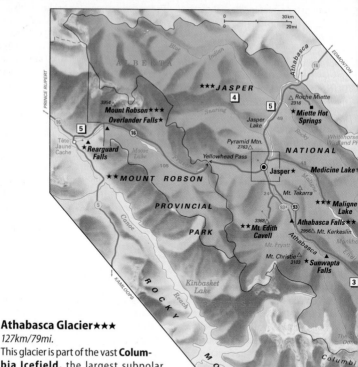

Athabasca Glacier★★★

127km/79mi.

This glacier is part of the vast **Columbia Icefield,** the largest subpolar icefield on the continent. The 325sq km/126sq mi Columbia lies along the Alberta-British Columbia boundary. The Athabasca and four other major outlet glaciers (Saskatchewan, Dome, Stutfield and Columbia), as well as smaller ones, flow off the icefield's eastern edge. Meltwater from these glaciers eventually feeds into three oceans: the Atlantic, Pacific and Arctic.

Situated along the high, remote tops of the Rockies at an altitude of more than 3,000m/10,000ft, the icefield was apparently unknown until 1898, when a mountaineering expedition from Britain's Royal Geographical Society discovered and named it.

From the parking lot of the Columbia Icefield Centre, a **view**★★★ encompasses the Athabasca, Kitchener and Dome glaciers.

Columbia Icefield Centre

⏱*Open mid-Apr–mid-Oct daily.* ☎*403-762-6700, or 877-423-7433.www.columbia icefield.com.*

This large, stone chalet-style building overlooking the Athabasca Glacier functions as an information centre and comfort station for travellers on the parkway. There are restrooms, eating places and a souvenir shop as well as a small museum featuring displays—including a large model of the glacier—and an audiovisual presentation on glaciology. A dining room is located on the second floor, and the third floor holds hotel rooms for overnight guests (⏱*see Address Book*). The centre also serves as the southern **visitor centre** (⏱*open mid-Jun–Aug daily 9am–6pm; May–early Jun & Sept–mid-Oct daily 9am–5pm;* ☎*780-852-6288; www.pc.gc.ca*) for Jasper National Park.

Across the parkway is Sunwapta Lake, fed by the Athabasca Glacier. From the parking area, a short trail ascends to the toe of the glacier. In recent decades the glacier has retreated dramatically. The progress of its recession is marked on signposts along the parking lot's road and the trail.

Ice Explorer Tours on the Glacier★★

Expect long lines in Jul & Aug, especially 10:30am–3pm). Tours (90min) depart from Icefield Centre daily Apr–Oct. Jun–Aug 9am–6pm.

Rest of the season times vary. $38. Brewster Tours ☎403-762-6700, or 877-423-7433; www.columbiaicefield.com. These specially designed ultra-terrain vehicles travel a short distance onto the upper end of the Athabasca Glacier and allow passengers to get off to briefly experience the glacial surface.

Sunwapta Falls★

176km/109mi; 400m/.3mi spur road to parking.

The Sunwapta River circles a small island, plunges over a cliff, makes a sharp turn around an ancient glacial moraine and enters a deep limestone canyon.

Soon after the falls, the parkway enters the valley of the mighty **Athabasca River** and follows it to Jasper. This impressive valley is dominated on the west by the distinctive off-centre pyramidal shape of **Mount Christie** (3,103m/10,180ft) and the three pinnacles of the Mt. Fryatt massif (3,361m/11,024ft). To the northwest the distance snow-clad summit of Mt. Edith Cavell slowly assumes prominence, while **Mount Kerkeslin** (2,956m/9,696ft), the final peak of the Castle Mountain Syncline, towers over the parkway to the east.

Athabasca Falls★★
199km/123mi; turn left on Hwy. 93A for 400m/.3mi.

The silt-laden waters of the Athabasca River roar over a lip of quartzite and down a canyon smoothed by the force of the rushing waters. Backdropping the cataract, Mt. Kerkeslin, slightly reddish from quartzite, has the same layering as the rock by the falls.

As the parkway approaches Jasper townsite, the Whistlers can be seen to the west. Straight ahead rises Pyramid Mountain, and to the east, the pinnacled peak of **Mount Tekarra.** At dusk elk are frequently spotted grazing alongside the parkway near the Wapiti Campground.

4 Jasper National Park★★★

The largest and northernmost of the four Rocky Mountain parks, Jasper National Park covers 10,878sq km/4,200sq mi, most of which is remote wilderness. In addition to spectacular terrain, Jasper also offers frequent opportunities to view a variety of wildlife.

A Bit of History

In the early 19C area indigenous peoples saw increased European presence as furtraders used the Athabasca River and Pass as a route through the Rockies. In 1801 Jasper Hawes, a clerk for the North West Company, established a supply depot on Brule Lake, 35km/22mi north of the present townsite. The depot became known as Jasper House and ultimately gave the current townsite its name. In the 1860s the Overlanders, a party of 125 gold seekers, passed through the region on their way to the goldfields of the Cariboo Mountains. Except for the mountaineers and trappers, the area had few inhabitants until the early 20C.

In 1907 Jasper Forest Park, as it was then called, was created in anticipation of completion of the Grand Trunk Pacific

Railway across the Yellowhead Pass. The townsite grew from a railroad construction camp set up in 1911.

Town of Jasper and Environs★

Situated at the junction of the Yellowhead Highway and the Icefields Parkway, the pleasant town of Jasper is the focal point of activity for the park. It contains a park **visitor centre** *(500 Connaught Dr. ◷ open daily mid-Jun–Labour Day daily 8:30am–7pm; rest of the year daily 9am, closing hours vary. ◷ Closed Jan 1, Dec 25; ♿☎780-852-6176; www.pc.gc.ca).* The town sits in the valley of the Athabasca River near its confluence with the Miette River. Small and very beautiful lakes—**Pyramid, Patricia, Annette, Edith** and **Beauvert,** site of the well-known Jasper Park Lodge—surround the townsite. The peaks of nearby mountains are visible on the horizon, most notably Mt. Edith Cavell to the south and rugged **Pyramid Mountain** (2,763m/9,063ft) to the north.

The Whistlers★★
Access by tramway (7min ascent) ◷ mid-May–mid-Jun daily 9:30am–6:30pm. Late Jun–mid-Aug daily 9am–8pm. Mid-Apr–early May & late Aug–mid-Oct daily 10am–5pm. ☎$25. ✕(at the top) ☎780-852-3093, or 866-850-8726.www.jasper tramway.com.

The tramway ascends more than 900m/3,000ft to the terminal perched on the ridge of these 2,470m/8,102ft peaks named for the sound made by resident marmots. The **panorama**★★★ from this elevation includes the townsite, the lake-dotted Athabasca Valley and the Colin Range to the northeast, and Mt. Yellowhead and the Victoria Cross Ranges to the northwest. If visibility permits, the great white pyramid of Mt. Robson can be spotted beyond them.

A trail climbs an additional 180m/600ft to the treeless ridgetop, offering a **view** to the south of Mts. Edith Cavell and Kerkeslin.

Mount Edith Cavell★★

24km/15mi from townsite. Access via Icefields Pkwy. to junction with 93A, then Mt. Edith Cavell Rd.

This massif (3,368m/11,047ft) was named for an English nurse executed by the Germans in World War I for assisting Allied prisoners of war.

The narrow, twisting access road climbs steeply into the high country, paralleling the dramatic Astoria River Valley. A short walk to **Cavell Lake** from the parking area for the Tonquin Valley Trail *(26km/17mi)* leads to a **view** of the mountain. The lake's bright-green waters feed from the fast-receding **Angel Glacier,** which is located on the mountain. At the end of the road *(2km/1.2mi drive)*, the trailhead is reached for the Path of the Glacier Trail, which follows the toe of this ice river.

Maligne Valley★★★

96km/60mi round-trip by Hwy. 16 and Maligne Lake Rd.

This valley cradles a magnificent lake and canyon, both named Maligne [Ma-LEEN], which can mean "injurious" or "mean-spirited" in French. Despite its name, the valley is among the most beautiful in the Rockies.

Maligne Canyon★★

7km/4mi from Hwy. 16 junction.

The most spectacular of the Rocky Mountain gorges, this great slit carved in limestone reaches depths of 50m/164ft, while spanning widths of less than 3m/10ft in some places. A paved trail follows the top of the canyon, descending with the drop of the Maligne River. Bridges crossing the canyon serve as viewpoints.

Medicine Lake★

22km/14mi.

The Colin Range to the north and the Maligne Range to the south hem in this lovely lake. From its highest levels during the snowmelt of early summer, the lake gradually shrinks as the season progresses, sometimes becoming only mud flats. Intriguingly the lake has no surface outlet, draining instead through sink holes in the limestone bedrock and resurfacing in the waters of the Maligne River. The road follows the edge of the lake for 8km/5mi with several advantageous viewpoints.

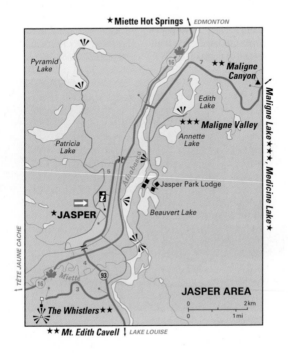

Maligne Lake★★★

For boat rentals, hiking and fishing trips or white-water rafting, contact Maligne Tours in Jasper. ☎780-852-3370 or 866-625-4463. www.malignelake.com.

At 23km/14mi long, Maligne is the largest natural lake in the Rockies and one of the most spectacular.

In 1875 surveyor Henry MacLeod was the first European to see the lake; it was initially explored in detail in 1908 by an expedition led by Mary Schaffer, a middle-aged widow from Philadelphia.

The road ends at the northern shore of this glacial lake. As seen from the road, the twin peaks of **Mounts Unwin** (3,300m/10,824ft) and **Charlton** (3,260m/10,693ft) on the southwest side are most prominent. However these peaks are best seen from a boat.

Boat Trip★★★

Departs from chalet at Maligne Lake early Jun until fall daily 10am–4pm hourly (5pm late-Jun–early Sept). Round-trip 1hr 30min. Commentary. ⊕$45. Maligne Tours. ☎780-852-3370 or 866-625-4463. www.malignelake.com.

As the boat proceeds down the lake, the water colour changes from green to deep turquoise because of the presence of glacial silt. After Samson Narrows, passengers can disembark near tiny **Spirit Island** to enjoy the **view**★★★ of the half-dozen glaciated peaks framing the south end of the lake.

⑤The Yellowhead Highway★★

This major highway (Hwy. 16) runs east-west through Jasper and Mt. Robson parks to Prince Rupert, BC. It was named for Pierre Bostonais, a fair-haired trapper in the 1820s known to the Iroquois as Tête Jaune ("yellow head"). The small town in BC is named for him.

From Jasper to Miette Hot Springs★★

49km/31mi

Heading east from Jasper, the highway enters the Athabasca Valley. The craggy pinnacles of the Colin Range are soon silhouetted in the east. For the remaining 40km/25mi, there are **views**★★★ of the braided course of the river and surrounding peaks. The road passes between **Talbot Lake** (east) and **Jasper Lake,** backed by the **De Smet Range.** At Disaster Point **animal lick,** pools on the road attract mountain sheep; cars have hit the animals, hence the name. From here on, the drive holds fine views of **Roche Miette** (2,316m/7,599ft).

Miette Hot Springs★

42km/26mi to junction with Miette Hot Springs Rd. ◷Open mid-Jun–Aug 8:30am–10:30pm. Mid-May–early Jun & Sept–early Oct 10:30am–9pm. ⊕$6.05. ✕&🅿☎780-866-3939 or 800-767-1611.

Spirit Island, Maligne Lake

©Travel Alberta

A road winds 18km/11mi through a green gorge. These natural minerals springs are the hottest in the Canadian Rockies (maximum temperature 54°C/129°F). A hot pool, warm pool and cold plunge pool are on-site. The natural **setting**★★ makes this the most spectacular location of the parks' bathhouses.

The highway continues 7km/4mi to the east gate of Jasper National Park.

From Jasper to Rearguard Falls★

100km/62mi

West of Jasper, Highway 16 follows the valley of the Miette River. At **Yellowhead Pass**—the lowest pass on the Continental Divide, and the boundary between British Columbia and Alberta—the road leaves Jasper National Park (24km/15mi) and enters Mt. Robson Provincial Park.

Mount Robson Provincial Park★★

East boundary at 24km/15mi.
🕐*Open year-round.* ☎*250-566-9174.*
This 224,866ha/555,650-acre park is named for its greatest attraction: 3,954m/12,972ft **Mount Robson**★★★, the highest peak in the Canadian Rockies. After entering the park, the road picks up the Fraser River, skirting Yellowhead Lake and larger Moose Lake. At **Overlander Falls**★ *(88km/55mi; accessible by trail)*, the blue-green river drops off a ledge and then narrows as it enters a canyon. Just beyond the falls, the park visitor centre has natural history exhibits (♿🕐*open mid-May–early Oct daily 9am–5pm; www.env.gov.bc.ca).*

Rearguard Falls★

🚶*3.2km/2mi walk.*
Part of a small provincial park by the same name, the low falls on the Fraser River are noted for chinook salmon leaping upstream in the spawning season *(Aug)*, having made a 1,200km/744mi journey inland, from the Fraser outlet on the Pacific Ocean to this point.

The crossroads town of Tête Jaune Cache lies 5km/3mi farther west.

6 Kootenay National Park★★

This park was formed in 1920, upon completion of Highway 93; it extends 8km/5mi from both sides of the road. With few attractions, Kootenay is a wilderness park explorable only on foot; venturing very far off the road demands wilderness expertise. ⚠Due to forest fires in 2003, some park trails may be closed. Contact the **Kootenay National Park Visitor Centre** *(7556 Main St. East, Radium Hot Springs* ☎*250-347-9505.* 🕐*open mid-May–early Oct 9am–5pm, Jul–Aug 6pm; in off-season, contact Yoho park visitor centre* ☎*250-343-6783).*

From Castle Junction to Radium Hot Springs

105km/65mi by Hwy. 93.
This **route**★★ leaves Highway 1 at Castle Junction and climbs steeply to the summit of **Vermilion Pass** (1,650m/5,412ft).

Marble Canyon★

17km/11mi from junction.
Tokumm Creek charges through this limestone gorge to the Vermilion River. The park's north entrance **visitor centre** (♿🕐*hours above;* ☎*403-762-9196, or 250-347-9615/winter)* is located here.

Paint Pots

20km/12mi from junction.
The ochre clay in these pools was used as body paint by Indians. Native tribes considered the three cold **mineral springs**★ places of spiritual power.

Radium Hot Springs★

103km/64mi.
🕐*Open mid-May–early Oct daily 9am–11pm. Rest of the year Sun–Thu noon–9pm, Fri–Sat noon–10pm.* 🎫*$6.50.* ♿ ☎*250-347-9485. www.hotsprings.ca.*
These waters (average temperature 47°C/117°F) contain sulphates and salts. The waters feed the huge swimming pools in the complex; the big pool is the largest hot-spring pool in Canada.
The road enters **Sinclair Canyon**★ and passes the park's south gate, in the town of Radium Hot Springs.

Kananaskis Country★★

MAP P 104

Albertans, and Calgarians in particular, have a second outdoor playground on their western border. It may not be quite as superlative as its neighbour, the Rocky Mountain Parks, but the vast Kananaskis [Can-nah-NASS-kiss] wilderness south and west of Banff National Park is truly a recreational paradise—without the day-use fees. Encompassing five provincial parks, four wildland provincial parks, an ecological reserve and several recreation areas, K-Country, as it's affectionately called, is crisscrossed by innumerable trails that afford access to the high country, the abode of black bears, bighorn sheep, coyotes and cougars. In fact, more than half of this 4,250sq km/1,641sq mi area of glacier-clad peaks, snowmelt freshets and wildflower-strewn meadows has been designated as protected parks and recreation areas; limited logging, gas drilling, hydroelectric activity, foresting and ranching have government sanction in other areas.

The recreation area itself is parcelled into more than half a dozen distinct zones, the most-popular of which are Kananaskis Valley, with its resort village, two 18-hole golf courses, hiking and cycling trails and a river for rafting and kayaking. Farther south lies immense Peter Lougheed Provincial Park, where the headwaters of the Kananaskis River begin their southeast course to Upper Kananaskis Lake before flowing northward along Highway 40 to meet the Bow River.

Kananaskis can be accessed on its eastern boundary from Calgary, which lies 100km/65mi away, as well as from eastern border towns Bragg Creek, Turner Valley and Longview. Canmore, sitting southeast of Banff along the Trans-Canada Highway, serves as the northern gateway to Kananaskis and a portal to neighbouring Banff National Park. The former coal-mining centre, whose booming development was spurred by recreational and real-estate demand during the 1988 Winter Olympic Games in southern Alberta, has been rejuvenated as a vibrant small town offering world-class recreational opportunities and visitor amenities.

- **Information:** Kananaskis Country park office: 800 Railway Ave. (2nd floor), Canmore. ☎403-678-5500. Alberta Tourism, Parks and Recreation: 866-427-3582; www.tpr. alberta.ca. *For where to stay and where to eat, see Lodging and Dining in K-Country.*

- **Orient Yourself:** Downloadable maps at www.tpr.alberta.ca. Several roads within Kananaskis are named Trail, even though they are vehicular roads. Hwy. 40 closed late Nov–late May for lambing season of area bighorn sheep. Hwy. 40 from Lakes Trail Rd. south to junction with Hwy. 541 closed Dec–mid-Jun. Check trail reports online at www.tpr.alberta.ca or phone the visitor centre. **Highway 40** is the roughly north-south route through the area: initiating from Highway 1, Exit 118 near Seebe, 23km/14mi east of Canmore, the highway curves southwest through Kananaskis Village, the area of most development, and along the Kananaskis River, before reining in near Highwood Pass, and proceeding southeast to Highwood House, where it continues south as Forestry Trunk Road. From Highwood House, **Highway 541** heads east and north out of Kananaskis Country to Longview. **Smith-Dorrien/Spray Lakes Trail** (*begins 50km/31mi south of Hwy. 1, off Hwy. 40*) is a gravel road that leads northwest from Kananaskis Lakes Trail road to Canmore. Just south of Bragg Creek, which sits east of K-Country's northern end, **Highway 66** (*closed from Elbow Falls westward Dec–Apr*) winds 28km/17mi into Kananaskis to terminate at the junction with Powderface Trail (*closed Dec–Apr*).

- **Organizing Your Time:** Highway 40 is closed to vehicular traffic late November to late May, so plan your trip accordingly. To thoroughly enjoy

K-Country and Canmore, allow at least 4 days, and more if you're an avid hiker or cyclist. Given the changeable temperatures, carry spare clothes, no matter what the outdoor activity, and a space blanket (the tinfoil-looking square packets, which cost $2 at any outdoor store).

Don't Miss: Peter Lougheed Provincial Park.

Especially for Kids: Trail rides and the bison paddock at Boundary Ranch.

Also See: THE KOOTENAYS.

A Bit of History

For centuries, the area was home to the nomadic Stoney Indians who trapped deer, bighorn sheep and other animals. As more and more European explorers and settlers encroached upon their land, the First Nations moved to more fertile hunting territory to the north and west. Like Banff, their rich cousin to the west, Kananaskis Country and Canmore were opened to the world with the arrival of the Canadian Pacific Railway in the mid-1880s. Before abundant coal seams were found here in the late 19C, Canmore was technically part of Banff National Park. However, the federal government determined that such resource development did not fit the vision for a pristine national park, and boundaries were redrawn in 1930 to exclude Canmore. Coal mining continued in the area, most notably on a mountainside below China-man's Peak (recently renamed Ha Ling Peak), until the mine was closed in 1979 due to declining demand and safety concerns. Another major mine oper-

ated in the Ribbon Creek area at Mount Allan, but only from 1947 to 1952, due to costs linked to having to haul coal by truck. The Alberta government created Kananaskis Provincial Park and Kananaskis Country (the two areas are now blended) in 1976. Construction of the Nakiska downhill ski area and Kananaskis Village began eight years later for the Winter Olympic Games in 1988. After the last mine closed, Canmore's growth remained dormant for a decade until the Canmore Nordic Centre was built for the Winter Olympic Games in 1988. Visitors and real estate developers flocked to the area as a more affordable alternative to Banff. Since Canmore did not face the growth restrictions and controls on non-resident property ownership imposed on the national park, high-end town-houses, resorts and golf courses were quickly built, quadrupling the population. Construction of the Three Sisters Mountain Resort, a residential/hotel community and three golf courses slated for completion by 2015, is expected to boost the population by 3,000 people.

©Travel Alberta

Mount Lorette and Barrier Lake

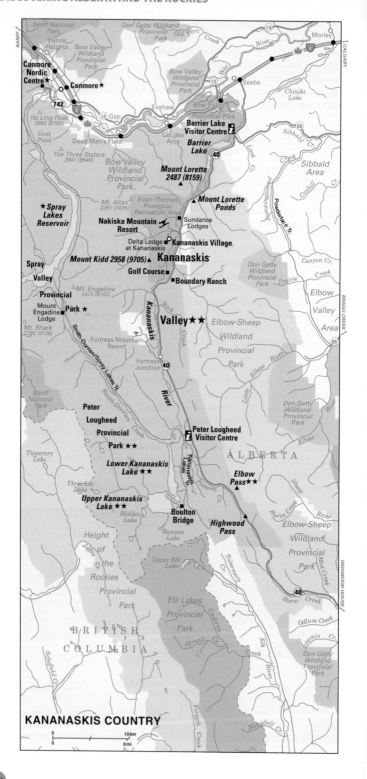

KANANASKIS COUNTRY

Natural Features

Climate – Like neighbouring Banff, Kananaskis and Canmore experience cold, snowy winters and warm, generally dry summers. Weather can change abruptly from a sunny day into a wind-whipped snowstorm. The east side of Kananaskis Valley is typically drier than the west side, where the higher peaks of the Kananaskis Range attract more precipitation.

Fauna and Flora – The area is diverse with bears, coyotes, deer, squirrels, elk, cougars (rarely seen) and many birds, including the golden eagle, whose annual spring and fall migration traverses K-Country. Backcountry travellers or even those strolling, hiking or cycling in more populated areas such as Kananaskis Village should stay aware of their surroundings so as to not surprise wildlife.

Most of the trees in this area are coniferous—the majority are varieties of pine and spruce—although the rocky spine of mountains that straddle much of the valley turn into softer foothills and alpine meadows as Highway 40 through the Highwood Pass descends into the Longview area in north Kananaskis. In the spring, **wildflowers** such as Black-Eyed Susans, lupines, crimson Indian paintbrush, blue flax, buttercups, white daisies and the blue swan river daisy can be found in meadows, green spaces and even growing abundantly along the highway.

Canmore★

Though not physically within Kananaskis Country, the fast-growing town of Canmore, located on the northwestern edge of the Kananaskis area, and just 6km/4mi east of the gates of Banff National Park, serves as a gateway both to K-Country and the Rocky Mountain Parks. Snuggled at an elevation of 1,309m/4,296ft at the base of soaring mountain peaks, Canmore shares the alpine beauty of nearby Banff half an hour west, but lacks the development restrictions facing communities that reside within the national parks. Once considered a poor cousin to Banff and Lake Louise, the former coal-mining town has been transformed into a charming, cosmopolitan and affluent community of 15,000 residents with world-class recreation, dining, accommodations and shopping. The town centre actually sits on an island bounded by Policeman's Creek (part of the Bow River system) along the eastern edge and the Bow River on the western side. Year-round the town's enviable location enables it to offer a range of recreational pursuits amid breathtaking scenery, like hiking, fishing, skiing, dogsledding, ice climbing, snowshoeing and golf. Many of Canmore's dining spots consistently make the Best Restaurant lists for the province, and shopping doesn't take a back seat, either. Main Street and surrounding avenues are chock-full of an array of boutiques selling clothing, outdoor gear, candy, coffee, art, and gift items reflective of the region and beyond.

- **Information:** Tourism Canmore, 907 7th Ave. ☎403-678-1295 or 866-226-6673. www.tourismcanmore.com. ⚲*For Where to Stay and Where to Eat in Canmore, see Canadian Rockies Address Book.*

▶ **Orient Yourself:** Canmore lies along **Highway 1**, about 30km/18mi southwest of Banff and some 100km/65mi west of Calgary. Take the first main exit from Highway 1 (signed to downtown), then follow Railway Ave. to Main St. (also known as 8th St.). Finding your way around the town's key attractions is easy: most of the shops and eateries are situated along Main Street (8th St.), which runs east-west. The downtown core is concentrated along Main St. from the NWMP building at the east end to 8th Ave. in the west end. Centennial Park lies two blocks south of Main St.

🅿 **Parking:** Free parking on Main Street and in lots on either side.

⊘ **Don't Miss:** Canmore Nordic Centre.

Especially for Kids: The Geoscience Centre at the Canmore Museum.

⚲ **Also See:** GREATER CALGARY.

Main Street, Canmore

Sights

Historic Buildings

Some eight historical sites are located in downtown Canmore *(obtain details for walking tour from the visitor centre)*. Two heritage buildings are especially noteworthy. The **North West Mounted Police Barracks** *(609 Main St.)* is the original structure, built in 1893, to house two officers of a police contingent responsible for maintaining law and order, particularly among the miners and railroad workers of the town. Restored to its 1921 appearance and furnished with period pieces, the mud-daubed log building, now painted white, functions today as a teahouse and gift shop. Another provincial heritage site, the **Canmore Hotel** *(8th St. & 7th Ave.)*, completed in 1891, is still in operation as a hostelry today.

Canmore Museum and Geoscience Centre

Civic Centre, 902B 7th Ave. ◷*Open mid-May–Aug Mon–Tue noon–5pm, Wed–Sat 10am–6pm. Rest of the year Mon–Fri noon–5pm, weekends 11am–5pm.* ⊜*$3.* ♿☏*403-678-2462. www.cmags.org.*
Housed in the striking Civic Centre building, this museum is devoted to Canmore's human past, especially its mining history, and the geology of the area's mountains. Well-presented dis-plays reveal the development of the area through artifacts, equipment, paintings, photographs, maps and clothing. A highlight of the museum's galleries, one exhibit focuses on the dangerous work of a miner and includes an assortment of mining lamps, miner's clothing, hard hat and tools. Kids will enjoy seeing a preserved life-size bison up close.

Additional Sight

Canmore Nordic Centre★

Spray Lakes Rd., 4km/2mi west of downtown Canmore. ◷*Open Dec–March daily (weather permitting) 9am–9pm. Rest of the year daily 9am–5pm.* ◷*Closed Dec 25. In winter cross-country ski lessons and rentals. In summer ⌁⌁guided tours, bike rentals.* ⊜*$7.50 for use of ski trails in season.* ✕♿🅿☏*403-678-2400. www. kananaskis-country.ca.*
Built to accommodate 1988 Winter Olympic cross-country events, including Nordic ski racing and biathlon, this facility boasts 70km/43mi of trails for all levels of cross-country skiers (though most trails are advanced). The centre often serves as a training site for competitive amateur and professional racers, allowing guests to rub elbows with Olympic hopefuls and medallists.
Amenities include a day lodge, recently renovated, which features a fireplace and views of Mount Rundle. Ski rentals

and lessons are available on-site. The trails, groomed and track set for both classic and skating ski techniques, wind through forested area with varying degrees of difficulty *(check website for map detailing difficulty levels)*. A 6.5km/10mi trail is illuminated for night skiing. In summer the centre's trails play host to mountain bikes.

Kananaskis★★

An assemblage of scenic river valleys, mountain ranges, lakes and creeks, provincial parks and wilderness areas, with few resorts, the vast expanse known as Kananaskis Country unfolds just east of the Rocky Mountains and west of Greater Calgary. The Kananaskis River and Kananaskis Range are major features of its geology; grizzly bears, mountain goats, moose, deer, elk, cougars (the latter rarely seen), coyotes and some 261 species of birds are its residents—humans are merely guests. Aspen trees and lodgepole pines thrive, creeks run clear, and turquoise-hued lakes glisten at the base of majestic rocky peaks. Metaphorically speaking, Kananaskis is shaped rather like an elongated, left-hand mitten, having just been pulled off: the "wrist" end begins along the Trans-Canada Highway (Highway 1) northwest of Canmore in the vicinity of **Canmore Nordic Centre Provincial Park;** the thumb dangles south to the

end of **Peter Loughheed Provincial Park;** the fingers portion hangs farther south into Don Getty Wildland Provincial Park and Plateau Mountain Ecological Reserve. Highway 40 (Forestry Trunk Road) is the north-south thoroughfare through the area.

Along Highway 40

50km/31mi from the Trans-Canada Hwy. (Hwy. 1) south to Smith-Dorrien/ Spray Trail road. ⌂Hwy. 40 closed late Nov–late May for lambing season of area bighorn sheep. Hwy. 40. from Lakes Trail Rd. south to junction with Hwy. 541 closed Dec–mid-Jun. To check status of closures, access the trail reports online at www.tpr.alberta.ca or phone the visitor centre.

Barrier Lake

Visitor Information Centre, 6km/3.5mi south of Highway 1 (⌚open year-round daily 9am–4pm; ⌚closed Dec 24-25; ☎403-673-3985. www.tpr.alberta.ca).
Along its 74km/46mi length, the **Kananaskis River** has been tamed by three hydroelectric projects of Calgary-based TransAlta Corp., primarily to supply peak-period demand: one here, one farther south at Upper and Lower Kananaskis lakes and one at Pocaterra (named for an area rancher from Italy who prospected for coal). Approximately 5km/3mi wide, Barrier Lake is a man-made reservoir, formed in 1947 when the waters of the

©Travel Alberta

Skating on Kananaskis Village Pond

Mt. Kidd Course, Kananaskis Golf Course

river were dammed. South of the visitor centre, both the dam and the lake are visible from the highway.

Kananaskis Valley★★
Along Hwy. 40, south of Hwy. 1.
Originating in the Rockies, the Kananaskis River ultimately courses north from Upper Kananaskis Lake up through Bow Valley Provincial Park near the Trans-Canada Highway to become part of the Bow River near Seebe. Bisected by Highway 40, along which the river flows, the heavily forested river valley stretches roughly from Canoe Meadows south to Fortress Junction at the valley's southern reaches. Prominent peaks, of which there are many, include the snow-capped, folded bulk of **Mount Lorette** and the massive, folded rocky face of **Mount Kidd.** Serene **Mount Lorette Ponds** (more lake-size than pond-size) attracts anglers to its trout-filled waters. A popular destination in the valley is Kananaskis Village with lodgings and a nearby golf course. Some 150km/90mi of hiking, mountain biking and cross-country ski trails thread the valley; the river attracts anglers, kayakers, canoeists and white-water rafters. Just past Mt. Lorette Ponds Day-Use Area, Sundance Road *(on the right side of Highway 40)* leads to Sundance Lodges (*see sidebar on Lodging and Dining in K-Country*), offering tepee and trappers' tent accommodation as well as camping sites.

Nakiska Mountain Resort
2.5km/1.5mi north of Kananaskis Village. ☎403-256-8473 or 800-258-7669. www.skinakiska.com.
This ski resort on 2,261m/7,415ft Mount Allan occupies the site chosen for the 1988 Winter Olympic's alpine events. In the late 1940s, coal was found at the mountain's foot, a discovery that led to some development in the area. Mining activity continued until the mid-1950s. But the real impetus came in 1986 when construction of the Olympic facilities began here. Today the resort (*see sidebar on Lodging and Dining*) draws skiers to its 304ha/750acres of skiable terrain.

Kananaskis Village
This cluster of hotels, shops and eateries was opened during the 1988 Winter Olympic Games to support athletes, staff and dignitaries for the downhill ski events at Nakiska. An international summit of G8 leaders met here in 2002, in part due to its rural location and limited access that allowed police and government officials to keep protesters at arm's length.
Today the village is a self-contained resort with paved trails heading down alongside the famous Kananaskis Country Golf Course, just south. Summertime fish ponds here become outdoor skating rinks in winter; tennis and basketball courts, a playground and several trails are on the premises. The 300-plus-room

Delta Lodge at Kananaskis is one of the village's two upscale hotels, with restaurants, a lounge and a spa. The other, the Executive Resort at Kananaskis, has a restaurant, pub, indoor pool, fitness centre and spa (see Lodging and Dining in K-Country). The village also accommodates a small grocery story and an equipment rental shop (skis, skates, snowboards, bikes, inline skates and tennis rackets).

If you're a cyclist, it's worth renting a bike at Kananaskis Village and pedalling the 7km/4mi to the south end of Highway 40, also known as the **Highwood Pass,** for a heart-thudding cycle back up the pass before the busy road opens to traffic in the spring (be bear aware, however).

Just south of the village, the popular **Kananaskis Country Golf Course** (403-591-7154 or 877-591-2525; www.kananaskisgolf.com) boasts two public 18-hole courses—each named for mountains soaring overhead and set amid a spectacular **setting**★★ —as well as a restaurant, clubhouse and pro shop. On the opposite side of the golf course, across Highway 40, **Bound-ary Ranch** (403-591-7171 or 877-591-7177: www.boundaryranch.com) offers trail rides, horse-drawn wagon rides and white-water rafting trips.

Peter Lougheed
Provincial Park★★
Approximately 15km/9mi south of Kananaskis Village. From Hwy. 40, turn right onto Kananaskis Lakes Trail road (opposite King Creek Day-Use Area) and drive 4km/2.5mi to the visitor centre (open year-round daily 9am–5pm; 403-591-6322; www.tpr.alberta.ca).

This vast park in the southwestern part of K-Country embraces the most spectacular scenery in all of Kananaskis. One of the province's largest parks, at 500sq km/193sq mi, it is named for Peter Lougheed, Alberta's premier from 1971-85 who was a leading force in Alberta's bid for the 1988 Winter Olympics. Among the park's highlights are two beautiful lakes, the **Lower and Upper Kananaskis lakes**★★. Kananaskis Lakes Trail road leads to the park visitor centre, which offers natural his-

tory exhibits, interpretive programs, trail maps and information about the park. Opposite the **visitor centre,** a road goes to **Canyon** Day-Use Area; **views**★★ from picnic tables along Lower Lake take in Mts. Warspite and Invincible, named for World War I battleships. South of the visitor centre, a trail just north of the spur road to William Watson Lodge, a facility for seniors and the disabled, heads west, following the lower lake's northeastern edge. Farther south, stop at the **Boulton Bridge** Day-Use Area for a bite to eat on the outdoor patio and browse in the trading post. Kananaskis Lakes Trail road continues south and then curves northwestward between the two lakes. The Canadian Mt. Everest Expedition Trail *(trailhead from White Spruce parking lot)* is a 1.7km/1mi round-trip ascent to a viewpoint for both lakes. Back on Highway 40, as it heads south toward Highwood Pass and out of the park's boundary, views of the jagged peaks of **Elbow Pass**★★ from the Day-Use Area along Pocaterra Creek, are not to be missed.

Along Smith-Dorrien/ Spray Lakes Trail

Gravel road, 60km/37mi from junction with Hwy. 40 north to Hwy. 1 at Canmore. Caution: This gravel road makes a steep descent into Canmore: be sure your vehicle, especially its brakes, are in good working condition. There are no fuel stations en route: it is advisable to start out with a full tank of gas.

Smith-Dorrien/Spray Lakes Trail is a gravel road its entire length. Beginning from Kananaskis Lakes Trail road, off Highway 40, it heads northwest through Peter Lougheed Provincial Park, cuts through Spray Valley Provincial Park and borders the boundary of Bow Valley Wildland Provincial Park before ending at Canmore.

Spray Valley Provincial Park★
Off Smith-Dorrien/Spray Lakes Trail. 403-591-6322.

Sitting atop Peter Lougheed Provincial Park like a coonskin cap, Spray Valley Provincial Park was created in 2000 to protect the wildlife and ecosystem

Lodging and Dining in K-Country

For dollar-sign categories, see the Legend on the cover flap.

WHERE TO STAY

$ Mount Kidd R.V. Park and Campground – *In Kananaskis Valley.* ☎403-591-7700. www.mountkiddrv.com. *229 campsites.* This year-round resort has a coin laundry, convenience store, coffee counter and registration desk in the main lodge, which also houses the lockers, showers, saunas, a whirlpool, games area and social room. Most sites are equipped for winter use. Families flock to the campground in summer for its two play areas and kids' wading pool, riverside picnic areas, amphitheatre for park interpretive programs and paved paths.

$ Sundance Lodges – *Sundance Rd., Off Hwy. 40, 22km/14mi south of Hwy. 1;* ☎403-591-7122; www.sundancelodges.com. *Closed late Sept–early May.* Sundance offers lodging in tepees and trappers' tents as well as camping sites for tents and RVs along the Kananaskis River. The family-run camp resort has showers, a coin laundry and a gift shop as well as sand volleyball and badminton courts. The Trading Post sells groceries and rents sports supplies such as volleyballs, badminton rackets and soccer balls. Pets are accepted for a nominal fee (some rules apply).

$$ Delta Lodge at Kananaskis – *In Kananaskis Village.* ☎403-591-6322 or 866-432-4322. www.deltahotels.com. *321 rooms.* ✕ Spa . This two-storey hotel is the village's largest resort, with two restaurants, a lounge and a combined deli and chocolate shop. Also on-site are a fitness centre, spa, saltwater pool and an indoor-outdoor hot pool. The Western-style **Fireweed Grill ($$)** serves international dishes.

Travellers seeking a higher-end experience can stay next door at the upscale, business-friendly **Delta Signature Club ($$$)**, which offers a lavish honour bar, wine and cheese events and complimentary breakfast in addition to luxurious accommodations. At the Signature Club, **Seasons Steakhouse ($$$)** specializes in prime Alberta beef and other regional fare; an excellent wine list includes selections from Western Canada.

$$ Executive Resort at Kananaskis – *In Kananaskis Village.* ☎403-591-7500 or 888-591-7501. www.executivehotels. net. *90 rooms.* . The rooms are a bit small, and the outside decor somewhat dated, but if you're on a budget, this is a decent option (beware: college spring break brings rowdy ski guests). A recent renovation has attracted more families. Situated on the village's back side, the hotel has a pub, indoor pool, fitness centre and spa. Open to the public, the **Wildflower Restaurant ($$)** serves Canadian dishes, such as an Alberta beefsteak sandwiches, trout, pasta and burgers.

$$$$ Mount Engadine Lodge – *Off Smith-Dorrien/Spray Lakes Trail road, in Spray Valley Provincial Park.* ☎403-678-4080. www.mountengadine.com. *8 rooms & suites.* ✕. This wood and fieldstone lodge and its cabins sit at an elevation of 1,845m/6,050ft overlooking a meadow where wildlife, especially moose, can often be spotted at dusk and dawn. Amenities include a hot tub and wood-fired sauna. The **dining room ($$)** *(open to the public by 24hr advance reservations)* serves a prix-fixe dinner *($35/person)* of international dishes. Rate includes three meals a day.

from human encroachment and habitat destruction along this wildlife corridor. Less crowded—even during high season—than its southern neighbour, the 35,800ha/88,426-acre park is largely untouched wilderness, save the area around **Spray Lakes Reservoir**★, which was created in 1947. The "tail" of the cap

hangs down in the Fortress Mountain area, site of the Fortress Mountain Resort *(www.skifortress.ca)*, opened in 1969, and long-favoured by area skiers, especially families *(the resort is currently closed for renovation)*. As Smith-Dorrien/Spray Lakes Trail enters the park's southern end, Mount Engadine rises

2,470m/8,102ft on the right; its namesake lodge perches above a meadow west of the highway (see *Lodging and Dining in K-Country*). Banff National Park borders the park, so watch off to the west (left side) for Mount Assiniboine's Matterhorn-like peak, which may be visible.

Bow Valley Wildland Provincial Park

Mount Buller, 2,805m/9,200ft tall, straddles Spray Valley park's boundary with Bow Valley Wildland Provincial Park. As Smith-Dorrien/Spray Lakes Trail follows the curve of the boomerang-shaped Spray Lakes Reservoir, it enters the Bow Valley park.

From the base of towering Mount Shark (2786m/9,138ft) in Spray Valley Provincial Park, the elongated body of water extends 20km/12mi to the shadow of The Three Sisters (2941m/9,646ft), which rises to the north of the reservoir.

Other massifs of the Continental Divide here include Ha Ling Peak (2,680m/8,790ft). In winter **dogsled tours** are popular in the area (*contact Canmore-based Snowy Owl Sled Dog Tours; ☎403-591-7154; www.snowyowltours.com*). After the reservoir, the road becomes narrow and winding.

Watch for a pull-out that affords an expansive **view** of Canmore as the road makes its steep descent into the Bow Valley.

Waterton Lakes National Park★★

MAP OF PRINCIPAL SIGHTS

Sitting apart from the other Rocky Mountain national parks, this lovely preserve—covering an area of 505sq km/195sq mi—is situated in Alberta's southwest corner. Waterton is the smallest of the Rocky Mountain national parks. Its tallest peak, Mount Blakiston, is 2,940m/9,645ft in height, compared to the 10,000 footers and higher of the Canadian Rockies. Because the park's gently rolling hills (rarely over 1,200m/4,000ft above sea level) meet a vertical rock wall towering another 1,200m/4,000ft or more above the plains, the park has been described as the place "where the prairies meet the mountains." A World Heritage Site (1995), the park is also a Biosphere Reserve (1979), created to provide insight into the relationship between humanity and nature. The jewels of the park are its three beautiful lakes: Upper Waterton Lake, at 148m/487ft, is the deepest lake in the Canadian Rockies, and Middle and Lower Waterton lakes. One of the most-oft photographed views in the Rockies is that of the Prince of Wales Hotel in the foreground, overlooking the lakes with dramatic mountains in the background. The hotel is one of Waterton's two National Historic Sites; the other is the Lineham Discovery Well, site of Canada's first producing oil well. The park's sole town, called Waterton Townsite, abides within the park boundaries, at the edge of Upper Waterton Lake. Many town merchants shut down during the winter months, but construction of several new inns in the past five years has added more year-round tourist bustle to the small town. As they have for decades, visitors keep coming to Waterton to boat its sparkling lakes, hike its mountain trails, and view its diverse flora and fauna.

Information: Visitor Information Centre: Park Entrance Rd. ☎403-859-2224. www.pc.gc.ca. Open early May–early Oct. Chamber of Commerce and Visitors Assn.: www.watertonchamber.com.

▶ **Orient Yourself:** Highway 6, off Highway 3, intersects with Highway 5 (from Cardston), which directly accesses Waterton park and the townsite. The Visitor Information Centre is located on the park entrance road as you approach Waterton townsite from Highway 5. The townsite sits at the centre of the park, along Upper Waterton Lake, and has extensive tourist and recreational facilities. Download a map of the townsite and of the park at www.pc.gc.ca. **Waterton Avenue** runs parallel to the lake. At the south end of the avenue are picnic shelters and a large RV park and campground, facing Cameron Bay. At the avenue's other end is the **marina,** where boats can be rented and lake cruises depart. There are public restrooms behind the post office on Fountain Avenue. At the western end of Cameron Falls Drive is Cameron Falls.

🕐 **Organizing Your Time:** The park is open year-round, although most facilities are closed in winter *(mid-Oct to early May)*. April and June see the most rain; July and August are usually warm and sunny. Spring is the best time to see wild-flowers, but the town's 10-day **Wildflower Festival** is held mid-June (www.watertonwildflower.com). Allow at least 3 days to leisurely enjoy the area.

🚗 **Don't Miss:** A cruise on the Waterton lakes across the Continental Divide and into Montana, and a ride on a rented moped or bike to Cameron Lake.

🧒 **Especially for Kids:** The Buffalo Paddock near the park entrance.

Natural Features

Climate – The park's mountains serve as weather antennae, intercepting the Pacific's warm, moist air and the Arctic's the cold, dry air. As a result of warmer air being forced upward, the park receives Alberta's highest average annual precipitation—most of it snowfall—of 1072mm/42in. Because it sits in a concentrated storm track, Waterton is one of the windiest places in the province. In fall and winter, gusts of100kph/60mph are commonplace. Chinook winds are created when cool air descends quickly from the peaks to the prairielands. Chinooks help to keep Waterton relatively warm in winter, when highs can reach 10°C/50°F; but temperatures can also dip to -40°C/-40°F.

Flora – The park is unique in its ecological diversity, in that it comprises over 1,000 species from three distinct, yet overlapping, ecological regions: prairie plants of the Great Plains, Rocky Mountain plant species from northern areas, and coastal plants, such as beargrass, from the humid Pacific Northwest. The park shelters dozens of varied habitats, from grasslands and evergreen forests to wetlands and lakes. More than half of the province's **wildflowers** can be found in the park, from lupines, lady slippers, fleabane and mariposa lilies to columbine and yellow paintbrush. Some 30 rare wildflowers grow in the park as well.

Fauna – Grizzly bears and black bears, white-tailed deer and mule deer, elk, coyotes and more rarely, cougars and wolves, plus an assortment of reptiles, two dozen fish species and some 250 species of birds make their home here in the grasslands and forests. The lakes of the park attract migrating ducks and geese, bald eagles, and even the rare trumpeter swan.

A Bit of History

The underlying sediment of these mountains, which once were part of an inland sea, was thrust up and sculptured by erosion and glaciation into sharp peaks, narrow ridges and interlocked U-shaped valleys. Among them, the three Waterton Lakes lie in a deep glacial trough.

Formerly a **Blackfoot First Nation** stronghold, the mountains of Waterton were first visited by **Thomas Blakiston** of the Palliser Expedition. Blakiston explored the area in 1858, and named the lakes for an 18C English naturalist, **Charles Waterton** (1782-1865). Oil was discovered in the 20C: the first strike came in 1902 at the **Discovery No. 1** site in Cameron Valley, Western Canada's first oil well. More oil was found near Cameron Falls, where Vancouver's Western Coal and Oil Co. set up offices and constructed a few buildings. Their settlement eventually grew into the Waterton townsite; the first lots were surveyed here in 1910. When the **Prince**

Prince of Wales Hotel, Waterton Lakes National Park

©Travel Alberta

of Wales Hotel opened in 1927, and its American builder, the Great Northern Railway, began passenger service from the US, Waterton's future as a tourist destination was assured.

The area was designated a national park in 1895, Canada's fourth national park. Pioneer **Kootenai Brown,** an area resident, was instrumental in establishing the park (*see Southern Alberta*). In 1932 the park was combined with Glacier National Park to become the first international peace park on earth. In 1979 Waterton was the first Canadian national park to participate in UNESCO's Biosphere Reserve program, designed to foster a greater understanding of mankind's relation with the natural world. In 1995 the Waterton Glacier International Peace Park was added to UNESCO's World Heritage List of sites of outstanding world value.

Visit

Park open year-round, but few facilities open late fall–early spring. Hiking, camping, horseback riding, fishing, boating, golf, winter sports. $8/day-use fee. 403-859-2224. www.pc.gc.ca. Bear sightings in the park are not unusual; hikers are urged to make noise and keep a respectful distance. Bear jams of camera-snapping drivers can cause hazards to wildlife and other motorists; if you stop for a moment, try to pull off the road. Never approach a wild animal. When camping, check with park wardens about wildlife warnings and fire bans; the Watertown townsite campground, situated along the windy lake, does not allow campfires. From Jun–early Sept, the park is usually busy enough to make advance reservations for accommodations, including campsites, a must.

Waterton Townsite

Built on delta materials deposited by Cameron Creek, the town sits at an elevation of 1280m/4,200ft above sea level. It edges Upper Waterton Lake, which is the largest and southernmost of the three Waterton lakes; elongated, it dangles like a pendant south into Montana in the US, separating the mountains of the Lewis and Clark Range, which tower steeply above it. The town has a lovely **site**★★ near the point where Upper Lake narrows into the Bosporus Strait, which separates it from Middle Lake. At times, deer and elk roam the cottonwood-lined streets, and mountain goats brazenly lick the salt from under parked cars. Perched on a mountain meadow overlooking the townsite is the stately Prince of Wales hotel. Behind the townsite, **Cameron Falls** can be seen dropping over a layered cliff. Just south behind the town, the flat face of **Mount Richards** can be distinguished. Beside it stands **Mount Bertha,** marked by pale

Bison or Buffalo?

While most people use the words interchangeably, purists will opt for the term bison when referring to the North American animal. Early settlers in the US called bison buffalo, since they saw a similarity to the buffalo of Asia and Europe. In fact, the ancestors of modern bison are thought to have migrated from Asia to North America across the Bering Strait thousands of years ago when the two continents were united by a land bridge. Some 200 years ago Plains bison inhabited the grasslands of the prairies. The larger wood bison, fewer in number, made the forested fringes of the northwestern prairie their home. Bison are wild bovids, members of the same family as cattle and sheep. An adult male can weigh as much as 2,200 pounds but can charge at a speed of 40mph. Calves weigh up to 70 pounds when born and can walk within 20 minutes. Mature at three years, a bison can live as many as 30 years.

Source: *Parks Canada*

green streaks down the otherwise dark green surface. The streaks were caused by snowslides that swept trees down the mountainside. Across the lake rise **Vimy Peak** and **Vimy Ridge.**

Boat Tours★★

🕐*Departs from Waterton Marina Jul–Aug daily 10am, 1pm, 4pm, 7pm. Mid-Sept–early Oct daily 10am & 2:30pm. Jun and early–mid Sept 10am, 1pm & 4pm. Advance reservations recommended. Round-trip 2hrs 15min; Commentary.* 💵*$32. Waterton Shoreline Cruise Co. Ltd.* ☎*403-859-2362. www.watertoncruise. com.* 🛈*The lake can be quite windy; best to bring a jacket, even in summer. Bring binoculars for wildlife viewing.*

Departing from Waterton Marina, the M.V. *International* takes passengers aboard for trips down **Upper Waterton Lake,** as it has been doing for years. The lake is 11km/7mi long and a half-mile wide *(.8 km)* at its broadest point. Two and a half miles of its waters *(4km)* extend south across the International Border into Montana. The boat features an enclosed viewing level and outdoor viewing level on the deck above. The vessel heads to the US ranger station at the southern end at Goat Haunt, Glacier National Park's northern gateway, for a 30min stop. This is also a jumping-off point for backcountry enthusiasts, and some trips include a stop at Crypt Landing for hikers headed for the rigorous but stunning Crypt Lake hike. En route, bears, mountain sheep, moose and bald eagles are often spotted along the shoreline.

Waterton Inter-Nation Shoreline Cruise

©Travel Alberta

Buffalo Paddock

Waterton Heritage Centre

117 Waterton Ave. ⏱*Open Jul–Aug daily 9am–8pm. May–Jun & Sept daily 9am–5pm.*💰*Contribution requested.* ☎*403-859-2624. www.wnha.ca/heritage.html.*
Located in the town's former fire hall (1952), this centre includes a small museum with displays on the natural history of the park. Maintained by the Waterton Natural History Assn., the centre also serves as its retail outlet and an art gallery.

Cameron Lake★★

17km/11mi from townsite by Akamina Pkwy., which is open first weekend May–Oct.
Before reaching the lake, the parkway passes the **site** of the first oil well in Western Canada *(a marker designates the site).*The jewel-toned lake, circuited by gentle hiking trails but with access to more challenging jaunts, is set immediately below the Continental Divide and, like Upper Waterton Lake, spans the international border. Dominating the view across the lake are, left to right, **Mount Custer** and **Forum Peak.** Grizzly bears can sometimes be spotted grazing in the alpine meadow across the lake. Canoe and paddle boats can be rented at the dock in the summer. A scenic trail *(1.6km/1mi)* traces the western shore of the lake.

Red Rock Canyon★

19km/12mi from townsite via Red Rock Canyon Pkwy., which is open first weekend May–Oct.; turn left at Blakiston Creek.
Offering good **views**★ of the surrounding mountains, the drive up the Blakiston Valley through undulating grasslands ends at this small canyon. In the summer *(Jun),* the roadside brims with wildflowers.
A popular **nature trail** follows the narrow canyon *(2km/1.2mi)* among scarlet-hued rock formations, where the characteristic colour is due to iron compounds in the rock that oxidized to form hermatite.
Red and green rocks, called argillite, are not an uncommon sight in the park. Argillite is fine-grained sedimentary rock composed largely of clay particles. While the red rocks contain oxidized iron, the green ones contain unoxidized iron. Rocks that are brownish-gray in colour are limestone or dolomite.

Buffalo Paddock★

400m/.2mi from park entrance.
Auto circuit 3km/2mi.
🧒Near the park's northern entrance *(off Hwy. 6),* a small herd of Plains bison occupies a large enclosure on a fine **site** backdropped by Bellevue Mountain and Mount Galway. A narrow road circles the paddock area (⚠*it is unsafe to get out of your car).*

GLACIER PARK REGION

Yoked like oxen since 1932, Alberta's Waterton Lakes National Park and Glacier Park in Montana share a similar topography and a history of cooperation. Together they form Waterton/Glacier International Peace Park. The Peace Park is one of North America's most awe-inspiring destinations with its jagged peaks, glacial lakes and U-shaped valleys straddling the US-Canada border. Far from major cities, relative isolation has enhanced its wilderness charms. During the ice ages, glaciers plowed down Rocky Mountain river valleys, shaving mountains into horns and arêtes and gouging the valleys.

Some glaciers flowed far enough south to impound the Clark Fork River at the present site of Lake Pend Oreille, creating glacial Lake Missoula. Larger in volume than Lakes Ontario and Erie combined, the inland sea spread from the Flathead region to the Bitterroot Mountains. Whenever an ice dam broke, floods raged down the Columbia River drainage to the Pacific; each time, another glacier plugged the outlet and the lake refilled. Fertile sedimentary deposits are the lake's legacy in the Mission and Bitterroot Valleys. Lewis' and Clark's 1804-06 odyssey took them across this ruggedly beautiful land: through the Bitterroot Valley, down the Columbia drainage. Even before the Corps of Discovery returned east, mountain men were headed west into these reaches. The pioneer influx led to conflict with Native Americans, whose free-roaming lifestyle disappeared into oppressive reservations.

Today, visitors can see bison and eagles, grizzly bears and mountain goats, they can meet real cowboys and Indians, stride across glaciers or into gold mines. America's Western heritage lives on through national and state parks, wildlife refuges, museums and historic preservation efforts.

Glacier NP MT

Mount Gould and Grinnell Lake, Glacier National Park

Address Book

🕯*For a legend of prices, see the cover flap.*

WHERE TO STAY

$$ The Copper King Mansion – *219 W. Granite St., Butte, MT.* ☎*406-782-7580. www.thecopperkingmansion.com. 5 rooms.* Built for a self-made copper millionaire in 1888, this opulent Victorian residence even offers a guided tour. It starts with the main hall's Staircase of Nations and moves to the ballroom, library and billiard room, all rich with stained-glass windows, gold-embossed leather ceilings, and inlaid woodwork.

$$ The Garden Wall Inn – *504 Spokane Ave., Whitefish, MT.* 🅿. ☎*406-862-3440 or 888-530-1700. www.gardenwallinn. com. 5 rooms.* With clapboard siding and claw-footed tubs, this charming Colonial Revival bed-and-breakfast inn is named for the sheer cliffs that form the Continental Divide. The innkeepers, keen outdoors explorers, concoct gourmet breakfasts that might include huckleberry-pear crepes.

$$ The Sanders – *328 N. Ewing St., Helena, MT.* ☎*406-442-3309. www. sandersbb.com. 7 rooms.* Most of the original furnishings remain in this charming 1875 bed-and-breakfast Victorian, home for 30 years (until 1905) of frontier politician Wilbur Fisk Sanders and his suffragette wife, Harriet Fenn Sanders. Listed on the National Register of Historic Places, it has been lovingly maintained by Rock Ringling (scion of the circus family) and Bobbi Uecker.

$$$ The Coeur d'Alene – *115 S. 2nd St., Coeur d'Alene, ID.* ✕🖥🅿🛆🆂🅿🅰. ☎*208-765-4000 or 800-688-5253. www. cdaresort.com. 336 rooms.* Consistently voted one of America's top resorts, this golf, sailing and tennis complex offers lodgings that range from economy to 18th-story tower penthouses. Housing four restaurants and saturated with amenities, it perches beside Lake Coeur d'Alene with a private beach.

$$$ Glacier Park Lodge – *US-2 at Hwy. 49, East Glacier Park, MT.* ✕🛆🅿. ☎*406-892-2525. www.glacierparkinc. com. 161 rooms.* The Great Northern Railway created rustic rooms in 1913 to attract wealthy travelers to the frontier. The vast lobby is a highlight of this grand building: 48ft timbers, with bark intact, create a rectangular basilica flanked by galleries and illuminated by skylights. Rooms are basic.

$$$$$ Averill's Flathead Lake Lodge – *Rte. 35, Bigfork, MT.* ✕🅿. ☎*406-837-4391. www.averills.com. 20 cabins. Open May–Sept.* This family-operated dude ranch, on the east shore of Flathead Lake, offers an experience of the new West. Log cottages surround a central lodge amid forestland. Visitors engage in horseback riding and fishing, or sailing and swimming at the private beach.

WHERE TO EAT

$$ Belton Chalet – *US-2, West Glacier, MT.* ☎*406-888-5000. www.beltonchalet. com. Dinner only.* **Regional**. Built in 1910 as a Great Northern Railway hotel, this Swiss-style chalet was filled with Arts and Crafts furniture and stone fireplaces. After a major historic preservation effort, it reopened in 2000 with a handful of guest rooms and a fine-dining restaurant. The Grill prepares dishes like rainbow trout, buffalo sausage and pheasant pot pie on an old boiler converted to an outdoor barbecue.

$$ The Bridge – *515 S. Higgins Ave., Missoula, MT.* ☎*406-542-0638.* **Italian & Seafood**. This cafe occupies two floors of a century-old "dime-a-dance" hall. A labor of love for its owners, the bistro serves pasta, pizza, fresh seafood and vegetarian entrees.

$$$ The Stonehouse – *120 Reeder's Alley, Helena, MT.* ☎*406-449-2552. Dinner only.* **American**. In the late 19C, fine dining meant white linen, even if atmosphere was rustic. This former miners' bunkhouse and four adjacent historic cabins perpetuate that theme. Specials include corn-fed steaks, stuffed catfish and wild game, and the Friday-night seafood buffet is always bustling.

Glacier National Park★★★

MAP OF PRINCIPAL SIGHTS

Shaped by glaciers, the Glacier Park area is characterized by rugged mountains, lakes and valleys. About 75 million years ago, a geological phenomenon known as the Lewis Overthrust tilted and pushed a 3mi- to 4mi-thick slab of the earth's crust 50mi east, leaving older rock atop younger Cretaceous rock. These mountains now rise 3,000-7,000ft above valley floors, partially forming the Continental Divide. A wet coniferous ecosystem on the west side of the Divide is balanced by dry, sparsely vegetated terrain on the east side.

- **Information:** ☎406-888-7800 or www.nps.gov/glac
- ▶ **Orient Yourself:** The park is about 67km/42mi south of Alberta via Hwy. 5 onto Hwy. 6 and then US-89 to Saint Mary Visitor Center at Going-to-the-Sun Road.
- **Parking:** On-site parking provided at the park.
- **Don't Miss:** Going-to-the-Sun Road.
- **Organizing Your Time:** Allow two days to enjoy the area.
- **Especially for Kids:** Keep an eye out for bighorn sheep.
- **Also See:** WATERTON LAKES NATIONAL PARK

Sights

Glacier National Park★★★

Going-to-the-Sun Road off US-2, 35mi east of Kalispell. △✕&P ☎*406-888-7800. www.nps.gov/glac.*
Known to native Blackfeet as the "Land of Shining Mountains," Glacier Park was homesteaded in the late 19C. Pressure to establish the park began in 1891 with the arrival of the Great Northern Railway; Congress gave its nod in 1910. The railroad built numerous delightful Swiss-style chalets and hotels, several of which still operate.

Glacier's rugged mountainscape takes its name not from living glaciers, but from ancient rivers of ice that carved the peaks, finger lakes and U-shaped valleys. The remoteness of the park's 1,584sq mi makes it an ideal home for grizzly bears and mountain goats, bighorn sheep and bugling elk.

Western Approaches

Coming from Kalispell, visitors pass through the village of Hungry Horse, named for two lost horses that nearly starved one long-ago winter. **Hungry Horse Dam** *(West Reservoir Rd., 4mi*

Bighorn sheep in Glacier National Park

©Sylvia Schug/iStockphoto.com

south of US-2; ☎406-387-5241), which impounds a 34mi-long reservoir, offers grand views up the South Fork of the Flathead River, into the BobMarshall Wilderness. Guided tours from a visitor center lead to the massive turbines and generators of the 564ft-high arched concrete dam.

Charming **West Glacier,** a park gateway town, is an outfitting center. Amtrak trains stop at a renovated depot that now houses the nonprofit Glacier Natural History Association. **Belton Chalet** (12575 US-2 East; ☎406-888-5000, www.beltonchalet.com), built by the Great Northern Railroad in 1910, is restored and listed on the National Register of Historic Places.

Going-to-the-Sun Road★★★
52mi from US-2 at West Glacier to US-89 at St. Mary. ◷*Closed mid Oct–late May due to snow.*

This National Historic Landmark may be America's most beautiful highway. Deemed an engineering marvel when completed in 1932, the narrow, serpentine roadway climbs 3,500ft to the Continental Divide at Logan Pass, moving from forested valleys to alpine meadows to native grassland as it bisects the park west to east. Passenger vehicles (size restrictions prohibit large RVs) share the route with Glacier's trademark red "jammer" buses, which have carried sightseers for more than 60 years.

Two miles from the road's beginning is **Apgar**, an assemblage of lodgings, cafes and shops at the foot of mountain-ringed **Lake McDonald**★. Like most park waters, this lake is fed by snowmelt and glacial runoff, and summer surface temperatures average a cool 55ºF. The launch *DeSmet*, a classic wooden boat handcrafted in 1928, cruises from the rustic **Lake McDonald Lodge** (Mile 11; ☎406-892-2525, www.lakemcdonaldlodge.com), open summers. There's been a hotel here since 1895.

At **Trail of the Cedars**★ (Mile 16.5), a wheelchair-accessible boardwalk winds through old-growth cedar-hemlock forest and past a sculpted gorge. Able-bodied hikers can amble uphill another 2mi to Avalanche Lake, fed by waterfalls spilling from Sperry Glacier. Beyond,

Bird Woman Falls cascades from Mt. Oberlin and the **Weeping Wall**★ gushes or trickles—depending on the season—from a roadside rock face.

At 6,680ft **Logan Pass**★★★ (Mile 33), visitors enjoy broad alpine meadows of wildflowers and keep their eyes open for mountain goats on the 1.5mi walk to **Hidden Lake Overlook**★★. White-flowered beargrass is beautiful in summer. Ripple-marked rocks more than 1 billion years old lie along the route to the observation post.

Descending Logan Pass, travelers may stop at the **Jackson Glacier Overlook** (Mile 37) or continue to **Sun Point**★ (Mile 41), where there is picnicking beside **St. Mary Lake** and a trailhead to **Baring Falls** (1mi). From **Rising Sun** (Mile 45), scenic 90min **lake cruises**★ aboard the 49-passenger *Little Chief*, built in 1925, are launched.

Eastern Valleys★★
A 21mi drive northwest from St. Mary leads to **Many Glacier**★★★ (12mi west of Babboff US-89). Three small glaciers provide a memorable backdrop to the valley above Grinnell Lake. They may be reached by a 5mi hiking path (part of Glacier Park's stalwart 735mi trail network), or viewed from the landmark 1915 **Many Glacier Hotel**★ (☎406-892-2525), or from a boat on sparkling Swiftcurrent and Josephine Lakes.

Two Medicine★ (13mi northwest of East Glacier Park off Rte. 49) is tucked into a carved glacial valley 38mi south of St. Mary via US-89 and has a general store and guided boat tours but no lodgings except a campground.

East Glacier Park
US-2 & Rte. 49.

This small town on the Blackfeet Indian Reservation is home to the 1913 **Glacier Park Lodge**★ (☎406-892-2525), whose lobby is columned with old-growth Douglas fir logs. The village boasts youth hostels, bicycle rentals, horseback outfitters and an Amtrak train depot.

Southern Boundary
Between East Glacier Park and West Glacier, a 57mi stretch of US-2 divides the park from the Great Bear Wilderness.

From 5,220ft **Marias Pass** on the Continental Divide, there are superb views of the Lewis Overthrust. Tiny **Essex** *(25mi east of West Glacier),* on the Middle Fork of the Flathead River, is home to the **Izaak Walton Inn** *(off US-2; ☎406-888-5700, www.izaakwaltoninn.com),* built in 1939 for rail crews. Today the half-timbered inn is a mecca for railroad fans and cross-country skiers.

Blackfeet Indian Reservation

US-2 & US-89. △✕🅿 ☎*406-338-7521. www.blackfeetnation.com.*

Bordered on the north by Canada, the Blackfeet Reservation stretches east from Glacier Park across 50mi of rolling hills and prairies notorious for hot, dry summers and wind-whipped winters. Today three Blackfeet confederacy tribes live in Montana and adjacent Alberta, earning livelihoods mainly in ranching and farming.

Flathead Region★

MAP OF PRINCIPAL SIGHTS

Wherever the eye rests in the Flathead Valley, mountains loom. They follow the traveller like a shadow. Ice Age glaciers left behind these jagged peaks and a fertile river valley that now supports an agricultural economy. The Flathead Indian Reservation and Flathead Lake are both found in this striking land, where outdoor recreation is gradually supplanting logging as the major industry.

- 🛈 **Information:** ☎406-756-9091 or www.fcvb.org
- ▶ **Orient Yourself:** Flathead Region lies to the southwest of Glacier National Park leaving from West Glacier via Hwy. 2
- 🜨 **Don't Miss:** Kalispell and the Conrad Mansion.
- 🕐 **Organizing Your Time:** Allow two days minimum to see the sights.
- 🄺🄸🄳🅂 **Especially for Kids:** Keep an eye peeled for bison along the road.
- 🜨 **Also See:** GLACIER NATIONAL PARK

Sights

Kalispell

US-2 & US-93 west of Glacier Park. △✕ 🅿♿ ☎*406-758-2800. www.kalispell chamber.com.*

Flathead County's commercial center, this town of 19,000 melds old and new Montana. The elegant **Conrad Mansion**★ *(313 6th Ave. E.; ☎406-755-2166, www.conradmansion.com),* a 26-room Norman-style home built in 1895, is Kalispell's crown jewel.

Whitefish★

US-93, 14mi north of Kalispell. △✕♿ 🅿. ☎*406-862-3501. www.whitefish chamber.com.*

This small town of 6,000 gracefully balances its dual identity as a Western community and resort center. **Whitefish Lake**★ draws anglers and water skiers in summer; in winter, 7,000ft **Big**

Mountain★ *(Big Mountain Rd., 8mi north of Whitefish; ☎406-862-2900, www.big-mtn.com)* lures snow-sport enthusiasts. Summer visitors ride the gondola to the summit for wonderful **views**★★ into Glacier National Park and the Canadian Rockies.

Flathead Lake★★

Between US-93 & Rte. 35, 11 to 38mi south of Kalispell. △

This 27mi-long lake, largest natural freshwater lake west of the Mississippi River, offers boating, sailing and fishing with gorgeous mountain **views**★.

With its Western-theme architecture and storybook lakeside setting, **Bigfork**★ *(Rte. 35, 17mi southeast of Kalispell;* △✕♿🅿 ☎*406-837-5888, www.bigfork.org)* is a center for the arts and fine dining. Galleries and gift shops line its main street, and the **Bigfork Summer Playhouse** *(☎406-837-4886, www.*

Where the Buffalo Roam

Fifty million bison once migrated across North America from central Mexico to Canada. For thousands of years they sustained generations of Plains Indians. Hides provided clothing and lodging; bones became tools and weapons; flesh and organs fed families. The herds flourished until the late 19C, when hunters slaughtered them for tongues and hides, leaving carcasses to rot.

The **National Bison Range**★★ *(Rte. 212, Moiese, 31mi south of Polson;* ♿ 🅿 ☎ *406-644-2211, www.fws.gov/bisonrange)* was set aside in 1908 to preserve a small herd of buffalo, by then approaching extinction. About 370 buffalo now roam the range and provide breeding stock for private North American bison ranches, where as many as 200,000 of the great beasts are raised. Visitor center displays examine the behavior and history of these strong, temperamental animals. Drivers on the 19mi Red Sleep Mountain tour may view not only bison but also pronghorn, bighorn sheep, elk and mountain goats on more than 18,500 scenic acres.

©Comstock, Inc

Bison grazing at the National Bison Range

bigforksummerplayhouse.com) draws sellout crowds to productions of comedies and Broadway musicals.

Flathead Indian Reservation

US-93 between Kalispell & Missoula. ✕ ♿ 🅿 ☎ *406-675-2700. www.cskt. org/vi.*

Montana's Salish, Kootenai and Pend d'Oreille tribes reside on this reservation, established in 1855. Every July, traditional **celebrations**★ in the villages of Elmo and Arlee welcome visitors to see Native American dancing, music and games.

The reservation's commercial center is **Polson** *(US-93 & Rte. 35, 49mi south of Kalispell & 65mi north of Missoula;* ☎ *406-*

883-5969; www.polsonchamber.com), a boating and outfitting hub that hugs the foot of Flathead Lake.

Six miles south of Polson, **The People's Center**★ *(US-93, Pablo;* ☎ *406-675-0160. www.peoplescenter.net)* relates the history of the Flathead tribes. Numerous prairie potholes, formed by glaciers 12,000 years ago, attract more than 180 bird species to **Ninepipe National Wildlife Refuge** *(US-93, 15mi south of Polson;* ☎ *406-644-2211, www.fws.gov),* a 2,000-acre wetland. The 1891 **St. Ignatius Mission**★ *(US-93, 29mi south of Polson;* ☎ *406-745-2768)* is graced with handsome frescoes and murals and backdropped by the majestic Mission Mountains.

SOUTHERN ALBERTA

Although hardly as travelled as the national parks of Banff and Jasper, this region offers a diverse landscape of prairie, badlands, foothills, river valleys and some of the most scenic mountain vistas in the province. Located south of Calgary, Southern Alberta encompasses the area along and south of Highway 3, stretching from the Crowsnest Pass in the Rockies east to Medicine Hat, near the Saskatchewan border. The area is in the "chinook belt," subject in winter to warm, dry winds from the Rockies, called chinooks, that can raise temperatures by 34°C/55°F in a day; some towns experience these winds as many as 40 days out of the year. Among the many water bodies here, the Oldman River, which flows 363km/225mi through historic Fort Macleod, the agricultural city of Lethbridge and points farther east, lends its lovely valley to much of the area; farther south, the Milk River, originating in Montana, flows into Alberta and runs north of and parallel to the border before returning to the US.

A vast swath of grassland where millions of buffalo once roamed now supports a largely agricultural economy of livestock and barley, flax, canola, rye and wheat crops, along with oil and gas drilling, mining, manufacturing and food processing. The region is home to two of five Treaty 7 First Nations bands—the Kainaiwa Nation based in Standoff, Canada's largest First Nations settlement, and the Piikani Nation at Brocket, west of Fort Macleod. An important heritage region, Southern Alberta boasts the UNESCO World Heritage Site of Head-Smashed-In Buffalo Jump, a landmark of First Nations culture dating back 10,000 years. At Writing-On-Stone Provincial Park, visitors can see ancient indigenous rock drawings and carvings. Cardston is noted for its Mormon temple and carriage museum. Alberta's second largest provincial park, the Cypress Hills marks a unique geological area of plains straddling the Saskatchewan border. Cornering the southwest portion of the province, Waterton Lakes National Park, recognized for its distinct mountain-prairie interface, is also a UNESCO site and Biosphere Reserve *(for a description of the park, see the Canadian Rockies chapter).*

Wind farm in Cowley, near Pincher Creek

©World Pictures/Photoshot

Practical Information

AREA CODES

The area code for southern Alberta is 403. For local calls, dial all 10 digits (area code plus the number, but without the 1-prefix for long distance). For more information: ☎1-403-555-1212 or www.telus.ca.

GETTING THERE AND GETTING AROUND

BY AIR

Calgary International Airport (YYC) 21km/17mi northeast of downtown, ☎403-735-1200, www.calgaryairport. com is served domestically and internationally by many airlines including Air Canada/Jazz (☎888-247-2262, Air North (☎800-661-0407), WestJet (☎800-538-5696), British Airways (☎800-247-9297), Lufthansa (☎800-563-5954) and United Airlines (☎800-241-6522)

Medicine Hat Municipal Airport, 5km/3mi west of downtown on Hwy 3 toward Lethbridge,☎403-526-4664, http://www.medicinehat.ca. Air Canada (☎888-247-2262, www.aircanada.com) offers 4 flights a day from Calgary. There is no public transit; taxi to downtown costs about $15.

Lethbridge County Airport, 8km/5mi south of downtown on Hwy 5, ☎403-329-4466, http://www.county. lethbridge.ab.ca. Air Canada (☎888-247-2262, www.aircanada.com) offers several flights a day from Calgary. There is no public transit; taxi to downtown costs about $20.

CAR RENTALS

Avis (☎800-879-2847 or www.avis. com) Hertz (☎800-263-0600 or www. hertz.com), National (☎800-227-7368 or www.nationalcar.com) and Enterprise (☎800-736-8222 or www. enterprise.com. Car rental services have counters at the airports including the smaller centres.

BY TRAIN

There is no passenger rail service in southern Alberta.

BY BUS

Greyhound Bus (☎800-661-8747; www. greyhound.ca) provides scheduled bus service to all cities and most towns in southern Alberta.

GENERAL INFORMATION

VISITOR INFORMATION

Alberta South Tourism Destination Region 3096 Dunmore Rd. SE. Medicine Hat. ☎888-486-8722. www.travel albertasouth.com offers information on attractions, accommodations, events and maps.

Chinook Country Tourist Assn. 2085 Scenic Dr., Lethbridge. ☎800-661-1222. www.chinookcountry.com features lodging, shopping, dining, recreation and other information on Southwest Alberta.

Travel Alberta's Aboriginal Tourism division ☎800-872-3782, www.travel-alberta.com/aboriginal has information on First Nations sites and activities.

ACCOMMODATIONS

♨ For a selection of lodgings, see the Address Book.

Alberta Hotel & Lodging Assn. features an online directory of more than 1,500 annually inspected lodgings and campgrounds. Online search function available. www.travelalberta.com.

Alberta Bed & Breakfast Assn. www.bbalberta.com

Alberta Country Vacations ☎866-217-2282; www.albertacountry vacation.com.

Charming Inns of Alberta ☎866-551-2281, www.charminginnsof alberta.com.

As well, contact the tourist information offices listed under each Sight heading.

RESERVATION SERVICES

Alberta Express Reservations ☎780-621-2855 or 800-884-8803. Free reservation service for some 300 hotels and motels throughout the province.

SHOPPING

Broxburn Vegetables and Café – Rural Rte. 8, Lethbridge. ☎403-327-0909. www.broxburn-vegetables.

com. *Cafe closed Sun.* Marked by a big windmill, this large farm store sells and serves its fresh produce in the on-site cafe, as well as pies made from scratch. The farm's greenhouses specialize in peppers, cucumbers, tomatoes, squash and lettuce grown without pesticides. U-pick crops include raspberries, strawberries and currants.

Head-Smashed-In Buffalo Jump
– *Near Fort Macleod. ☎403-553-2731. www.head-smashed-in.com.* The on-site museum shop offers an array of native crafts, jewellery and works of art.

Medicine Hat Clay Industries District
– *713 Medalta Ave. S.E., Medicine Hat. Closed Sun & Mon in winter. ☎403-529-1070. www.medalta.org.* The gift shop at the district's museum sells reproductions of the pottery in the form of bowls, jugs, crocks and mugs as well as apparel, books and souvenirs.

Peigan Crafts Ltd. – *In Brocket. ☎403-965-3755 or 800-800-1478. www.peigancrafts.com.* Handcrafted clothing, moccasins and other items by members of the Piikani Nation.

Southern Alberta Art Gallery – *601 Third Ave. S., Lethbridge. ☎403-327-8770. www.saag.ca. Closed Mon.* Housed in the former public library, the gallery showcases the works of its members and sells them in the gift shop, including pottery, works in blown glass, accessories, handmade soaps and other artistic creations.

RECREATION

Southern Alberta's many lakes and rivers offer opportunities for **boating** and **fishing;** beginners should preferably hire a guide or consult with a local outfitter or organizations such as the Alberta Recreational Canoe Association (☎877-388-2722, www.abcanoekayak.org) about flooding, low water levels or other potential hazards. The Milk River offers some of the most interesting desert scenery but is best paddled in spring when water is high and rocks are less exposed; the Oldman and South Saskatchewan rivers provide long stretches of placid waters that are easily explored by the inexperienced. For information about **trail rides** and guided horseback adventures, contact the Alberta Outfitters Association (☎800-742-5548 or www.albertaoutfitters.com), which offers a detailed listing of approved operators. Visitors seeking an authentic western ranch experience can head to Claresholm, 120km/70mi south of Calgary, to Skyline Ranch & Outfitting (☎403-625-2398 or www.skylineranching.com). Here in the pretty **Porcupine Hills,** you can help with ranch chores or head for the hills on a guided pack trip or daily trail ride; also offered are mountain biking, trout fishing, wildlife photography and all-inclusive vacation packages.

©Travel Alberta

Trail Riding in Medicine Hat

FESTIVALS

early Jun **Spectrum Festival:**
Medicine Hat ☎403-977-2227 http://
nonprofit.memlane.com/spectrum

mid-Jun **Cowboy Poetry Festival:**
Pincher Creek ☎403-627-5855
or 888-298-5855.
www.pincher-creek.com/agsociety

late Jun **Medicine Hat JazzFest**
☎403-529-4857
www.medicinehatjazzfest.com

mid-Jul **Rum Runner Days:**
Blairmore ☎403-563-2217
www.rumrunnerdays.com

mid-Jul **South Country Fair:**
Fort Macleod ☎403-388-4414
www.scfair.ab.ca

late Jul **Blue Grass and Country Music
Festival:** *Hillspring* ☎866-626-3407
http://gcbd.ca/blue-grass-festival

late Jul **Exhibition and Stampede:**
Medicine Hat ☎403-527-1234
www.mhstampede.com

early Aug **Doors Open & Heritage
Festival:** *Crowsnest Pass*

Midway, Rum Runner Days

©Travel Alberta

www.discovercrowsnestheritage.
com or www.frankslide.com.

mid Aug **Whoop-Up Days:**
Lethbridge ☎403-328-4491
www.exhibitionpark.ca

mid–late Aug **Taber Cornfest:** *Taber*

Address Book

🍴For dollar-sign categories, see the
Legend on the cover flap. For lodgings in
Brooks, 🍴see Alberta Badlands.

WHERE TO STAY

$ Bluebird Motel – *5505 1st St. W.,
Claresholm (40km/25mi north of Macleod
via Hwy. 2).* ☎403-625-3395 or 800-661-
4891. *www.bluebirdmotel.ab.ca.* 22 units.
🅿. Now for something completely
different: this out-of-the-way motel
attracts guests with quirky, no-holds-
barred charm. The exterior sets the
tone with a gabled blue roof on a white
clapboard building. With names such
as the Gene Autry Room, the Calgary
Stampede Room or more reassuring,
the well-ordered RCMP Room, guest
rooms are delightfully western-themed,
and sport antiques, 1930s-style
cabinets and other authentic touches.
All units have a private bathroom, a
full kitchen and large-screen cable TV;
computer data ports and fax service on
request. Pets allowed in some rooms.

$ Historic Cosmopolitan Hotel
– *13001 20th Ave., Blairmore (Crowsnest
Pass).* ☎403-562-7321. 13 rooms and
3 suites. 🅿✕. Once a bustling hotel for
businessmen here for the coal mines,
this early 20C brick block in central
Blairmore is fully renovated, still offers
great mountain scenery and is easily
accessible to Highway 3.
The street-level restaurant (**$**) serves
home cooking and lunch specials, and
the bar is friendly, with entertainment
on weekends.

$ Safe Haven Bed & Breakfast –
8126 Hwy. 3, Coleman (Crowsnest Pass).
☎403-563-5030 or 800-290-0860.
2 rooms & 1 cabin. 🅿 ⌐. This modern
establishment is furnished with sturdy,
hand-made rustic furniture, comple-
mented by soft furnishings in reposeful
colours. Each room has an en suite
bathroom, phone and high-speed cable
Internet. The two-bedroom cabin offers
a kitchen, sitting area and patio. In the
B&B living room, guests enjoy TV, music
and deep chairs. Breakfast menus are
flexible: state your preferences and your
hosts will comply.

$$ Crowsnest Mountain Resort

– *Blairmore.* ☎*403-562-7993 or 866-562-7993. www.albertaresort.com. 5 cabins. 47 RV sites.* ✖🅿. Modern rustic-themed cabins afford lovely alpine views in this tiny, former coal mining town on the Crowsnest Pass route. The cabins have one bedroom, a bathroom and a full kitchen with sitting area, satellite TV and phone. The **Lodge ($$)** serves lunch and dinner in a light-filled dining room with log walls. As the chef is Swiss, so is the cuisine, with specialties such as Zurich-style veal cutlet with a mushroom cream sauce and roesti. Also worth trying are the fondue selections, the mushroom risotto and the steaks. Swiss chocolate stars in the dessert mousse. Nearby activities include hiking, mountain biking, white-water kayaking, climbing, fishing, golfing and horseback riding.

$$ Elkwater Lake Lodge and Resort –

Off Hwy. 41, Elkwater. ☎*403-893-3811 or 888-893-3811. www.elkwaterlakelodge. com. 37 rooms, 11 condos, 6 cabins.* ♿🅿✖♨🆂🅿🅰. This four-season resort within the Cypress Hills Interprovincial Park offers 37 guest rooms, 6 cabins and 11 condominium units, with amenities that include an indoor saltwater pool. Lodge accommodations are modern and functional, but not luxurious, with kitchenettes; some have decks and fireplaces. The grounds, of course, are gorgeous: one of Canada's great parks. The **Bugler's ($$)** dining room serves Canadian fare such as bison medallions with goat cheese and roasted pumpkin, or mustard-glazed rabbit with spinach fettuccini, with perhaps a Saskatoon berry and spinach salad to start. There is a children's menu as well as a Sunday brunch; the resort's lounge offers a pub menu. The Woodstock Massage and Spa sees to guests' beauty and revitalization needs. Pet friendly.

$$ Heritage House Bed and Breakfast

– *1115 8th Ave. S., Lethbridge.* ☎*403-328-3824. www.ourheritage. net/bb.html. 2 rooms, shared bath.* 🅿🛏. Built in 1937 in the minimalist International style, this large house has Art Deco lines. The exterior evokes a sophisticated 1930s period movie, perhaps a Thin Man or Hercule Poirot feature. Set in lovely gardens with mature trees, the house has remained in the Haig family all these years. Now operating as a B&B, it overflows with family mementos and eclectic furnishings, rather than the sleek modernist pieces one would expect. Its well-preserved interior features have earned it a designation as a provincial historic site. Reservations in summer essential.

$$ Lethbridge Lodge – *320 Scenic Dr.,*

Lethbridge. ☎*403-328-1123 or 800-661-1232. www.lethbridgelodge.com. 190 rooms.* ♿🅿✖🛏. This large hotel and conference centre offers all modern amenities (indoor pool, fitness room, business facilities) and a central location in downtown Lethbridge. Room options include family suites and extended-stay suites with kitchenettes. The **Botanica ($)** restaurant offers a pleasant garden setting for light meals,

Heritage House Bed and Breakfast, Lethbridge

including dinner buffets *(Sun–Tue)*. Dinner options include steaks as well as stir-fry dishes, pasta, and breaded fish. Sunday brunch is served in the **Antons ($)** ballroom. Essies, a cowboy-themed bar and poolroom, can get pretty noisy on weekends; ask for an exterior room to avoid dreams with a deep-bass rhythm.

$$ Medicine Hat Lodge – *1051 Ross Glenn Dr. SE, Medicine Hat.* ☎*403-529-2222 or 800-661-8095. www.medhat-lodge.com. 221 rooms.* ♿🅿✕⌁Spa. This very large hotel and conference centre is almost a vacation in itself with a huge indoor water park of slides, swimming pool, wading pool and steam room. Other entertainment includes a video gaming room and casino. The Alberta Massage and Spa is an urban oasis. Rooms are modern and functional, while the bathrooms offer polished granite surfaces. The **M Grill Steakhouse ($$)** prepares generous cuts of beef as well as bison and venison with the respect Albertans give their meat. The **Jungle Cafe ($)** offers family-friendly fare of steaks and finger food. Two lounges serve drinks and noshes.

$$ Norland Bed & Breakfast – *5801 1st Ave. S., Lethbridge.* ☎*403-380-2348. www.thenorland.com. 4 rooms.* 🅿✕⌁. A bit of the Old South that found its way to Lethbridge, this three-storey 1910 mansion with a towering white portico worthy of Scarlett O'Hara stands on five-acre landscaped grounds on the edge of town, where it used to house a dairy farmer and his family. The house has 7 bedrooms, of which 4 are now used for guests; 3 rooms have private bathrooms. The decor is vaguely antebellum, but recently renovated, with modern, tiled bathrooms. Amenities include a lap pool, hot tub, fitness room and Internet. Breakfast on the deck, weather permitting, is heavenly.

$$$$ Bent Creek Resort – *11km/7mi east of Fort Macleod on Hwy. 3. Turn left on Meadowlark Rd. After 7km/4.5mi, follow sign for ranch.* ☎*403-553-3974 or 866-553-3974. www.bentcreek.ca. 4 rooms in ranch house. All meals provided.* ✕🅿⌁. Indulge your inner cowboy with rambles on horseback through spectacular range and coulee country

near Fort Macleod, where Mounties used to face down bad guys. Beginners or advanced riders can sign up for clinics to improve their horsemanship, or opt to wrangle cattle from horseback. With instruction, you will learn to sense your mount's every mood. Three homey bedrooms share a bathroom, one bedroom has en suite bathroom. The sprawling ranch house holds spacious common rooms, including a living room with a fireplace.

WHERE TO EAT

$ Cobblestone Manor – *173 7th Ave. W., Cardston.* ☎*403-653-2701or 866-653-2701. www.thecobblestonemanor.com. May–Sept closed Sun. Rest of year closed Sun & Mon (lunch & dinner only).* **Canadian.** This restaurant is located in a two-storey, 14-room stone house, originally an 1889 pioneer cabin, modified over the years by a lovelorn Belgian for a bride who never arrived. The dining room serves simple but well-prepared home-style dishes such as veal cutlets or poached salmon, but most especially Alberta steaks, including a buffalo version. The apple pie is a must-try. In summer breakfast, lunch and dinner are available. This being Mormon country, no alcoholic beverages are served. Two guest rooms **($)** are also available.

$ Macleod's Restaurant & Lounge – *271 23rd St., Fort Macleod.* ☎*403-553-8841.* **Canadian.** The decor is a little tired, but this local favourite south of town on Highway 3 delivers decent pub-style fare and pizza without breaking the bank. Pizza, chicken wings, pitchers of beer.

$ Stone's Throw Cafe – *13047 20th Ave., Blairmore (Crowsnest Pass).* ☎*403-652-2230. www.stonesthrowcafe.ca. Closed Tue.* **Canadian.** A small place in Blairmore's formerly hopping business district, this local favourite serves breakfast and lunch. Choices are sandwiches, soup and a few salads, with delicious baked goods such as fruit scones and brownies, smoothies, and a full espresso bar. Sit back, open a newspaper, smile and you'll seem like a local. Wi-Fi available. For those going on a hike, the cafe supplies box lunches.

$$ DeVine Grill – *501 3rd St. SE, Medicine Hat.* ☎*403-580-5510.Closed Sun.*

Italian. This pretty restaurant, with its terra-cotta walls and flower-filled courtyard, has been through several incarnations over the past decade, the present state being the most recent one. DeVine serves up pizzas, pastas, a range of entrées and a satisfactory wine list. Special live performances during events such as the Jazz Festival in June.

$$ La Bella Notte – *402 2nd Ave. S., Lethbridge. ☎403-331-3319. www. labellanotte.com.* **Italian.** Situated in a former fire hall, this restaurant is the buzz of the city; from its giant garage doors that are opened on nice days to the thorough wine list and seasonal variations. The menu leads with steak, of course, but has options such as the ginger sirloin, with a piquant ginger sauce and red sweet peppers. The pasta selection is extensive and inventive: try the Venezia, served with a curried coconut sauce, or the boscaiulo, with chorizo sausage, peppers and mushrooms. The hip and vibrant Red Room Lounge makes for a great night out.

$$ Paradise Canyon Golf Resort – *185 Canyon Blvd. W., Lethbridge. ☎403-381-4653 or 877-707-4653. www.playin-paradise.com.* **Canadian.** Celebrated for a challenging 18-hole golf course, this resort requires no athletic skills to enjoy its pleasant restaurant, open all day long. Service begins with hearty breakfasts, through snacks to accompany 19th-hole drinks, a lunch selection of inventive sandwiches (try the chicken wrap with pineapple chutney), and dinners that feature well-prepared steaks, pastas, seafood (salmon and halibut) and specials. Meals can be taken on the terrace overlooking the beautiful course. The resort offers one- and two-bedroom villas **($$)** plus a range of vacation amenities that include a pool.

$$ Ric's Grill – *#200, 103 Mayor Magrath Dr. S., Lethbridge. ☎403-317-7427. www. ricsgrill.com.* **Canadian.** The location of this restaurant, part of a chain in Alberta and British Columbia, requires some explanation: it sits at the top of a former water tower that once accommodated 300,000 gallons. An elevator goes to the first floor, where there is a lounge; the restaurant, with windows all around it, occupies the second floor (stairs are an option). The menu features Alberta beef and lamb, expertly grilled, with some fresh grilled tuna so you can bring an out-of-province date. The tapas menu, to accompany drinks, is extensive, and the little plates arrive in artistic arrangements. Good choices include the crispy coconut prawns or the almond crusted goat cheese.

$$ Thai Orchid Room – *336 Strachan Court SE, Medicine Hat. ☎403-580-8210.* **Thai.** For a decade locals drove to Bow River for a meal at this restaurant, which recently moved into Medicine Hat. It is garnering local accolades for its pleasant setting—in a spacious room with windows overlooking the prairie—and for a varied menu that leans towards the Indian side of Thai cooking, with curries, satays and spicy meat dishes. In the essential tradition of Thai cooking, the chef (who is indeed Thai) searches for the freshest produce and adapts recipes to what he finds. The green curry can't miss, but try the seasonal dishes.

A Bit of Geology

Southern Alberta lies within the grasslands of the Great Plains that stretch from the Gulf of Mexico through the central US and into all three prairie provinces of Canada (Alberta, Saskatchewan and Manitoba). The geological story of Southern Alberta, much of which is gently rolling rangeland, is long—with a dramatic last chapter. For millions of years, starting in the Precambrian era some 700 million years ago, a succession of oceans covered this area, and about 550 million years ago, life forms appeared in the oceans. Over the eons, dead plant life and sea creatures, along with other detritus, accumulated as layer upon layer of sediment. In the late Cretaceous period, some 100 million to 65 million years ago, most of Southern Alberta was covered by a shallow subtropical sea, in a climate much like that of the Gulf of Mexico, at about whose latitude Southern Alberta then lay. Southeastern Alberta's **Red Rock Coulee** Natural Area evidences the action of this ancient sea. In the marshes around present-day

Brooks, dinosaurs roamed and their remains are often dug out of the sediment that covered them. But water still submerged Southern Alberta, and along the edge of the sea, as it expanded and retreated over time, sand accumulated, compressing into several sorts of sandstone depending on mineral composition, that can be seen here wherever erosion has worn away upper layers of sediment. Around the **Cypress Hills,** also in southeastern Alberta, layers of sediment accumulating over millions of years built up small mountains. To the west, about 75 million years ago, colliding tectonic plates began thrusting up the Rocky Mountain Cordillera. Then about 1.8 million years ago began the Pleistocene era, during which four successive advances and retreats of ice sheets up to 2km/1.25mi thick have profoundly re-worked the landscape of all of Canada. Uniquely, the Cypress Hills, lying between the Laurentide ice sheet to the east and the Cordilleran to the west, were not completely covered. The glacial Lake Lethbridge, as it expanded and retreated, left behind great piles of sediment that today provide rich farmland. As the Wisconsin glacier retreated about 10,000 years ago, surges of meltwater carved out deep valleys at the bottom of which now flow tranquil rivers such as the Milk River, which crosses Writing-on-Stone Provincial Park, or the Oldman River, along whose bluffs lie Fort Macleod and Lethbridge. The underlying sandstone today appears in dramatic scenery that attracts tourists, while deposits of fossil fuels—coal and gas—formed by decayed plants and animals in the ancient seas, have brought wealth and the railroad to small towns from Crowsnest Pass to Medicine Hat.

A Bit of History

The first traces of human habitation in Southern Alberta go back to the retreat of the glaciers; stone tools fashioned by the Clovis people some 11,000 years ago have been found near Crowsnest Pass. Totally dependent on the buffalo for survival, aboriginal peoples followed the vast herds across the prairies and left traces of their culture at places such as Head-Smashed-In Buffalo Jump and Writing-on-Stone Provincial Park. By the late 18C, French and British fur traders were exploring central and northern Alberta, following waterways that led north; the less accessible Southern Alberta remained largely terra incognita. However, an Irish landowner named **John Palliser** (1817-1887), while on a hunting trip in 1847-48 to the American plains, became intrigued with what might lie along the long border with Canada. Coincidentally, the British government, about to take over the vast territories of the Hudson's Bay Company, wanted to know what it could expect. The Royal Geographical Society accepted Palliser's proposition to undertake a scientific expedition to explore and map out the area between the Red River Colony in Manitoba and the west coast. Between 1857 and 1860, Palliser and his party performed such a thorough job that their reports are cited to this day.

Yet Southern Alberta remained wild and unsettled; the Blackfoot resisted white encroachment, and the Canadian government fretted that Americans would move into the void and possibly annex the area, as had happened to Mexico's territory. When whisky trading with Indians was outlawed in Montana, American traders moved north to posts such as Fort Whoop-Up near Fort Macleod. The 1873 massacre of Nakoda Indians at Cypress Hills by drunken Canadian and American wolf hunters prompted the formation of the **North West Mounted Police** in 1874 specifically to tame Southern Alberta (the force was renamed the Royal Canadian Mounted Police in 1920). In 1877 the Blackfoot ceded 130,000sq km/50,000sq mi of territory, and later retreated to reserves. The opening of **coal mines** at Lethbridge in 1870 and at Crowsnest Pass in the late 19C, plus the bonanza of natural gas at Medicine Hat, followed swiftly by the arrival of the **Canadian Pacific Railway,** launched towns, and towns drew settlers. Crowsnest Pass mines were shut down by the 1980s and the last Lethbridge coal mine closed in 1957, although it is estimated that possibly 800 million tons remain to be exploited in Southern Alberta.

The region, particularly semiarid southeastern Alberta, experienced many droughts over the years, which prevented sustained agriculture and reduced community water supplies to critical levels. The Canadian Pacific Railway introduced massive irrigation systems along its rail lines in the early 1900s, including the Brooks Aqueduct, that transformed unproductive lands into areas of successful cultivation. In the late 1980s the provincial government began the Oldman River Dam project. In 1991 the **Oldman River Reservoir** was the result of the damming of the Oldman, Crowsnest and Castle rivers; the reservoir not only stores water for dry periods but also offers abundant recreational opportunities north of Pincher Creek.

In mid-2007 the future development of a $1.8 billion, eco-friendly condominium resort on **Crowsnest Lake** was announced. Designed to use solar, wind and geothermal energy, the complex, known as Bridgegate, is expected to be completed in 2010, and will consist of a hotel, casino, spa, fitness centre, shops and restaurants as well as more than 500 lakefront condominiums.

Crowsnest Pass

POPULATION 5,700 – MAP OF PRINCIPAL SIGHTS

The Crowsnest Pass across the Great Divide in the Rocky Mountains is both a spectacular natural sight and a place of great commercial and historical significance. The pass runs east-west in the valley of the Crowsnest River, which drains eastwards into the Oldman River in Alberta; as the pass lies on the Continental Divide, rivers also flow west, as does the Elk River in British Columbia. Crowsnest (elevation 1,357m/4,451ft) is one of the three major passes through the Canadian Rockies, along with the Yellowhead Pass (elevation 1,133m/3,716ft) in Jasper National Park and Kicking Horse Pass (elevation 1,625m/5,330ft) connecting Yoho and Banff national parks. The most southerly of the three and the lowest pass between New Mexico and Yellowhead, Crowsnest Pass lies on the Alberta-British Columbia border, and is traversed by a Canadian Pacific Railway line and by Highway 3, the Crowsnest Highway. The drive across is scenic, and a stop at Crowsnest Provincial Park on the British Columbia side provides an opportunity to appreciate the surroundings without worrying about the driving.

- **Information:** An Alberta Tourism visitor centre is situated in the Frank Slide Interpretive Centre (*see below*), which also provides information about the Leitch Colliery Provincial Historic Site and the Hillcrest disaster.
- **Orient Yourself:** Crowsnest Pass is situated on the Alberta/British Columbia border in the southwestern corner of Alberta; Hwy. 3—the Crowsnest Highway—crosses the pass.
- **Don't Miss:** The town of Frank, where a mountain fell on a town in 1903.
- **Organizing Your Time:** Allow at least a day in the area. If you are an outdoor enthusiast, allow more time, since there are two major ski areas, Castle Mountain near Pincher Creek and Fernie just across the BC border, which offer abundant downhill powder in the winter and mountain biking and hiking in the summer.
- **Especially for Kids:** The Frank Slide Visitor Centre does a fine job of explaining the dramatic tale to younger visitors; several of the rescued survivors were small children.
- **Also See:** THE CANADIAN ROCKIES

A Bit of History

Members of David Thompson's party first entered the pass in 1800. It had already served, for thousands of years, indigenous peoples who mined high-altitude chert here to make stone tools. Some of the oldest archaeological remains in North America have been found near Frank, stone tools bearing the distinct fluting of the Clovis People, some 11,000 years old. The name Crowsnest may be a reference to Crow Indians who "nested" here during an expedition over the pass.

Along the route the Crowsnest Highway runs parallel to the Canadian Pacific Railway line, pushed through in 1897 to permit exploitation of the coal deposits in the area. The term "Crow's Nest Pass," spelled in three words, is notorious in Canada as an agreement reached in 1897 between the Canadian Pacific Railway (CPR) and the Canadian government that set "in perpetuity" low rates for grain and flour travelling eastwards, and for agricultural products travelling west, over the pass. The agreement benefited western farmers, but left the CPR with insufficient earnings to improve the railway, rolling stock and services, so it pressed for change. Long term, the agreement also undermined western economic growth, as it was substantially cheaper to ship out agricultural products for processing elsewhere, than to build a manufacturing base in the region. After years of heated arguments, the federal government finally abrogated the agreement in 1993, compensating farmers. It is this tussle that produced the classic Prairie story: A farmer's dog dies, his wife takes sick, the well goes dry and a tornado wipes out the homestead. The farmer stands in his field, shakes his fist at the sky and cries, "Curse the CPR!"

From the late 19C until the 1980s, coal mining was the principal industry of this area, despite major disasters. The 1903 collapse of Turtle Mountain in the mining town of Frank killed 70 people, while the explosion at the Hillcrest Mine in 1914, Canada's worst mining disaster, killed 189 miners. As mining activity shifted to British Columbia, where the conditions were safer, residents looked elsewhere for their livelihoods. The municipality of Crowsnest Pass, created in 1979, incorporates little towns whose names resonate with mining history: Bellevue, Hillcrest, Frank (the smallest), Blairmore and Coleman. The economy today depends on tourism, both historical and recreational.

Sights

Frank Slide Visitor Centre★

1.5km/1mi off Hwy.3, in Frank (Crowsnest Pass). ◐*Open mid-May–mid-Sept daily 9am–6pm. Rest of the year daily 10am–5pm.* ◐*Closed Jan 1, Easter Sunday & Dec 25.* ⊜*$9.* ♿🅿✕☎*403-562-7388. www.frankslide.com.*

The sheered-off side of the **Turtle Mountain** and great boulders here and there provide dramatic witness to a natural disaster that may have been caused by mining activity exacerbating a naturally unstable site. Because water seepage continues to dissolve the limestone, the site is still monitored today. The area's indigenous people had apparently known about the mountain's instability, naming it "the mountain that moves."

©Travel Alberta

Coal Scuttle, Bellevue Underground Mine Tour

The disaster, whose cause has never been definitively established, occurred at 4:10am on April 29, 1903, when the east flank of Turtle Mountain collapsed and sent some 90 million tons of rock cascading over the coal-mine entrance and the eastern corner of the town of Frank. The rock slide covered 3km sq/1.2sq mi, burying all in its path (although the main town miraculously escaped). All 17 miners trapped underground managed to dig themselves out after 14 hours of desperate struggle, while 23 of the townspeople buried in seven houses and farm buildings were pulled out. An approaching passenger train was flagged down metres before it hit the slide. In all, 70 people, or 12 percent of the town's population of 600, perished, but after a brief evacuation, the town and mine reopened, and the Canadian Pacific quickly repaired its rail line.

The town continued to boom until 1918, when the mine closed permanently due largely to safety concerns.

Re-opened in fall 2008 after a thorough renovation by Alberta Tourism, the visitor centre provides interactive exhibits and audio-visual displays to describe not only the 1903 disaster, but also the geology and coal-mining history of the area. The museum presents displays on the 1914 Hillcrest Mine explosion, where 189 miners died at a supposedly safe site.

Besides touring the **visitor centre** and talking to the helpful guides, you will find it worthwhile to walk the **interpretive trails** (⊘allow 2hrs) around the tiny community (pop. 200), where old houses and remains of the mining days are still evident; on the tour, the ghost town of Lille can be visited. The mountain setting is, of course, beautiful, and local people are delighted to welcome tourists.

In the nearby community of **Bellevue,** visitors can take an underground tour of the West Canadian Collieries Mine, a former coal mine that closed in 1961 (access road at 21814 28th Ave. in Bellevue: helmet and lamp provided). A guide offers commentary through 300m/984ft of underground tunnels, where visitors see a coal seam, loading chute, a coal room, mining equipment and artifacts. 🐾Tours mid-May–Labour Day daily 10am–5:30pm every half hour; $9; ☎403-564-4700 or 403-563-3217; www.crowsnestpass.com/bellevuemine.

Leitch Collieries Provincial Historic Site

On Hwy. 3 at east end of Crowsnest Pass. ◷Open mid-May–Aug daily. Staff and washrooms on-site. The rest of the year, visit is self-guided and washrooms are closed. ✍Contribution requested. ♿🅿 ☎403-562-7388. www.tprc.alberta.ca.

The picturesque remains of this massive mine—one of the most advanced coal and coke operations of its day and the only completely Canadian owned and operated mine in the area—can be explored via self-guided interpretive walking trails. The mine, which opened in 1907, at its prime included 101 coke ovens, a 27m/90ft washery where the coal was cleaned of dust, and a tipple that could move from 1,000 to 2,000 tons of coal each day. Buildings of stone were meant to last, but the mine closed after only eight years as a result of several events: strikes, disagreements with the Canadian Pacific Railway, soft markets that never produced big contracts and finally, World War I.

Today what is left of the washery, mine manager's house, power plant and coke ovens stand in a neatly maintained park. The remains of Passburg, built as a community for the miners, stand 1km/.6mi west of the site, although most buildings were moved elsewhere.

Excursion

Lundbreck Falls

42km/26mi east of Crowsnest Pass, via Hwy. 3.

This provincial recreation area makes a good place to take a break. Right alongside the road, near the bridge over the Crowsnest River, you can see the swift-flowing waters plunge 12m/39ft over flat-topped rocky outcroppings. Steps beside the road lead down to the river.

Pincher Creek

POPULATION 3,666

Located east of Crowsnest Pass, along Highway 6, about 7km/4mi south of Highway 3, this small community of less than 4,000 residents bases its economy on agriculture, natural gas and wind generation. Apparently a horse-shoeing tool was left near a creek by Montana gold seekers en route to Kootenay in the late-1860s; the North West Mounted Police found the rusted pincers in 1874 and named the creek for them. Their horse ranch eventually grew into a settlement that took on the same name. In 1906 the town was incorporated.

🛈 **Information:** Pincher Creek Chamber of Commerce, 1037 Bev McLachlin Dr. ☎403-627-5199. www.pincher-creek.com.

▶ **Orient Yourself:** Main Street is intersected by Hwy. 6A, south of Hwy. 6. Bev McLachlin Dr. is also a major downtown street.

🅿 **Parking:** Attractions have designated parking.

🕓 **Organizing Your Time:** Allow a day to enjoy the sights.

Kids **Especially for Kids:** Kootenai Brown Pioneer Village.

Sights

Kootenai Brown Pioneer Village★

1037 Bev McLachlin Dr. Log building, Pioneer Place, on Bridge Ave. serves as the entrance to the village. 🕓*Open mid-May–mid-Sept daily 10am–6pm. Rest of the year Mon–Fri 10am–4:30pm.* 💲*$6.* 🅿 ☎*403-627-3684. www.telusplanet. net/public/kootenai.*

Kids Set in a spacious, tree-shaded park near the centre of town, a dozen restored historic buildings, several moved from other locations, feature displays, furnishings and artifacts of

Southern Alberta's pioneering 1890s. The cabin of famed frontiersman **John George "Kootenai" Brown** (1839-1916) *(♨see sidebar)* forms the centerpiece of this re-created log village.

The original building serves as a **museum** with displays on topics ranging from antique guns and ammunition to First Nation Peigan culture; even a period dentist office has been replicated. Sparsely furnished with a few hand-hewn pieces, the **Kootenai Brown cabin** served as the home of Brown and his second wife in the Waterton area until 1911. The sturdy **Doukhobor barn**★ was rescued from

Kootenai Brown Pioneer Village

©Travel Alberta

Kootenai Brown

Irish-born **John George Brown** (1839-1916) was known across Western Canada as a pioneer with a heart and a respected rebel. After military service in India, he prospected for gold in British Columbia, surveyed land, rode for the Pony Express, and hunted wolf and buffalo. He also worked as a guide and scout. Brown was 26 years old when he trod an aboriginal trail through South Kootenay Pass. His good standing with the local Kootenay tribe gave him his nickname. Local lore has it that he was wounded by a Blackfoot arrow and pulled it out on his own. He was captured by Sitting Bull and a band of Sioux, but the wily frontiersman escaped, as he did from many other escapades. Acquitted of murder in Montana in 1877, he eventually settled in the Pincher Creek and Waterton areas of Southern Alberta. With his wife and children in tow, he ran a trading post in Waterton for many years, but later turned to ranching and fishing. Self-appointed promoter of this part of Alberta, Brown became a conservationist and politician, pushing for Waterton's status as a national park. He served as the park's first superintendent until his death in 1916. Brown was buried on the shore of the lower Waterton Lakes.

flooding during construction of the Oldman River dam; Doukhobors came to Alberta in the early 1900s to escape persecution in Russia. Vintage buggies, farm tools, butter churns and horse tack can be viewed in the barn. Moved from nearby Fishburn, the one-room **school-house** was built in 1894 and used until 1963. The 1894 ranch house from the former 100,000-acre Walrond cattle ranch features a collection of **antique saddles**★ as well as exhibits on area ranching. A blacksmith shop, a log NWMP outpost, a bathhouse, laundry, and other structures as well as a quarry car, can be seen. An exhibit on the Canadian Pacific Railway is passed en route to an authentic CPR caboose. Don't miss the outdoor display of century-old, horse-pulled farming machinery on the grounds.

Lebel Mansion

696 Kettles St. ◷*Open Jun–Aug daily 9am–noon & 1pm–5pm. Rest of the year Mon–Fri 1pm–5pm.* ☎*403-627-5272.*
Completed in 1910 this spacious, three-storey brick house was the residence of a local businessman and later served as a hospital. The name is believed to stem from the French *la belle,* meaning "the beauty." In its corner turrets and decorative veranda, the structure embodies Queen Anne features as well as an element of French Canadian architecture in its multiple roofline. The mansion now serves as the home of the local arts council. Visitors are welcome to take

Oldman Dam

©Travel Alberta

a self-guided tour of the building during its hours of operation and view the works on exhibit in the art gallery.

Additional Sight

Oldman Dam Provincial Recreation Area

Hwy. 785, off Hwy. 3, about 10km/6mi north of Pincher Creek. Dam at southeast end of reservoir after Hwy.785 curves right. ○Open daily year-round. ☎403-627-5554.

Completed in 1991, the 76m/249ft-high earth-and rock-fill dam impounds the waters of the Oldman, Crowsnest and Castle rivers. The view of the dam's spillway is especially dramatic. The 2,429ha/6,000-acre recreational area edges portions of land along the Oldman River Reservoir, providing campgrounds, RV sites, picnic areas, hiking trails, boat launches and beaches for public enjoyment. The most extensive recreational facilities are found at the dam site in the Boulder Run, Windy Point and Island View day-use areas.

Fort Macleod★

POPULATION 3,072 – MAP OF PRINCIPAL SIGHTS

Situated 165km/102mi south of Calgary, this small town edges the Oldman River along Highway 3. The river derives its name from a Blackfoot legend about a spirit in the form of an old man living in the mountains. Today Fort Macleod is a thriving agricultural community. Grain is grown with the aid of irrigation, thanks to the Oldman River Dam near Pincher Creek, and cattle are raised on the ranchland of Porcupine Hills to the west. The prairie surrounding the town has been inhabited for thousands of years, as witness the Carmangay Tipi Rings Provincial Historic Site north of Fort Macleod and west of the town, Head-Smashed-in Buffalo Jump, where natives regularly drove buffalo over a cliff for millennia. Fort Macleod is famous for two historic sites—the buffalo jump and a reconstructed North West Mounted Police fort.

- ⓘ **Information:** Tourism Information Centre, east end of Main St. Open Victoria Day–Labour Day daily 9am–5pm. ☎403-553-4955. www.fortmacleod.com.
- ▶ **Orient Yourself:** Fort Macleod lies at the intersections of Hwy. 2 (the Edmonton-Lethbridge Hwy.), and Hwy. 3, the Crowsnest Hwy. Main downtown streets within the historic core are 23rd Street (Chief Red Crow Blvd.) and 24th Street (Col. Macleod Blvd.) and 2nd and 3rd avenues.
- Ⓟ **Parking:** Major attractions have designated parking.
- ○ **Organizing Your Time:** Don't overlook Fort Macleod's lively downtown core, with its frontier buildings, shops and restaurants.
- Kids **Especially for Kids:** The Musical Ride at the Fort Museum should thrill kids; they can also visit the stables.
- ⓖ **Also See:** GREATER CALGARY

A Bit of History

The town was the site chosen for the first NWMP post in the West, established only one year after the force's founding in 1873. In 1874 men were quickly trained at Fort Dufferin, Manitoba, to stop the illegal whisky trade and border incursions, such as the one that had led to the Cypress Hills Massacre the pre-

vious year. Dispatched from Fort Dufferin in October, the band of weary men arrived at the notorious Fort Whoop-Up (ⓖ *see Lethbridge*) after a long and arduous trek from Manitoba. Providentially they found it abandoned by its rowdy inhabitants. The expedition commander, Col. **James Macleod,** who was also the force's assistant commissioner, was unable to negotiate a purchase

Empress Theatre, Fort Macleod Historic District

price with the fort's lone caretaker, so he moved the men west where they built permanent barracks on an island known as Blackfoot Crossing, on the Oldman River. The celebrated Mountie **Sam Steele** spent time at the fort, before the headquarters were moved to Fort Walsh in Saskatchewan (*see Cypress Hills Interprovincial Park*) in 1878. The island post was occupied until 1884, when the garrison moved to the south side of the river.

The downtown area, with some 30 historic buildings dating to the early 20C, was designated the province's first Provincial Historic Area *(walking tour brochure available from tourism centre; guided tours Jul–Aug, call to book ☎403-553-2500)*. Among the landmarks is the 1910 **Empress Theatre** *(235*

Sam Steele

The title of most famous Mountie belongs without doubt to **Sir Samuel Benfield Steele** (1849-1919), known as Sam Steele. His exploits in bringing law and order to the Prairies and the Yukon without, it is said, ever firing his gun contributed to uniting a far-flung nation. Born near Orillia, Ontario, then a frontier town, Steele was reared to be a soldier and early on sported a ferocious moustache. A graduate of the Royal Military School in Toronto, Steele had a colourful military career pursuing Fenian raiders along the US border and Louis Riel's troops in Manitoba before joining the newly formed North West Mounted Police as a Troop Sergeant Major in 1874. He participated in the famous March West that established order and Canadian sovereignty in Southern Alberta. For more than 20 years Steele, promoted to superintendent in 1887, chased criminals, horse thieves, smugglers and rebels while diplomatically resolving disputes among Indians, Métis and settlers. In 1898, during the Klondike gold rush, he was dispatched to the Yukon to do the same thing there.

In 1900, as the Boer War raged, Sam Steele led a cavalry unit to South Africa, where he set up the South African Constabulary. While commanding Canadian troops in Britain during World War I, Steele died of influenza, in bed, which no doubt surprised him. In the nick of time, King George V had knighted him. In June 2008 it was revealed that Sam Steele's personal papers, hidden away in family attics in Britain, had been purchased by the University of Alberta for $2 million. The ceremony to hand over the papers was held at Trafalgar Square, presided over by Prince Edward, stopping London's rush hour traffic for seven minutes.

Main St.; guided tours Jul–Aug daily 2:30pm & 4:30pm depart from the lobby; ☎403-553-4404 or 800-540-9229;www.empresstheatre.ab.ca), the province's oldest continually operating theatre; it hosts a May chamber music festival, a full summer theatre program and concerts all winter.

Sights

Fort Museum★

On Hwy. 3, one block from centre of town. 219 25th St., Fort MacLeod. ⊘*Open Jul–Labour Day daily 9am–6pm. Jun daily 9am–5pm, last 3 wks May Tues–Fri 9am–5pm, Sept–mid-Oct Wed–Sun 10am–4pm.* ✆*$8.* ♿☎*403-553-4703 or 866-273-6841. www.nwmpmuseum.com.*

The museum is dramatically set behind a palisade of sharpened stakes, with blockhouses at the four corners. Life on the North West Mounted Police post has been well re-imagined, with reconstructed buildings, demonstrations, displays of artifacts and audio-visual presentations. Modern **dioramas** show how early settlers and aboriginal peoples lived, explain the arrival of the railway and the development of ranching, and give a lively description of the force's own history.

Inside the wooden, palisaded walls stand a number of log structures. A lawyer's office and an early church are reconstructed, with fascinating information about the actual people who occupied these places. The re-created interior of the **chapel** typifies those of log churches built throughout Alberta during its early settlement. Named for a trader named Fred Kanouse who survived a bullet in a scuffle at Fort Whoop-Up, the **Kanouse Trading House** has walls of poplar tree logs and a sod roof that vividly evoke the hardships of early settler life: imagine living under a mud roof when it rained, or in the hot summer when dust drifted down continuously. The first post on Blackfoot Crossing Island was just such a building, and even brave Sam Steele found it miserable. An original building on its original site, the Kanouse House holds a museum of commerce, showing how the whisky trade evolved into proper businesses. The **Mounted Police Building** houses a model of the first fort and exhibits about the police. In the Dispensary, primitive equipment and instruments such as those used by area doctors is on view.

The **Centennial Gallery** contains a superb collection of native arts and crafts. Because aboriginal peoples moved constantly to follow the buffalo, they could not create large artworks, but instead adorned themselves and decorated their housewares and implements. The gallery describes the ancient origins of this art, but concentrates on artifacts from 1860-1930, when aboriginal peoples cleverly adapted materials and

©Travel Albertaa

The North West Mounted Police at the Fort Museum

RCMP Musical Ride

There are few more colorful and fitting tributes to the country's heritage than the RCMP Musical Ride, a tightly choreographed ballet performed by scarlet-clad Mounties on horseback. This show is a highlight of summer visits to historic Fort Macleod, the site of Canada's first Musical Ride demonstration in 1876, three years after the mounted police force was formed. The show has its roots in a stylized variation of British Army cavalry drills, which evolved during peacetime into elaborate demonstrations of horsemanship set to the music of regimental bands. Today, the Musical Ride is performed around the world at 40 to 50 venues each year.

Each show involves 32 horses with riders wearing traditional red serge uniforms. Manoeuvres named Diamond, Bridal Arch, Cloverleaf and Maze are just a few of the complicated movements. The pinnacle of the show is the Charge, when horses break into a gallop while riders lower their ceremonial lances. Under tradition set by an early RCMP commissioner, all Musical Ride horses are black, usually thoroughbreds though some Hanoverians are also used. Fort Macleod's Musical Ride is performed amid the faded log slats of the 1874 RCMP Fort Museum's ceremonial grounds. Presented four times a day, shows last 30min *(Jul–Labour Day Wed–Mon 10am, 11:30am, 2pm & 3:30pm, weather permitting)*. *For more information:* ☎403-553-4703 *or www.nwmpmuseum.com.*

techniques learned from white men to go off in new artistic directions.

In 1870s Alberta, horses were a vital means of transportation. They were invaluable to the work of the North West Mounted Police. The [Kids] **stables** at the Fort Museum are open to visitors, weather permitting *(Jul–Labour Day Wed–Mon 9am–4pm).*

In summer riders dressed in the police uniforms of 1878 (red jackets, black breeches, white pith helmets) perform a [Kids] **musical ride** in the central parade grounds (see sidebar).

Head-Smashed-In Buffalo Jump★★

18km/11mi northwest by Hwy. 785 (Spring Point Rd.). Open mid-May–mid-Sept daily 9am–6pm. Rest of the year daily 10am–5pm. Closed Jan 1, Easter Sunday, Dec 24–25. $9. ☎403-553-2731. www.head-smashed-in.com.
This buffalo jump, a UNESCO World Heritage Site since 1981, has the most extensive deposits of butchered bones (11m/33.5ft deep) of any jump in North America. For more than 5,500 years, buffalo were driven to their deaths over this cliff to provide the food, shelter and tools necessary for the survival of the Plains Indians: meat, hides for clothing

and shelter, and bone for scrapers and needles.

Before the arrival of horses and firearms in North America, hunting the buffalo was very dangerous work, as hunters had to creep into the herd to make the kill close-up with spears and arrows. A jump, of which some 150 have been found on the continent, made the hunt much more productive. Even with horses and guns, people often died; the redoubtable **George McDougall** (1821-1876), the missionary who set up Methodist churches at Fort Edmonton and Victoria Crossing, was killed on a hunt. The aboriginal jump consisted of the vast gathering basin where the buffalo grazed; the wide path, or drive lanes marked by hundreds of stone cairns, into which the animals were funneled; the drop; and then a very large area for butchering and processing the kill, all accomplished with stone knives and tools, some of which have been recovered from the site. The meat was dried on racks, while bones were boiled in pits to render out grease; grease, fat and meat were pounded together to make **pemmican,** a nutritious food that remained edible for years. The jump, which is only about 10m/30.5ft high, did not kill the buffalo, but only broke their legs; they were dispatched and butchered at the bottom. At Dry Island

Cliff at Head-Smashed-In Buffalo Jump

Buffalo Jump Provincial Park near Red Deer (𝒞 *see Red Deer*), the higher jump actually killed the animals.

Built into the sandstone cliff, a dramatic **interpretive centre** contains excellent displays on five floors about the history and culture of the Blackfoot people, based on archaeological evidence, as well a film *(10min)* on buffalo-hunting cultures. Stand near a taxidermied buffalo in the interpretive centre to get an idea of the size of these beasts, up to 2m/6.6ft tall at the shoulder and weighing up to 910kg/2,000lbs. A vivid **diorama** shows three buffalo about to go over the jump. Displays explain the mechanics of the hunt. Western and traditional native food such as Blackfoot fry bread or *iimistsikitaan*, is served in the cafeteria.

Outside, paths lead to the top of the cliff, where visitors are afforded a spectacular **view**★★ of the vast grassy, largely treeless surroundings; at the bottom, visitors can follow another trail to the area where the buffalo were skinned and

Tepee Camping

Tepee Camping at Head-Smashed-In Buffalo Jump

If you've always wondered what it would be like to sleep in a tepee (or tipi), here's your opportunity to find out. Overnight and two-night tepee camping is available *(mid-May–mid-Sept)* at Head-Smashed-In Buffalo Jump. The site is remote enough to assure a starry night, if the weather is clear. Bring your own sleeping bag or rent one there *($15/night)*. Canvas tepees, inflatable air mattresses, camping stoves and flashlights are supplied, and showers are available at the interpretive centre. You'll help set up a tepee, dine on buffalo burgers and buffalo stew with bannock, listen to Blackfoot legends around the campfire, and take a guided walk before a breakfast of fry bread and Saskatoon berry jam. Lunch and a guided hike to a nearby archaeological dig site revealing aboriginal petroglyphs are included in the two-night package *(90-day advance reservations requested; for cost and other information ☎403-553-2731 or www.head-smashed-in.com)*.

Great Canadian Barn Dance

You can't help but kick up your heels at this sprawling, family-run resort sitting in the tiny hamlet of Hillspring, about 50km/30mi southwest of Fort Macleod. The popular country compound, recognizable by its huge, gambrel-roofed barn, makes a great escape for people of all ages.

Among the fun activities is a country BBQ dinner of Alberta roast beef with potatoes, baked beans and all the trimmings. Live music by the Kunkel Family band gets people toe-tapping on the main floor of the 94-year-old barn. Upstairs in the dance hall, people from all over the province, country and beyond learn the two-step or line dance. Once your feet have lost their dance fever, take a horse-drawn **wagon ride** around a small lake, before retiring to your B&B lodge, cottage or RV campground on the premises.

The facility also hosts year-round special events such as an annual bluegrass festival and regular Family Fun Dances. *Tickets for the barn dance and dinner are $27.50 adults; $20 for youth 10-17, $7.50 for children age 9 and under. Camping/dance packages are available. For directions and details, call ☎403-866-626-3407 or access www.gcbd.ca.*

Great Canadian Barn Dance, Hillspring

©Travel Alberta

processed. Archaeological work on this rich site remains in progress, and visitors can observe active digs.

Every Wednesday during summer, **drum and dancing** performances are held on the plaza at the interpretive centre *(Jul-Aug 11am & 1:30pm)*. Every Sunday year-round, workshops and activities offer visitors the opportunity to try their skill at native handicrafts; registration is required, but there is no charge for classes, except in some cases for materials.

It is possible to stay overnight in a tepee on the site, have lunch the next day and hike to an archaeological excavation *(see sidebar Tepee Camping)*.

Claresholm

POPULATION 3,850

This quiet town of nearly 4,000 people is often bypassed by motorists heading to Lethbridge or the Crowsnest Pass. Split in two by north-south Highway 2, it makes a practical stop for gas or a snack at the service stations and convenience stores lining the route. Visitors who detour one block west to downtown are rewarded by well-preserved heritage buildings housing cafes and shops; several are adorned with elaborate **murals** paying homage to the town's history and location "where the wheatfields meet the range." Claresholm was born when the railway between Edmonton and Calgary was extended south to this agriculturally rich area in 1891. Its residents come from diverse backgrounds; their pioneer ancestors arrived from distant places like North Dakota, Oregon and Minnesota, as well as Eastern Canada, in response to a massive late-1800s advertising campaign ("Canada West—free homes for millions.") by the federal government that was designed to populate the Prairies. West of town, Highway 520 leads through a stunning stretch of the Porcupine Hills, a range of foothills between the plains and the Rockies that stretches from Nanton, known for its antique stores, south to Head-Smashed-In Buffalo Jump near Fort Macleod. The forested hills shelter moose, elk, deer, beaver, turkey and other wild denizens.

- **Information:** Visitor Information Centre in Claresholm Museum, 5126 1st St. W. (east side of Hwy. 2). Open late-May–early-Oct, daily 9:30am–5:30pm. 403-625-3131. Town office: 403-625-3381. www.townofclaresholm.com.

- **Orient Yourself:** Claresholm lies at the junction of Hwy. 2 and Hwy. 520; it is 40km/25mi north of Fort Macleod. The downtown core sits just west of Hwy. 2 and is centred on 2 St. W.

- **Organizing Your Time:** Allow at least a half day to appreciate the attractions.

- **Especially for Kids:** At the museum, Claresholm's first schoolhouse.

Sight

Claresholm Museum

5126 1st St. W. (east side of Hwy. 2) in train station. Open late-May–early Oct daily 9:30am–5:30pm. Contribution requested. 403-625-3131.

Housed in a historic sandstone railway station (1886), this museum portrays daily life in a prairie town in the late 19C; exhibits include a dentist's office and train ticket office. Claresholm's first **schoolhouse** (1903) sits on the site.

The museum serves as the town visitor information centre; a walking tour guide is available of the town's historic buildings.

Excursion

Willow Creek Park

About 34km/22mi northwest of Claresholm, via Hwy. 2 to Stavely, then west on Hwy. 527, cross Pine Coulee; at four-way intersection turn left, go over the canal and Willow Creek and at the three-way intersection, turn left (paved road all the way). Open May–Oct (call in advance for hours). 403-549-2218.

Snug within the Porcupine Hills, this former provincial park was for centuries a traditional camping and hunting place for Blackfoot tribes; several tepee rings can be found in the area—notably at Carmangay—and a rim of cliffs where buffalo were often stampeded to their death. Tree-fringed Willow Creek beckons bathers, and along its banks, bird watchers and hikers. The day-use area is especially popular with families.

Cardston

POPULATION 3,452 – MAP OF PRINCIPAL SIGHTS

Bisected by Lee Creek, this small town, 25km/16mi north of the Montana border, is an important Mormon centre. It was founded in 1887 by Charles Ora Card, a son-in-law of Brigham Young, and his followers, who arrived by wagon from Utah. Also known as the Church of Jesus Christ of the Latter-Day Saints, the sect was established in 1830 by Joseph Smith (1805-44) at Fayette, New York; its doctrine is based on the Bible, the *Book of Mormon* and Smith's writings. After Smith's death, most of his followers moved to Utah under the leadership of Brigham Young, establishing Salt Lake City in 1847. The Mormons contributed much to Southern Alberta's prosperity, building at the end of the 19C a network of irrigation canals using water from the nearby St. Mary River; this system, now much expanded and reputedly the largest irrigation district in the country, has made Lethbridge and surrounding communities thriving agricultural producers. Cardston's economy is agrarian-based, and the city is justly proud of its million-dollar agricultural and equestrian centre, the large Agridome, which occupies 8ha/20acres on the outskirts of town; many rodeo events take place there in its indoor arenas such as barrel races and roping demonstrations. Other than several Mormon Church notables, the town's most distinguished former citizen was Fay Wray (1907-2004), the glamorous actress carried by King Kong to the top of the Empire State Building in the 1933 movie.

- **Information:** Tourist Information, 67 3rd Ave. W. ☎403-653-3366. www.town.cardston.ab.ca
- **Orient Yourself:** Downtown Cardston is centred on north-south running Main Street and east-west 3rd Avenue.
- **Parking:** Parking lots provided; street parking downtown also available.
- **Don't Miss:** The Remington Carriage Museum is one of the world's best of its kind.
- **Organizing Your Time:** As the Mormon temple cannot be visited, the most important stop is the carriage museum, where at least 2hrs are needed.
- **Especially for Kids:** Carriage rides at the Remington Museum, which also has several displays and programs just for children.

Remington Carriage Museum

©Travel Alberta

Sights

Town Centre

Along the Cardston's wide boulevards lie early 20C homes and buildings, including the **Carriage House Theatre** *(353 Main St. ☎403-653-1000. www.the carriagehousetheatre.com)*, opened as the New Palace Theatre in 1912 but much modified today; people congregate from considerable distance to watch theatre performances, dinner theatre in the summer, and movies. Charles Ora Card's first home, a tiny **log cabin,** still stands near the town centre and can be visited *(✆open July–Aug 1:30pm–5pm; ☎403-653-3366)*, as can the 1907 sandstone **courthouse,** now a museum, where visitors can see the original judge's bench, witness stand and even the jail cells *(89 3rd Ave. W.; ✆open July–Aug 9am–12:30pm; ☎403-653-3366)*.

Remington Carriage Museum★★

Kids *623 Main St. ✆Open mid-May–mid Sept daily 9am–6pm. Rest of year daily 10am–5pm.✎$9; seasonal carriage ride $4.
♿✕🅿 ☎403-653-5139. www.remington carriagemuseum.com.*

This museum houses some 250 restored carriages, wagons, sleighs and other vehicles displayed in a vast, 5,900sq m/63,000sq ft building. The collection was started as a Rotary Club project by Don Remington, who collected 45 vehicles before persuading the provincial government to build the museum. Most carriages are on loan from the Glenbow Museum in Calgary.

In the exhibit area, 16 displays showcase 55 remarkably well-restored carriages, standing in historical context as if ready to head off at a moment's notice. Other carriages are on view in an adjacent storeroom. Most of the carriages in the collection were found in the west, and are ranch vehicles, such as wagons and carts. However, elegant carriages are also present: anyone who enjoys historical drama or literature will appreciate viewing close-up a "victoria" or a "phaeton." Non-motorized hearses, omnibuses, hansom cabs, school vans, sleighs and stagecoaches occupy plenty

Cardston Alberta Temple

of space, so visitors can see them from every angle. Highlights include a late-19C bullwagon, a veteran from the Oregon Trail; a sheepwagon, the Great Plains version of a mobile home; and a Concord stagecoach. Explanatory panels clear up questions about vintage and purpose. Also among the displays are a fire hall and a complete **carriage manufacturing works,** with an explanatory video *(8min)*, as well as the workshop where the carriages are restored.

Out in the spacious courtyard, Clydesdale, Canadian or quarter horses are hitched to vehicles, and visitors can ride about, imagining days of bonnets and top hats. Interactive and audio-visual presentations and a carriage **restoration shop** tell the story of the evolution of transportation from pioneer wagons and buggies to motorized vehicles.

Cardston Alberta Temple

348 Third St. W. ⚊Temple not open to the public. Visitor centre ♿ ✆open mid-May–Labour Day daily 9am–9pm. ☎403-653-3552.www.ldschurchtemples. com/cardston.

This white-granite structure features stark vertical lines and horizontal supports that reference the pueblo architecture of the American southwest and Aztec pyramids from Mexico, with perhaps a touch of Frank Lloyd Wright. The imposing building sits on 4ha/10acres of landscaped lawn near the centre of town. Started in 1913 and completed in 1923, this temple was the first one constructed outside of the US, and remains one of the few Mormon temples in Canada, where the church is most active in Ontario, Alberta and British Columbia.

Lethbridge★

POPULATION 81,692 – MAP OF PRINCIPAL SIGHTS

Located 216km/134mi southeast of Calgary, Alberta's fourth largest city overlooks a wide riverbed cut by the Oldman River. Constructed into the side of this riverbed are the striking buildings of the University of Lethbridge, and crossing over it is the dramatic High Level Railway Bridge, 1.5km/1mi long and 96m/314ft high, constructed by the Canadian Pacific Railway in 1909. The city is the centre of a productive agricultural region. Widespread irrigation and the relatively mild winters moderated by the warm chinook winds have made the cultivation of hay and grain crops for livestock feed as well as of vegetables, canola (also called rapeseed, a food oil seed) and sugar beet, very profitable. Lethbridge also prospers from food processing plants, particularly flour milling and production of potato products. Also thanks to irrigation, intensive livestock operations, particularly cattle and hogs, provide employment in transportation and processing. Wind, sunshine and cultivation of biofuels today mean energy, and Lethbridge is working with other Southern Alberta cities to develop an alternative energy industry.

- 🛈 **Information:** City offices, 910 4th Ave S. ☎403-329-7355. www.lethbridge. ca. Chinook County Tourist Assn., 2805 Scenic Dr. ☎403-320-1222 or 800-661-1222. www.chinookcounty.com.
- ▶ **Orient Yourself:** Lethbridge is a highway hub: Trans-Canada Hwy. 3 passes through the city while Hwy. 2, connecting to Calgary and Edmonton, meets Hwy. 3 some 30km/19mi to the west. Several provincial highways also pass through. Downtown is situated off Scenic Drive.
- 🅿 **Parking:** Permitted parking times vary in the downtown area; check signage.
- ☺ **Don't Miss:** Stroll through the city's lovely parks, trails and walking paths, especially in the Oldman River Valley.
- 🕐 **Organizing Your Time:** Lethbridge is a pleasant place to stop for a night or weekend base camp to explore the area.
- **Kids Especially for Kids:** Fort Whoop-Up.

High Level Bridge

Susan Mate/Michelin

Nikka Yuko Japanese Garden

©Travel Alberta

A Bit of History

Once the summer hunting territory of the Blackfoot, the Lethbridge area was settled after 1870 when coal deposits were discovered in the valley. The first mine was established by Sir **Alexander Galt** (1817-1893), a prominent Canadian politician, and his son; Galt laid out the city's first street plan and is remembered in several local place names. The community thrived when the Canadian Pacific Railway sent a spur to the North Western Coal and Navigation Company's mine in 1885; the town was named in 1884 after the company's president, William Lethbridge. It is thanks to its strategic position as a CPR divisional point linked to the US via Montana, the Crowsnest Pass into British Columbia and to markets in eastern Canada that the city prospered as Southern Alberta's commercial centre. The notorious Fort Whoop-Up, a whisky and firearm trading post located not far west of the city, gave the area a certain lively reputation.

Founded in 1967 the University of Lethbridge, with campuses in Calgary and Edmonton, is particularly strong in the sciences and information technology and has a notable program for integrating aboriginal students; it has some 7,500 full-time students.

The city is proud of its extensive park system, with pathways linking the green spaces. The Oldman River valley is largely given over to an extensive network of parks, paths and recreation areas, with kayaking, canoeing and boating on the water.

Sights

Nikka Yuko Japanese Garden★

Mayor Magrath Dr. and 9 Ave S, next to Henderson Lake. ⏰*Open Jul–Aug daily 9am–8pm. Mid-May–Jun & Sept–mid-Oct daily 9am–5pm.* ⏣*$7.* ♿ 🅿 ☏*403-328-3511. www.nikkayuko.com.*

The city built this lovely 1.6ha/4-acre garden in 1967 as a symbol of Japanese-Canadian amity (*Nikka Yuko* is formed from the words Nihon, Kanada, and yuko, meaning "Japan-Canada friendship"). The garden was designed by landscape architect Tadashi Kubo and installed by Masami Sugimoto, both from Osaka Prefecture University in Japan. It is a wonderfully serene place where visitors can gain an appreciation for traditional Japanese landscape architecture, as interpreted through features such as rocks and prairie plants found in southwestern Alberta. Water, a preoccupation in this irrigated rangeland, bubbles and flows throughout the garden. The structural elements, such as the pavilions, bridges and the bell-tower, were shipped from Kyoto.

The garden was prompted by an unfortunate event in Canadian history, which still pricks the national conscience. When Canada declared war on Japan in

1941, about 22,000 Japanese-Canadians living on the West Coast were placed in internment camps in central British Columbia and Alberta, although in many cases they were Canadian citizens. About 6,000 of these were resettled in Lethbridge, where most chose to stay after the war.

Five types of formal landscapes are linked by meandering paths. At the centre of the garden lies a **pavilion** of Japanese cypress wood, overlooking a calm pond and laid out for a tea ceremony. In the distance, the "borrowed view" glimpsed along pathways incorporates the adjacent Henderson Park and the shores of its lake.

Henderson Park

Adjacent to the Nikka Yuko Japanese Garden. ⏰*Open year-round dawn-dusk.* Situated near the city centre, this 47ha/117-acre park surrounds a 24ha/60-acre man-made lake that offers children an opportunity to fish in summer and skate in the winter. Although swimming is not permitted in the lake, the park has a nice pool with a grassy border for sun-bathing.

Fort Whoop-Up★

In Indian Battle Park, access from west end of 3rd Ave. S. off Scenic Dr. ⏰*Open Jul–Aug Tue–Sun 10am–5pm. April–May & Oct Wed–Sun 1pm–4pm. Rest of the year Sat–Sun 1pm–4pm.* ⏰*Closed major holidays.* ⬟*$7.* ♿☎*403-329-0444. www.fortwhoopup.com.*

📷 In the deep valley of the Oldman River stands a replica of this once-notorious whisky trading post, whose proud motto is "Founded by Scoundrels." A visit here today offers a glimpse of how the Canadian West was won, rescued from a band of Americans and their illegal dealings by the newly formed Mounties.

The scoundrels in question, employees of the T.C. Power Company, hailed from Fort Benton, Montana, and the site's official name was **Fort Hamilton,** after one of the company owners. The operation flourished from 1869 to 1874, the most important of many forts that sprang up all over Southern Alberta and Saskatchewan in the early 1870s to trade furs and

other goods as well as to market illegal liquor and firearms, hence the sobriquet Fort Whoop-Up. The post attracted Indians from far and wide to trade buffalo skins, furs and indeed almost anything for a particularly lethal brew bearing little resemblance to whisky: ingredients included chewing tobacco, red peppers, Jamaican ginger and black molasses, as well as alcohol. In 1873 the Canadian government formed the **North West Mounted Police** to put an end to this American encroachment into Canadian territory and to stop a trade that was demoralizing the Indians. In October 1874 the force arrived at the gates of Fort Whoop-Up, only to find it abandoned except for one lone caretaker. The subsequent founding of Fort Macleod nearby, and of Fort Calgary the following year, effectively ended the illegal trade and brought law and order to the West. Fort Whoop-Up continued legal operations, with Mounties renting space within the fort, until at least 1890, after which the buildings deteriorated and were swept away in a flood.

The reconstructed fort (not on the original site, which was nearer Fort Macleod) flies the trading flag of the original T.C. Power Company; it was the flying of this non-British flag that raised concerns about sovereignty and brought in the Mounties. Below it, wooden buildings form a fortified enclosure, defended by canons; living conditions inside the fort were crowded and rough, and the many artifacts collected over the years give a good idea of daily life. Interactive exhibits tell the complex story not only of the fort, but also of the North West Mounted Police, the Blackfoot and the settlers who replaced the whisky traders. Intriguingly, the tough guys liked to be photographed and their grim-jawed portraits form one of the most arresting portions of the exhibits. In the visitor centre, a video *(20min)* presents the history of the post in the context of the development of the Canadian West.

Galt Museum and Archives

502 1st St. S. ⏰*Open mid-May–mid-Sept daily 10am–6pm. Rest of the year daily 10am–4pm.* ⏰*Closed Jan 1, Easter Sunday, Dec 31.* ⬟*$5.* ♿🅿☎*403-*

320-4258 or 866-320-3898. www.galt museum.com.

The vast glass windows of the 2006 expansion to this municipal museum look out over the prairie and the escarpments of the Oldman River Valley, including the High Level Bridge and the buildings of the University of Lethbridge. The sturdy brick original building, built in 1891 and once a hospital, provides quite a contrast. With a sizeable volunteer staff to augment the professionals, the museum specializes in the history of southwest Alberta, with a 20,000-artifact collection and a large archives. The museum's name is derived from that of the hospital built by Sir Alexander Galt, a Canadian politician and Father of Confederation, who with his son, established the first coal mine on the Oldman River and thus became co-founder of the city of Lethbridge, although he didn't live here.

The permanent collection in Discovery Hall includes mostly personal possessions of settlers, miners and the 6,000 Japanese-Canadians evacuated here from the west coast during World War II. Many of the articles are clearly family heirlooms, and interesting stories are attached to them, providing a vivid insight into prairie life.

Great Horned Owl

©Travel Alberta

opportunity to take part in guided visits with the birds and most especially to have an owl or falcon perch on your arm or shoulder; some visitors get to hold a captive-bred, just-hatched chick.

Picture Butte

30km/18mi north of Lethbridge by Hwy. 3 to Hwy. 25 north, then east on Hwy. 519. The ranching town of Picture Butte, which bills itself as "the Livestock Capital of Canada," sits at the junction of Highways 519 and 843.

Prairie Acres Heritage Village

3 A St. (Hwy. 843), 1.6km/1mi south of town. ⏱*Open daily year-round.* ♿🅿🎟*403-329-4758, www.picturebutte.ca/visitors.* 🎟*$5.*

Known locally as the Prairie Tractor and Engine site, the "village" is a collection of heritage buildings and farm machinery that embodies the trades and daily life of bygone times. The highlight is the display of more than 100 antique tractors, combines, threshers, binders and other farm equipment as well as old automobiles at the Farm Equipment Museum. The Prairie Tractor and Engine Society restored the on-site structures, several of which were moved here; they include a Canadian Pacific Railway station, a post office, a garage with a vintage gasoline pump, a homesteader's shack and a one-room school. Every year since 1982, the society has hosted an annual jamboree and **threshing show** the third week-

Excursions

Alberta Birds of Prey Centre

15km/9mi west of Lethbridge, in Coaldale. From Hwy. 3 turn left at second traffic light, cross the tracks and follow the signs. ⏱*Open mid-May–mid-Oct daily 9:30am–5pm. Bird programs* 🎟*$7.* 🎟*403-345-4262. http://members.shaw.ca/colin.weir/index.htm.*

This conservation and rehabilitation centre is devoted to the care and rehabilitation of raptors such as falcons, many varieties of owl, eagles, hawks and other birds of prey. An interpretive building showcases wildlife art, and wall displays explore the history, lifecycle and habitat of the birds.

Outside, visitors can wander within the 28ha/70acres of wetlands along several trails past cages of injured birds under rehabilitation. The highlight is the

end in August. Plowing and threshing demonstrations, rope making, horse and tractor pulls and a parade are some of the fun events.

Picture Butte Reservoir

Just north of town, off Hwy. 843.

Not far from town, this reservoir is a nesting site for geese and other birds, which can be seen from a tangle of **walking trails.** During fall migration hundreds of white pelicans, Canada geese and American coots have been counted here in one day. There's also good fishing on the reservoir—it's not unusual to land a 10-pound pike.

Lethbridge Corn Maze

Robin Pick Berry Farm, just south of Picture Butte; follow signs to the corn maze. ⏱*Open Aug–late-Oct daily.* ⬛*$8; without maze $3.* ✕ ♿ 🅿 ☎*403-381-3775. www. lethbridgecornmaze.com.*

🧒 The maze at the Robin Pick Berry Farm is open from August until late October. The farm's 2.8ha/7acres delight young and old as they wind their way through the labyrinth of towering rows of corn. A different pattern is carved by the farm's owner into the corn each year. There are also hayrides, a kid-sized maze, bale jumping contests, a pumpkin slingshot, a petting zoo, a pumpkin patch and picnic areas.

Writing-on-Stone Provincial Park★

MAP OF PRINCIPAL SIGHTS

Well off the beaten path, this 1,780ha/4,400acre park near the Montana border is notable for its remarkable carvings made by aboriginal peoples on the soft sandstone cliffs, for which it has been designated a National Historic Site. As well, a reconstructed North West Mounted Police outpost meant to deter trouble that never arrived offers insight into the often bleak life of a prairie cop. The landscape affords magnificent vistas of sweeping grasslands stretching over deposits of sandstone formed along the shoreline of a Late Cretaceous-era (100-65 million years ago) sea. A fine provincial park campground draws big summer crowds due to its location along a shallow and gentle section of the Milk River. The park offers children's and interpretive programs, a beach, showers, firewood, amphitheatre, fire pits and a playground. RV travellers are provided power hookups and sewage disposal.

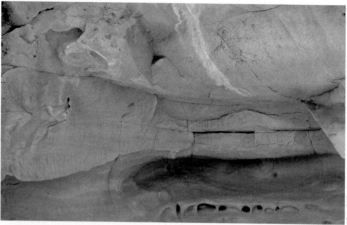

©Travel Alberta

Thunderbird Cave, Writing-on-Stone Provincial Park

Information: ☎403-647-2364. http://gateway.cd.gov.ab.ca.

▶ **Orient Yourself:** The park lies some 80km/50mi southeast of Lethbridge via Hwy. 4 to the town of Milk River, then east 32km/20mi via secondary road 501, and 10km/6.25mi south on secondary road 500. All roads are paved.

Parking: Designated parking at the site.

Don't Miss: If possible, take one of the guided rock art tours.

Organizing Your Time: Unless you are camping, plan a day trip from Lethbridge. The park also offers camping, canoeing and kayaking, swimming at a beach, hiking and fishing. There are no food services at the park. Be sure to bring along plenty of water and a picnic lunch.

Especially for Kids: The park has a swimming beach and recreational areas.

A Bit of Geology

As the glaciers receded more than 10,000 years ago, the meltwaters created a surging torrent that ripped out a great valley with steep sandstone cliffs, badlands and coulees, through which the peaceful Milk River, which arcs across the Montana border into Alberta, now flows south to meet the Missouri. The river's cloudy colour, the result of the sediment it carries, caused Lewis and Clark, they when observed it in Montana during their 1804-1806 expedition, to name it the Milk River. In many spots, harder rocks called cap rocks, sitting like hats on the top of softer stone, have protected the column underneath from being worn away by erosion, forming the weird monuments called **hoodoos.** More distortion takes place as harder rock deposits fall out of the sandstone columns, forming holes that are then worked further by erosion. These eerie shapes mystified settlers (the word "hoodoo" comes from "voodoo") and caused the indigenous peoples to consider the area sacred. Along the river cluster leafy stands of poplar, cottonwood and willow trees, as well as bushes such as wild roses, chokecherry, juniper and Saskatoon berry. Sage and cactus dot the grasslands, where profusions of wildflowers bloom.

Some 100 species of birds have been sighted in the park, where the thick greenery offers nesting spots for songbirds. Marmots and beaver are often seen, along with the occasional pronghorn antelope, mule deer, muskrat, coyote, or mink. Rattlesnakes are not uncommon. In the southern distance, particularly from the lookout of the new visitor centre, visitors can glimpse the three jagged buttes of the Sweet Grass Hills (max. elevation 2,291m/6,983ft) of Montana over the flat prairie.

It was through this splendid landscape that the Blackfoot and other aboriginal peoples followed the buffalo for 10,000 years, leaving on sheer sandstone cliffs **carvings** and **rock paintings** that describe the important events in their existence up to 3,000 years ago. A generally accepted transliteration of the Blackfoot name of the area is A'i'sinai'pi.

Visit

Park open year-round. Visitor centre open Jun–Aug daily 9am–7pm, last 2 wks May & Sept–early Oct Thu–Mon 9am–4:40pm. ☎403-647-2364. http://gateway.cd.gov.ab.ca.

The stunning new (2007) $3.2 million A'i'sinai'pi **visitor centre** overlooking the Milk River valley has made an excursion to this beautiful park even more rewarding. The circular building, with its traditional eastward facing door to catch the morning sun, was designed in consultation with the Mookaakin Cultural and Heritage Society, a Blackfoot public education group. The centre offers interactive exhibits on the history and culture of the Blackfoot and the history of the North West Mounted Police. In the tepee-shaped theatre, a film *(7min)* shows images of the park.

The Pictographs★★

By guided tour (2hrs) only Jul–Aug daily 10am and 2pm, mid-May–Jun & Sept–early Oct daily 2pm. Tour includes a short shuttle-bus ride. 👁 *$8. Tickets from visitor centre 1hr before tour.*

Guided interpretive tours are the only means to view most of the art, which is within an archaeological preserve. However, the short, self-guided **Hoodoo Trail** permits visitors a view of some of the largest and best of the artwork. Carvings and some pictographs in red ochre found on the sheer sandstone cliffs form the most extensive pictographs on the North American Plains, dating back some 3,000 years and continuing until the late 19C. Some 50 sites contain several thousand figures, many depicting humans; the more ancient figures, carved with bits of bone, carry shields, while more recent figures, carved with metal tools, ride horses, introduced here in the early 18C, at which point shields were abandoned. Scenes are clearly depicted, and after a little prompting by guides, it is possible to pick out the story being recounted, such as battle scenes or hunts. Some scenes can be dated to a specific time, based on oral traditions of battles. Due to the natural processes of erosion, the art is slowly being worn away, despite protection afforded by the park.

North West Mounted Police Outpost

👁 *Visits by guided tour (3hrs) only, depending on availability of staff.*

Deep within the park, near the Montana border but visible from the visitor centre, is a white frame building, a 1977 reconstruction of a North West Mounted Police outpost based on archaeological evidence from the original building that was destroyed by fire. The interior is furnished to approximate the year 1897. The group of 275 Mounties who traveled from Manitoba to found the post at Fort Macleod camped here for four days in September 1874, and some of them scratched graffiti into the rock art. In 1887, a summer police outpost was established here to control whisky trading, native horse stealing raids, and incursions from Montana; a permanent frame building was erected in 1889. A police post was maintained until 1918.

Tepee Rings

Phantom remains of an ancient nomadic way of life, tepee (or tipi) rings are found throughout the Prairies—often along river courses, where aboriginal peoples used to set up their conical tepees. These portable, tentlike dwellings consisted of three or four tall, sturdy lodge poles over which buffalo skins were stretched. The bottom edges of the skins were anchored to the ground with heavy rocks; when the tepee was dismantled and taken away, the circle of stones remained. Often, discarded tools and weapons indicate the age of the ring: rings found along the South Saskatchewan River date to 5,500 years ago. Sometimes tepee rings surround a medicine wheel; 46 such wheels have been found in

Tepee, Medicine Hat

Alberta. These cairns, some of which were started thousands of years ago, may mark the burial of famous warriors or may have cosmological meaning. Notable traces of encampment can be seen north of **Carmangay Provincial Historic Site** *(62km/39mi north of Lethbridge, via Hwy. 23; interpretive signs on-site)*, where nine circles of stone stand along the Little Bow River. A stone arrowhead found here dates the encampment to between AD 200 and 1700. Tepee rings are also located at **Head-Smashed-In Buffalo Jump** *(see Fort Macleod)*. Thousands of rings dot Southern Alberta, where they are treated with reverence; many people here have found them on their property.

Taber

POPULATION 7,000

This one-time coal-mining town is famous in Canada for its abundant crops of sweet corn, which along with sugar beets, have made the community an important contributor to Alberta's economy. The introduction of large-scale irrigation in the early 1900s transformed Taber's hot, dry real estate into an agriculture breadbasket. Taber corn is a hot commodity every August and September, when it is sold in grocery stores, markets and food stands across the province. (Roadside vendors in Calgary are required by law to display a permit proving the corn was grown in Taber.) The Taber Sugar Beet Factory is Alberta's only sugar producer; its sugar-beet crops benefit from the region's hot, sunny days and cool nights. A service and supply centre for the oil and gas industry, the town has used income from this base to help build recreational facilities, geared to its youth (30 percent are age 15 and under), including a skateboard park, and sports fields, tennis courts and baseball diamonds at Confederation Park *(corner 50th Ave & 50th St.)*. The annual Cornfest, held in late August, celebrates the harvest with a fair, a fun run, pancake breakfasts, kids' games and hot-air balloon rides.

- **Information:** Town Office 4900A 50th St. ○Open Jun–Sept Mon–Fri 8am–4pm. Rest of the year Mon–Fri 8:30am–4:30pm. ○Closed major holidays. &☎403-223-5500, www.taber.ca.com.
- **Orient Yourself:** 51km/32mi east of Lethbridge, along Hwy. 3, just west of north-south Hwy. 36.
- **Especially for Kids:** The Aquafun Centre's waterslide.

Sight

Aquafun Centre
4712 50th St. ○Public swims daily 1pm–3:30pm & Mon–Fri 7pm–8:30pm. ☞$5; family and multi-use passes available. ✕&P☎*403-223-5500.*
Situated within the community centre, this recreational complex boasts three water features: a pool with a 70m/200ft **waterslide,** a children's play lagoon, and a rapids channel. State-of-the-art saltwater technology is used to disinfect the water, and its salinity is kept at the same level as fluid around the human eye to reduce irritation. A sauna, steam room and hot tub appeal especially to adults. The community centre also is home to two ice arenas, a four-sheet curling rink, a private health club, an archery range and a 600-seat auditorium for concerts and other special events.

©Travel Alberta

Pools at Aquafun Centre

Brooks

POPULATION 13,581

Situated 100km/62mi north of Taber by way of Highway 36, Brooks is a community of just under 14,000 people, many of whom are engaged in the city's economic mainstays of livestock, grain and vegetable production. Brooks benefits from long-time extensive irrigation of the area as well as large deposits of natural gas; a number of oil and gas firms maintain regional offices here. With the coming of the Canadian Pacific Railway in the early 1880s, settlement began in earnest. To further develop the area, the CPR initiated large-scale irrigation projects in the early 20C, which included the nearby Brooks Aqueduct, now a provincial historic site.

A meat-packing facility, one of the largest in the country, is a major employer in the area, and western Canada's largest producer of ring-neck pheasants is located in Brooks: the Canadian Pheasant Company raises more than 200,000 of these birds annually. On the second weekend in June, the community heads to the local rodeo grounds for the annual Brooks Kinsmen Rodeo, which includes a parade, pancake breakfasts, midway rides and a greased pig chase in addition to rodeo competitions.

- **Information:** ☎403-362-3333. www.brooks.ca. The visitor centre is in the Brooks & District Museum, 568 Sutherland Dr. (near Cassils Rd.). Open late-May–Labour Day daily 8:30am–5pm. ☎403-362-5073.
- ▸ **Orient Yourself:** Brooks sits just west of the junction of the Trans-Can Hwy. and Hwy. 542 (Cassils Rd.). The downtown edges the north side of One-Tree Creek along 1st Ave. between Centre St. on the east and 3rd St. W.
- **Don't Miss:** Brooks Aqueduct and Lake Newell.
- **Organizing Your Time:** Allow a minimum of one day for this area, with an overnight stay. Spend a half day at Lake Newell. Dinosaur Provincial Park lies 40km/25mi north (*see Alberta Badlands chapter for description*).
- **Especially for Kids:** The caboose and fire truck at Brooks & District Museum.

Sights

Brooks & District Museum

568 Sutherland Dr. ◷Open late May–Labour Day daily 8:30am–5pm. ☎403-362-5073.

In a grassy, treed compound, half a dozen historic buildings, transport vehicles, farm machinery and other artifacts illustrate life in the area between 1900 and 1950. In the museum building, exhibits range from irrigation and ranch life to the war years. A re-created dentist's office displays medical instruments, and a replica of the interior of a 1910 general store is stocked with early 20C goods; note the ornate cash register.

On the grounds, restored structures moved here from other sites include a schoolhouse, barn, blacksmith shop and NWMP outpost. A CPR **caboose** sits near the train station; also of interest are a 1903 oil rig and a 1941 **fire truck**.

Crop Diversification Centre South

301 Horticultural Station Rd. E., 3km/1.8mi east of Brooks. ◷Open year-round Mon–Fri 8:15am– noon & 1pm–4:30pm. 🅿☎403-362-1300.

Spread out over 128ha/316 highly productive acres in the midst of semiarid short-grass prairie, this research centre exists to keep Alberta's producers at the forefront of today's horticultural and agricultural markets. It is also a delightful place to visit if you like gardening. CDCS maintains four farms, a 10,500sq ft laboratory, research and production greenhouses, a machine shop and a storage area.

Brooks Aqueduct and Interpretive Centre

Early in the 20C, the Canadian Pacific Railway built an irrigation system to water its millions of acres in Southern Alberta. As part of the irrigation plan, **demonstration farms** were established along the rail line. In 1918 this site was created as the headquarters farm; by 1935 it had become a tree nursery and breeding ground for native plants as well as a research facility for horticultural crops. That same year, the CPR divested itself of the irrigation business; the provincial government later took over management of the farm and acreage. Construction of new state-of-the-art greenhouses to replace those that are 40 years old is expected to be completed in 2009.

Visitors are welcome to tour the rose garden, rock garden, arboretum, and pinetum with its conifers, some of which were planted in the 1950s.

Kinbrook Island Provincial Park
13km/8mi south of Brooks via Rge. Rd. 14.5 to Lake Newell Resort Rd. ◷Open year-round. ☎403-362-2962.

A portion of this tree-dotted park occupies an island in one of Canada's largest man-made lakes. **Lake Newell** covers 117sq km/45sq mi, inviting a host of water sports such as canoeing, kayaking, windsurfing, swimming and water-skiing. Anglers have plenty of fish to go after like rainbow trout, brown trout, lake whitefish, northern pike, walleye

and yellow perch, to name a few. There are hiking and biking trails as well. Three sanctuaries attract migrating birds; some 250 species have been sighted at the park, including great blue herons, common terns, American white pelicans and cormorants. The marshes are home to ducks, coots, geese and other waterfowl, and deer and antelope inhabit the forests.

Brooks Aqueduct
About 7km/4mi southeast of Brooks, off Rge. Rd. 14.2. ◷Open mid-May–Labour Day daily10am–5pm (call to confirm the site is open). ☎403-362-4451 (summer) or 403-653-5139. http://culture.alberta.ca.

A component of the Canadian Pacific Railway's irrigation system for the area, the 3.2km/2mi-long aqueduct took two and a half years to build and was in use from 1915 to 1979. Constructed of steel-reinforced concrete, the flume was held 20m/66ft above the valley by massive concrete columns. From the beginning there was leakage, and over time natural forces such as wind, frost and hail caused deterioration, but it did deliver the water that made area crops thrive. Today modern pipelines and canals have rendered the aqueduct outmoded. It stands, however, as a remarkable engineering feat and a testament to the ingenuity of its builders.

The provincial historic site has a small interpretive centre and a picnic area.

153

Medicine Hat

POPULATION 56,997 – MAP OF PRINCIPAL SIGHTS

Thanks to its setting at the junction of three rivers, the driest city in Canada, surrounded as it is by semiarid prairie terrain, benefits from a dramatic cityscape of escarpments and coulees, interspersed with green parks. The Seven Persons River and Ross Creek empty into the South Saskatchewan River here, providing a green oasis in an area that receives just 230mm of rain, but 2,512 hours of sunshine a year. Medicine Hat maintains an extensive park system and 92km/57mi of trails along its watercourses; during the hot summer months, the South Saskatchewan River is dotted with boaters. The beautifully restored brick and sandstone heritage buildings downtown house retail shops, cafes and restaurants. Oil and gas as well as agriculture are the primary sources of the city's wealth, with manufacturing and information technology developing from these natural assets as well as from the community's fortunate location on a Canadian Pacific Railway line and the Trans-Canada Highway.

- **Information:** Tourism Medicine Hat, 8 Gehring Rd. S.W. near the Saamis Tepee. ⏱Open mid-May–Aug Mon–Fri 8am–7pm, Sat–Sun & holidays 9am–5pm. Rest of the year Mon–Fri 9am–5pm, Sat 10am–3pm. ⏱Closed major holidays in winter hours. ♿☎403-527-6422 or 800-481-2822. www.tourismmedicinehat.com.
- ▶ **Orient Yourself:** Located on Trans-Canada Hwy. 1, Medicine Hat is a sprawling city. Streets run east-west, while avenues are north-south. The east-west boundary is Division Ave.; the north-south is the South Saskatchewan River.
- 🅿 **Parking:** Permitted parking times vary in the downtown area; check signage.
- ⊛ **Don't Miss:** A stroll through the historic downtown district.
- ⏱ **Organizing Your Time:** Allow at least a day to visit Medicine Hat. It provides a good base for visiting Cypress Hills Interprovincial Park, which requires another full day.
- 🧒 **Especially for Kids:** Clay Industries National Historic District.

A Bit of History

Originally a North West Mounted Police fort and later a CPR construction camp, the city was founded in 1886. Gas deposits discovered in 1883 when the CPR was drilling a well have since been revealed as one of the world's largest reserves; Rudyard Kipling, during a 1907 stop in the city, described these deposits as "all hell for a basement." But it was these gas deposits that literally fueled the city's industrial growth. The name Medicine Hat refers to the eagle-feather bonnet *(saamis)* worn by Blackfoot medicine men, but why the name applies to this site, long a meeting place for tribes following buffalo herds, is pure conjecture; the CPR chose it. Locals tend to call their city "The Hat."

A century ago, the clay deposits along the river launched a now-defunct clay pottery industry, and today the 60ha/150-acre Historic Clay District provides a lively insight into the daily activities of workers here. To the southeast some 45km/28mi lies lovely Cypress Hills Interprovincial Park, while the vast grasslands of Canadian Forces Base Suffield, which includes a 458sq km/177sq acre National Wildlife Area *(⊘ public access prohibited)*, are 56km/40mi northwest. CFB Suffield, 2,690sq km/1,039sq acres in total, is the largest expanse of unplowed grassland on the Canadian Prairies.

Sights

Esplanade Arts and Heritage Centre

401 1st St. S.E.; ☎403-502-8580; www.esplanade.ca.
Opened in 2005 the centre presents concerts, exhibitions and other events in

Saamis Tepee

a 750-seat state-of-the-art theatre and the smaller Studio Theatre. A museum (◔open Mon–Fri 9am–5pm, weekends & holidays noon–5pm; ◔closed Dec. 25-26 & Good Friday; ◗$4, free Thu; ☎403-502-8582) displays exhibits about area history and artifacts related to the cultural history of aboriginal peoples, settlers and business enterprises of the area. An art gallery (◔same hours and conditions as museum) displays works by regional artists or art related to the area, as well as travelling exhibits.

Saamis Tepee★

Off Trans-Canada Hwy. ◔*Open year round. Self-guided walking tours of the Saamis archaeological site.* ☎403-527-6422, or 800-481-2822. www.tourism medicinehat.com.
Built to commemorate First Nations during the 1988 Winter Olympics in Calgary, the tepee (or tipi), 58m/36ft, or about 20 storeys high, is the city's most visible landmark. "Saamis" is a Blackfoot word referring to an eagle tailfeather used for feather bonnets, and is the origin of the town's name. Within the open-sided structure is a series of ten storyboards, each painted by a different aboriginal artist, recounting legends about the area and customs of First Nations people. Originally sited at Calgary, where the Olympics were centred, the structure

was purchased by a Medicine Hat businessman, brought here and significantly modified to make it structurally more solid to withstand the area's sometimes brutal winds and winter cold. Nearby, in Seven Persons Coulee, is a buffalo jump where an archaeological dig has uncovered arrowheads and stone tools. A self-guided walking tour is a pleasant expedition.

Medicine Hat Clay Industries National Historic District★

Museum: 713 Medalta Ave. S.E., off Hwy. 41A South. ◔*Open mid-May–Aug daily 9:30am–5pm. Rest of the year Tue–Sat 10am–4pm.* ◔*Closed major holidays.* ☞*Guided tours mid-May–Labour Day daily 10am & 11am, and hourly from 1pm–4pm.* ◗$10. ♿ 🅿 ☎403-529-1070. www.medalta.org.
This large museum, which also takes in a 61ha/150-acre section of the city where pottery factories once flourished, celebrates an industry that grew up around the providential combination of deposits of stoneware clay along the South Saskatchewan River, abundant natural gas to fuel kilns and a railway to haul the heavy products to markets across Canada.
Initially, a local brick-making operation evolved into a manufacturer of clay products such as sewer pipes, tiles and

Red Rock Coulee Provincial Natural Area

chimney flues, for which there seemed to be an insatiable market. Alberta Clay Products, the city's colossus of clay, founded in 1907, created Medicine Hat Potteries in 1937 to make crockery (pitchers, pots, dinnerware, spittoons, artware, teapots etc.) for domestic use; the company's symbol, stamped onto each piece, was an Indian with a feather in his sombrero. Alberta Clay Products' great rival was Medalta Potteries, established in 1912, whose image was an Indian in a full feather bonnet. While Alberta Clay concentrated on the western market, Medalta had great success shipping stoneware crockery to Ontario and points east. Labour-intensive clay industries employed many local people, another reason for nostalgia about their heyday. By the 1960s most pottery making had ended; Hyland, the last company, closed in 1989. Today, items manufactured by these companies are collectors' items, traded on E-Bay.

A brick plant still operates in the district, while the Medalta and Hycroft China (the successor to Medicine Hat Potteries) factory complexes, across the street from each other, can be visited as part of the museum. The site includes children's programs and a gift shop, where reproduction of the pottery can be purchased, along with pottery classes and exhibits.

Excursion

Red Rock Coulee Provincial Natural Area

About 60km/37mi southwest of Medicine Hat by Hwy. 3 to Seven Persons, then Hwy. 887 south.

⊘ Caution: this is rattlesnake territory. Vehicles are not permitted on the natural area.

A coulee is a deep ravine or gulch carved out of the land by water erosion. Many of Alberta's coulees resulted from the rushing meltwaters of glaciers. The lunar-like topography at this natural area is distinguished by remarkable, round **boulders,** rather like big loaves of brioche dotting the terrain; their reddish colour derives from iron oxide. The formations are sandstone concretions, measuring as much as 2.5m/8ft in diameter, making them among the largest such formations in the world. Created by the withdrawal of ancient seas, the concretions increased in size as swirling waters deposited more layers of sand, iron oxide and calcite around their cores, which were accumulations of fossilized shells or bones.

Cypress Hills
Interprovincial Park★★

MAP OF PRINCIPAL SIGHTS

Straddling the Alberta-Saskatchewan boundary, north of Montana, the plains give way to rolling, forested hills cut by numerous coulees, valleys, lakes and streams. These verdant hills rise prominently in the midst of otherwise unbroken, sunbaked, short-grass prairie. On their heights grow the tall, straight lodgepole pines favoured by Plains Indians for their tepees or lodges—thus the name. The trees were probably mistaken by early French voyageurs for the jack pines (cyprès) of eastern Canada. A bad translation compounded the error, and the name Cypress Hills was born. The Cypress Hills area covers some 2,500sq km/965sq mi, while the park encompasses the highest part of the Cypress Hills, with 204sq km/79sq mi on the Alberta side and 182sq km/70sq mi on the Saskatchewan side.

- **Information:** Park office at Elkwater Lake. Visitor centre ☎404-893-3777 (Alberta) or ☎306-662-5411 (Saskatchewan). Visitor centre ☎403-893-3833. www.cypresshills.com.
- **Orient Yourself:** Cypress Hills lies on the Alberta/Saskatchewan border, some 66km/40mi southeast of Medicine Hat via Trans-Canada Hwy. 1 and Hwy. 41 South, about 70km/43mi north of the state of Montana.
- **Don't Miss:** Displays in the new visitor centre at Elkwater Lake.
- **Organizing Your Time:** Devote a full day to the park; pack a picnic lunch or plan to eat at the on-site cafe.
- **Especially for Kids:** Farwell's Trading Post at Fort Walsh re-creates frontier life.

A Bit of Geology

The hills present unique geographical features. The highest elevations in Canada between Labrador and the Rocky Mountains, they rise to a maximum elevation of 1,460m/4,450ft, or nearly 600m/1,970ft above the surrounding prairie, providing an area of cool breezes, where balsam poplar, white spruce and aspen trees, along with the lodgepole pine, thrive in an ecosystem more like that of the Rocky Mountains than the plains. Unlike the Rockies, these hills were not formed by jostling tectonic plates, but rather by the slow accumulation of sediment over eons. Elsewhere on the prairies, this accumulation was displaced by succeeding ice sheets but here, uniquely, a 200sq km/80sq mi area at the top 100m/62.5ft level protruded as *nunatuks*, or mountain tips, over the Wisconsin-Laurentide ice sheet, which covered most parts of Canada with ice more than 1km/.6mi deep. The hills form a divide between two great watersheds: the Hudson Bay and the Gulf of Mexico. Streams flow south to the Missouri-Mississippi system and north to the South Saskatchewan River, Lake Winnipeg and Hudson Bay. The flora and fauna of the hills offer remarkable diversity. Wildflowers and song birds normally associated only with the Rockies flourish here, cactus grows on the dry, south-facing slopes and orchids thrive beside quiet ponds.

A Bit of History

In 1859 John Palliser, exploring the western domains for the Royal Geographical Society, described this area as "A perfect oasis in the desert we have travelled." Aboriginal peoples wintered here to escape the cold prairie winds and to hunt abundant game. Archaeological research has found traces of human habitation going back some 6,800 years, and visitors in the 19C observed that

View from Horseshoe Canyon, Cypress Hills Interprovincial Park

the area was inhabited by Nez Perce, Assinaboine, Cree and Métis. In the late 19C, settlers found the hills ideally suited for ranching, a vocation the area maintains today.

In the early 1870s, several trading posts were established in the Cypress Hills by Americans from Montana. In exchange for furs, they illegally traded, among many other items, "firewater," an extremely potent alcoholic brew. In 1873 Nakoda Indians camped near the trading post of Abel Farwell were joined by a party of Canadian and American wolf-hunters, whose horses had been stolen by Cree raiders. Thinking the Nakoda were the thieves, the drunken "wolfers" attacked the Indian camp on June 1, 1873, killing 36 people. When news of this massacre reached Ottawa, then-Prime Minister Sir John A. Macdonald acted quickly. He created the **North West Mounted Police** (renamed the Royal Canadian Mounted Police in 1920) and dispatched them to the Northwest to stop such border incursions and end the illegal whisky trade. The perpetrators of the massacre were arrested but later acquitted for lack of evidence. However, the fact that white men had been arrested impressed the Indians and helped establish the force's reputation.

Visit

Park office at Elkwater Lake. For road and trail conditions check at park office ☎403-893-3777(Alberta) or 306-662-5411 (Saskatchewan). ⏱Park open year round. Visitor centre open mid-May–Labour Day daily 9am–7pm. Rest of the year Thu–Sun 9am–4pm. ♿✕☎403-893-3833. www.cypresshills.com.

For thousands of years Cypress Hills has offered a welcome recreation area in the midst of a sere landscape. In the past, aboriginal people rested and hunted here. Today, vacationers arrive from far and near to enjoy the extensive recreational facilities. The 14 **hiking trails** of varying difficulty, several of which are also used for cycling and cross-country skiing, take visitors through the woodlands, around the lake and along streams. The Trans-Canada trail system spans the park across 29km/18mi. ♿Shoreline Trail and Soggy Bottom Trail are wheelchair accessible. The park also offers **swimming** at Elkwater Lake *(Jul–Aug 11am–6pm)* as well as boat and bike rentals. Seventeen campgrounds, three of them open year-round, provide some 692 campsites. Hidden Valley Ski Area, a small alpine ski resort on the Alberta side, offers a 1,400ft elevation and one quad chairlift. The family-oriented nine-hole Cypress Hills Golf Course (☎306-662-4422; ⚲$20 green fee) is located on the Saskatchewan side.

The new **visitor centre** at Elkwater Lake provides an excellent introduction to the park, and interpretive programs are offered all year. Birdwatchers will appreciate the 220 species of birds sighted here, including the yellow-bellied sapsucker, the ruby-crowned kinglet and the Oregon junko. Animals that may be sighted include white-tailed and mule deer, moose, elk, bobcat and many small creatures such as red squirrels and porcupines. Some 700 plant species, including 18 species of orchid, flourish here.

From Elkwater Lake an interesting drive (40km/25mi) leads past **Horseshoe Canyon** to **Head of the Mountain,** which affords pleasant views of coulees and hills as far as the Sweet Grass Hills and Bear Paw Mountains of Montana. The drive proceeds to Regsor Lake and the park boundary. This road continues to Fort Walsh, approximately 18km/11mi south, just across the Saskatchewan border. Within the park are a general store, a cafe, a resort hotel (⚲See Address Book), boat and bike rentals at the Loch Leven Marina, two gas stations and some snack counters. Visitors so inclined can bring their own horses to the West Block camping area. The nearest substantial town is Maple Creek, Saskatchewan.

Fort Walsh National Historic Site★

In Saskatchewan, 52km/32mi southwest of Maple Creek by Hwy. 271. ◷*Open mid-May–Labour Day daily 9:30am–5:30pm (in Sept, call for hours).* ⚲*$10.* ✕⚲☎306-662-3590. www.pc.gc.ca.

A part of Cypress Hills Interprovincial Park since 2000, this North West Mounted Police post, named for its builder, **James Walsh,** lies near the site of the Cypress Hills Massacre. From 1878 to 1882 it was the force's headquarters, established to deal with the influx of Nez Percé and Lakota Indians displaced by fighting over the border in the US. The post was closed once the First Nations people were established on reserves. In 1942, the Royal Canadian Mounted Police (RCMP) opened the Remount Ranch here to raise and train the famous black horses used in the Musical Ride; the ranch closed in 1967, but the buildings are now part of the reconstructed fort. At the **visitor centre** displays and films provide a good introduction to an area where remains of ancient abo-

Sitting Bull in Canada

In 1876 a force of Sioux warriors under their great chief, Sitting Bull, exterminated an American army detachment under Gen. **George Custer** on the Little Big Horn River in southern Montana. Fearing reprisals from the enraged Americans, Sitting Bull crossed into Canada with nearly 5,000 men. Inspector **James Walsh** of the North West Mounted Police was given the difficult task of trying to persuade the Sioux to return, in order to avoid war between the Sioux and their traditional enemies, the Cree and the Blackfoot, who inhabited the region. Riding into the sizable Sioux encampment near Wood Mountain (350km/217mi east of Fort Walsh) with only four constables and two scouts, he informed

Portrait of Sitting Bull (c.1885)

US Library of Congress

Sitting Bull that he must obey Canadian law. Although this act of bravery won the respect of the chief, it was four years before Sitting Bull consented to return to the US to live on a reservation.

Ranch Getaways

$ Brown Creek Ranch Vacations – *Claresholm*, ☎403-625-4032. *www.brown creekranchvacations.com.* Cabins, RV and tent camping. Trail rides, cattle care and other farm work. All-inclusive packages or self-catered/B&B options.

$$ Bent Creek Western Vacations – *Fort Macleod*, ☎403-553-3974. *www.bent creek.ca.* Cabins, host house, RV camping. Branding, roping, riding lessons, cattle drives, nature excursions, hourly trail rides for non-guests. Hosts speak English, French and Cree.

$$ Lucasia Ranch Vacations – *Claresholm*, ☎403-625-2295. *www.lucasiaranch. com.* Cabins, lodge or host house. Branding, riding lessons, team roping, cattle drives, hourly trail rides for non-guests with the Rockies as a backdrop. Also hiking and bird-watching in 4,000 acres of open range.

$$ Rangeview Ranch Vacations – *Cardston*, ☎403-653-2292. *www.rangeview ranch.com.* Rustic log cabins, tepee and RV camping. Branding, roping, riding lessons, cattle drives, hourly trail rides for non-guests. Also guided and self-guided hiking, rafting, swimming, bird-watching.

$$ Sierra West Ranch Vacations – *Lundbreck*, ☎403-628-2431. *www.sierrawest-777.com.* Self-catered log cabins, tepees, RV and tent camping. Outfitter tents with cots or beds available. Situated on Todd Creek near the base of the Livingstone Mountain Range. Trail rides, cattle drives, roping, rodeo participation. Guided backcountry trips.

$$ Skyline Ranching and Outfitting – *Claresholm*, ☎403-625-2398. *www.skyline-ranching.com.* Cabins, tent camping and RV camping. Cattle drive in the scenic Porcupine Hills, brand cattle, riding lessons, trail rides *(open to non-guests)*.

Herding cattle in Southern Alberta

riginal wintering sites are still evident in tepee rings. Self-guided trails along Battle Creek ridge provide a good view of the area. The fort can be reached by foot or by park bus service. The surprisingly small whitewashed log buildings include barracks, stables, a workshop and the commissioner's resi-dence. At Kids **Farwell's Trading Post**★ *(2.5km/1.5mi south of the fort, access by park bus; ↩visit by 45min guided tour only)*, visitors are shown around by cos-tumed guides who depict the historical figures of the trading post's notorious past, when it was a proud way station in Whoop-Up country.

©Susan Scott/Michelin

Grain elevator in Skiff, Alberta

Cathedrals of the Plains

Visible for miles across the flatlands of the Prairie provinces, brightly painted wooden grain elevators rise beside the railroad tracks of many rural towns. Beginning in the 1800s, the silent sentinels followed the railways west across Manitoba, Saskatchewan and Alberta. It was in these silos that farms stored their grain to protect it from ruin by insects and the elements. By the 1930s the landscape was dotted with 6,000 of them.

Grain elevators derive their name from the process of elevating grain from a low-level pit, into which it is delivered, up to the bins where it's stored and cleaned. The long steel belt that performs this function is called a "leg," with buckets attached to it. The buckets scoop the grain and carry it to the top of the elevator—typically about 23m/75ft high. When the grain is ready for shipment, it's first dropped from the bottom of the bins onto a huge scale, where it is weighed. From there it's elevated again to the top bins where it falls through long chutes into the waiting boxcars.

Built of wood and often colourfully painted, the original rectangular, pitched-roof country elevators developed distinctive architectural features like the narrow cupola that crowns traditional types. The early wood elevators were often lost to fire—grain dust is extremely volatile: one stray spark could cause a disastrous explosion. Consequently, later structures were sheathed in sheet metal or built of concrete to lessen the risk of fire. At first, horses were used to haul wagonloads of grain into the elevator, where the cargo was dumped into the pit. But the elevators became increasingly mechanized with the advent of steam engines in the early 19C; in 1897, electricity eliminated the need for steam power.

These icons that once characterized every prairie town are now disappearing. Since the government is no longer granting freight subsidies, many branch lines have been abandoned by the railway companies. And huge new cement-and-steel grain terminals—run by computers and located in larger towns— are replacing the wooden silos, which are being demolished. Computerized elevators handle grain faster: 115 railcars are filled in one eight-hour shift, versus the wooden elevators' fastest rate of about two cars per hour.

Near the Saskatchewan border, in Acadia Valley, 30km/19mi southeast of Oyen on Hwy. 41, the **Prairie Elevator,** in working condition, is open to the public (◯Jul-Aug daily 10am–5pm; ☎403-972-2028, www.mdacadia.ab.ca/mdacadia/interest.htm). On-site is a garden plot where wheat, oats, rapeseed and other grains are grown.

ALBERTA BADLANDS

The **Alberta Badlands**★★★ are a vast and striking glacier-hewn panorama of steep bluffs, fluted gullies and lunarlike rock formations that marks parts of southeastern Alberta. These badlands are found notably at Writing-on-Stone Provincial Park on the Milk River along the Montana border, but the most dramatic terrain stretches some 300km/190mi along the Red Deer River Valley. The valley spans a width of 2km/1mi to 28km/17mi, running east of the town of Red Deer, through Dry Island Buffalo Jump Provincial Park and southeast to Dinosaur Provincial Park, a UNESCO World Heritage Site, where visitors can observe fossils in situ; the tourist epicentre is the town of Drumheller.

The exposed Cretaceous rock that surrounds this small town has yielded coal-mining riches, along with fossil beds so abundant that the Royal Tyrrell Museum of Palaeontology opened here in 1985 to excavate and study them. More than 375,000 people a year pass through the museum gates to see full-sized skeletons, reproductions, petrified plants and other evidence of prehistoric life. The museum is also a working research station, and would-be archaeologists can take part in real-life fossil expeditions in the area and throughout the badlands. Tourism, mostly dinosaur-related, has revived faded economic fortunes in towns such as Drumheller and nearby communities like the hamlet of Rosebud, where for nine months of the year a rural professional theatre attracts some 60,000 visitors annually. Summer is extremely busy across the badlands, with hotels, motels and campgrounds booked months in advance. Spring and fall are much less hectic, and offer a welcome respite from the often scorching summer heat.

A Bit of Geology

The surging meltwaters of the Wisconsin ice sheet, which retreated some 14,000 years ago, cut deep valleys across the rolling prairies of southern Alberta, exposing sedimentary deposits formed during the Upper Cretaceous period (65 million to 99 million years ago) when the area was a subtropical river delta, inhabited by dinosaurs. Subsequent erosion (still going on) by wind and

Horse Thief Canyon, Alberta Badlands

©Travel Alberta

Address Book

⌂ *For dollar-sign categories, see the Legend on the cover flap.*

WHERE TO STAY

$ A Lakeshore B&B and Spa – *Off Young Rd., Brooks.* ☎*403-501-5275 or 866-501-5275. www.alakeshorebb. com. 3 rooms.* 🅿️ 🛏 Spa . Overlooking Lake Newell, about 40km/25mi south of Dinosaur Provincial Park, this modern house, constructed as a B&B, offers comfortable rooms with private baths; two have private lakeside entrances. Breakfast is served in the sitting room that faces the lake, or on the terrace in fine weather. Spa treatments include massage, facials, herbal body wrap and a verbal relaxation session with a body talk practitioner.

$ Douglas Country Inn B&B – *Hwy. 873 (2nd Ave. W.) at Hwy. 542 (Cassils Rd. W.), Brooks.* ☎*403-362-2873. www.bbcanada.com/10098.html. 7 rooms.* 🅿️🛏 . Located on a large lot, this rambling one-storey house offers quiet comfort and modern lodgings. Guest rooms, which can accommodate children with an added cot, have antique touches such as iron beds and patchwork quilts. All rooms have en suite bathrooms, television, Internet and air-conditioning. A continental breakfast comes in the rate. Other meals are available at extra charge. Families are welcome.

$$ Best Western Jurassic Inn – *Hwy.9, Drumheller.* ☎*888-823-3466. www. bwjurassicinn.com, 48 units.* 🅿️🛏 . The tidy suites and indoor pool are family favourites at this two-storey motor inn with the bright blue roof ; it's located along the highway as you enter Drumheller. Rooms have microwave, fridge, coffee, iron, hairdryer, TV and high-speed Internet; a complimentary continental breakfast comes in the rate. Kids love the fresh popcorn in the lobby and the dinosaur motif on the walls.

$$ Econolodge – *392 Centre St., Drumheller.* ☎*403-823-3322 or 877-823-0022. www.econolodgedrumheller.com. 54 rooms.* 🅿️🛏 . This fully renovated motel, formerly the Lodge at Drumheller, is centrally located near the tourist information office. Newly refurbished rooms offer wireless Internet, fridges, microwave ovens; for families, there is a suite with a kitchenette. Breakfast is included in the rate.

$$ Heritage Inn – *1217 2nd St. W., Brooks.* ☎*403-362-6666 or 888-888-4374. 106 rooms.* 🍽🛏🅿️ . This full-service hotel is as a welcome relief after a hot summer day. Rooms have standard amenities; six are suites and one has a kitchenette. There's a fitness centre, lounge and restaurant. **Season's Café (** *$$* **)** offers salads and sandwiches; dinner fare such as steak and chicken dishes; a children's menu; and Sunday brunch. Essie's Nightclub can get lively Tuesday to Saturday nights, so ask for rooms away from the action. Small pets welcome.

Next door **Heritage Inn and Suites (** *$$* **)** *(1239 2nd St. W.;* ☎*403-362-8688;* 🅿️🛏 *)* offers 61 business-style rooms with kitchenettes and suites with kitchens; amenities include an indoor swimming pool, a complimentary breakfast and on-site parking.

$$ Lakeview Inn and Suites – *1307 2nd St. W., Brooks.* ☎*403-362-7440. 78 rooms.* 🍽🛏🅿️ . This modern hotel offers amenities such as microwave ovens and refrigerators in the room, on-site laundry facilities, a fitness centre and indoor swimming pool. Guest rooms are spacious and comfortable, and suites have fireplaces. Children are welcome.

$$ Ramada Inns & Suites – *680 2nd St., Drumheller.* ☎*877-807-2800. www. ramadainn.com. 48 units.* 🛏🅿️ . This centrally located, modern motel has spacious rooms (no kitchenettes) along with an indoor pool, waterslide and fitness centre. The free breakfast goes one solid step beyond the usual sugary continental fare (get to the breakfast area early, as it gets busy).

$$ Taste of the Past Bed and Breakfast – *281 2nd St. W., Drumheller.* ☎*403-823-5889. www.bbalberta.*

com/tastethepast. *3 rooms.* P ⌐.
This early 20C prairie-style house is
spacious and sports a gabled roof. It's
located in central Drumheller, and is
appointed with comfortable modern
furnishings and a few antique touches.
The three bedrooms, all with private
bathrooms, are located on the second
floor. The ground-floor sitting room is
sunny, and the full breakfast is served in
a pleasant dining room.

$$ Travelodge Drumheller –
*101 Grove Place, Drumheller. ☎403-823-
5302 or 877-464-0646. 49 units.* ⚐P.
Boasting a great location across the
bridge from the World's Largest Dino-
saur, this motel is popular with leisure
and business travellers. Perks include
high-speed Internet, oversized vehicle
parking, guest laundry and kitchen-
ettes. A waterpark and aquaplex centre
are nearby.

$$$ Inn and Spa at Heartwood –
*320 North Railway Ave. E., Drumheller.
☎403-823-6495 or 888-823-6495.
www.innsatheartwood.com. 10 rooms.
2 cottages.* P Spa . This charming,
family-run inn sits within in a heritage
house. Decorated with striking paint-
work, each room has antique furniture,
a gas fireplace, air conditioning and
cable TV. A day spa offers facials, mani-
cures, pedicures and specialty massage.
The owners are longtime local residents
who know the area well. A hearty
breakfast *($10),* notably a waffle with
flambéed strawberries, is served in the
elegant dining room. Rosebud dinner
theatre packages are also available.

$$$ Rosebud Country Inn – *111 2nd
Ave. E., Rosebud. ☎403-677-2211.
www.rosebudcountryinn.com. 14 rooms.*
P ⚐. It's hard to believe this lovely
gabled inn, painted sunshine yellow,
with a wide, deep porch, is not a herit-
age building. Antique-furnished guest
rooms are cosy and quiet; the pretty
dining room-tea room provides a good
view of the valley. Breakfast is offered
at an extra charge; limited lunches and
dinners are also available *(reduced hours
in winter).*

WHERE TO EAT:

$ Bernie and the Boys Bistro –
*305 4th St. West, Drumheller. ☎403-
823-3318.* **Canadian.** You can eat in or
take away at this casual fast-food joint,
with its faded decor. Bernie's is locally
famous for its all-dressed beef burgers
(try the Mammoth Burger, for dinosaur-
sized appetites), creamy milkshakes,
fries and onion rings.

$ Café Italiano – *35 3rd Ave. W.,
Drumheller. ☎403-823-4443.* **Italian.**
A favourite place for lunch, this cafe
serves paninis, salads, desserts and an
assortment of coffee.

$ Molly Brown's – *233 Centre St.,
Drumheller ☎403-823-7481.* **Canadian.**
This popular lunch spot serves up a
variety of soups, sandwiches and sushi
as well as an assortment of coffees.

The Inn and Spa at Heartwood

Inn and Spa at Heartwood, Drumheller

$ Rosedeer Hotel and Last Chance Saloon – *555 Jewel St., Wayne (southeast of Drumheller).* ☎*403-823-9189.* **Canadian.** This near-ghost town, population 40, is reached by crossing 11 one-lane, plank-floored bridges over a 6km/4mi road (Highway 10X) from Rosedale. Since 2,500 people once lived here, the abandoned buildings and mining machinery are a big draw, but so is the three-storey clapboard hotel (1913) and adjacent saloon, which has a trendy outdoor terrace. The restaurant menu includes buffalo burgers, steaks and apple pie. For overnight stays there are seven guest **rooms ($)** (with shared bathrooms), but only on the first two storeys; the third is reputedly occupied by a ghost. Two bullet holes in the ceiling are a reminder to pay bills promptly.

$ Sizzling House – *160 Centre St., Drumheller.* ☎*403-823-8098.* **Asian.** Serving Chinese (Szechuan and Peking) as well as Thai cuisine, this restaurant offers lunch buffets weekdays and on Friday and Saturday evenings.

$ Whifs Flapjack House – *801 N. Dinosaur Trail, Drumheller.* ☎*403-823-7595.* **Canadian.** During peak season there's always a lineup for the heaping omelettes and pancake breakfasts at this nondescript-looking eatery adjacent to the Badlands Motel. Lunch and dinners are less hearty—mainly burgers that are tasty, and fries. Situated en route to the Royal Tyrrell Museum, the diner varies its hours with the season, so call ahead.

$$ Athens Greek Restaurant – *71 Bridge St., N. Drumheller.* ☎*403-823-3225.* **Greek.** Located across the street from the dinosaur, this popular restaurant serves substantial plates of Greek fare such as souvlaki and lamb dishes as well as pizza and steak. The restaurant has a casual atmosphere with touches of traditional Greek blue and white decoration.

$$ O'Shea's Eatery & Ale House – *680 2 St. S.E., Drumheller,* ☎*403-823-2460.* **Pub Fare.** One of Drumheller's newest watering holes is situated in a strip mall just outside downtown. O'Shea's features the dark wood interior and lively music of a traditional British pub. Kilkenny beer-battered fish and chips are on the menu (the fries are homemade), along with other British pub fare and an extensive selection of beer.

$$ Stavros Family Restaurant – *In the Best Western Ramada, 1103 Hwy. 9 South, Drumheller.* ☎*403-823-6362.* **International.** The decor is casual and a little dated, but the spacious and comfortable eatery does a solid business with locals and travelers. Pizza, fresh sandwiches, pasta and deep-fried fare such as battered mushrooms and chicken fingers are the order of the day. Open for breakfast, lunch and supper.

rain has further exposed the ancient sediments, creating the striking panorama—in marked contrast to the rolling grasslands all around—of rivers running down through steep bluffs and fluted gulleys in a landscape of both stark beauty and desolation. Harder rocks capping the soft rock have protected it from eroding, forming the unusual finger formations known as **hoodoos.** Barren of vegetation, steep slopes, ravines and coulees bear testimony to the work of erosion.

The word *dinosaur* is derived from Greek, meaning "terrible lizard." **Dinosaurs** first appeared during the Late Triassic Period, 227-206 million years ago, and evolved continuously before disappearing at the end of the Late Cretaceous Period (99-65 million years ago). Fossils in the Red Deer River Valley are from this last period. Remains have been found on every continent, including Anarctica; dinosaurs roamed the planet for more than 160 million years. Over that time, climates and topography evolved as continents broke apart and drifted away from each other. Earth's flora gradually altered as coniferous and deciduous trees as well as flowers appeared alongside ferns; many of the plants that grew at the time of dinosaurs survive today.

The largest dinosaurs were the plant-eating *sauropods,* tall enough to reach the tops of trees; the giant **brachio-**

saurus weighed as much as 32tonnes/35tons and grew to 25m/82ft in length. Some meat-eating dinosaurs, such as the *compsognathus,* were as small as cats or chickens. Most dinosaurs were plant-eating, however. The **duckbilled dinosaur** (hadrosaur), the dominant Late Cretaceous plant eater, walked on its hind feet, which were webbed for swimming, and sported a snout resembling a duck's bill. Its contemporary, the **horned dinosaur** (ceratopsian) walked on four feet and had horns—usually one over each eye and one on the nose. Carnivorous dinosaurs, some of which have been found with their prey inside them, include the **Albertosaurus,** which measured 10m/30.5ft long and weighed 2tonnes/1.8tons; it could run at a speed of 40kph/25mph.

Some 65 million years ago, dinosaurs became extinct. The most widely accepted theory as to what caused their disappearance is that a large asteroid, about the size of Mount Everest, hit the earth near the Yucatan peninsula, causing conflagrations and sending so much debris into the atmosphere that sunlight reaching the earth was greatly reduced for a very long time; recently gathered evidence indicates that this collision occurred when life was already under great stress due to consequences of massive volcanic eruptions.

Today, about 1,000 species of dinosaur are known, representing perhaps one-fifth of what must have existed. The dinosaurs' descendents are still among us: birds are evolved from *saurichia* dinosaurs, some of which were carnivorous.

A Bit of History

The badlands are a sacred place for First Nations, who consider the wind-sculpted hoodoos a source of spiritual power. The name badlands is taken from the early French explorers' description of similar *terres mauvais à traverser* farther to the south, who found the terrain difficult to cross.

The first fossil dinosaur (later classified as *Albertosaurus sarcophagus*) was discovered near Drumheller in 1884 by geologist Joseph Burr Tyrrell (*see sidebar*). Since then, remains of more than 300 specimens, comprising 39 species have been unearthed here and are on display in many world museums, including the Royal Ontario Museum in Toronto.

In the late 19C, this largely uninhabitable valley was a choice hideout for outlaws such as Butch Cassidy, as well as for horse thieves, whisky traders and, during Alberta's 1916-1923 flirtation with prohibition, moonshiners. The area's Wild West heritage and singular landscape have made it a popular filming spot for Hollywood movies, which have included *Unforgiven* (1992, Clint Eastwood, Gene Hackman) and *Shanghai Noon* (2000, Jackie Chan, Owen Wilson).

Thanks to the abundant tropical life that surrounded the dinosaurs, the area holds one of the world's richest deposits of fossil fuels: coal, oil and gas. The discovery of coal early in the 20C brought prospectors and fortune hunters to the area, boosting the population of Drumheller to more than 30,000 people in the 1930s when coal was at its peak.

The arrival of the Canadian Northern Railway in Drumheller in 1912 had fostered the success of the industry. From 1911 until the 1960s, Drumheller was surrounded by coal mines, which gradually closed down as oil and gas came to the fore as energy sources.

The **West Drumheller Field** holds Alberta's second largest natural gas deposit; several thousand oil wells also produce across the region.

Elsewhere in Alberta, coal mining still thrives, with a dozen active mines producing 70 percent of Canada's coal.

Along with oil, agriculture has become a principal economic engine in the area, which is engaged primarily in grain farming as well as raising cattle and horses. Courtesy of Canada's most extensive irrigation system, the grasslands that surround the badlands support fields of wheat and bright yellow canola as well as ranges where cattle feed.

Dry Island Buffalo Jump Provincial Park★

MAP OF PRINCIPAL SIGHTS

Encompassing 1,600ha/3,950 acres, this provincial park straddles the Red Deer River at the northern end of the badlands. It is named for a 200m/609ft mesa that rises above the dry landscape amid fantastic formations of eroded rocks. At the rim of the valley, where the vast grassy plains sweep up to the very edge of the badlands, are cliffs over which aboriginal peoples stampeded bison 700 to 2,800 years ago. Dry Island's buffalo jump is the highest of those in Alberta, at nearly 61m/200ft. The site is particularly rich in *Albertosaurus* remains, and recently a member of the *Triceratops* group was discovered here. Cree and Blackfoot Indians who found monstrous bones sticking out of the sedimentary strata recognized them as being extremely ancient: they called the bones "fathers of the buffalo." The park is a popular recreational site; during summer months, canoeists and kayakers can descend the Red River all the way to Dinosaur Provincial Park, stopping at convenient campgrounds along the way. Greatly favoured by bird watchers, the park hosts both nesters and migrating birds; some 150 species have been sighted here. Anglers can also try their luck catching trout, perch, dace, whitefish and pike.

In Alberta, it is illegal to remove fossils from provincial and federal parks or to sell or take fossils out of the province without a government certificate.

- **Information:** There is no park visitor centre. For information, call ☎403-823-1749. www.gateway.cd.gov.ab.ca.
- **Orient Yourself:** The park is located some 94km/59mi northwest of Drumheller. The park entrance lies northeast of Trochu. From Drumheller, take Hwy. 56 north to Hwy. 585 and head west to Hwy. 21 (you will pass through the park's Tolman camping area); then drive north on Hwy. 21 to Township Rd. 34-4, an access road that leads east into the park. The steep entrance road to the river valley is impassable during wet periods; access is gated in winter months.
- **Parking:** Parking is available at the day-use picnic site and at the Tolman Bridge Recreation Area camping grounds.

Dry Island Buffalo Jump Provincial Park

©Travel Alberta

Dry Island Buffalo Jump Provincial Park

- **Don't Miss:** Reasonably fit visitors will enjoy remarkable scenery on some of the informal trails that meander around the park. Be sure to wear hiking boots and a hat, and carry plenty of drinking water.
- **Organizing Your Time:** If you are only driving through the park, a half day is sufficient. The park gate is closed at night and in winter; during wet weather, when the roads and trails are dangerous, access is denied.
- **Kids:** The trails are not appropriate for the stamina of small children.
- **Also See:** RED DEER AREA

A Bit of Geology

The exposed rocky areas include **hoodoos,** the strange pillars of soft sedimentary capped by protecting boulders of hard rock. The park's rugged rock formations emerge from fields of green buffalo grass that stretches like a carpet over the valley floor. Along the Red Deer River, the riparian habitat is lined with cottonwoods, willows, poplars, aspens, balsams and other towering trees. Flowering plants bloom in profusion in early summer: some 450 plant species, many flowering from late May through June, are found here. Wildflowers include wild blue flax, prairie coneflower, globemallow, tiger lilies, three-flowered avens, Western wild bergamot (also called horsemint) and delicate harebells; prickly pear cactus grows on the driest spots. The park's many animals include mule deer, white-tailed jackrabbits, muskrats, beavers and badgers. Birders often hike here to observe turkey vultures, golden eagles, cliff swallows, mountain bluebirds, belted kingfishers and great blue herons, among many others.

A Bit of History

Hunting buffalo before Europeans introduced horses to North America was an extremely dangerous and uncertain enterprise, as a buffalo weighed 800kilos/1,760lbs and could run at 50km/hr/30mph. **Stampeding** was a common hunting method all over the plains; about 100 buffalo jump sites have been found in North America, including the spectacular one in Alberta at Head-Smashed-In Buffalo Jump (*see Fort Macleod*), a UNESCO World Heritage Site.

Today scientists excavate in Dry Island Buffalo Jump Provincial Park during the summer, and finds from here can be seen in museums around the world. The site is particularly rich in *Albertosaurus* remains: fossils of some 22 individual animals have been identified here, out of some 30 in existence, indicating this reptile moved in herds. The *Albertosaurus* was a much smaller cousin of the *Tyrannosaurus*, weighing in at a mere 2tonnes/1.8tons; still, a herd of them must have provided considerable excitement. Other unusual fossils include freshwater fish.

Located within Midland Provincial Park near Drumheller (♿ *see Drumheller*), the Royal Tyrrell Museum of Palaentology, a premier research institute as well as a museum, announced in 2007 the discovery in this park of a beast they named **Eotriceratops xerinsularis** (the last word means "dry island" in Latin), which lived 67 to 69 million years ago and was a very early member of the triceratops group, the popular horned dinosaur with the big neck frill. The assembled skeleton is now on view in the museum's Ceratopsians gallery.

Visit

🕐 *Park open year-round daily. Vehicle access May–early Oct only; access road gated at night, during wet periods and in winter.* ♿ *The road is very steep and impassable in wet weather. There is no park visitor centre.* 🅿 🚶 ☎ *403-823-1749. www.gateway.cd.gov.ab.ca.*

As the Township Road 344 approaches the park from the west, the prairie stretches green into the far distance, making the sudden 200m/656ft cliff that plunges into the valley seem a dramatic punctuation. The access road follows the rim of the valley for a good distance, offering excellent views. From the picnic area and canoe launch on the river (♿ *descending road passable only in dry weather*), a network of informal footpaths crosses the park, some leading to the Dry Island mesa, from which there are spectacular **views**★★, after a strenuous climb. The flat surface of the mesa, covered in fescue grass, also provides a pristine example of ancient prairie.

Hikes on the west side of the park, along the base of the valley cliffs over which aboriginals stampeded bison, reveal a variety of ecosystems, as well as ancient buffalo bones.

Archaeologists have found traces of aboriginal habitation, including pottery and gravesites, along these cliffs.

Because the river serves as a reference, hikers are unlikely to get lost here.

One way to explore the park is on horse or mule: Buffalo Jump Canyon Ranch in Huxley offers **guided trail rides** through the park (*1hr $35; 3hrs $90*); for details, ☎ 403-442-2277; www.buffalo jumpcanyon.com.

Horses graze near Drumheller Valley

©Travel Alberta

Drumheller ★

POPULATION 7,932 – MAP P 173

As visitors approach Drumheller, crossing a fertile, wheat-growing plain dotted by bobbing "donkey head" oil pumpjacks, the townsite comes as a surprise. Nearly 120m/400ft deep and 1.6km/1mi wide, the extensively eroded valley in which the town sits is the very image of desolation. But it is due to this erosion that the Dinosaur Capital of the World is one of Alberta's most visited sites, overflowing with tourists in summer. Named after Samuel Drumheller, who launched coal mining here, the town amalgamated with 14 others over the years and since 1997, spreads across 111sq km/43sq mi, making it Alberta's largest town in terms of physical size. A few of the old coal-mining centres now part of Drumheller are East Coulee, Midland, Rosedale and the near-ghost town of Wayne. On the outskirts of town, an annual theatrical spectacle called the Canadian Badlands Passion Play (www. canadianpassionplay.com) portrays the story of the resurrection of Jesus Christ in a dramatic natural amphitheater that seats 2,500 people (Jul).

- **Information:** Information Centre, 60 1st Ave. W. Open Jul–Aug daily 9am–9pm. Rest of the year daily 10am–5pm. ☎403-823-8100 or 866-823-8100. www.traveldrumheller.com. or www.canadianbadlands.com.
- ▶ **Orient Yourself:** The main entry point to town is Hwy. 9 heading east from the Trans-Canada Highway, which turns into 5th Street, a route of strip malls with hotels, fast-food restaurants and retail stops. The tourist information centre is situated on this route just past Bridge Street, which crosses north over the Red Deer River. The south side of the river and downtown (South Railway Ave.) turn into the **South Dinosaur Trail** through near-ghost towns such as Wayne and Rosedale. The north side of the river is **North Dinosaur Trail,** which turns into Hoodoo Trail. The Royal Tyrrell Museum is situated in Midland Provincial Park on the town's northwest edge.
- **Parking:** Badlands attractions and the town itself have plenty of designated public parking; the streets around the town visitor centre have free street parking, but plan to walk a few blocks if visiting during the peak summer months.
- **Don't Miss:** The Royal Tyrrell Museum, the hoodoos, and a float down the placid Red Deer River (see sidebar below).
- **Organizing Your Time:** Downtown is easily explored on foot, but a car is needed to see most other sites such as the museum, Horseshoe and Horse Thief canyons and the Atlas Coal Mine. Tour the Dinosaur Trail early in the morning or late in the day for the best colours. Plan at least three hours for the Royal Tyrrell Museum. Also popular are day-long dinosaur digs in the hills surrounding the Tyrrell museum.
- **Kids:** The interactive computer game at the Royal Tyrrell Museum allows kids to create their own dinosaur.
- **Also See:** CALGARY

A Bit of History

In 1884 the dauntless geologist, historian, cartographer and explorer **Joseph Burr Tyrrell** (see sidebar) was searching the Red Deer River Valley for bituminous coal deposits known to lie in the area. On June 9, as he was poking around Kneehills Creek a few kilometres from the present-day Royal Tyrrell Museum, he stumbled upon the skull and bones of what was later christened an *Albertosaurus sarcophagus*, a smaller version of the fearsome Tyrannosaurus rex. With immense effort, Tyrrell bundled his very heavy discovery off to Calgary, then off to the famous palaeontologist Edward D. Cope of the University of Pennsylvania, who called it a *Laelaps incrassatus*. In short order the Geological Survey

©Travel Alberta

View of the Red Deer River

sent out Thomas Weston to see what else could be found. Later discoveries around what is now Dinosaur Provincial Park brought scientists rushing to the Badlands, particularly after the arrival of the Northern Canadian Railway to Drumheller in 1912 made travel easier (prior to this, fossil-hunters floated down the river on rafts). The period between 1910 and 1917 is known as the **Great Canadian Dinosaur Rush.** A few days after discovering the dinosaur, Tyrrell found the largest seam of bituminous coal in Canada. His later career was equally glittering, as he turned to gold mining.

On the heels of the geologists, ranchers arrived in the late 19C to raise stock on the rich grasslands once roamed by buffalo. Coal deposits had to wait for the arrival of the Canadian Northern Railway to haul them out. In 1907 **Samuel Drumheller** (1864-1925), an American from Walla Walla, Washington, came through the badlands looking for ranchland to buy. Noticing that a rancher was using a bucket of coal to heat his shack, Drumheller traced snowy footprints to a surface seam of bituminous coal. Apprised that the railroad was coming through, he bought the rancher's land. By 1911 the first coal was being shipped out, although not from Drumheller's mine; owners of the Newcastle mine beat him to it, but Sam's mine opened the next year and made him very prosperous; for many years Mrs. Drumheller

reigned over the **Women's Institute,** an affiliate of a British charitable, educational and social organization (every respectable town had a building that belonged to the Women's Institute). Thousands of prospectors and miners from Eastern Europe, Great Britain and Nova Scotia flocked in and by 1921, some 27 mines were operating. The grateful railway, which had bought Drumheller's land, agreed to name the town after him. At its peak in the 1930s, the city population reached 30,000, and between 1911 and 1966, some 124 mines opened here, producing 67 million tons of coal; all are now closed. The boom town acquired the nick-name "Hell's Hole," something of an exaggeration because the low-sulphur sub-bituminous coal produced little explosive methane gas, and because Canadian miners had already acquired important working rights. A miners' strike in 1925 briefly established the Mine Workers' Union of Canada as a rival to the United Mine Workers, which notoriously conspired with coal mine

☺ A Bit of Advice ☺

When hiking near any of many closed-down mine entrances in this area, be very careful. Abandoned machinery can be dangerous. Never climb on slag heaps—the red shale can burn for years without producing any warning smoke.

owners. Conditions were certainly rough but much less dangerous and grueling than for previous generations. Still, what with palaeontologists, ranchers, farmers, coal miners from the fringes of Europe, moonshiners defying prohibition, desperadoes lurking in the coulees and the ladies of the Women's Institute, Drumheller in its early days must have been a lively place indeed.

Downtown

The Red Deer River gently flows through the town between narrow green banks. The downtown streets, a jumble of faded historic buildings that stretch for about 10 square blocks, are lined with brightly coloured concrete dinosaur statues (which kids inevitably try to climb). Drumheller is typically hot and dry in summer, making the river a well-used recreational venue. A children's water park next to the giant dinosaur is popular with locals and visitors, and an **aquaplex** next to the water park has indoor and outdoor pools.

Dominating the entrance to the **visitor centre** (60 1st Ave. W.; *see Information above*) is an 25m/86ft-high, 46m/151ft-long fibreglass **replica** of a Tyrannosaurus rex that contains a stairwell leading to a viewing platform within the beast's toothy jaws (*$3*).

The **view**★ of the river valley is worth the climb (106 steps). The centre serves as the departure point for **bus tours** of Dinosaur Provincial Park (*see description and details below*), which must be reserved one day in advance. The centre also provides a wide selection of brochures about accommodations, attractions and sights. A useful brochure is the self-guided **walking tour** of the downtown area. Occasionally during the year, there are guided tours of the downtown, the cemetery (with stories about people under the tombstones) and area mines. Inevitably, the centre includes a gift shop with "you won't believe where I am" souvenirs.

Badlands Historical Centre

335 1st St. E. Open Jun–Sept daily 10am–6pm. Rest of the year by appointment. *$4.* 403-823-2593.

This centre offers a good overall view of the ancient history and geology of the area; it has information about the tropical sea that once lay here, and the plants and animals that have been preserved as fossils. Some displays are interactive. There is also a rather quirky but scholarly **collection** of fossils, Indian artifacts, art objects and natural oddities amassed by Lawrence A. Duncan, a Scottish-born London police officer who came to Canada with the British army; he was hired by the Drumheller police force in

Royal Tyrrell Museum, Drumheller

©Travel Alberta

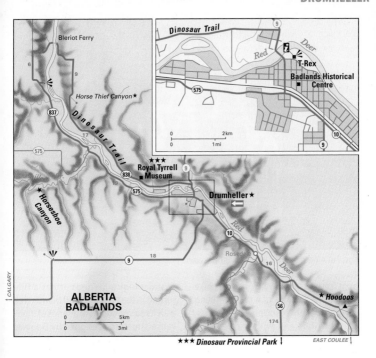

Bleriot Ferry

Dinosaur Trail

Red Deer

T-Rex

Badlands Historical Centre

Horse Thief Canyon ★

★★★
Royal Tyrrell
Museum

Drumheller ★

Horseshoe Canyon

Rosedale

Red Deer

ALBERTA
BADLANDS

★ Hoodoos

CALGARY

★★★ *Dinosaur Provincial Park*   EAST COULEE

1926 to clean up the rather wide-open town, then known as "Hell's Hole." After serving as chief of police for many years, he moved to Calgary in 1944 to work as an insurance investigator. There, he was a founder of the Calgary Rock and Lapidary Club.

Homestead Museum

901 N. Dinosaur Trail. ◷*Open May–mid-Oct daily 10am–5pm (mid-May to Labour Day til 8pm Thu–Sun).* ⊜*$5.* ✕&☎*403-823-2600. www.traveldrumheller.com/homestead-museum.*

Parts of this museum's collection are clearly overflow from local attics, but out of 10,000 items on the premises there are some, such as the notorious stuffed two-headed calf, that catch the eye. There are native artifacts, household implements and furniture, items of clothing, musical instruments and more. Outside, farm equipment and a stagecoach sit on the lawn.

Dinosaur Trail

&*See map. 51km/32mi circular drive via Hwy. 838, Hwy. 837 and Hwy. 575. Begin from Drumheller on the north side of the river.*

Connecting the sights of the Drumheller area, this scenic driving tour makes a loop on the plains above the Red Deer River Valley. Offering good views of the badlands, it can be travelled in either direction. The colours of the rock vary throughout the day: brilliant rose in early morning, bleached white under full sun, showing shades of coral, yellow and pink later on, and burnt orange with deep violet shadows at dusk. The striations are much more apparent in early morning or late afternoon. Seams of dark coal can be seen at some places.

Midland Provincial Park

☎*403-823-1749. www.albertaparks.ca.* From 1912 to 1959 this park was the site of a large coal mine, where the Royal Tyrrell Museum of Palaeontology now stands. An oasis of greenery along the Red Deer River and on McMullen Island, the park provides opportunities to

Fossil of Albertosaurus, Royal Tyrrell Museum

boat (canoes and kayaks), fish and hike around the remains of a once-thriving town under the canopies of poplars, cottonwoods and willow trees. The former 1912 Midland Mine office holds an exhibit on mining lore.

Royal Tyrrell Museum of Palaeontology★★★

6km/4mi northwest of Drumheller by Hwy. 838. ⏱*Open mid-May–early-Sept daily 10am–9pm. Early-Sept–early-Oct daily 10am–5pm. Rest of the year Tue–Sun 10am–5pm.* ⏱*Closed Jan 1, Dec 24-25.* ◉*$10.* ⮞*Guided tours Jul–Aug daily 11:30am & 3:30 pm; mid-May–late-Jun weekends 11:30am & 3:30pm; Sept daily 2:30pm.* ◉*$3; free in Sept.* ✕⛳☎*403-823-7707, or 888-440-4240. www.tyrrell museum.com.* ✏*A museum floor plan can be printed from the website.*

This splendid museum, opened in 1985 and operated by the Alberta government, is one of the largest in the world devoted to the study of life-forms from past geological periods. It has a fine setting in the badlands and blends well with its surroundings in a series of innovative structures designed by Douglas Craig of Calgary. Like other first-class museums, the Royal Tyrrell is actively involved in ongoing palaeontology research here and around the world; scientists participate in expeditions (a recent group went to Mongolia) and new finds from Alberta are quickly put on display here. The museum also offers public educational programs, lectures with experts and an opportunity to take part in archaeological expeditions for a day or longer.

The museum highlights are the enormous **Dinosaur Hall 1** and **Dinosaur Hall 2,** where some 40 mounted skeletons of dinosaurs formerly inhabiting the area are re-created, some with original fossils, others with modern casting materials (more than 75 percent of the fossils displayed are original). The huge *Tyrannosaurus rex, Albertosaurus* (whose

The Tyrrell for Tykes

🧒The museum's unique sleepover program "Snore with the Dinosaurs" allows families and youth ages 5 to 13 (parental accompaniment required for every 5 campers) to spend a night in the Dinosaur Hall. The campers are provided supper, an evening snack and breakfast; admission to the museum is included. Activities include creating a cast of a dinosaur fossil. Kids will also love interactive computer stations where they can build a virtual dinosaur and see if it would have survived in harsh ancient ecosystems.

Joseph Burr Tyrrell

Joseph Burr Tyrrell (1858-1957) was born in Weston, Ontario, a town his wealthy, Irish-born father founded. An unlikely start for a great explorer, childhood scarlet fever damaged his eyesight and hearing, and a later bout of pneumonia weakened him. An arts graduate of the University of Toronto, Tyrrell articled to a lawyer, but had no strength for the work. So, in a very Victorian solution, he joined the Canadian Geological Survey, and in 1883, at age 25, headed out west with renowned explorer **George Mercer Dawson** (1849-1901) to scout the Rocky Mountain foothills in advance of the transcontinental railway. In 1884, while leading a rafting expedition on the Red River, Tyrrell found a large dinosaur skull emerging from the rock. Shortly thereafter, he discovered, near Drumheller, the largest seam of bituminous coal in Canada. Recognizing the significance of both discoveries, he packed the dinosaur bones off to Philadelphia, but was most pleased about the coal.

Tyrrell's subsequent adventures involved mapping the Barren Lands from Lake Athabasca to Hudson Bay, travelling by canoe, dogsled and snowshoes; discovering copper, zinc and nickel in northern Manitoba; and reporting in 1898 that, indeed, there was gold in the Klondike. He parlayed expertise in geology into a glittering career that saw him strike gold at Kirkland Lake, Ontario in 1924. He served as general manager of the Kirkland Lake Gold Mining Company until age 69, but remained president until 1955, retiring at age 97.

In his expeditions Tyrrell had relied on the journals of early explorer **David Thompson** (1770-1857). When he discovered Thompson's lost *Narrative,* he edited it and got it published in 1916. He published many scientific articles, notably pioneering theories on the advance of glaciers that are now universally accepted. George Dawson named a 2,755m/8,397ft mountain in Banff National Park in honour of his assistant, and the eminent Royal Tyrrell Museum in Drumheller bears his name.

fossil Joseph Burr Tyrrell discovered in 1884), the armored Stegosaurus and some smaller birdlike dinosaurs can be seen. The skeletons are set in dramatically lit dioramas that help visitors understand the ancient environment; some are encased in blocks of stone, so visitors can appreciate how palaeontologists inch them out from ancient mud. One part of the hall represents the bottom of the ancient Bearpaw Sea, which covered the western Canadian interior 70 million years ago. Here, large marine reptiles up to 15m/50ft long can be viewed.

Other areas of the museum such as the **Devonian Reef** take visitors back more than 3.9 billion years to the dawn of life on earth. In the **Cretaceous Garden,** visitors can admire a large collection of plants descended from those living in the Drumheller Valley 65 to 70 million years ago, when dinosaurs roamed. It is interesting to learn that the movie *Jurassic Park* should have been called Upper Cretaceous Park. The **Ice Ages and Time Tunnel,** with dramatic

blue lighting and elaborate skeletons, shows a time when sheets of ice over one mile thick covered Canada. See life-sized skeletons and reproductions of creatures such as the sabretooth tiger,

Little Church, Drumheller

Hunting Fossils

Look for fossils where sedimentary rocks are exposed such as in quarries, along road cuts, cliffs and seashores. **Always get permission** from local authorities or landowners before you begin your search. **Be aware of legal restrictions:** in Alberta, it is illegal to remove fossils from provincial and federal parks or to sell or take fossils out of the province without a government certificate. Check with the Royal Tyrrell Museum regarding excavation permits. Whether surface collecting or excavating, you need a map, compass, magnifying glass, notebook, small paintbrush, knife, trowel and geological hammer. Safety gear includes gloves, goggles and a hard hat. Take paper towels or newspaper to wrap the fossil and plastic bags for carrying it. Give the specimen a number and handle it properly to maintain the scientific information held within. Record the location and date of your find in your notebook. Also describe the colour and texture of the rocks in which the fossil was found (for example, hard limestone block).

In Drumheller, you can buy fossils and related materials at the **Badlands Historical Centre,** the **Fossil Shop** *(61 Bridge St., ☎403-823- 6774; www.thefossil shop.com)* or the **Museum Shop** in the Tyrrell Museum. The Tyrrell offers day-long and week-long field research in Dinosaur Provincial Park and the hills around the museum; shorter 🔲 day-long **archaeological digs** near the Tyrrell museum welcome young dinosaur hunters (the longer expeditions do not).

R. Corbel/Michelin

mastodons, giant bison and the massive woolly mammoth, which roamed the cold fringes of these glaciers. The exhibit also traces human migration to North America across the Bering Sea land bridge.

Displays in the museum change constantly as new information emerges about ancient life, and as new specimens are excavated from the badlands. The recently discovered **Eotricerotops xerinsuleris,** found in Dry Island Buffalo Jump Provincial Park and a probable ancestor of the familiar Triceratops, with its big neck ruff, can be seen in the gallery called Ceratopsians: the Horned Herbivores.

In the Preparation Lab, watch through glass windows as scientists using tools ranging from toothbrushes to chisels prepare fossils for research and display.

The Dinosaur Trail Golf & Country Club *(www.dinosaurtrailgolf.com)* is a pretty course near the museum; the coulees and cliffs make it quite challenging, particularly the back nine holes.

The next attraction on the Dinosaur Trail is the aptly named **Little Church** *(6km/4mi west of Drumheller on Hwy. 838),* a 1990 replica of a tall-steepled, white frame church built in 1958 by local contractor Trygyve Seland. The small edifice seats, as its caretakers explain, thousands of worshippers, but only six at a time.

With its rounded, almost barren hills stretching to the river, **Horse Thief Canyon★** *(16km/10mi west of Drumheller)* is a gorge 122m/400ft deep, with steep walls of striated sedimentary rock and towering hoodoos with boulders balanced on their tops. Its expansive ruggedness can be admired from the lookout on its rim, or visitors can choose to descend, although the trail is not well-marked. The canyon was used by rustlers in frontier days to hide stolen horses and cattle that would emerge with different brands and very quickly, different owners, some as far south as Montana (where, indeed, some of the stock originally hailed from).

To cross the Red Deer River at the trail's halfway point, 27km/16.2mi northwest of Drumheller, take the **Bleriot Ferry** (🕐 *operates 8am–10:45 pm daily, only when the river is not frozen)*. One of Alberta's last cable ferries—and the last of nine such ferries once operating in this valley—the ferry shuttles eight vehicles at a time the short distance between the north and south banks of the river, saving a much longer route by road. It is named for a rancher, André Bleriot, and has operated since 1913.

Once past the river, the road climbs to a fine **view**★ of the valley from the Orkney Hill Lookout. The green pastures beside the river provide an interesting contrast to the cactus-strewn bluffs and gullies immediately below.

The site of the Canadian Badlands Passion Play, a stony natural amphitheatre lies near the Drumheller Ski Area, close to town. The large, white statue of Jesus on the hillside has stood there since the 1930s.

Additional Sights

Horseshoe Canyon★
18km/11mi southwest of Drumheller by Rte. 9.
This canyon, which has no exit, extends for some 3km/1.8mi, covers 200ha/494acres and reaches a width of 1.5km/.9mi. The view from the canyon viewpoint pullover is quite breathtaking, and has been justly compared to a miniature Grand Canyon. Try to see it early or late in the day, when the colours are the most pronounced. Paths leading through the hillocks to the river provide some of the best **views** of the badlands in the area. A portion of the canyon is a nature conservancy area. A gift shop sells fossils.

Suspension Bridge
In Rosedale, 9km/5.5mi southwest of Drumheller by Rte. 10.
In the small community of Rosedale, take the time to walk across the 117m/357ft suspension bridge crossing the Red Deer River, where miners working at the Star Mine used to pass twice daily to get to work. A cool breeze often wafts up from the slow-moving waters below, but you might prefer not to look down. The bridge was built in 1931; previous to that, miners crossed over the chasm in slings that slid over a cable. The coal came out the same way.

©Travel Alberta

Rosedale Suspension Bridge

Hoodoos

From Rosedale, Highway 10X leads southwest to the near ghost town of Wayne (population 40), an interesting detour. Moonshiners operated here during Alberta prohibition (1916-1923) and the town has, of course, a Last Chance Saloon (*see Address Book*).

Hoodoos★

17km/10mi southeast of Drumheller by Rte. 10.

These strange rock formations, which look like giant mushrooms, consist of boulders balancing on the top of wind-shaped buttes, and illustrate the work of erosion in the valley. The boulders on the top are hard rock that has protected the softer sedimentary rock of the columns from erosion. If the cap boulders tumble off, the shafts melt away in a few hundred years. Cree and Blackfoot Indians had spiritual beliefs about these formations, which do indeed inspire awe: the name hoodoo seems to be a variation of the word voodoo.

Excursions

Atlas Coal Mine National Historic Site★

110 Century Dr., East Coulee, 22km/14mi southwest of Drumheller by Rte. 10. Open May–mid-Oct daily 10am–5pm;

extended hours in summer. $7, or $21 per family. Guided tours throughout the day. 403-822-2220. www.atlascoalmine.ab.ca.

The first Atlas Coal Mine opened in 1917, producing in 1921 at its height 135,000tons a year. The mine closed in 1929, but not before making its four original investors—a disparate group that included an Irish adventurer and a physician—wealthy men. At its height, the town of East Coulee had 3,800 inhabitants, now dwindled to about 180. The last mine at this site, Atlas #4, shipped its last coal in 1979 and closed definitively in 1984, when it was sealed. It was the last operation in Drumheller, victim of dwindling yields and the emergence of clean-burning gas and fuel oil as preferred energy sources for household heating and cooking.

At the **visitor centre,** a 20min documentary, *Thunder in the Valley,* includes footage showing how a living was pieced together from mining and labouring in off-times on farms and ranches.

The guided tour visits the eight-storey wooden **tipple,** the largest one still standing in Canada, where visitors can see how chunks of ore were pulled from the rocky hills and transported above ground via miles of conveyor belts to the valley bottom. The tour includes a short ride in a coal car (called a "man trap"), in

Paddling the River

Paddling down the placid lower Red Deer River by canoe or kayak and camping on the shore enjoys great popularity with Albertans. You can choose a guided tour with all equipment provided, or rent your own gear and float on your own. Family-run **River Getaways Inc.** (☎403-235-5995; www.rivergetaways.com) offers badlands floats and rentals from its base camp 20 km/12 mi upstream of Dinosaur Provincial Park; a two-day self-guided package including gear, an equipped campsite and food starts at $159/adult and $99/child.

A pleasant day trip begins at the **Bleriot Ferry Provincial Recreation Area** (open year-round; 28 sites; $15/night; no reservations; www.gateway.cd.gov.ab.ca), about 24km/15mi west of Drumheller, where a shady campground lies on the west side of the river; plan to paddle 3-6 hours (depending on river speed and depth) to pull out at the Drumheller bridge.

The Dinosaur Trail RV Resort in Drumheller (☎403-823-9333; www.holidaytrails resorts.com/dinosaurtrail) rents canoes by the hour and provides transport to the Bleriot Ferry. For longer expeditions, the **Mountain Equipment Co-op** stores in Calgary and Edmonton (www.mec.ca) rent canoes, kayaks, paddles, lifejackets, roof racks and other gear. The best deals can be found through the **University of Calgary Outdoor Centre** (☎403-220-5038www.calgaryoutdoorcentre.ca; credit card deposit required, boat, paddles and PFDs start at about $30/day).

Routes and campgrounds include several options. A 2-day float starts at the Tolman Bridge 60km/43 mi north of Drumheller, where the lovely campground (open year-round; 36 sites east side, 30 sites west side; $13/night; ☎403-378-4342;www.gateway.cd.gov.ab.ca) at the Dry Island Buffalo Jump Provincial Park sprawls along the east and west bluffs overlooking the river (the best sites are on the east). A full day of paddling down the river takes you to the **Morrin Bridge Recreation Area,** an open and largely treeless site along the river; the full moon illuminates the canyon shadows. There are campgrounds at McLaren Dam (12 sites), Michichi Dam (18 sites) and **Starland Recreational Area** (50 sites) ($10/night; ☎403-772-3793; www.starlandcounty.com/campgrounds/htm). Novices in particular will enjoy the float from Drumheller to Dinosaur Provincial Park

©Travel Alberta

Canoeing on Red Deer River

south of the town. As you pass through prairie grassland, you're likely to see mule deer, whitetail deer, rabbits, coyotes, beavers and plenty of bird life along with flowers, cactus and cottonwood trees. On hot summer days, wear your swimsuit so you can hop into a swimming hole to cool off or float behind your boat on an inner tube.

Caution: The upper Red Deer River, as it winds northwest of the badlands through the towns of Sundre and Innisfail, is not for novices. Expert paddling skills or guided whitewater rafting are required to navigate its many hazards such as ledges and tree sweepers. For more information access the **Alberta Recreational Canoeing Assn.** at www.abcanoekayak.org.

Atlas Coal Mine National Historic Site

which miners crouched as ponies, protected by little helmets, dragged them deep into the mine shaft.

On their own, visitors can look at a miner's shack built of cow dung, mud and straw (not much lumber around here), a wash house (considered a real perk when introduced), a battery office and other abandoned buildings.

On the rough-and-tumble frontier, people organized schools and clubs, lived as neatly as they could and planted large gardens. The **East Coulee School Museum** housed in the town's surprisingly spacious 1930 school, gives an idea of life for children and families in coal-mining days. Exhibits include a typical classroom (it is quite large; the town once had many children) and a re-created home. There is a gift shop, a cafe and a picnic area. ◷*Open mid-May–Labour Day Mon–Fri 10am–5pm, weekends 10am–6pm. Rest of the year Mon–Fri 10am–5pm (Wed til 1pm). ☜$5. www.ecsmuseum.com. ✕☏403-822-3970.*

Hand Hills Ecological Reserve

About 28km/17.5mi southeast of Drumheller via Hwy. 573.

◷*Open year-round daily. 🚶☏403-823-1749. ⊘No vehicle access; cars not permitted; no visitor facilities.*

This 2,227ha/5,500-acre expanse of prairie enables visitors to observe some 130 bird species and many animals from its **hiking trails** *(no trailheads)*. The reserve abuts Little Fish Lake Provincial Park. Although not pristine (the land is used for stock grazing), the reserve provides a good notion of what the northern mixed grasslands in this area looked like before Sam Drumheller arrived. There are no facilities.

Alberta's Official Symbols

Provincial **flower**:	Wild Rose
Provincial **tree**:	Lodgepole Pine
Provincial **bird**:	Great Horned Owl
Provincial **mammal**:	Rocky Mountain Bighorn Sheep
Provincial **gemstone**:	Ammolite
Provincial **motto**:	"Strong and free"

Dinosaur Provincial Park★★★

MAP OF PRINCIPAL SIGHTS

This 81sq km/31sq mi park on the Red Deer River would be a spectacular recreational area based only on the great natural beauty and wildlife of its badlands, but its fame and its status as a UNESCO World Heritage Site are also due to events that took place here over 75 million years ago, when the terrain was a tropical marshland on a river delta teeming with life. Layers and layers of sedimentary rock built up over the ancient swamp as geological processes continued for eons; periods of glaciation have worn away much of the accumulated sediment. Today about 3 million years of strata is visible on the valley walls. So far, some 39 species of dinosaurs have been found here, along with other finds such as skin impressions, prehistoric plants, ancient fish and birds. Palaeontologists have unearthed 150 complete skeletons in the park as well as piles of bones (bone beds) washed down by the ancient river; excavations continue and every year the Royal Tyrrell Museum in Drumheller produces a report. The richness of the discoveries of dinosaur fossils in the park might lead some people to believe that in Late Cretaceous fossil beds, it is standing room only. In fact, worldwide, dinosaur fossils are extremely rare and fragmentary. The Royal Tyrrell Museum exhibits feature about 75 percent real fossils (the casts are lighter in colour), which is quite unusual. Most exhibits in the world's museums, including the Royal Ontario Museum in Toronto, are largely casts. Only about .0001 percent of all dinosaurs left a fossil trace. That is why every fossil site is precious. The province set up the park in 1955 largely to protect the dinosaur remains. Some 90,000 visitors pass through the park every year.

- **Information:** Park open daily year-round. Visitor Centre open mid-May–Labour Day daily 8:30am–7pm, Sept–early Oct 10am–5pm. Rest of year hours vary. ☎403-378-4342. www.tprc.alberta.ca.
- **Orient Yourself:** The park lies 174km/108mi southeast of Drumheller by Hwy. 10 south to Hwy. 56 south to the Trans-Can Hwy. 1 east to Brooks. From Brooks, take Hwy. 873 north 10km/6mi, turn right onto Hwy. 544, and left on Hwy. 551 to Dinosaur Park Rd. The **visitor centre** is just south and west of the parking lot, and 5km/.3mi north of the park entrance.
- **Parking:** A large parking lot is located about .5km/.3mi north of the park entrance, off the loop road that leads through the park. Walking paths lead to the visitors' centre. Vehicles are not allowed within the park, except on designated roads.
- **Don't Miss:** As most of the park is a protected nature reserve, the only way to see the remote areas is by the park's guided interpretive hikes or by a tour bus (details below).
- **Organizing Your Time:** Give yourself at least a day to explore Dinosaur Provincial Park. If you are at all fit, it is worthwhile to take the hikes; the average high temperature at the park in July is 35°C/95°F. Reserve well in advance of your visit for a guided hike or the bus tour, as these fill up. An overnight in Brooks, about 40km/25mi south of the park, is recommended. Man-made Lake Newell, located 13km/ 8 mi south of the park, provides welcome aquatic relaxation.
- **Kids:** The exhibits in the Tyrrell field station, inside the visitor centre.
- **Also See:** SOUTHERN ALBERTA

A Bit of Geology

Ancient Life – More than 75 million years ago, when the park's terrain was a tropical marshland on a river delta, great ferns, towering palm trees, giant redwoods, huge insects and exuberant flora shared the land with multitudes of ancient animals, culminating in the dinosaurs. Early forms of birds, lizards,

©Travel Alberta

Dinosaur Provincial Park

turtles, sharks, crocodiles, amphibians, fish, mammals, marsupials and an astonishing array of dinosaurs died over the eons and were covered by river silt, then by the waters and sediment of the ancient Bearpaw Sea—in rare cases being preserved by a chemical process that turned them into fossils. About 65 million years ago, after a series of events whose nature is still unclear, culminating in the terrible meteor impact that created the huge Chicxulub crater in the Yucatan Peninsula, mass extinctions brought the Late Cretaceous Period to a close, at which point dinosaurs disappeared, launching the Tertiary Period. This event is known as the KT boundary (K standing for Cretaceous period, T for the Tertiary).

Then, a mere 14,000 years ago, the most recent great ice sheet, the Wisconsin, began its last retreat. Meltwater accumulated behind ice dams, forming lakes from which great rivers cascaded, ripping through the land and creating the deep river valleys characteristic of this area of Alberta. Wind and rain continued this process, which was very rapid

😊 A Bit of Advice 😊

😊In Alberta, it is illegal to remove fossils from provincial and federal parks or to sell or take fossils out of the province without a government certificate.

in geological terms, and the Cretaceous layer was uncovered for one Joseph Burr Tyrrell to recognize in June 1884, when he found, within days, a dinosaur skeleton and bituminous coal. In 2007 Royal Tyrrell palaeontologists excavated a bone bed of **hadrosaur,** or duckbilled dinosaur, remains; over the winter of 2007-2008, they removed the skull of a **corythosaurus** (crested duckbilled dinosaur) by pulling it in a sled across the frozen Red Deer River.

Today's Habitats – The park's UNESCO World Heritage Site citation mentions first and foremost its natural setting and great cottonwood trees. Within the park are three distinct habitats, where live many animals, including 160 bird species, and plants under stress elsewhere. In the **riparian habitat** along the river stand groves of prairie cottonwood and willow trees, along with wild roses (Alberta's provincial flower), strawberries and gooseberries as well as Saskatoon, chokecherry and buffalo berry bushes. Migrating warblers pass through while Baltimore orioles, robins, least flycatchers nest here and waterfowl such as loons, grebes, great blue herons, pelicans, cormorants, and geese and tundra swans are sometimes seen. Farther off, in the **arid badlands** of the valley floor, cacti (which bloom in early June) and sage predominate with flowers such as Soloman's seal, prairie primrose, blue flax and asters, and visitors often spot Nuttal's cotton-tail rabbits, mule deer and the occasional coyote. Golden eagles, kestrels, mountain bluebirds, nighthawks and great-horned and short-eared owls all nest within the park. High up, on the prairies above the valley, extend the **grasslands** of the dry mixed-grass subregion, where pronghorn antelope, western meadowlarks, mourning doves, blackbirds, ring-necked pheasants and grouse reside.

A Bit of History

The discoveries of Joseph Burr Tyrrell occurred when the scientific world was primed to receive them. The 19C was a period of great scientific ferment, nowhere more so than in geology where it was becoming apparent that the earth was very old indeed, and that strange events had taken place. Dinosaur bones that had cropped up in Europe and America were now recognized as remains of very old animals, deeply confusing naturalists who couldn't place them in any sort of reasonable category. In 1842, Richard Owen, a great British taxonomist, coined the term *dinosauria*, identified them as reptiles and laboured to name the specimens that had been found. Bones slowly piled up, as scientists adjusted world history to account

for them, and dinosaur reconstructions were a prime exhibit at the Great Exhibition of 1851 in London. By the time Tyrrell made his discovery, scientists knew what they were looking at. Within four years of his find of the *Albertosaurus,* the **Geological Survey of Canada** sent Thomas Weston to investigate the site; what he found in Dead Lodge Canyon, now a part of the park, confirmed Tyrrell's discovery. In 1897 the Survey dispatched Lawrence Lamb, who wrote systematic descriptions and made drawings. When the Canadian Northern Railway reached Drumheller in 1912, palaeontologists were among the first to leap to the platform. Americans Barnum Brown of the American Museum of Natural History in New York City and Charles H. Sternburg, progenitor of three generations of distinguished palaeontologists, floated down the Red Deer River on rafts, conducting extensive excavations between 1910 and 1917, a period known as the Great Canadian Dinosaur Rush.

Visit

Park open daily year-round. Visitor centre open mid-May–Labour Day daily 8:30am–7pm; Sept–early Oct 10am–5pm. Rest of year hours vary. 🅿🚶♿*(some trails accessible; ask ahead; bus tour by advance arrangement).* ☎*403-378-4342. www.tprc.alberta.ca.*

©Travel Alberta

Dinosaur Provincial Park Visitor Centre

©Travel Alberta

Dinosaur Provincial Park tour

Just south of the parking lot, the new (2006) park **visitor centre,** an expansive, low-lying building that blends in well with the landscape, is an essential stop. Displays describe the landscape visitors will encounter, including the rare cottonwood habitat on the floodplains along the river. A film *(35min)* describes the creation of the park site. Park interpreters in a fossil laboratory give demonstrations *(25min)* of how fossils are prepared and skeletons assembled. The **field station** of the Royal Tyrrell Museum of Palaentology, with its galleries of ancient life, is housed in a separate wing. Sunday evenings *(Jul & Aug)*, the park organizes badlands-themed entertainment at the Deadlodge Canyon amphitheatre, with visitors recruited to help out on stage.

Immediately upon entrance to the park, an splendid **viewpoint**★★★ overlooks nearly 3,000ha/7,000 acres of badlands cut by the Red Deer River. The scene includes mesas, canyons and hoodoos, the wind-sculpted columns protected by boulders of harder stone on the tops; the best colours are seen early or late in the day.

Through the park runs the thin green floodplain of the Red Deer River, in dramatic contrast to the arid badlands, and in the distance stretches the vast expanse of the prairies. The road then descends to the valley. A **circular drive** *(5km/3mi)* takes the visitor through this wild and desolate, almost lunar, landscape, where little except cacti and sagebrush flourish. At several points, short walks lead to dinosaur bones preserved where they were found. Explanatory panels offer details on the type of dinosaur and its size. Longer **nature trails** enable visitors to better appreciate this pristine terrain. Two outdoor sites provide displays of dinosaur lore. Since 70 percent of the park is a natural preserve, the best way to see it is by one of several themed **guided hikes** led by an interpreter, ranging from 2.5hrs to all day *(reservations ☎403-378-4344; prices vary)*, or by a special **bus tour**★ *(2hrs.; departs from the Drumheller Visitor Centre plaza mid-May–Labour Day Mon–Fri 9am–noon & 1pm–4pm, weekends 10am–noon & 1pm–4pm; 1-day advance reservations required; ⊛$8; ♿by arrangement; ☎403-378-4344).*

As these tours are extremely popular, it is essential to reserve ahead, and to allot enough time. Most tours occur only in July-August, while some tours are also offered in May and September.

Occasionally, visitors can glimpse research teams hard at work on digs that take place every summer during a frantic 10-week period starting in June, after which the finds are taken to the Royal Tyrrell Museum in Drumheller for cataloguing.

Rosebud
POPULATION 90

Named for the multitude of wild rose bushes that bloom in the valley of the Rosebud River, this tiny town of fewer than 100 residents has known a renaissance as an outpost of culture in the midst of the prairies. The town's setting, in the eroded badlands valley surrounded by wheat fields, is beautiful and the town, like the rose bushes, has bloomed into a very attractive place. Its rebirth is due entirely to the Rosebud Theatre and School of the Arts, which has taken over many buildings to house its programs, staff and students, who have done much to add animation to the town. Operating nine months a year, the theatre brings in about 40,000 visitors a year. By Western standards, the 100km/63mi trip from Calgary is a short hop. Services in town revolve around the theatre. Life in pioneer Rosebud is evoked in the Centennial Museum located in a little red building that was once Mah Joe's Chinese Laundry.

- 🛈 **Information:** ☎403-677-2271. www.rosebud.ca.
- ▶ **Orient Yourself:** 35km/21mi southwest of Drumheller by Hwy. 9 west, then Hwy. 840 south.
- 🅿 **Parking:** There is ample parking in the town.
- 👁 **Don't Miss:** Explore the theatre scene in Rosebud.
- 🕐 **Organizing Your Time:** Consider an overnight stay in order to take in a performance at the theatre, although matinees are offered. Otherwise, allow a half a day to visit Rosebud.
- **Kids:** Plays at the Rosebud Theatre are generally appropriate for older children.
- 👶 **Also See:** GREATER CALGARY

A Bit of History

Ranchers and farmers, many of them from Scotland and the US, scraped out a difficult living here in the late 19C, until the arrival of the Canadian Northern Railway in 1912 made it possible to ship out grain and join the larger economy. Years of relative prosperity followed, and the population once reached the dizzying total of 300, served by a hotel, store, Chinese cafe and laundry, a dance hall and a grain elevator. But by the 1960s, Rosebud had turned into a boarded-up ghost town as services such as education, the railroad and banking moved to larger population centres, a fate of many small prairie towns.

Begun as an outreach program for Calgary youths in 1973 by the Crescent Heights Baptist Church of Calgary, the Rosebud Theatre and School of the Arts presented their first play in 1983, and events progressed from there. Today the school mounts productions nine months a year and offers accredited certificate programs in theatre arts.

©Travel Alberta

Rosebud Mercantile Building

Sights

Town Centre

Along Main Street.

The small centre of the community holds a restaurant-tea room in the bright yellow Victorian-style Rosebud Country Inn, several other B&Bs, a general store, and two art galleries in addition to the theatre. A self-guided **walking tour** of the town takes in 12 points of historical interest, each with an interpretive sign *(details from the Centennial Museum)*. Rosebud has several excellent gift shops including one in the basement level of The Mercantile building and two across the street selling fair-trade clothing, handmade jewellery, pottery, soaps and household items. A pretty nine-hole golf course stretches along the river.

Rosebud Theatre

102 Railway Ave. Box office open Mon–Fri 8am–4:30pm and Sat 8am–4pm, ⏰ *Closed Sun and major holidays.* ☎403-677-2001, or 800-267-7553. www.rosebudtheatre.com.

This local professional theatre company marked its 25th anniversary in 2008 with a stellar roster of shows and stay-and-play packages with local inns such as the Rosebud Country Inn *(see Address Book)* and the Heartwood Manor and Spa in Drumheller *(see Address Book)*. The extensively renovated 220-seat **Rosebud Opera House** is the venue for five major productions during the year, with five to seven shows a week, including matinees; recent plays have included *On Golden Pond, Fiddler on the Roof,* and *For the Pleasure of Seeing Her Again* by Québec's Michel Tremblay. The 70-seat Studio Stage on the "outskirts of town," that is to say, five minutes away on foot, hosts productions during the summer season as well as students' theatre workshop productions. Sets, music, lighting and venue are surprisingly elaborate and visually effective. As befits the theatre's Baptist origins and continuing connection with the ministry, the majority of these plays, especially the heartwarming Christmas performance, are family friendly.

A dinner theatre ticket will get you a seat at The Mercantile restaurant and an all-you-can-eat country buffet lunch or supper. Ticket prices vary depending on day and time, whether the meal is included, size of group and high or low season; check the website for details.

Rosebud Centennial Museum

117 Main St. ⏰*Open same hours as general store, mid-May to Labour Day Mon–Sat 9am–5pm except on theatre nights, when open to 8pm. Sun 10am–2pm.* ⏰*Closed Sun in winter.* ☎403-677-2271. www.rosebud.ca/museum_home.htm.

This museum maintained by the Rosebud Historical Society shares the premises of the Little Country Blessings

Rosebud welcome sign

Rosebud Theatre production

General Store, formerly the Mah Joe's Chinese Laundry, directly across the street from the Rosebud Theatre. Inside the low-lying building with its false front is a lovingly assembled collection of artifacts showcasing the region's coal mining and agricultural history; the exhibit of old tools is especially popular.

Local lore includes that about 6-feet-tall rancher "Wild Horse" **Jack C. Morton** (1879-1944), also known as Big Jack and Manitoba Badboy, seemingly a character of boundless charm and terrific initiative, who ran one of the biggest spreads in the area, then switched to farming when winters proved too hard for cattle. He was an initiator of the Calgary Stampede. A photo of Jack and his family, all looking grim enough to stare down a charging buffalo, hangs near the checkout counter.

The Rosebud Theatre

Back in its heyday from the end of WW II and the 1950s, the mining-farming town of Rosebud was a social and economic hub. Set among the deserted hills of the Rosebud River Valley, the town of 300 had a bank, twice-daily train service to Calgary, a school, three churches and three grain elevators. But the realities of urbanization of the railroad, farming and government services, which devastated many towns on the prairie, turned Rosebud into a real-life ghost town until the early 1970s. About this time, a group of theatre enthusiasts from the Crescent Heights Baptist Church in Calgary visited the hamlet and decided to make their home in an empty white clapboard building. The nonprofit Rosebud School of the Arts and its resident company, Rosebud Theatre, was born.

Today more than 40,000 people a year attend shows in the town of only 90 residents. The primary venue is the 220-seat Rosebud Opera House, a converted granary. The arts school educates about 25 to 30 students at any one time in a variety of disciplines, including acting, vocals, set design and construction, and wardrobe. Most students cut their teeth on the theatre stage. The theatre company celebrated its 25th anniversary in 2008.

RED DEER AREA

Edging the banks of its namesake river, the city of Red Deer and its surroundings lie deep in Alberta's parklands of gently rolling hills interrupted by moraines— long ridges of gravel formed when ice sheets stopped pushing forward and began melting. The roadside landscape is one of wheat fields and crops of canola, an oil seed alternately known as rapeseed that in summer turns a brilliant yellow as far as the eye can see. The region is also a major producer of barley and corn; cattle grazing on the rich grasslands support local meat-packing plants. Embracing 2 million people within a 160km/100mi radius, Alberta's densest population centres are here, in a north-south corridor running from Edmonton to Lethbridge and encompassing Calgary and Red Deer, Alberta's third most populous city. Speckled with lakes and crisscrossed by dozens of rivers and streams, the area boasts world-class fishing and boating, not to mention other recreation. Prairie towns to the east, such as Stettler, offer attractions like the Alberta Prairie Railway Excursions, and to the west, the Nordegg and Rocky Mountain House national historic sites, en route to Banff and Jasper national parks, are easily reached via Highway 11, the David Thompson Highway.

A Bit of Geology

Covering some 12 percent of Alberta's territory, the **parklands** are a transitional ecozone lying between the prairie region to the south and the boreal forests to the north. Vegetation types characteristic of this area are low bushes, grasslands, stands of aspen trees and wetlands, although little pristine parkland has survived the introduction of farming in the late 19C. The area is well-watered and rarely suffers drought, in contrast to the dry prairies in the southeast of the province.

Weather in the parklands varies according to the proximity to the Rocky Mountains, but in the area surrounding the town of Red Deer, expect January weather to average minus 15°C/4°F and July weather to average 16°C/61°F. Frost-free days per year total only 99, but

Canola field, near Red Deer

©Travel Alberta

Address Book

For dollar sign categories, see the Legend on the cover flap.

WHERE TO STAY

$ Duchess Manor Retreat – *4813 54th St., Red Deer.* ☎*403-346-7776. www. dmanorretreat.com. 3 rooms.* P Spa ⌣. This 1905 house in the city centre offers calm amid the bustle. Rooms are furnished in a vaguely retro style, with flowered fabrics and some antiques. Shared bathroom. Guests have access to a patio and porch, as well as to a pleasant sitting room. Breakfast comes in the rate, and lunch is available at cost. Spa services include facials, hand and foot treatments, aromatherapy. No children, no pets.

$ Ol' MacDonalds Resort – *On Buffalo Lake, east of Lacombe. Turn east off Hwy. 2 at Lacombe onto Hwy.12 to Alix, then left onto Hwy. 601. 4 motel rooms, 10 cabins, 200-plus campsites. www.olmac donalds.com.* Choose a cabin (each with cooking utensils, a firepit and picnic table, but no bedding), motel room or camping spot at this tree-lined summer resort on the shores of Buffalo Lake. Campsites, many right on the sandy beach, are serviced or unserviced and family sites are available. Resort amenities include a beach snack shack, playground, baseball diamond, petting zoo, rentals of water-sports equipment, mini-golf, and daily hay rides. Travellers looking to escape the squeals of happy kids should stay elsewhere. Pets permitted in the campground only.

$ Roslyn Hills B&B – *Off Hwy. 595, near Hwy. 808.* ☎*403-347-0206. www. roslynhills.com. 3 rooms plus guest house.* P ⌣. Out on the range, yet near to city lights, this property offers guests B&B lodgings with shared bathroom or a self-catering guest house that accommodates 8 people, with a kitchen and fireplace. The B&B sitting room has convertible couches that can do service as beds. Rooms are clean and comfortable. A former granary, the guest house is decorated in western style with log furniture, a stone fireplace and

Ol' MacDonalds Resort

©Travel Alberta

colourful throws; beds are all in one room, bunk style. The Purdie family has worked this land for five generations, and invites guests to enjoy ranch activities such as horseback riding and looking after stock.

$ Shunda Creek Hostel – *Shunda Creek Recreation Area Rd., west of Nordegg, 3km/1.8mi north of Hwy.11.* ☎*403-721-2140 or 888-748-6321. www.hihostels. ca/alberta. 47 beds.* This place is a well-kept secret, but not that secret—you will need to make reservations in peak season. Spend time inexpensively in a gorgeous natural setting in the vicinity of Nordegg, near Lake Abraham and Lake Goldeneye. Part of the Hostelling International group, this site offers both shared and private rooms available year-round; linens provided. Guests have access to a self-catering kitchen, laundry facilities and common room. The front desk will point you to great hikes, mountain bike rentals, and places to ice-climb, golf and fish.

$$ Aurum Lodge – *On Whitegoat Lake, 45km/28mi west of Nordegg, off Hwy. 11.* ☎*403-721-2117. www.aurumlodge. com. 6 rooms, 3 housekeeping units.* ✕⌣P⌣. Modified American plan available. This Bighorn Country eco-retreat sits at an elevation of 1,350m/4,500ft within a 1hr's drive of

Banff and Jasper national parks. Set in pristine woods overlooking Abraham Lake, the destination resort hugs the front ranges of the Rocky Mountains. Fully recyclable materials have been used in the construction of the solar-powered lodge, which boasts European-styled rooms. More rustic, the housekeeping units are self-contained, with kitchens. Breakfast included; dinner available by prior request (**$$**). The lodge provides bicycles, horseback riding, guided canoe tours and guided walks of the Athabasca Glacier. On their own, guests can hike amid stunning mountain scenery. The largely untrammeled wilderness area can be explored year-round, but summer brings out its best.

$$ Capri Centre – *3310 50th Ave., Red Deer.* ☎*403-346-2091 or 800-662-7197. www.capricentre.com. 219 rooms.* ✕ ⟨⟩ 🅿 ⟳. This 14-storey hotel caters to business travellers (wireless Internet), but welcomes tourists as well. Rooms have a vaguely western theme, with pine-paneled walls and fancy headboards, but furnishings are otherwise standard. A heated outdoor pool, three restaurants, a fitness club, hair salon and in-house liquor store are on-site. Entertainment includes a country music dance hall for those so inclined, but also **Barbero's Restaurant ($$)**, serving Alberta beef and a buffet in white-linen-and-crystal surroundings; the Sunday champagne brunch is lavish *(reservations suggested* ☎*403-346-2091 ext 3168)*. **Joe's Deli ($)** provides soup, salad, sandwiches and large mugs of Second Cup coffee at lunch time.

$$ Cheechako Cabins – *Grouse Meadow Lane, Nordegg. Off Shundra Creek Rd. from Hwy. 11.* ☎*403-721-2230. www.cheechakocabins.com. 4 cabins. 2-night minimum stay.* These modern versions of coal-miners' cabins are trim and comfortable, with indoor plumbing, satellite TV and DVD player, fully equipped kitchen, a wood-burning stove and a BBQ out on the patio. All bedding and linens are provided. An old-time miner would think he'd died and gone to heaven. Interiors are a bit snug, but newly decorated with pine panelling and polished wood floors,

patchwork quilts on the beds, comfortable chairs, a dining area and windows looking out on the woods.

$$ La Solitude B&B and Spa – *From Hwy. 2 and 32nd St. overpass, take Calgary-Edmonton trail .5km/.3mi, then turn left at Woodland Hills sign. Go 2.3km/1.4mi on paved road, then left on TWP 380 gravel road 1km/.6mi.* ☎*403-340-0031. www.lasolitude.com. 2 suites.* 🅿 Spa ⟳. Despite its rural site, this B&B is only a short drive from downtown Red Deer. Attired in romantic decor of lace and florals, large, sunny rooms look out on spacious grounds. Included in the rate, the breakfast is a choice of hot and cold menu items. Spa treatments include facials and beauty treatments, and full-body treatments such as massage, scrubs and a mud bath.

$$ Red Deer Lodge – *4311 49th Ave., Red Deer.* ☎*403-346-8841 or 800-661-1657, 233 units. www.reddeerlodge. ca.* ✕ Spa ⟳ 🅿. Popular with business travelers for its conference facilities, this six-storey hotel (part of an Alberta chain) is a good bet for families as well, given its child-friendly extras such as kids' suites (adjoined to the parents' room), nightly milk and cookies, movie night and special packages. A fitness centre with a swimming pool and a hot whirlpool, an indoor courtyard garden with pond, and a great location on the south end of downtown are added perks. There's also a hair salon and day spa. The **botaniCa ($$)** restaurant, open 7am to 8pm, is set in the tropical garden atrium and offers a range of fare including kids' noshes like chicken fingers. On weekends, try the breakfast buffet and brunch. For dinner, it's best to take the Alberta prime rib buffet. Nothing fancy, but hearty portions and good service.

$$$ Chateau Suites at Sylvan Bay – *5100 Lakeshore Dr., Sylvan Lake.* ☎*403-887-6699 or 877-8265. www. chateausuites.ca. 61 rooms.* ⟨⟩ 🅿. This five-storey beachside resort hotel sits on 2.2ha/5.5 acres at Sylvan Lake. It is situated next to the Wild Rapids Water Slide and near restaurants, boat rentals and other tourist amenities. Shopping is not far off. Each spacious one- or two-bedroom suite includes a fully equipped kitchen that opens to a sitting area and balcony, with gas BBQ, overlooking the lake. Suites have gas fireplaces, washers and dryers. Decoration includes plenty of blond wood and relaxing neutral colours. Ideal for a family vacation at the beach or for a winter getaway; the nearby provincial park offers skating, and there are many snowmobile trails in the area.

$$$ Prairie Creek Inn – *About 19km/12mi south of Rocky Mountain House, off Hwy. 22.* ☎403-844-2672. *www.theprairiecreekinn.com. 2 suites, 1 cottage. Minimum 2-night stay.* ♿🅿🍽. Extending over 60ha/150acres of wooded wilderness, this secluded luxury lodging makes an ideal spot to hibernate or recharge amid nature. Edging a brimming creek, the compound offers suites with a fireplace, soaking tub, plush furnishings, duvets on the beds and bathrobes. Included in the rate, a hot gourmet breakfast might feature crab and dill egg scramble or blueberry cream-cheese French toast, among other choices. Besides fishing for brown trout, activities include bocci ball on the lawn, walks along the creek and evening marshmallows roasts.

WHERE TO EAT

$$ Earls Red Deer – *2111 Gaetz Ave., Red Deer.* ♿🅿. ☎403-342-4055. *www.earlsreddeer.ca.* **Canadian.** This downtown restaurant serves a convivial lunch and dinner. Appetizers are the sort best eaten with a stiff martini or Margarita (which Earls does quite well), such as chicken wings, potato skins and nachos. Main courses include a variety of pizzas, chicken and rib combos, steaks and a pasta selection, plus a salmon dish. Earl believes spicy is better, so check for red pepper and garlic: Cajun blackened chicken, spicy seafood penne (with cracked chilis), spicy Thai green curry. The steaks are unspiced, but the potatoes are rich in garlic. Salads are less intense: the spinach and berry salad with roast chicken offers a pleasant alternative.

$$ Las Palmeras – *3630 50th Ave, Red Deer.* ♿🅿. ☎403-346-8877. **Mexican.** Over the past 15 years, this family-run eatery has changed locations several times, and a devoted clientele has lately followed it to the south side of Red Deer, just off Gaetz Avenue (west side). It's the city's only authentic Mexican restaurant, and it dishes up favorites such as tacos, burritos and enchiladas along with combo platters (mix and match) that include tasty Spanish rice and refried beans. Specialties include grilled seafood, pork and beef. The mole sauce is especially good, as is the homemade salsa.

$$ Smuggler's Inn – *5000 Lakeshore Dr., Sylvan Lake.* ♿🅿. ☎403-887-0213. *www.smugglersatsylvan.ca.* **Canadian.** In the Alberta tradition, this restaurant, a branch of the popular Calgary eatery of the same name, offers an excellent selection of prime beef, with one roast chicken dish and a little taste of shrimp and lobster, but only if taken with some beef. There's a generous salad bar. The interior vaguely resembles a pirate ship, with dark wood paneling and comfortable upholstered chairs, enlivened by portraits of fierce one-legged brigands and kegs of rum. A modern frame structure, the building is sited near the beach at Sylvan Lake.

$$$ Redstone Grill and Wine Bar – *5018 45th St., Red Deer.* ♿🅿. ☎403-342-2180. *www.redstonegrill.ca.* **Canadian.** This bistro serving 'Canadian' fare is a solid addition to Red Deer's restaurant scene. The candlelit dining room is sleek, with dark wood furnishings and olive-hued walls. There's a good selection of wine and an upscale menu. An extensive offering of appetizers includes savoury lobster cakes, fanciful mini-cheeseburgers and warm duck confit salad; mains include rack of lamb with a cranberry-mustard coating, St. Louis spareribs basted with bourbon, seafood and, of course, Alberta steaks. The lunch menu is lighter, with gourmet paninis and other sandwiches, salads and pasta. On weekends, there's often live music.

hours of sunshine are plentiful, and in midsummer (late June) the sun doesn't set until 10pm.

A Bit of History

Traces of human habitation here go back 10,000 years, following the retreat of the last ice sheet. Aboriginal inhabitants of this area when European settlers arrived included the Blackfoot, the Cree and the Stony Indians, as well as the Métis, who are descended from European fur traders and aboriginal women. Today, First Nations members make up a small but significant portion of the area's population; less than 5 percent of Red Deer's population is indigenous.

Beginning in 1800 geographer **David Thompson** (🖙 see sidebar) made Rocky Mountain House his base for exploration of the Red Deer and Bow rivers, and parts far beyond. In 1811 he set out from here and crossed the Athabasca Pass to establish the first practical trade route to the Pacific; his feat confirmed the British claim to British Columbia, reinforced by the Royal Navy. Today, Highway 11 from the city of Red Deer to Jasper and Banff national parks commemorates this renowned explorer.

In the 1940s the discovery of large tracts of oil and gas transformed the region's inhabitants into "blue-eyed sheiks," and sparked a population boom. Recent high energy prices and ancillary economic development are bringing in another wave of newcomers. Strong **petrochemical** and **energy** service industries have developed to complement natural resources extraction; the Joffre/Prentiss area just 15km/9mi northeast of Red Deer is home to several major petrochemical plants, such as NOVA Chemicals, BP Petroleum, Praxair and ME Global, one of the largest such clusters in North America. The jobs at these plants pay extremely well and most require a high level of education, reinforcing the area economy. Local spin-offs include manufacturing industries that produce and use plastics, film, fibres and other petrochemical products.

Red Deer marks the halfway point between Calgary and Edmonton along the Queen Elizabeth II Highway (Highway 2). This location makes Red Deer a providential meeting point for corporations with offices in both major cities. The great economic importance of the Highway 2 corridor has fueled debate about resurrecting passenger train service from Edmonton to Lethbridge.

David Thompson

Considered one of North America's greatest geographers, David Thompson (1770-1857) was born in dire poverty to Welsh parents living in London. His widowed mother enrolled him in a charity school, where he studied mathematics. The Hudson's Bay Company took promising students as apprentices, and at age 14, Thompson embarked for Rupert's Land, the vast HBC territory in northern Canada. At 18 Thompson suffered a broken leg, which nearly killed him; during convalescence he learned navigational measurement using the sun and stars, blinding one eye in the process but setting him on a brilliant surveying career. Working successively for the HBC and its rival, the North West Company, Thompson traveled 90,000km/55,000mi—twice the earth's circumference—locating the headwaters of the Mississippi, crossing the Rocky Mountains and mapping the entire Columbia River. He noted his travels in minute detail, including aboriginal people he encountered. In 1799 he married Charlotte Small, who was half Cree; their marriage lasted 58 years and produced 13 children. In 1812, Thompson crossed Canada to Terrebonne, north of Montreal, to retire. As a wealthy partner in the North West Company, he continued to receive commissions to draw maps and survey canals. He established the US/Canada boundary from Rainy Lake, Ontario, to Quebec for the International Boundary Commission. Unfortunately, unsuccessful business ventures drained his fortune. At 87 he died in poverty. His *Narrative* remained in the family until the great geologist Joseph Burr Tyrell got it published in 1916.

Red Deer ★

POPULATION 85,705 – MAP P 198

Red Deer is an important trade and commercial centre whose population has climbed from 65,000 just over a decade ago to nearly 86,000. A major destination for conventions and trade shows (the annual Agri-Trade Show draws more than 75,000 visitors), the community serves a regional population of some 200,000 people. Boasting amenities out of proportion to its size, the city hosts the 115acre/46.5ha convention and event centre Westerner Park, many shopping malls, large hotels with conference centres, 80km/50mi of paths along the Red Deer River, manicured parks such as Bower Ponds and picturesque natural areas such as the Gaetz Lake Sanctuary. Its compact core includes restored heritage buildings as well as gingerbread houses, riverside cottages and modern residences. The city's economy is based primarily on agriculture (grain and cattle), oil and gas, manufacturing and retail services. As is usual for Prairie towns, volunteer community organizations abound, supporting everything from refugee placement to sports for the handicapped to Irish and Scottish country dancing. The annual five-day Westerner Days fair in mid-July includes rodeo activities, a midway and concerts.

- **Information:** Tourism Red Deer Visitor Centre, north of 32nd St overpass on Hwy. 2. ⊙Open Mon–Fri 10am–5pm, Sat–Sun and holidays 9am–5pm. Slighter longer hours in the summer. ✕⟨♿⟩P☎403-346-0180, or 800-215-8946. www.tourismreddeer.net or www.reddeer.ca
- ▶ **Orient Yourself:** Red Deer is a sprawling but easily navigated community. The main street is Gaetz Avenue, running north-south, which curves off Hwy. 2 at the city's south end just past the refueling strip known as **Gasoline Alley** and runs past several big-box shopping centres and strip malls, then through downtown Red Deer. Gaetz Ave. intersects with several major east-west routes such as 32nd St. (access to Heritage Ranch, Alberta Sports Hall of Fame and Museum) and 67th St. (leading to large retail and industrial addresses at the north end of town).
- P **Parking:** Most of downtown parking is paid under a new system established in 2008 (☾see Parking in Practical Information).
- ☺ **Don't Miss:** Waskasoo Park, Fort Normandeau.
- ⊙ **Organizing Your Time:** Red Deer is a good weekend stop with easy access to both northern and southern Alberta as well as nearby sights worthy of several days' time.
- Kids **Especially for Kids:** Alberta Sports Hall of Fame, Kerry Wood Nature Centre.
- ⚲ **Also See:** GREATER CALGARY

A Bit of History

The Cree called the Red Deer River waskasoo or "elk." Early Scottish fur-traders apparently confused local elk with the large-antlered red deer native to the Highlands. The name **Waskasoo** reappears often in modern Red Deer, notably in the name of a city park and a residential area.

Like rivers and lakes across Canada, the Red Deer River was part of a vast and ancient aboriginal trading network; a trail leading up from Montana to present-day Edmonton crossed the river some 7km/4.5mi upstream from the present-day city of Red Deer. When Fort Calgary was established in 1875, this fort gained commercial importance on what became the Calgary-Edmonton Trail. A trading post, **Red Deer Crossing,** was set up in 1882, and in 1884 one Robert McClellan set up a "stopping-house," or rough inn, at this site. During the 1885 Northwest Rebellion, the militia built Fort Normandeau at Red Deer Crossing. The present town site was definitively established when the Calgary

Practical Information

AREA CODES

The City of Red Deer has just one area code (403). For local calls, dial all 10 digits (area code plus the number but without the 1-prefix for long distance). Long-distance calls to Edmonton and northern Alberta require the 1-780 area code in advance of the number. For Calgary and southern Alberta, dial the (403) area code. More information: ☎1-403-555-1212 or www.telus.ca.

GETTING THERE

BY AIR

Red Deer's regional airport does generally not support tourist travel between Calgary and Edmonton. Your best access is by bus, your own vehicle or rental car from both cities. **Calgary International Airport (YYC)** can be reached at ☎403-735-5000; www. calgaryairport.com.; contact information for Edmonton International Airport is 780-890-8382 or www.edmontonairports.com.

BY BUS

Both **Greyhound Canada** (*☎800-661-8747; www.greyhound.ca*) and **Red Arrow Motorcoach** (*☎403-531-0350 or 800-232-1958; www.redarrow.pwt. ca*) service Red Deer direct from both Calgary and Edmonton (stops in Red Deer three to four times a day).
Red Arrow rates are about 15 percent higher than Greyhound but offer extras such as computer ports and plug-ins, wider aisles and seats, and self-serve cookies, other snacks and hot and cold drinks. Greyhound's depot is located at 4303 Gaetz Ave. (☎403-343-8855); find Red Arrow at 5315 54 St. downtown (☎403-343-2396).

BY CAR

From Calgary International Airport to Red Deer: 17.5km/10mi northeast of downtown. Follow the signs directing you to Hwy 2 (Deerfoot Trail) and take the north exit to Red Deer (which takes about 90 minutes).
From Edmonton International Airport to Red Deer: This airport is actually about 14 mi (20 km) south of Edmonton city limits at the town of Leduc; the airport road runs east for about 2 km (1 mi) to intersect with Hwy 2 running north to Edmonton or south to Red Deer), about 80 minutes by car or bus.

CAR RENTALS

Car rental services have counters at the airports including the smaller centres.
Avis (☎800-879-2847 or www.avis.com)
Hertz (☎800-263-0600 or www.hertz.com)
National (☎800-227-7368 or www.nationalcar.com)
Enterprise (☎800-736-8222 or www.enterprise.com)

GETTING AROUND

BY PUBLIC TRANSPORTATION
By Bus
Transit passes and tickets can be purchased at the city cashier on the first floor of downtown's **city hall;** adult $2.50; youth $1.50, Day passes $6.75 adults. $4.50 youth; they are also available at other locations such as the Bower Place and Parkland Mall information booths; also community services on the fourth floor of city hall. ☎403-342-8225 daytimes or transit@reddeer.ca.

BY TAXI
Associated ☎403-346-2222 or **Chinook Cabs** ☎403-341-7300, or **Alberta Gold Taxi** ☎403-341-7777.

BY CAR
Downtown Red Deer is easy to navigate on foot, though for the most part there is plenty of available on-street meter parking and pay-parking lots along with free 2hr parking in some inner-city areas. Bus service is frequent between north and south Red Deer along Gaetz Avenue, which is not pleasant, however, to travel on foot (exhaust, noise, etc.).

Parking
Most of downtown parking is paid under a new system established in 2008. You can pay at a meter or official city lot (look for the 'P') with a prepaid parking smart card (not helpful for most visitors), or by coins such as the loonie ($1), the twoonie ($2) or in some places quarters. Some private lots accept credit card payments. Downtown parking on weekdays costs 50 cents to 75

cents an hour depending on location and times; parking is free on Saturdays, Sunday and holidays in some city lots (watch for signs).

GENERAL INFORMATION

VISITOR INFORMATION

Tourism Red Deer Visitor Centre, north of 32nd Street overpass on Hwy. 2. Open Mon–Fri 10am–5pm, Sat–Sun and holidays 9am–5pm. Extended hours in summer. ☎403-346-0180 or 800-215-8946. www.reddeer.ca or www.tourismreddeer.net.

ACCOMMODATIONS

For a selection of lodgings, see the Address Book.

Alberta Hotel & Lodging Assn. features an online directory of more than 1,500 annually inspected lodgings and campgrounds. Online search function available. www.travelalberta.com.

Alberta Bed & Breakfast Assn. www.bbalberta.com.

Alberta Country Vacations ☎866-217-2282; www.albertacountryvacation.com.

Charming Inns of Alberta ☎866-551-2281, www.charminginnsofalberta.com. As well, contact the tourist information offices listed under each Sight heading.

RESERVATION SERVICES

Alberta Express Reservations ☎780-621-2855 or 800-884-8803. Free reservation service for some 300 hotels and motels throughout the province.

LOCAL PRESS

Newspapers: *Red Deer Advocate, Red Deer Express* plus numerous weekly publications from towns in the area, including the *Lacombe Globe, Olds Gazette,* and the *Didsbury Chronicle.*

Radio/Televsion: GKGY (country and news); Zed 99, Big 105.5, 106.7 The Drive; CFRN, City TV, CH Television, Shaw Cable.

ENTERTAINMENT

Red Deer College Centre for Performing Arts – *off Hwy. 2 and 32nd Ave.* Home to a leading-edge arts centre that offers a year-round array of ballet, plays, concerts, poetry readings and other cultural/arts events. The **Red Deer Symphony Orchestra,** founded in 1987, performs a full season of concerts at the Arts Centre of Red Deer College.

USEFUL NUMBERS

Red Deer RCMP 911 (emergency) or ☎403-341-2000 (non-emergency).

Red Deer Regional Hospital ☎403-343-4422.

SHOPPING

MALLS

Parkland Mall – *50th Ave. (Gaetz Ave) at 67th St.* ☎403-343-8997. www.parkland-mall.ca. From the province that brought you the world's biggest indoor mall (Edmonton), here is Red Deer's answer, with some 100 shops, restaurants, salons and entertainment venues.

Bower Place – *4900 Molly Bannister Dr.* ☎403-342-5240. www.bowerplace.com. This is Red Deer's premier indoor mall for fashion shopping, with more than 100 shops.

South Pointe Common – *Gaetz Ave. and Delburne Rd.* ☎403-253-3311. www.qualicocommercial.com/southpointe. The newest Red Deer mall, with 700,000sq ft of commercial space, is outdoors, with store façades resembling an early 19C western town, false fronts and fanciful details. Shops are mostly upscale and trendy.

FARMERS' MARKETS

Red Deer Public Market – *Red Deer Arena.* Open mid-May–mid Oct Sat 8am–12:30pm. This farmers' market has operated since 1970, and now attracts some 12,000 people every Saturday. Vendors arrive here from far and near, including fruit growers from British Columbia. Buskers entertain shoppers, and shoppers can sit down to breakfast.

Lacombe Farmers' Market – Open early-May–early Oct Fri 9am-1pm. *Lacombe Centre Mall.* Local farm produce, baked goods and crafts, along with stalls selling snacks and bargain goods.

LEISURE

Collicutt Centre – *3301 30th Ave., Red Deer.* ☎403-358-7529. www.reddeer.ca/collicuttcentre. Kids This enormous fitness centre (250,000 sq ft) contains a wave pool and children's swimming area as well as hot tubs and a steam room, a field house with facilities for tennis, basketball, volleyball and badminton,

Riverbend Golf Course, near Red Deer

©Chris Duthie/Travel Alberta

a 290m/950ft four-lane running track, a gym, 2 indoor soccer pitches, a climbing wall and more, as well as shops, a food court, spa facilities and a chess board (oversized, of course), as well as a well-used chiropractic clinic—all of which are a reminder that, for at least half the year, the outdoors is a bit nippy.

Kids Heritage Ranch – *25 Riverview Park, Red Deer. Open year-round daily 9am-5pm.* ♿☎*403-347-4977.www. heritageranch.ca.* For aspiring cowboys, this equestrian centre near the Albert Sports Hall of Fame and the visitor information centre offers trail rides *($35/hr)* along the Red Deer River for inexperienced riders and children; pony rides around the corral *($3/ride Jul–Aug daily, weekends May–Jun & Sept–Oct)* introduce small children to horses; hay rides in summer, sleigh rides in winter *($150/wagon/hr)*, romantic carriage rides on order.

RECREATION

The Red Deer Area boasts dozens of golf courses, trails for hiking and horseback riding (🍃*Also see Leisure, above*) and wildlife-watching spots. Boaters, rafters and anglers appreciate the **Red Deer River,** which, near its headwaters in the Rockies, is legendary for adrenaline-rush rapids; the water's current and the natural hazards ease as the river weaves from west to east through downtown Red Deer. Other waterways such as the Little Red Deer, the Battle River and the Medicine River are also popular recreational venues. Central Alberta's scattered lakes,

bordered by towns and hamlets, offer lovely local parks and campgrounds, while the resort town of **Sylvan Lake,** 23km/14mi west of Red Deer, has seen a population explosion over the past decade; the town and its giant water slide have been a summer destination for families since the early 20C. **Sylvan Lake Provincial Park** west of Red Deer and six other provincial parks lie within an easy drive of Red Deer. **Pigeon Lake Provincial Park** to the north and Crimson Lake and Buck Lake parks to the west are especially popular.

AREA FESTIVALS

mid-Feb **Winterfest (and polar bear dip):** *Sylvan Lake* ☎403-887-1192 ext 504, www.town.sylvan-lake. ab.ca

late-May **Fort Normandeau Days:** *Red Deer* ☎403-347-7550. www.waskasoopark.ca

mid-Jul **Westerner Days:** *Red Deer* ☎403-343-7800, www.westerner.ab.ca

end Jul **CentreFest:** *Red Deer* ☎403-340-8696, www.centrefest.ca

early Aug **Cream Day:** *Markerville* ☎403-728-3006, www.touralberta.com/creamery
Alberta Railfans Day: *Stettler-Big Valley* ☎403-742-2844, www.absteamtrain.com

mid-Aug **David Thompson Days Fair** ☎403-845-5450, www.rockymtnhouse.com
Jazz at the Lake Festival: *Sylvan Lake* ☎403-882-5050, www.sylvanlakejazzfestival.com

and Edmonton Railway (later part of the Canadian Pacific Railway) arrived in 1891; the city shortly afterwards became a railway hub, with the Canadian Pacific, Alberta Central and Northern Canadian railways all passing through.

Besides Waskasoo, another name that crops up frequently in Red Deer is Gaetz: **Annie L. Gaetz,** a history teacher and newspaper columnist, came to Red Deer from Nova Scotia in 1906. She wrote several books celebrating the area, including *The Park Country History of Red Deer Alberta and District* (1948); a park, an elementary school and of course, Gaetz Ave., carry her name.

Sights

Downtown

Plans to improve the attractiveness of the downtown core include the Alexander Way project, where 48th Street *(formerly Alexander St.)* is being transformed into pedestrian-friendly corridor with sculpture, murals and street furniture linking Barrett Park to the Riverlands area, and connected to the city trail system. **Centennial Plaza Park** *(52nd St., adjacent to Alexander Way)* offers formal gardens and a fountain celebrating the Canadian Pacific Railway. Throughout the downtown are 11 **bronze statues** of local heroes, including Francis the Pig, who escaped captivity for five months only to perish tragically in a senseless accident, and six **murals** depicting local historical events. These artworks, continually augmented, are part of the Ghost Project (the statues being the ghosts) commissioned by the Downtown Business Association to interest residents in local history.

Red Deer Museum and Art Gallery

4525 47A Ave. ◷*Open year-round daily noon–5pm (Wed until 9pm).* ◷*Closed major holidays.* ✺*Contribution requested.* ♿ 🅿 ☏*403-309-8405. www.museum. red-deer.ab.ca.*

While lacking the sandstone grandeur of Calgary's Glenbow Museum or the capaciousness of the Royal Alberta Museum in Edmonton, this understated museum and gallery offers an interesting look at local history from First Nations prior to European contact to the world wars, the Depression and more recent times. The museum collection is particularly strong in western Canadiana and personal artifacts. The art gallery's permanent exhibit comprises artworks from Inuit and First Nations sources as well as from around Canada and abroad. Don't miss the **Swallow Collection of First Nations** or the new **Discovery Room,** where items from the museum collection are highlighted each month, with opportunities for visitors to handle artifacts and to attend talks. There's also an extensive assemblage of costumes

©Travel Alberta

Aerial view of the city of Red Deer

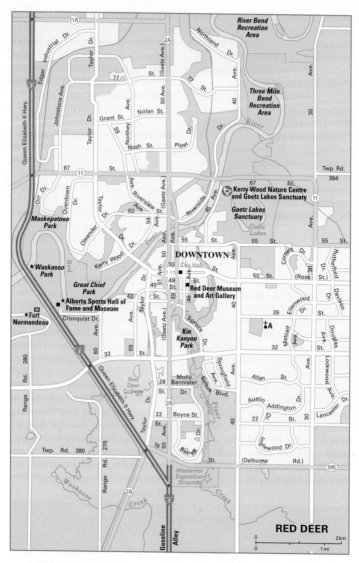

RED DEER

0 — 2km
0 — 1mi

and textiles. An Inuit art exhibit includes a rare, 3m/9ft-long engraved Narwhal (toothed whale) tusk.

St. Mary's Catholic Church★★

A on map. 6 McMillan Ave. (between 30th and 40th Ave. off 39th St.) ⏱*Open year-round Mon–Fri 10am–4 pm; services Sat 5pm, Sun 9am, 11am & 7pm. Self-guided tours* ☙*by contribution. Phone ahead to book a guided tour.* ℗&✆*403-347-3114. www.stmarys-reddeer.ca.*

With its curved and folded walls, rounded towers and massive roof, this

striking church is at once futuristic and ancient in appearance. It presages Frank Gehry's Bilbao museum, while evoking adobe missions of the American Southwest. The use of exposed brick as the sole building material, without adornment, gives the structure exquisite uniformity and solidity. Completed in 1968, the edifice was the first major work by Métis Canadian architect **Douglas Cardinal** (b.1934) and the one that brought him into the architectural limelight. Cardinal went on to build other landmarks including the Canadian Museum of

Tourism Red Deer

St Mary's Catholic Church

Civilization in Quebec, Grande Prairie Regional College in northwest Alberta and the National Museum of the American Indian in Washington, DC.

The building's dark, 650-seat interior reveals sloped floors and a sunlit altar, illuminated by two deep skylights. Oversized curved brick confessionals also dominate the interior. Sculpture by German artist Alois Marx graces the inside. A cross made of two large yellow cedar logs measures 6.5m high and weighs 3,500 pounds.

Kerry Wood Nature Centre and Gaetz Lakes Sanctuary

6300 45th Ave., on south bank of Red Deer River. ◐*Open mid-May–Aug daily 10am–8pm. Rest of the year daily 10am–5pm. Holidays opens 1pm.* ◐*Closed Dec 25.* ◉*Contribution requested.* ♿ 🅿 ☎*403-346-2010. www.waskasoopark.ca. Gaetz Lakes Sanctuary (next to the nature centre)* 🅿 ◐*open year-round daily.* 🚫*No cycling, jogging, skiing or pets allowed.*

A lush labyrinth of red-shale trails, spruce forest and meadows immerse visitors in the region's ecosystems and varied plant and animal life. Volunteer and staff naturalists are knowledgeable about local wildlife as well as the rare moss and lichen here. Winter and summer afford diverse perspectives, both worthy of a visit. The modern **Kids** **interpretive centre,** aimed chiefly at children, displays taxidermied animals such as foxes and large birds. Most notable are the exhib-

its illustrating how Alberta's landscape was formed by successive ice sheets and mega-floods that occurred as the ice retreated. The centre is named for writer and radio and TV broadcaster **Kerry Wood** (1907-1998), an avid nature lover who came to Red Deer with his Scottish parents, via New York City, as a child. He helped found 26 wildlife sanctuaries across North America.

The 118ha/300acre federally protected migratory **bird sanctuary** has recorded sightings of 170 species, including loons, grebes, Sandhill cranes, bald eagles, peregrine falcons, ruffed grouse, great-horned owls and many more. Visitors will enjoy walking along the 5km/3mi of trails and a boardwalk where there are two bird blinds and a viewing deck,

Alberta Sports Hall of Fame and Museum★

30, Riverview Park, off Hwy. 2. ◐*Open mid-May–mid-Oct daily 9am–6pm. Rest of the year daily 10am–5pm.* ◐*Closed major holidays.* ◉*$3.* ♿ 🅿 ☎*403-341-8614. www.albertasportshalloffame.com.*

Kids You don't have to be an athlete, armchair or otherwise, to enjoy this 651sq m/7,000sq ft museum on the city's west side. Plan to spend a couple of hours inside the sprawling redbrick building, which also houses the city's visitor information centre. More than 7,000 sports artifacts are housed here, from Stanley Cup jerseys in the Alberta Hockey Hall of Fame to outdoor equip-

Alberta Sports Hall of Fame and Museum

ment in the Ice and Snow winter gallery. It's the interactive exhibits that really shine: play virtual basketball, football, soccer or hockey, or pretend you're a sportscaster in an official-looking press box. Hop into a wheelchair and test a virtual, 200m/656ft paralympic racetrack, or hone your skills on the baseball pitching field. There's also a 40-seat theatre showing highlights of Alberta sports, an innovative climbing wall, a simulated alpine ski racing machine and a three-hole putting green.

Waskasoo Park★

Follows the Red Deer River Valley within the city. ☎403-346-2010 or 403-342-8111. www.waskasoopark.ca.

This natural area, which follows Piper Creek and the Red Deer River through the city, is a sanctuary from urban life, with paved and shale trails that lead through forests and over brooks. Sightings of animals such as white-tailed deer and many birds are common. Threaded by more than 200km/124mi of trails, this park includes the Gaetz Lakes Sanctuary, historic Fort Normandeau and Kerry Wood Nature Centre, along with the Bower Ponds (canoeing and kayaking in summer, skating and tobogganing in winter) and **Three Mile Bend Recreation Area,** which attracts joggers, cyclists, inline skaters and walkers. In summer, visitors to Three Mile Bend can try—or watch others trying—a freestyle ski jump set atop a deep pond. The Cron-

quist House overlooking Bower Ponds is a restored 1911 farmhouse. The **Kids** **discovery centre** within Bower Ponds is a delightful series of small ponds on a descending slope connected by streams along which children can safely bob on inner tubes *(available for rent)*, sprayed at the bottom by a gentle jet of water in the final pool.

Additional Sight

Fort Normandeau★

Take 32 St. west of Hwy. 2 for 1km/.6mi. ⊙Open mid-May–Jun daily noon–5pm. Jul–Aug daily noon–8pm. ⊘Contribution suggested. ⏰✕🅿️☎403-347-7550. www. waskasoopark.ca.

At this point, where the Calgary-Edmonton Trail crossed the Red Deer River at a relatively safe ford, the little settlement of Red Deer Crossing appeared in 1882. During the **Northwest Rebellion** of 1885 led by Louis Riel, local settlers feared for their safety as Cree and Métis battled government troops, prompting militia under the command of Lt. J.E. Bédard Normandeau of the 65th Mount Royal Rifles to establish a log fort here in 1885. The North West Mounted Police, which later became the Royal Canadian Mounted Police, took over the fort and remained until 1893.

The present structure is a replica, incorporating some of the original fort's logs, constructed by the RCMP in 1974, the centennial of their founding. The park has now become a celebration of early First Nations, Métis and European culture. In late May, a weekend of **Fort Normandeau Days** recalls the turbulent times of 1885 with battle reenactments and Cree dances, all in good fun and with activities for children.

Costumed interpreters invite visitors to make bannock (unleavened bread) over a fire, work an old-fashioned ice-cream churn, participate in Highland activities such as throwing the caber or dancing to lively Métis fiddle music or Native drums. The **interpretive centre** shows a film *(10min)* describing the history of the fort and its significance. History and culture aside, the original river crossing point is a pleasant picnic spot and a great launching point for paddlers who can wend through the city and Waskasoo Park on a half-day float.

Excursion

Sylvan Lake★

18km/11mi west of Red Deer on Hwy 11A. ☎403-887-2141. www.town.sylvan-lake. ab.ca.

This 22km/14mi-long lake, which like others in the region such as Gull Lake and Pigeon Lake offers moderately warm waters, boasts 5km/3mi of sandy white beaches that get quite busy in the summer months, especially with families. In and around the town of Sylvan Lake (pop. 10,208), a resort destination since the early 20C, are half a dozen golf courses, a variety of newer condo-style resorts plus some older motels and hotels that are well suited to family travellers.

Dominating the skyline as visitors approach the lake is the Kids**Wild Rapids Waterslide** (*⏰open late-Jun–Labour Day daily 11am–7pm; $30; ♿✕🅿☎403-887-3800; www.wildrapids.ab.ca*), a towering network of twisting tubes looming over the water. This version dates from 1983, but a giant slide has propelled swimmers into the lake from this site since 1928.

The park boasts more than 10 giant slides, including the Hell's Gate raging river slide and several speed slides. There's also a children's wading pond. Paddleboats and sailboards can be rented. Boats can also be rented at the Sylvan Marina (*☎403-887-2950*).

More tranquil than the waterslide area, **Sylvan Lake Provincial Park** (*☎403-340-7691; http://gateway.cd.gov.ab.ca*) offers a 1.6km/1mi sand and grass beach with picnic facilities. In the winter, the park opens two large skating rinks. Fish in the lake include whitefish, walleye pike, northern pike, burbot and emerald shiner.

Wild Rapids Waterslide, Sylvan Lake

©Travel Alberta

Rocky Mountain House
National Historic Site ★

MAP OF PRINCIPAL SIGHTS

Set on a spectacular 202ha/500-acre natural site on the banks of the North Saskatchewan River, this park was established to commemorate the two fur-trading posts established here in 1799 by the Hudson's Bay Company and its great rival, the North West Company. The particular fame of Rocky Mountain House is due to the achievements of explorer and cartographer David Thompson (*see sidebar*), who worked for both companies at different times. Thompson used Rocky Mountain House as a base for exploring vast regions of present-day western Canada and the US, establishing trading posts as he went. His most famous achievement was crossing through the Athabasca Pass from Rocky Mountain House and reaching the mouth of the Columbia River, which he mapped.

- **Information:** Parks Canada: ☎403-845-2412. www.pc.gc.ca.
- ▶ **Orient Yourself:** The site lies 81km/50mi west of Red Deer. From the community of Rocky Mountain House, take Hwy. 11A west 7km/4mi.
- **Don't Miss:** The film on David Thompson in the visitor centre.
- **Organizing Your Time:** A half day is sufficient, but allow more time if you want to partake of the many recreational activities the site affords.
- **Especially for Kids:** The visitor centre has a puppet show describing the life of David Thompson (*Jul–Aug Wed–Sun 2pm; mid-May & Jun weekends 2pm*). A miniature reconstruction of a fur fort allows children to pretend being traders.
- **Also See:** THE CANADIAN ROCKIES

Visit

Open mid-May to Labour Day daily 10am–5pm. Tue after Labour Day–early Oct Mon–Fri 10am–5pm. Jul–Aug guided tours of the exhibits. $2.40. ☎403-845-2412. www.pc.gc.ca.

Only two chimneys remain from the rival fur-trading posts, but Parks Canada has created two self-guided interpretive trails along the river that bring the old days vividly to mind. Eight listening posts along the paths detail the life of a fictional James Robertson, employee

York boat, Rocky Mountain House National Historic Site

©Travel Alberta

of the North West Company and, like so many of the early traders, a Scot.

Along the trails are exhibits that aid in understanding the rugged life of the fur trader.

A reconstructed **York boat** shows how furs were floated down the river, then across the 5,000km/3,125mi network of waterways and portages to Lachine, just outside Montreal, for shipment to Britain. A fur press shows how pelts were compacted so they could be fit into a canoe and back-packed over portages. At the **visitor centre** is an excellent exhibit of artifacts excavated on site, as well as samples of equipment David Thompson would have used, aboriginal clothing and crafts, with fine examples of embroidery, and a model fort storeroom. Four films are screened on request: the story of David Thompson (45min); a Métis child's visit to Fort William (now Thunder Bay) (24min); the story of frontier artist Paul Kane (14min); and the story of the voyageurs (20min).

Besides the history, Rocky Mountain Historical Site offers hiking and bicycling trails, canoeing and kayaking on the North Saskatchewan River, camping and picnicking, fishing in the river and bird-watching. A herd of bison grazes within the park, and can often be seen from the road.

From here, **Highway 11** (David Thompson Highway) continues west on into the Rockies, joining the Icefields Parkway 174km/108mi beyond Rocky Mountain House and affording an alternate route to either Jasper (turn north) or Banff (turn south) national parks.

On the north side of Highway 11, **Crimson Lake Provincial Park** (☎403-845-2330; http://gateway.cd.gov.ab.ca) offers boating, canoeing and kayaking, fishing and swimming along sandy beaches at Crimson Lake and Twin Lakes. Hiking trails are easy, and lead into the forest and around lakes; bicycles are allowed. In winter, there is cross-country skiing.

Excursion

Nordegg

6km/4mi west of Rocky Mountain House via Hwy 11. www.travelnordegg.com.

Climbing gently out of parklands and forest surrounding Rocky Mountain House, the David Thompson Highway (Hwy. 11) moves into the thick forests that cling to the eastern slopes of the Canadian Rockies. Lying in the valley of the North Saskatchewan River, the former coal-mining town of Nordegg has a population of about 125. In addition to the mine site, the town, which is emerging as a tourist destination, offers several resorts and beautiful scenery.

Abraham Lake, created in 1972 behind the Bighorn Dam, is a recreational lake coloured turquoise by glacial silt, over which looms 2337m/7,123ft Mount Michener; **Crescent Falls,** on the Bighorn River, is worth the difficult hike to get there; Shunda Lake (Fish Lake) lies in a scenic mountain setting. Many excellent day hikes and longer treks start from here. Outfitters in the area organize horseback tours, as well as camping excursions.

In its heyday, Nordegg was a bustling community of 3,800, to which the Canadian Northern Railway had built a special spur line. The town was named for Martin Nordegg, the representative of the German Development Co., one of the mine's founding partners; at the outbreak of war in 1914, Herr Nordegg was escorted out of Canada but the town kept his name. The mine closed in the mid-1950s when locomotives switched to diesel fuel.

Nordegg Heritage Centre

Main street. ◐Open mid-May–mid-Sept daily 9am–5pm; ✕ ♿ ☎403-721-6265.

The coal-mining era is recalled with exhibits and memorabilia at this centre, operated by the Nordegg Historical Society. The museum has a display of historic newspaper articles and a photo archive. A small gift shop and a cafe serving lunches are on the premises. Ask for the brochure outlining a self-guided tour of the town (but not the mine site) at the reception desk. Mine tours depart from the centre.

©Travel Alberta

Abraham Lake along David Thompson Highway, near Nordegg

Nordegg National Historic Site★

Visit to the mine site by guided tour only; tours leave from Nordegg Heritage Centre mid-May–mid-Sept daily 1pm. $8. Best to reserve ahead. ☎403-845-2412. www.pc.gc.ca.

The **Brazeau Collieries,** which excavated 10 million tons of coal from 1911 to 1955, were exceptionally advanced in their use of technology, and the abandoned site remains largely intact. Anyone with the slightest interest in how things work will enjoy taking one of the daily tours. Visitors can follow the path of the coal as it left the mines and was transported by trolleys to be cleaned, transformed into briquettes, then lifted by conveyer belts to towers, from which it was poured into waiting railway cars.

Red Deer Area Guest Ranches

$$ Red Lodge Guest Ranch – *Bowden,* ☎403-224-3082. *www.redlodgeoutfitters. com.* Cabins, host house, RV and tent camping, restaurant. Hay or wagon rides, general farm help, riding lessons, wildlife watching. Hourly trail rides for non-guests.

$$ Ride the Wind Ranch – *Rocky Mountain House,* ☎403-845-5997. *www.ridethe windranch.com.* Cabins. Riding lessons, trail rides, farm help, wildlife watching, fishing, hiking, boating. Situated in scenic David Thompson Country in north-central Rocky Mountains. English and German spoken.

$$ Rolyn Hills B&B and Guest Ranch – *Near Red Deer,* ☎403-347-0206, *www.rolyn hills.com.* B&B and self-catered guest house, RV and tent camping. Riding lessons, cattle branding, hourly trail rides for guests and non-guests, wagon/sleigh rides on 2,000 acres.

Lacombe★

POPULATION 11,562 – MAP OF PRINCIPAL SIGHTS

Tucked into the hills east of Highway 2, this attractive community is noted for its Main Street lined with well-restored Edwardian brick and sandstone houses and buildings. One story has it that after a devastating fire in 1906, town fathers forbade further construction in wood. The town of Lacombe was in its early years a rival to Red Deer as a regional centre. When the single-track Calgary-Edmonton Railway line passed through here, a siding permitted one train to stop while another passed by. In 1893 the railway established Siding No. 12 as a settlement named for **Father Albert Lacombe** (1827-1916), (ⓘ see St. Albert) an Oblate missionary who accompanied the voyageurs and was much appreciated for his peacemaking skills among the Cree, Blackfoot and pioneer settlers. The town received important education institutions (notably the present-day Canadian University College), but the major railways passed through Red Deer, leaving Lacombe blessed with lovely buildings, parks and lakes, but a limited economic base dependent on agriculture and, today, oil and gas.

- **Information:** Lacombe Tourism: ☎403-755-6935, www.lacombetourism.com.
- ▶ **Orient Yourself:** Lacombe lies 30km/19mi north of Red Deer off Hwy. 2 or 2A
- **Don't Miss:** The heritage structures of the town centre.
- ○ **Organizing Your Time:** A half day is sufficient to enjoy the sights.
- **Especially for Kids:** The many birds at Ellis Bird Farm and the activities at the Lacombe Corn Maze.

Downtown

A stroll through downtown is most pleasant. The most photographed of the heritage sites is the **flatiron building** at 100-5005 50th Avenue, built at a triangular street corner. The building now houses the **interpretive centre** (○ mid-May–late Oct Tue–Sat 10am–6pm; rest of the year Tue–Sat noon–4pm; ☎403-782-9786), with exhibits about local history.

Roland Michener (1900-1991) was a revered politician and diplomat who served as Canada's governor general from 1967 to 1974. The two-storey, white clapboard house where he was born is preserved at 5036 51st Street as the **Michener House Museum** (○ open mid-May–late Oct, Tue–Sat 9am–5pm; ☎403-782-3933) and contains items donated by the Michener family as well as extensive archives. The house is kept in a style appropriate to the early 19C.

Additional Sight

Ellis Bird Farm★

8km/5mi east of Lacombe by Hwy. 12 east, then RR 26-0/Prentiss Rd. south 8km/5mi. ○ Open mid-May to Labour Day Tues–Sun & holiday Mon 11am–5pm. ♿✕🅿☎403-885-4477. http://ellisbirdfarm.ab.ca.

©Travel Alberta

Flatiron building, Lacombe

Bird Houses, Ellis Bird Farm

Kids Open to the public only in summer, this working farm claims a beautiful natural setting where you can pet a lamb or roam trails dotted with ponds, orchards and gardens, through fields with native wildflowers such as black-eyed Susans and blue flax. Special events such as the **Bluebird Festival** or **Bug Jamboree** draw many visitors, especially families. In an interesting arrangement, Union Carbide Corp. purchased the farm when its elderly owners, who had created the bird sanctuary literally with their own hands, could no longer maintain it. An ethelyne glycol plant opened in 1984 on a corner of the property near the ghost town of Prentiss, but the remainder of the farm is operated by a nonprofit charitable company largely funded by MEGlobal Canada, successor to Union Carbide; naturalist organizations and local groups appoint representatives to the board. The objective is to protect native cavity-nesting birds; the gardens have been designed to please them. Wheelchair-accessible, the farm can be explored solo or guided by a naturalist *(reservations recommended)*. The teahouse serves light refreshments and Saskatoon berry tea.

Nest boxes for mountain bluebirds, tree swallows, black-capped chickadees, purple martins and flickers are sited around the grounds, many on tall poles. Avian recreation is not neglected, with several bird-baths and feeding stations artfully placed. Try, if possible, to glimpse a mountain bluebird, whose intense blue colour with a lighter blue breast is quite dramatic: in flight the bird is like a fluttering bit of Alberta sky. Its song is a short whistle with a little rasp to it.

Additional Sight

Lacombe Corn Maze

Take Hwy. 12 from the Hwy. 2 overpass west of Lacombe. After 1.6km/1mi, turn left (south) on RR#27-3 and drive .8km/.5mi. Maze is well signposted. Open late-Jul–Labour Day Mon–Sat 11am–9pm. Rest of Sept–mid-Oct Wed–Thu 4pm-8pm, Fri 4pm–9pm, Sat 11am–9pm. Labour Day & Thanksgiving Mon noon–6pm. $9 (rides extra). 403-782-4653, www. lacombecornmaze.com.

Kids Set within a 6ha/15-acre cornfield, the maze is divided into three sections. Friendly guides are on hand to make sure visitors find their way out. In late summer, corn stalks reach as high as 3m/9ft high. A petting zoo, a tricycle trail, mini-mazes, a straw mountain, tube slides and other games delight children.

Stettler
POPULATION 5,418

Set amid wondrously flat, rich farmland and pastures northeast of Red Deer, this town was founded by Swiss-German settlers and retains its tidy character today. It also possesses one of the increasingly rare "cathedrals of the prairies," a grain elevator. The highlight of a Stettler visit, however, would be a lively journey on an old steam or diesel train.

- **Information:** Town of Stettler ☏403-742-8305. www.stettler.net.
- **Orient Yourself:** Stettler lies off Hwy. 12, about 29km/18mi east of Red Deer via Hwy. 11. Its Main Street (50th St.) is one block north of the railroad tracks. A color map of the town can be download at www.stettler.net.
- **Don't Miss:** An excursion on the Alberta Prairie Railway.
- **Organizing Your Time:** The railway excursion takes 5hrs to 6hrs; allow some time to see the town as well. Book the railway adventure as far in advance of your visit as possible.
- **Especially for Kids:** Children will love the Railway Excursion, especially if a staged "robbery" takes place.
- **Also See:** ALBERTA BADLANDS

Sights

Town and Country Museum
6304 44th Ave.🕐Open May–Labour Day, 10am–5:30pm. 💰$3. ☏403-742-4534. This museum is an open-air museum consisting of 26 heritage buildings spread over 2.8ha/7 acres. Among the historic structures are an old courthouse, a church and a rail station.

Alberta Prairie Railway Excursions★
Board at Stettler Station, Main St. 🕐Open mid-May–mid-Oct for summer excursions. Dining excursions offered Nov–Apr. 💰$85 for probable train robbery and meal; $135 for guaranteed train robbery and even better meal. 5hr-6hr round-trip: timetable varies; check the website, regularly updated. Reservations recommended. Special train tours, such as a mystery murder tour, are also offered.

©Travel Alberta

Staged train robbery, Alberta Prairie Railway Excursions

☎403-742-2811 or 800-282-3994 (for Canada only). www.abssteamtrain.com. This old-fashioned train, which may be pulled by either a steam or diesel engine, runs from Stettler Station at the end of Main Street south to the hamlet of Big Valley, some 30km/19mi away, and back. The trip lasts a good five hours or more, because so much happens: an outlaw gang is very likely to attack (perhaps they have the train

schedule) and the Métis chief Gabriel Dumont usually succeeds in rescuing the passengers, but not before some are forced at cap-pistol-point to contribute to a children's charity. A friendly buffet lunch is included, either in Big Valley or in Stettler, and musicians entertain guests who still have the nerves for it. Some passengers may think it fortunate that there is a fully-licenced saloon car.

Innisfail

POPULATION 7,691

The largest town between Calgary and Red Deer, this agricultural community owes its roots to Anthony Henday, who was the first European to see the Canadian Rockies, in 1754. Accompanied by Cree and Assiniboine guides while he and his party were exploring the area for the Hudson's Bay Company, he spotted the snow-capped peaks from just northeast of Innisfail. Highway 54, the Anthony Henday Highway, is named for him. In the 19C Icelandic and Danish pioneers, many from the Dakotas, Wisconsin and Nebraska, began settling here and in neighbouring communities, such as Markerville and Dickson. Originally a stopping house along the stagecoach route between Fort Calgary and Fort Edmonton, Innisfail was named by a Canadian Pacific Railway (CPR) worker for the Celtic term meaning "isle of destiny." The CPR arrived in Innisfail in 1891, and by 1900 the village had its own opera house. Today the town earns its livelihood largely from grain and livestock farming. Every year in mid-June the Innisfail Pro Rodeo is held at the nearby Daines Rodeo Ranch.

- **Information:** Town of Innisfail Information Centre, 4943 53rd St. ☎403-227-3376. www.innisfailtourism.com.
- **Orient Yourself:** Most businesses, attractions and residential communities are west of Hwy. 2 and Hwy. 2A; major arteries around the central core are 42 St., 60 Ave. and 50 St., the latter anchoring the downtown streets. Dodd's Lake sits north of the centre and Napoleon Lake to the west. A colourful town map can be downloaded from www.innisfailtourism.com.
- **Parking:** Attractions have designated parking.
- **Don't Miss:** RCMP Police Dog Service Training Centre.
- **Organizing Your Time:** Innisfail and surrounding attractions can be explored in half a day.
- **Especially for Kids:** Innisfail Historical Village, Dog Training Centre and ice cream at the Markerville Creamery Museum.

Sights

Innisfail Historical Village★
42nd St. and 52nd Ave., one block south of the school grounds. ☎403-227-2906. www.innisfailhistory.com. Contribution requested. ◷Open year-round Mon–Sat. 10am–5pm; Sun and holidays noon–5pm.

The donation of an 1884 log home that served as a stopping house on the old stagecoach road between Calgary and Edmonton was the impetus for creating this village in 1970. Spread over 5ha/2acres on the town fairgrounds, some 17 structures have been refurbished to depict life in the area from its earliest days until the mid-1930s.

RCMP Police Dog Service Training Centre

The buildings include an old bank, a 1938 church, a 1915 blacksmith shop, a cattle barn, a livery stable, and a train station complete with period luggage. The Parker Cabin is furnished with period antiques. Several vintage cars and a collection of farm equipment are also on display.

Rhubarb and herbs can be found along with a variety of vegetables in the pioneer garden. The heritage garden has domestic plants that were common in early homestead gardens such as horseradish.

There's a tea room and a day-use picnic area at the village for visitors to enjoy.

Additional Sight

RCMP Police Dog Service Training Centre★

4 km/2.5mi south of town on Hwy. 2 northbound. Take exit 365 at Innisfail, travel east and follow the signs. ⏱*Public demonstrations (45min) Wed 2pm in summer.* 🅿 ☏*403-227-3346. www.rcmp-grc. gc.ca/pds/cntr/visit_e.htm.*

Kids Set among several acres on the east side of Highway 2, this facility serves as a national training centre for police service dogs and handlers within the Royal Canadian Mounted Police force as well as other police agencies. The RCMP began using dogs in police work in 1935; a training school was founded in Calgary in 1937. The Innisfail centre was established in 1965. Only purebred, usually male, German shepherds and Belgian shepherds are used. The breed is favoured for police work because the dogs are courageous and adaptable. They are physically strong and their heavy coats allow them to withstand the cold Canadian winters.

Dogs begin school when they are a year to 18 months old and undergo basic training for 17 weeks. The RCMP also has a breeding program, testing puppies for their potential for the rigorous police work.

In an outdoor compound, visitors can watch as uniformed trainers put dogs-in-training and their RCMP handlers through a variety of obedience and agility exercises. The dogs are trained

RCMP Police Dog Facts

- A dog can search a vehicle in 3 minutes.
- The cost to train handler and dog is $60,000.
- On average a police dog retires at age 7.
- Dogs have only a 17 percent chance of success in the training.

Source: *www.rcmp.gc.ca/factsheets*

©Travel Alberta

Stephansson House, Markerville

for tasks such as avalanche rescue, narcotics detection, suspect tracking and explosive detection.

Excursions

Markerville

About 30km/18mi northwest of Innisfail via Hwy. 54 to Rge. Rd. 10 north then Hwy. 592 west.

In the late 1880s, settlers from Iceland established the village of Markerville, which edges the Medicine River. One particular Icelander of note was **Stephan G. Stephansson** (1853-1927), who moved here from Wisconsin in 1889 to raise livestock. Considered Iceland's greatest modern poet, Stephansson wrote his verse in his native tongue after a long day of farm chores. Now a provincial historic site, the **house** that he constructed for his large family (five sons, three daughters) may be visited; restored to the 1920s, it includes the writing desk that he himself built (🕐 *open mid-May–Labour Day daily 10am–6pm; ⬭$3;* 🅿 ☎*780-427-3995; http://culture.alberta.ca/museums*).

Markerville's other famous attraction is its Kids **Creamery Museum.** Built in 1902 with government funds, the creamery turned out butter using cream from local farms until 1972. Now restored to its 1932 appearance, the creamery is open for guided tours. An on-site cafe serves Icelandic specialties and delicious ice cream (🕐 *open mid-May–Labour Day daily 10am–6pm; ⬭$3;* 🅿 ☎*403-728-3006*).

Danish Canadian National Museum and Gardens

In Spruce View, about 27km/17mi west of Innisfail via Hwy. 54. 🕐*Open mid-May–Labour Day Mon–Sat 10am–5:30pm, Sun 12:30pm–5:30pm. Rest of Sept Fri–Sat 10am–5:30pm, Sun 12:30pm–5:30pm.* ⬭*$2.50.* ☎*403-728-0019 or 888-443-4114. www.dancanmuseum.ca.*

In Alberta, the Danish first settled in Dickson in 1903. This museum opened in 2002 in Spruce View, just 3km/1.8mi south of Dickson, seeks to preserve Danish heritage in the province.

Housed in a former school (1933), the museum comprises rooms displaying Danish memorabilia, a library, a room dedicated to Hans Christian Andersen, a gift shop and coffee house.

On the 5ha/13acre grounds are vegetable gardens and Danish flower gardens planted with linden trees. A pioneer church is typical of those in Denmark. Two structures moved here from other communities are under renovation. Kids The **children's garden** features a storytelling hut, a bust of Hans Christian Andersen, a castle with a drawbridge and paths with panels illustrating Andersen's famous fairy tales such as *The Ugly Duckling* and *The Little Mermaid.* Of special interest is an assembly of large rocks known as a **stendysse;** typical of burial mounds or tombs dating to 3,000BC, these upright boulders, usually three, were topped by a horizontal capstone.

For the best little places, follow the leader.

Looking for the latest news on today's best hotels and restaurants? Pick up the Michelin Guide and look for the Bib Gourmand and Bib Hotel symbols. With 45,000 addresses in Europe, in every category and price range, the perfect place to dine or stay is never far away.

MICHELIN
A better way forward

GREATER EDMONTON

Lying near the centre of the province, this region of Alberta includes the city of Edmonton as well as Parkland County to the west, Leduc County to the south, Strathcona County to the east and Sturgeon County to the north. The population of some 1,035,000 is projected to expand by some 12,000 annually over the next few years. Blessed by abundant lakes and rivers, generous rainfall and rich farmland, the region claims great natural beauty as well as economic advantages in agriculture and forestry. What is more, oil and gas discoveries starting in Leduc County just south of Edmonton in 1947 have revealed the second largest proven oil reserves in the world, after Saudi Arabia's. The area is not only rich, but aspires to cultural achievement as well, with a symphony orchestra, excellent museums, a large theatre and of course the constant festivals, some 30 per year. Particularly north and west of Edmonton vast tracts of forests and lakes offer recreation at many provincial parks as well as some 70 golf courses (in summer at this latitude, you can tee off at 6pm and expect to finish a round in daylight). Elk Island National Park, a wilderness area 30km/19mi east of the city, offers sanctuary to diverse wildlife including rare birds and wood bison.

Like most of Canada, this area was initially explored and mapped by fur traders. The region was part of the vast territory of **Rupert's Land** ceded to the Hudson's Bay Company by Charles II in 1670, and not relinquished by the HBC until 1870, when Canada acquired it under the British North America Act. Both the HBC and the North West Company built forts near here, on opposite banks of the North Saskatchewan River, in the late 18C, near present-day Fort Saskatchewan. When the two companies merged in 1821, the HBC set up Fort Edmonton. When Fort Calgary was founded in 1875, a well-travelled trail (now Highway 2) led north to Edmonton.

Advertisements in the late 19C drew farmers from the US, Eastern and Central Europe and Great Britain as well as a substantial number of French Canadians to the area, which despite its bitterly cold winters (average daily temperature in January is -11°C/10°F), proved to be rich agricultural land. The town of **Vegre-**

Skyline, Edmonton

©Travel Alberta

Address Book

🔖 *For dollar sign categories, see the Legend on the cover flap.*

WHERE TO STAY

$ HI Edmonton – *10647 81st Ave., ☎780-988-6836 or 877-467-8336. www. hihostels.ca. 88 beds.* 🅿. This hostel in a modern building, just off Whyte Avenue in Old Strathcona, couldn't be better located for activities, and the University of Alberta is only a few blocks away. It provides private and shared rooms, a family room, Internet access, laundry facilities, a TV room, a self-catering kitchen and free parking (limited). About half the rooms have private baths. The staff organizes activities such as a travelogue series and holiday parties that guests appreciate.

$ University of Alberta – *Main campus located south of the river, extending to 82nd (Whyte) Ave. ☎780-492-6056. www.ufaweb.ualberta.ca/conference services.* Student dorm rooms are offered at excellent prices and afford surprising comfort; apartments and other visitors' lodgings offer condo- or hotel-level comfort at reasonable prices. Dormitory rooms available *(May-Aug)* at the Lister Centre *(corner 116th St & 87th Ave.)* and Résidence St-Jean *(in Francophone district, entrance on 91st St. between 84th & 86th Ave., 6km/4mi from main campus)* come with a bed, desk, Internet and private washrooms. Other summer accommodations include one-bedroom suites at the HUB Mall *(209-9005 112th St. NW)* and International House bachelor suites (no children permitted), located on the east side of the main campus, all rented by the month. Michener Park Town Houses *(entrance at 112 St. & 48th Ave.)* also rent by the month. Located at Listre Centre, the Conference Centre ♿🅿🛏. **guest rooms ($$)** available year-round for stays of a day or more, are like hotel rooms with all the usual amenities.

$ Villa Maria Country Inn – *9910 213th St. ☎780-488-6089 or 866-488-6089. www.villamariacountryinn.com. 4 rooms.* 🅿🛏. A bit away from the thick of things, this inn, located on a large property in west Edmonton, offers spacious, comfortable rooms with en suite bathrooms. The West Edmonton Mall is close by, and the inn provides a shuttle service to the airport, train station and bus station. A copious breakfast, served in the dining room, includes specialties by the owner, a former restaurateur.

$$ Crowne Plaza Chateau Lacombe – *10111 Bellamy Hill. ☎780-428-6611 or 800-661-8801. www.chateaulacombe. com. 307 rooms.* ✕🅿. The location of this 24-storey, 18-sided tower on Bellamy Hill in downtown Edmonton is convenient. The 1967 architecture gives the building a quirky charm, inside and out, and the lobby rotunda seems to echo the Legislature Building. Wedge-shaped rooms surround a central service core, affording panoramic views. All have been thoroughly renovated and all amenities are provided such as Internet and a fitness room; for the stressed-out, a Sleep Advantage program puts guests in bedrooms zoned extra-quiet, with scientific sleep-inducing CDs, earplugs and tactful wake-up calls.

The **LaRonde ($$)** revolving rooftop restaurant, another 1960s delight, serves dinner and Sunday brunch. Menus, based on seasonal local produce, offer dishes like free-range turkey *paillard* with buckwheat fettucini, Katahdin lamb from a farm in Maplethorpe, or fennel-crusted Arctic char with new potato and onion salad. Inventive side dishes include sage spaetzle with sweet grass jus, okra and sage beignets, or bedrock seed hemp crepes.

$$ Glenora Inn – *12327 102nd Ave. NW. ☎780-488-6766 or 877-453-6672. www. glenorabnb.com.com. 26 rooms.* 🅿🛏. Situated in the former Buena Vista apartment block, built in 1912 in west Edmonton, this inn provides accommodations ranging from small but pretty B&B rooms **($)** with a shared bathroom to larger studios with private baths and kitchenettes **($$)**, and apartment suites **($$)** with kitchen, sitting and dining rooms, not to mention a fireplace. The rooms are tastefully decorated with a slight retro touch (flowered wallpaper and coverlets), clean-lined woodwork and hardwood floors. Breakfast is served in the trendy **Glenora Bistro ($$)** on the street level, and a large guest parlour offers comfortable chairs and a pleasant Edwardian environment. The area is in the midst of shops and galleries, and is a short hop from the river valley and downtown attractions.

$$ La Bohème – *6427 112nd Ave. ☎780-474-5693. www.laboheme.ca. 6 suites.* ✕ P ⌑. Located in the Gibbard Block, a splendid former apartment building dating to 1912, this Edmonton inn lies in the Highland residential district in the city's northeast, just off the river valley park, with easy access to downtown attractions. The rooms carry wildly romantic names (the Greta Garbo suite, the Buenos Aires suite, etc.) and feature Edwardian furniture and comfortable sitting areas. The breakfast is continental, served in the restaurant to guests only. La Bohème's first-floor **restaurant ($$$)** is adventurously French, with main courses such as medaillon of wapiti (elk) in a blueberry demi-glace or a royal Moroccan couscous, as well as a beautifully prepared Alberta filet mignon. A Sunday brunch, with champagne and bellinis as well as espresso, fresh pastries and omelets and of course beef, has gained a devoted following.

$$ The Varscona Hotel on Whyte – *8208 106th St. ☎780-434-6111 or 866-465-8150. www.varscona.com. 89 rooms.* ✕ P ⌑. Set in the lively Old Strathcona district, this venerable hotel offers modern rooms and suites that make up in efficiency what they lack in period charm. Internet access, a fitness room and a complimentary continental breakfast are some of the amenities. The hotel's **Murietta's Bar and Grill ($$)**, a chic, modern restaurant with an extensive menu, serves the likes of duck breast with fig and shallot *tarte tatin*, a bouillabaisse incorporating West Coast seafood, and plenty of Alberta beef. The fish and seafood selection is particularly good. The hotel also houses a pleasant bar, O'Bryne's Irish Pub, offering Irish music on some evenings, and a Second Cup cafe.

$$$ Union Bank Inn – *10053 Jasper Ave. ☎780-423-3600 or 888-423-3601. www.unionbankinn.com. 34 rooms.* ✕ P ⌑. This downtown boutique hotel is housed in a 1910 Italianate building, faced in the same Indiana limestone as the Hotel Macdonald. It was originally built as a bank and today, is one of the rare old buildings in downtown. Reinvented as a hotel with a modern 20-room addition for business guests, the building offers elegance inside and out. Every room boasts a fireplace, goose-feather duvet, Internet, temperature control and windows that open, while suites offer whirlpool baths. Decoration is subdued modern, with light Edwardian touches. There is a business centre and fitness room, and a complete breakfast is included. **Madison's Grill ($$$)**, a modern space set among the pillars and potted palms of the old banking hall, serves breakfast, lunch and dinner weekdays, but no lunch weekends. The inventive dinner menu includes bison carpaccio with truffled peaches, Alberta venison with mushrooms and sweet-potato purée, or roasted striped bass with prawn dumplings. Salads such as zebra tomatoes with talegio cheese, or a Caesar salad with apples and pumpkin seeds, are especially creative.

$$$$ Fairmont Hotel Macdonald – *10065 100th St. ☎780-424-5181 or 800-441-1414. www.fairmont.com/mac donald. 199 rooms.* ✕ ⅙ P ⌑. This 1915 chateau-style landmark, whose green copper roof appears high on a bluff overlooking the North Saskatchewan River, offers every sort of comfort, along with Edwardian splendour. Originally constructed by the Grand Trunk Pacific Railway, the hotel emerged completely renovated in 1991, after purchase by Canadian Pacific Hotels, now Fairmont. Several public areas have heritage status, retaining virtually the same appearance as when new. Guest rooms seem a tad small by modern luxury standards, but are sumptuous; the Grand Trunk doorknobs are original. Celebrities visiting the city congregate here (the most prestigious suites are high up in the turrets), and Edmontonians like to share a drink amid the potted palms of the **Confederation Lounge.** Hotel

©Travel Alberta

Confederation Lounge, Hotel Macdonald

amenities include a fitness centre with a tiled pool, a staffed business centre, and airport shuttles. At 3pm on Sat and Sun afternoons, the hotel serves a bountiful **Royal Tea** (*$33, reservations essential*) that includes a hotel tour. The **Harvest Room ($$$)** restaurant, an art deco delight with awesome views of the river valley, serves breakfast, lunch and dinner. Cuisine is based on fresh products, as local as possible, and the dinner menu offers main course selections such as a roasted veal chop from Innisfail, served with quinoa (a seed vegetable from the Andes, ground into flour) risotto and cauliflower purée, or sablefish from British Columbia, served with spaetzle, pickled shallots and winter squash. The **Sunday brunch** buffet (*$44, 10am-2pm*) in the **Empire Ballroom** is a treat, both for the fare and the surroundings. The ceiling, 8m/24ft above the floor, displays a remarkable hunting scene, hidden under a false ceiling for decades.

WHERE TO EAT

$ Thai Orchid – *4009 Gateway Blvd. NW. ☎780-438-3344. Closed Mon.* **Thai.** What this eatery in an industrial area of south Edmonton lacks in curb appeal (it's housed in an EconoLodge), it makes up for with fresh, authentic Thai food. The house specialties are flavourful curries (red, green, yellow) made with rich coconut milk, and a Pad Thai and other noodle dishes. For those sensitive to spicy food, the helpful staff will cheerfully turn down the heat. Word is out

among locals, so count on waiting for a table if you don't arrive early.

$$ La Tapa Mediterranean Restaurante – *10523 99th Ave. ☎780-424-8272. www.latapa.ca. Closed Sun.* **Spanish.** This modern, trendy downtown restaurant resides within a 70-year-old house with a terrace out front. It brings a touch of Iberia to the prairies. Starting with an apéritif accompanied by assorted tapas (shared small plates of exquisite noshes), meals can flow on forever. Some 30 sorts of tapas figure on the menu: try the *patatas* aioli (roasted potatoes in a garlic mayonnaise sauce) or the traditional tortilla Espanola (potato and onion omelet sliced into wedges), one of the chorizo sausages, or perhaps the *gambas a la crema*, (shrimp in Pernod sauce). For many, this first stage is a meal in itself, but it would be a mistake to miss the paella, offered in four varieties, or perhaps the classic *zarzuela de mariscos*, best translated as a seafood love story.

$$ Lemongrass Café – *10417 51st Ave. NW. ☎780-413-0088. No dinner Mon, no lunch weekends.* **Vietnamese.** This bright and busy eatery off Calgary Trail in south Edmonton offers Vietnamese cuisine adapted to local produce. An example is the Autumn Salad, which isn't salad at all but mixed root vegetables lightly battered and flash-fried with a spicy dip. The *banh xeo*, or plate of sprouts, mint and grilled meat that diners wrap in lettuce or rice crepes, is popular, as are noodle soups like the pungent *pho* or the *bun bo Hué*, flavoured with lemon grass. The bar makes a decent martini, and other drinks as well.

$$ Sofra – *108-10345 106th St. NW. ☎780-423-3044. No lunch. Closed Mon.* **Turkish.** This downtown restaurant offers a relaxing repast with Turkish music softly playing in the background. Meals are eaten in stages, begun with appetizers such as *yaprak sarma*, or stuffed grape leaves with pine nuts and raisins, or perhaps a red lentil soup. An array of meat and vegetable kabobs arrives with saffron-infused rice pilaf and mixed greens; the honey mustard dressing is especially tasty. The attention given the grilled vegetables makes them a surprise star. Through a glass window, diners can watch the cook expertly roll dough, slide it into the wood-burning oven and later remove puffy, crisp pita bread, which is served with a dip such as hummus (garlic-flavoured chick pea purée). The smoky baba ganoush eggplant is a favourite, though it's not always on the menu. For dessert, try Turkish coffee and a little baklava. The bar offers a good selection of wine and mixed drinks.

$$ Wild Tangerine – *10383 112th St. ☎780-429-3131. www.wildtangerine. com. No lunch Sat. Closed Sun.* **Asian.** Health-conscious Asian cuisine is served in this lower-level space, furnished in edgy black lacquer, with mandarin red accents and spot lighting. The owners, well-known local restaurateurs, demonstrate an inventive hand for Chinese-inspired cuisine. The shrimp lollipop (a prawn wrapped in noodles, mounted on a skewer and deep-fried) is the signature dish, but don't hesitate to try other creations such as the tofu pancakes with hoisin glaze, the bison short ribs with sesame sushi rice, or perhaps peppercorn-encrusted yellowfin tuna with hemp-oil tomato coulis. Dessert has to be the warm ginger-bread pudding. The owners prove fearless at the bar as well, with combinations involving gin and green tea, or whisky and cranberry-orange juice.

$$$ Culina – *9914 89th Ave. NW. ☎780-437-5588. www.culinacafe.ca. Closed Sun.* **International.** Open for three meals a day, this bohemian bistro has great food, funky decor and eclectic music, which have combined to make this restaurant a local favourite. The dishes on the menu are creative, with such entrées as pork tenderloin, steaks in almond-cardamom cream sauce over couscous, or a goat cheese and *channa dal* in phyllo with tomato chutney and Chinese greens. Also delicious is the roasted garlic custard appetizer. Like the food, the wine list is vast and varied. On Sunday nights *(5pm–8pm)*, a special prix-fixe dining experience called Family Night, offers food on large platters.

$$$ Hardware Grill – *9698 Jasper Ave. ☎780-423-0969. www.hardwaregrill. com. Dinner only. Closed Sun, holidays & first 10 days Jul.* **Canadian.** Located downtown in the 1912 Goodridge Block, this 5,000sq ft former hardware store has emerged as one of the city's premier dining spots. A subdued interior sports olive-coloured walls and bits of hardware-store adornment such as wall framing and steam pipes. The kitchen issues forth exuberant inventiveness, such as the mocha-crusted venison with a chocolate-balsamic syrup paired with bison meatloaf and BBQ glaze, gnocchi and dried cherries. Portions are quite small, so the unexpected juxtapositions can be amusing, not overwhelming. Vegetables undergo identity crises as well: a butternut pear hash with pine nuts and mascarpone fork-crushed potato accompanies the soya-lacquered duck breast. Food is served in fanciful arrangements, and it's all good fun, for a price.

$$$ Jack's Grill – *5842 111th St. ☎780-434-1113. www. jacksgrill.ca. Dinner only. Closed first 10 days of Jan.* **Canadian.** Despite its strip-mall setting next to a gas station in Edmonton's southern Lendrum neighbourhood, this bistro offers genuine chic with oak floors, sand-colored walls and well-spaced tables. Fare includes grilled duck breast in black currant sauce, pork chops stuffed with prunes and served with risotto, or rack of lamb with mushroom ragout. Alberta beef is simply prepared and served with interesting sides such as tomato and goat cheese tortellini and creamed spinach. Save room for Jack's bread pudding with raisins and caramelized rum sauce, or his famous chocolate lava cake.

$$$ Red Ox Inn – *9420 91st St. ☎780-465-5727. www.theredoxinn.com. Dinner only. Closed Mon.* **Canadian.** This small 12-table restaurant, located north of downtown, has gained a following for its attentive service and menu focusing on Canadian cuisine with a reach for the exotic. Try the shiitake-mushroom-crusted crab cakes, or the pancetta-wrapped Arctic char with garlic stuffing. The Alberta beef tenderloin with mushroom cognac cream sauce comes with rich-flavoured roast root vegetables. To end your meal, order the warm pecan pie with caramel sauce or the lemon tart with pine nut crust.

ville, some 65km/41mi east of Edmonton, celebrates its Ukrainian traditions with a huge, roadside Easter egg and the nearby Ukrainian Cultural Heritage Village, but in fact the population is a famously harmonious blend of several nationalities. Archaeological evidence of human settlement in the area found on the banks of the North Saskatchewan River goes back some 5,000 years. European fur traders found several tribes living in this area (Cree, Blackfoot, Blood, Peigan, Salteaux), hunting buffalo, and fishing and trapping along the watercourses and in the forests.

As Europeans began passing through, there quickly appeared a third group, the **Métis,** who were children of fur traders and aboriginal women. The Métis were divided into English-speaking children of British fathers and French-speaking descendents of the voyageurs. The Métis language, Michif, is a Creole composed of French, English and Cree vocabulary combined with Cree syntax and grammar, although it is now rarely heard. The Métis were a force in the area during the **Red River Rebellion** of 1869-70 and the **Northwest Rebellions** of 1885, when, allied with First Nations, they protested against the destruction of the buffalo herds and consequent starvation. In 1990, after long years of legislation and negotiation, the eight Métis settlements achieved substantial autonomy and legal rights under the Métis Settlement Act. A new cultural centre at Smoky Lake 104km/65mi northeast of Edmonton, called Metis Crossing Historical Park, celebrates the culture and history of the Métis.

Today **Fort Saskatchewan,** on the northeast edge of Edmonton, is the epicentre of the area's refining and petrochemical industries, an area covering 330sq km/127sq mi, where more than 30 companies are located, and where some $25 billion has been invested to date. Industrial development this intense, in an area with significant recreational and historic sites, not to mention residents, provides a prime example of the balancing act between economic growth and conservation that Greater Edmonton faces. Recent dramatic increases in the price of oil have given economic impetus to exploitation of the Athabaska oil sands near Fort McMurray, 440km/274mi to the north, for which Edmonton is the transportation and distribution centre. Oil sands production has raised serious issues of environmental pollution, both in terms of damage to the immediate surroundings and in carbon emissions into the atmosphere. Yet Edmontonians, who have survived economic booms and busts over the years, naturally welcome the new wealth; the optimism of local business organizations can reach Texan levels.

The effect of oil money can be seen throughout the area: construction cranes tower over building sites, enthusiastic shoppers crowd the malls, the petrochemical complex at Fort Saskatchewan announces new plans, and a big new city ring road is under construction. Statistics Canada reckons that the economy of the greater Edmonton area will grow at a rate of 4.4 percent a year until 2012; some $150 billion in oil and gas investments is projected over the next few years. Wealth is creating new jobs, significantly increasing incomes and bringing to a relatively out-of-the-way location workers from across Canada and the world.

Some 22 per cent of the greater metropolitan population is now composed of immigrants to Canada, and some 40 percent of these come from South, Southeast and East Asia, enriching the area's already diverse ethnic mix. Although some problems have resulted—notably a shortage of skilled workers and a tight housing market—the Greater Edmonton area is generally adapting happily to an economic growth rate that, the Edmonton Chamber of Commerce claims, approaches that of China. Mindful of the fickle nature of resource-based wealth, the region also rejoices in its diversified economy, with major and growing investments in agri-foods, forest products, manufacturing, health care, bio-technology, software development, financial services and retail. In addition, the presence of the provincial government and its many civil servants contribute to a strong service sector, as do ten post-secondary educational institutions, including the University of Alberta.

Edmonton★★

POPULATION 730,372 – MAPS P 225 AND P 231

The capital of Alberta is North America's northernmost metropolis, although it is not, by world standards, particularly Nordic, being at about the latitude of Dublin or Liverpool. But the city undeniably lies well north of the great commercial and industrial centres of Canada and the US. The North Saskatchewan River snakes through the centre of the city. Edmonton's site, along the steep banks of the river, is strikingly beautiful, and intelligent urban planning has made the city—although devoid of historical charm outside of the Old Strathcona conservation district—a pleasant, livable place with a low population density and much green space. Continually rebuilt over the years, Edmonton retains few old buildings, but the great sandstone Legislature Building and Government House on the riverbank provides a striking contrast to the towers all around; the Legislative Building is a spectacular sight at night when illuminated. The Shaw Conference Centre, spilling down the river bluff in a series of terraces, is a remarkably sensitive use of topography. The magnificent 1915 chateau-style Fairmont Hotel Macdonald, a Grand Trunk Pacific Railway hotel named after Canada's first prime minister, Sir John A. Macdonald, stands on a high bluff above the river, its green copper roof and turrets dramatic above the greenery. A brutal cement 1955 addition so offended Edmontonians that it was demolished in 1986.

- **Information:** Visitor Centre, 9990 Jasper Ave. (World Trade Centre) ☎780-426-4715 or 800-463-4667. www.edmonton.com/tourism.
- ▶ **Orient Yourself:** The principal downtown artery, **Jasper Avenue,** lies north of the river while Old Strathcona, centred on **Whyte Avenue,** lies to the south. **Whitemud Drive,** a freeway that runs east to west through south Edmonton, affords easy access to sites such as West Edmonton Mall and Fort Edmonton on the city's west side. Construction of a ring road around the city, called Anthony Henday Drive or Hwy. 216, was launched in 2005; the southern half of the ring is completed and in service, while a substantial portion of the northern side will be completed in 2011. This is why Whitemud Drive manages to run into Anthony Henday Drive at both its east and west ends. The Trans-Canada Hwy. 16 (the Yellowhead Highway) crosses the city east-west in the north, while the Calgary-Edmonton road, Hwy. 2, turns into the Calgary Trail

Muttart Conservatory

Practical Information

AREA CODES

The City of Edmonton has one area code (780). For local calls, dial all 10 digits (area code plus the number, but without the 1-prefix for long distance). For more information: ☎1-403-555-1212 or www.telus.ca.

GETTING THERE

BY AIR

Edmonton International Airport (YEG) (☎780-890-8382; www.edmontonairports.com) is 30km/20mi south of downtown.

Air Canada (☎888-247-2262 Canada/US; www.aircanada.com) flies from numerous Canadian and US cities. Aside from these direct routes, connections are offered from many major US and other Canadian cities and from major international cities. Domestic air service is offered by Air Canada as well as its affiliated regional airlines and by Calgary-based **WestJet** (☎800-538-5696 or 877-952-0100 TDD; www.westjet.com).

Shuttle

Transportation to downtown:
Sky Shuttle to various central points downtown starts at $14 one-way; for schedules, access www.edmontontaxiservicegroup.com/skyshuttle or call ☎780-465-8515. Wheelchair-accessible service is available by advance booking. Numerous hotels also offer free shuttle service.

By **taxi:** About $45 (for taxi companies, see By Taxi below). There is no public transit service to the airport.

BY TRAIN

Canada's passenger line, **Via Rail,** runs its scenic transcontinental Canadian train through the city (☎888-842-7245 or www.viarail.ca).

BY CAR

From airport to downtown: The drive from Edmonton International Airport to downtown takes about 45min; from airport follow Highway 2 (QEII Hwy.) north about 17km/11mi to Edmonton city limits. The highway becomes Calgary Trail (also Gateway Blvd. or 103 St. northbound, 104 St. heading south), which feeds into the North Saskatchewan River valley and then into downtown (the route is well signed).

Main routes to downtown

From the south: Take Hwy. 2 north from the airport, which turns into Calgary Trail (also known as 103 St. or Gateway Blvd.). Travel north through Old Stratchona and follow signs across the North Saskatchewan River to downtown (just north of the river).

From the west or east: Enter the city on the Yellowhead Hwy. north of downtown; head south on 97 St. You can also enter the city from the west on Stony Plain Road, which joins up with the Yellowhead (Hwy. 16) on the city's edge. Hwy. 16 heading east takes you to Lloydminster and then the Saskatchewan border. The westbound highway offers the best access to Jasper National Park.

From the north: There are three main routes entering the city. From Athabasca and Slave Lake, head south on Hwy. 2, which becomes St. Albert Trail. From Fort McMurray, take Hwy. 28 to downtown. Hwy. 15 to Fort Saskatchewan turns into Manning Drive as you wind through the city's northeast edge and intersects with major routes such as Jasper Avenue.

BY BUS/MOTORCOACH

Both **Greyhound Canada** (☎800-661-8747; www.greyhound.ca) and **Red Arrow Motorcoach** (☎780-425-0820 or 800-232-1958; www.redarrow.pwt.ca) service Edmonton.

GETTING AROUND

BY PUBLIC TRANSPORTATION

Edmonton Transit System operates an extensive public transit system of regular buses and express buses plus light-rail transit (LRT) service along a 12km/7mi route between northeast Edmonton and the University of Edmonton. It also operates zero-emission electric **trolley buses** through the city core as well as the **High Level Streetcar,** which runs between Old Strathcona and downtown. Transit hours of operation (individual services may vary): Mon–Fri 5am–1:30am, reduced service weekends and holidays. Exact fare required, adult

$2.50; youth and seniors $2.25. Day Pass $7.50 over age 12. Purchase tickets and tokens at stores displaying the Edmonton Transit ticket decal. Free transfers between buses & LRT within a 90-minute timeframe. System maps & timetables available free of charge. Route information ☎780-496-1600 *(automated service)*, ☎780-496-1611 or www.edmonton.ca.

BY CAR

Use of public transportation or walking is encouraged within the city as streets are often congested and street parking may be difficult to find. Edmonton has a strictly enforced tow-away policy. Motorists should park in designated **parking** areas which are identified by a sign with a green 'P'; there is usually a 2hr limit, though some all-day parking is available; public, off-street and meter parking facilities are located throughout the city. For a free map and information about parking fees, call ☎780-396-3100 or go online to *www.edmonton.ca*.

Car rentals: Avis ☎780-448-0066 or 800-879-2847; www.avis.com. **Budget** ☎780-448-2000 or 800-267-0505; www.budget.com, **Hertz Canada** ☎780-415-5283 or 800-263-0600. www.hertz.ca, **Thrifty Car Rental** ☎780-890-4555 or 800-847-4389. www.thrifty.com. Most offer free pick-up and drop-off services from hotels.

BY TAXI: Checker Cabs (☎780-484-8888), Prestige Cabs (☎780-462-4444) and Yellow Cab (☎780-462-3456).

GENERAL INFORMATION

VISITOR INFORMATION

Edmonton Tourism ☎780-424-9191 or 800-661-1678 (Canada/US). www.edmonton.com/tourism Visitor information centres are found in three locations: Main office downtown (see above, 9990 Jasper Ave. across from Fairmont Hotel Macdonald). There is an information kiosk at Edmonton International Airport and a large visitor centre as you enter the city northbound from the airport at Gateway Park. Website for all: www.edmonton.com/tourism

ACCOMMODATIONS

For a listing of suggested hotels, 👜see the Address Book. For **hotels/motels** contact Tourism Edmonton ☎780-426-4715 or 800-463-4667 *(Canada/US)*. www.edmonton.com/tourism. Reservation services: Hotels.com ☎800-224-6835 *(Canada/US)* http://deals.hotels.com.

LOCAL PRESS

Daily: *Edmonton Journal, Calgary Sun, Globe and Mail, National Post.* **Weekly:** *Edmonton Examiner* and *The Vue Weekly,* plus many suburban weeklies such as the *St. Albert Gazette* or *Leduc Representative.* **Monthly:** *Avenue* magazine *(www.avenuemagazine.ca)* and free guides to entertainment, shopping, and restaurants: *Where* (www.whereedmonton.com). Broadcast Media: Global TV Edmonton, CFRN-TV, CFCW, CJSR FM88, CKUA Radio, CBC Radio, Access Television, A-Channel.

ENTERTAINMENT

Consult the arts and entertainment supplements in local newspapers *(Thursday or Friday editions)* for schedules of cultural events and addresses of principal theatres and concert halls. Ticketmaster *(☎780-451-8000 for concerts or 416-872-1111; www.ticketmaster.ca)* sells tickets for theatre and the arts. The website www.festivalcity.ca also offers good information.

USEFUL NUMBERS

◆ **Police: 911** (emergency) or ☎780-945-5330 (non-emergency).
◆ **Edmonton International Airport** – ☎780-890-8382.
◆ **Canadian Automobile Assn.** – ☎403-989-6250 or 800-222-6400.
◆ **CAA Emergency Road Service** (24hr) – ☎780-222-4357.
◆ **Shoppers Drug Mart** (24hr pharmacy) with many locations – ☎800-746-7737.
◆ **Road Conditions** – ☎877-262-4997.
◆ **Weather** – www.weatheroffice.gc.ca.

SHOPPING

SHOPPING MALLS

The city boasts numerous mega-malls including the world's biggest shopping centre, **West Edmonton Mall,** as well as big-box mega-centres

Deep Sea Adventure Lake, West Edmonton Mall
©Travel Alberta

like the sprawling **South Edmonton Commons** on the city's northeast edge, with more than 100 stores, as well as **Londonderry Mall.** Downtown shopping malls include **ManuLife Place** and the **City Centre** mall. Southwest of Old Strathcona, **Southgate Centre Mall** sits off Highway 2.

West Edmonton Mall – 170th to 178th Sts., 87th to 90th Aves. Shopping hours Mon–Sat 10am–9pm, holidays 10am–6pm, Sun 11am–5pm. Hours and fees vary for waterpark and rides. Some 800 stores and an indoor amusement park. ☎780-444-5200. www.westedmontonmall.com.

Old Strathcona Antique Mall – 7614 Gateway Blvd. ☎780-433-0398. This large emporium features rows upon rows of antiques for sale by some 200 vendors. Artworks, collectibles, furnishings, housewares, jewellery and more.

SPECIALTY SHOPS

Alberta Craft Council Gallery and Shop – 10186 106 St. ☎780-488-5900 or 800-362-7238 (Alberta only). High-quality stoneware, glass works, wood carvings and bowls, scarves and other woven articles, toys, Christmas decorations, clothing, dolls and many other gift items handmade by the council's 200-plus members throughout the province.

Italian Bakery Co. – *Main outlet at 4118 118th Ave.* ☎780-474-2248. Much more than a bakery, this unassuming market in a strip mall on Edmonton's south side is jammed with everything from rows of olive oils and balsamic vinegars to an endless array of fresh breads and baked good. A good supply of interesting produce including seasonal specialties like chanterelle mushrooms. The deli counter has cheeses and meats from around the world; their take-out panini sandwiches wrapped in brown paper are a meal in themselves. A longstanding second location in Chinatown *(10646 97th St.; ☎780-424-4830)* has the same fresh-baked goods but a smaller deli/grocery section.

Planet Organic Market – *12120 Jasper Ave.* ☎*780-452-4921, www.planet organic.ca.* Health-conscious foodies—especially those with dietary needs such as yeast-free, vegan or gluten-free—won't go hungry at this well-stocked grocery store and deli counter on the west side of downtown. There's a good selection of cheeses, meats, organic local produce and tasty take-out goods like samosas, wraps, salads and baked goods. A second location in the city's north side *(7917 104th St.; ☎780-433-6807)* offers similar fare.

Sunterra Markets – *Main location at Lendrum Shopping Centre, 5228 111th St.* ☎*780-434-2610. www.sunterramarket. com.* Owners of this family business have ensured top-quality products by raising and producing their own meat and game through sustainable and often organic practices. The market offers a good variety of pre-made food to go (meat, side dishes, sandwiches, salads, soups and desserts) along with groceries and deli foods such as olives, cheeses and baked goods. Also a good selection of specialty items such as gluten (wheat)-free and sugar-free products; cooking classes, tastings and demos are also offered. A smaller second location with companion wine/beer store recently opened in Commerce Place mall on Jasper Avenue downtown (☎780-426-3791).

FARMERS' MARKET
Old Strathcona Farmers' Market
(ⓒ see address book for more) is the city's best known; it runs Saturdays in **Old Strathcona.** Most of the suburban towns such as Sherwood Park, Leduc and St. Albert also have weekly farmer's markets between late May and mid-October, check www.albertamarkets.com for more information.

SECOND-HAND WARES
For upscale chic and vintage clothes, head to the boutiques along Whyte Avenue in the **Old Strathcona District** or toward 109 Street near the University of Edmonton.

GALLERIES AND ART
A cluster of galleries and craft shops within a seven-block area of Jasper Avenue downtown offer a diversity of wares from expensive First Nations and Inuit paintings to funky folk art carvings and jewellery. Indigenous works are represented by the **Gallery Walk Assn.** (www.gallery-walk.com). One of the best-known of these shops is **Bearclaw Gallery** (☎780-483-1204), featuring a wide range of high-end and more affordable Aboriginal art. There are also many art, craft and jewellery shops, both new and consignment, along Whyte Avenue in three-block radius around 103rd Street and 106th Street. Many artists also sell their wares at the Strathcona Farmers' Market (ⓒ see above).

SPORTS AND LEISURE

SPORTS
Edmonton Oilers (ice hockey): season Oct-May at the Skyreach Centre (next to Northlands Park), ☎780-414-4625, www.edmontonoilers.com. **Edmonton Eskimos** (football) play from mid-Jun–Nov at Commonwealth Stadium,

☎780-448-3757 or ☎800-667-3757, www.esks.com.

PERFORMING ARTS
More than 15 theatre companies operate in Edmonton, with the majority found in the downtown theatre district. Cultural anchors include the capacious **Citadel Theatre** (☎780-425-1820, www.citadeltheatre.com), which, within the space of one full city block, features not only five theatres, but also an indoor garden with ponds and waterfall. Another major venue for world-class musical performers is the **Winspear Centre** (☎800-563-5081; www.winspearcentre.com), renowned for its pitch-perfect acoustics and home of the **Edmonton Symphony Orchestra** (☎780-428-1414). The **Walterdale Playhouse** (☎780-439-2845) in the Strathcona District is the city's oldest theatre; set in a restored turn-of-the-century fire hall, the playhouse features mostly offbeat, alternative and historical shows. The past is also showcased at the historic **Princess Theatre**, which runs old movies, alternative flicks and foreign films. Both the **Alberta Ballet** (☎780-428-6839, www.albertaballet.com) and **Edmonton Opera** (☎780-429-1000; www.edmontonopera.com) call the University of Alberta's **Jubilee Auditorium** home; the aging theatre recently underwent an extensive renovation.

NIGHTLIFE
For bars in Old Stratchona, the city's most colourful district, ⓒ see the sidebar. Other popular bets are **Cowboys** (10102 180th St.; ☎780-481-8739), a lively country bar known for its young crowd, long lineups on weekends and party-'til-you-drop atmosphere. There's a huge dance floor and the bar attracts some big-name country acts from across North America. Another hot spot is the **Cook County Saloon** (8010 Gateway Blvd.; ☎780-432-2665), where the dance floor is perpetually packed with two-steppers and line-dancing enthusiasts, especially on the weekends. Big-name artists come here also, and dance lessons are available on some weekday evenings.

SPAS

EvelineCharles Salon and Spa, second level, near the ice palace in West Edmonton Mall (☏780-424-5666; www.evelinecharles.com) is a spacious spa, offering a full slate of aesthetic services. Stop in for a 45min neck and back massage or a pedicure. More time? Take the hydrotherapy or try the hydro tub with its 144-jet massage. Reservations suggested (required for packages).

The Board Room (www.boardroom-spas.com) is a newer men's-only spa in Commerce Place downtown that bills itself as "the world's finest spa for men." The 2,900-sq ft space offers a full range of wellness, aesthetic and medical (i.e. botox) services in an upscale setting aimed at the urban professional male. The spa's executive lounge boasts leather recliners, a big-screen TV, complimentary beverages, men's magazines and newspapers.

The 5,000sq ft **Pink Lime Salon and Spa** (10334 108 St.; ☏780-422-7465; www.pinklimeed.com) features a range of services in a spacious downtown setting dominated by wood floors, sleek curved counters and lots of bright windows. This "spa with a conscience" is known for supporting many charitable causes and fund-raisers. Treatments include the usual array of aesthetic and salon plus pedicures including the signature Royal Treatment, a 90min nail and foot pampering from the comfort of a heated recliner.

RECREATION

The river valley has been preserved as a stretch of parkland spanning 27km/17mi with 30km/19mi of trails for **walking, biking** and **skiing.** City officials, ever vigilant with world-class comparisons, point out that the green space is 21 times bigger than New York's Central Park; even better, Edmonton's park comes with official warnings about urban coyotes and a coyote hot line. Whatever the statistics, any visit to Edmonton must take in this lush corridor, where **kayakers** paddle in the river, **in-line skaters** whiz past, picnickers stretch out on the grass, and **anglers** try their luck—and all on their lunch breaks. The valley has room for three municipal **golf courses,** including Canada's oldest municipal course, the Victoria, and many individual neighbourhood parks. Several of the city's 30 annual festivals take place in the parks here, which are a welcome refuge when summer temperatures reach 20°C/68°F to 25°C/83°F, with high humidity.

Parks in the City

Edmonton has more than 460 parks, a statistic that is considered to be the most urban parkland in North America. There are 22 major parks in the river valley section (◔see above) alone, most of them wheelchair-accessible. **William Hawrelak Park** (9930 Groat Rd.), west of the university, is one of the city's finest and a popular venue for festivals and other special events such as Canada Day celebrations on July 1.

Ice-skating at William Hawrelak Park

©Travel Alberta

With a small manmade lake (kids love the paddle boats), fountains, an outdoor amphitheatre and treed pathways, Hawrelak Park is a nice spot for a picnic or family reunion. The lake is cleared for **ice-skating** in the winter, when cross-country skiers and snowshoers take to its trails. Other major parks include the 460-acre **Terwillegar Park** (159th St. and 45th Ave. in the west end, near city limits), a former gravel pit that has a large off-leash area for dog walkers plus trails for cyclists, in-line skaters and cross-country skiers. **Emily Murphy Park,** on the south bank of the river, runs from Groat Road to the High Level Bridge. This 11ha/27acre park is linked to **Kinsmen Park** to the east and feature seven interpretive signs along the trails to teach users about Edmonton's urban forest. The action-packed **Rundle Park** (28th St. and 118th Ave.) on the river valley's northeastern edge is another scenic venue boasting many amenities such as a river footbridge, an aquatic centre, baseball diamonds, soccer and football fields, disc golf, an 18-hole mini-golf, tennis courts, horseshoe pits, paddleboats and many paved and shale trails. There's also a par 3 golf course. Website for all parks (hours vary and change seasonally) is www.edmonton.ca, click on the Parks and River Valley.

PRINCIPAL FESTIVALS

Edmonton's year is enlivened by some 30 festivals. The 10-day Edmonton **International Street Performers Festival** runs in early July. In mid-July, the gigantic (no other word will do) 10-day **Capital Ex** extravaganza at the Northland fairgrounds brings all of Edmonton to a state of high excitement. Mid-July also plays host to the **Grand Prix of Edmonton.** The **Edmonton Folk Music Festival** takes place the second weekend in August in Gallagher Park, while the **Fringe Theatre Festival** takes place the same month in Old Strathcona, a bustling area south of the river along Whyte Ave notable for cafes, restaurants, boutiques, artisan shops, galleries and second-hand stores (see sidebar). In the colder months (generally mid-Oct to May) events move to indoor venues such as the Francis Winspear Centre for Music or Citadel Theatre north of the river downtown. Two such events are the **Edmonton International Film Festival** (usually lasting a week in late-Sept/early Oct) and the five-day **Global Visions Film Festival** in early November. The **Canadian Finals Rodeo,** which attracts top talent from across the country, is held annually in early November.

once it enters the city and cuts through the heart of the historic Old Strathcona area. After an abrupt turn west, it becomes Whitemud Drive NW.

P **Parking:** Downtown Edmonton is tied together by a 13km/8mi system of "pedways," or covered walkways and tunnels connecting most of downtown's principal buildings to Edmonton Light Rail Transit stations. This LRT system, North America's first when introduced in 1978, covers 13.8 km/8.6mi and has ten stations, with a further 7.5km/4.7mi scheduled for completion in 2010. Try to use this system whenever convenient. Downtown and in Strathcona, plan to walk a few blocks because lots fill up early, especially off Whyte Avenue during the wildly busy Saturday Old Strathcona Market. City parking meters charge $2/hr to $6/hr, depending on the area and day of the week; there are also numerous large pay lots. On Sundays, meter parking is usually free.

🚲 **Don't Miss:** Fort Edmonton is a lively, interactive introduction to the city's fur-trading roots.

🕐 **Organizing Your Time:** Plan a visit during one of Edmonton's many festivals: they are held throughout year.

Kids **Especially for Kids:** The West Edmonton Mall has attractions and amusements galore.

👟 **Also See:** RED DEER AREA

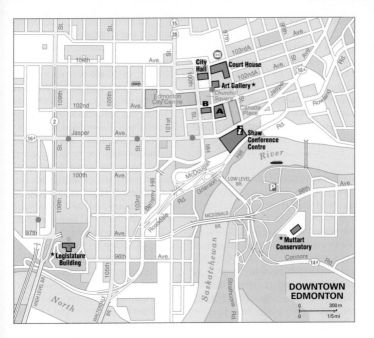

City Hall
Court House
Art Gallery ★
102ndA
Edmonton City Centre
Churchill Square
B
A
Canada Place
Shaw Conference Centre
River
LOW LEVEL BR.
Jasper Ave.
Jasper Ave.
103rdA
Rowland Rd.
Saskatchewan
MCDONALD BR.
★ Muttart Conservatory
Connors
★ Legislature Building
North
Saskatchewan
DOWNTOWN EDMONTON
0   300 m
0   1/5 mi

A Bit of History

By the end of the 18C, posts near present-day Edmonton were trading blankets, guns and other goods to Cree and Blackfoot Indians in exchange for animal pelts. A fur-trading port was established in 1795 by the Hudson's Bay Company next to the smaller Fort Augustus, operated by the Northwest Company. The settlement grew as goods arrived by wide-bottom **York boat** (stable and wide to ply shallow waters such as the North Saskatchewan River) and overland from Winnipeg by **Red River cart**—the major means of pioneer transportation on the prairies (the axles never required greasing and the wheels were easily removed for river crossing). Traders had already discovered that the river valley and surrounding area, forested with spruce and poplar, were rich in fur-bearing animals such as muskrat, beaver and fox.

In 1821 **Edmonton House** emerged as the Hudson Bay Company's most important post in the West. The decision of the Canadian Pacific Railway Company to route its line through Calgary was a blow, but other rail lines arrived in

Edmonton by the end of the century. Fort Edmonton moved in 1830 to the site where the Alberta Legislature building stands today. During the Klondike Stampede of 1896-99, Edmonton became known as a "Gateway to the North." Primarily due to its strategic location between central farmland and the northern regions, Edmonton became Alberta's capital in 1904. It might have remained a quiet administrative centre had oil not been discovered in 1947 in **Leduc,** a small community to the south, followed by other many discoveries in the region. The latest big development is the Athabasca oil sands project to the north near Fort McMurray, for which Edmonton is a today major service and distribution centre. The largest percentage of the province's producing oil wells and gas pipelines are concentrated in the Edmonton area.

While the oil and gas industry has driven the economy during the past half century, many Edmontonians also work in the civil service for the provincial and municipal government as well as in burgeoning research, biotech and agricultural technology sectors.

Downtown

Despite strong competition from suburban malls, the downtown district is a lively place, due in great part to the construction of high-end condominium towers overlooking the North Saskatchewan River, whose occupants support the services, shops, restaurants and entertainment venues. Office space in the glass towers is at a premium here, and the 30-odd schools in the area bring 40,000 students downtown daily. Sir Winston Churchill Square, the centre of the Arts District, generally hops with activity, amid cafe tables, greenery, a waterfall, festival venues, the **Court House** and the Centennial Plaza Park. At no. 1 Winston Churchill Square stands **City Hall,** designed by Dub Architects Ltd., recognizable by its eight-storey glass (43m/131ft) pyramid, 65m/200ft clock tower holding a 23-bell carillon and reflecting pool, where Edmontonians cool off in the summer and skate in the winter. **The Art Gallery of Alberta** (👜 *see below*) at 2 Winston Churchill Square, currently being rebuilt, presents a tangle of girders and cranes. It has moved during renovations to Enterprise Square at 10230 Jasper Ave until at least late-2009. Nearby, at 4 Sir Winston Churchill Square, the Edmonton Symphony Orchestra performs at the **Francis Winspear Centre for Music,** as do popular, jazz and classical musicians. The 1,932-seat "shoebox" style concert hall, opened in 1997, was designed by

Douglas McConnell of Cohos Evamy Partners and is renowned for excellent sightlines and acoustics. The elegant glass and brick **Citadel Theatre** (*9828 101A Ave.; ☎780-426-4811; wwwcitadel-theatre.com)*, the city's premier venue for theatrical performances, houses the Lee Pavilion, which provides an urban refuge (especially in winter) filled with exotic plants surrounding a waterfall. The **Metro Cinema** (*www.metrocinema.org*), within the theatre, screens educational, documentary and generally noncommercial films. The four-storey **Stanley A. Milner Library** (*☎780496-7000; www. epl.ca)*, main branch of Edmonton's public library system, stands at 7 Sir Winston Churchill Square; its 1967 architecture with a great glass façade still appeals to modern taste. Two blocks south, the steel and glass structure of Edmonton's **Shaw Conference Centre** (👜*see below)* rises from the steep riverbank opposite **Canada Place,** which houses offices of the federal government. Eclectic shopping can be found at 104th Street, above 97th Avenue, including the City Market (*mid-May-Sept Sat 9am-3pm; ☎780-429-5713; www.city-market.ca.)*, a century-old farmers' market where dwellers in the towering condos can connect with their roots. Starting at 102nd Ave. and continuing north on 97th St. is the city's small Chinatown, entered through the Chinatown Gate.

Downtown malls, where Edmontonians can escape their seriously nippy winters to spend money in comfort,

Francis Winspear Centre for Music

©Travel Alberta

Old Strathcona

Just across the river from downtown, well-restored buildings line Whyte (82nd) Avenue in Edmonton's historic Old Strathcona, a vibrant 10-block hub packed with coffeehouses, restaurants, pubs and some 300 shops (☎780-437-4182; www. oldstrathcona.ca). Look for Canadian and native art at **Fort Door** (10308 81st Ave.; ☎780-432-7535) or fair-trade handicrafts at **The Ten Thousand Villages** (10432-82nd St.; ☎780-439-8349). For a break, sip a latté at one of the many coffee or tea shops, or enjoy an Italian lunch at **Chianti's** (10501 82nd Ave. NW; ☎780-439-9829;www.chianticafe.ca) in the Italianate Old Post Office, with its clock tower. **O'Byrnes Irish Pub** (10616 82nd Ave.; ☎780-414-6766), in the Varscona Hotel, offers Irish cheer and music. **The King & I** (8208 107th St.; ☎780-433-2222) is a longtime favourite that serves excellent, albeit expensive, Thai cuisine; the Rolling Stones have stopped in. **Blues on Whyte** (10329 82nd Ave.; ☎780-439-3981) features live blues from bands performing nightly. Enjoy jam sessions Saturday afternoons; some little-known big talent is often at the microphone at this grungy but entertaining venue. Every August the district hums when Canada's largest fringe theatre festival (10330 82nd Ave; ☎780-448-9000; www.fringetheatreadventures.ca) draws crowds to venues such as the Fringe Theatre and Walterdale Playhouse. Every Saturday year-round, the Old Strathcona **farmers' market** sells local produce and crafts (Sat 8am–3pm; 10310 83rd Ave; ☎780-439-1844; www. osfm.ca). This busy market offers everything from produce and prepared foods to handmade crafts and jewellery. Specialty vendors sell cheese and meat including exotic choices such as bison, elk and even ostrich. There are also bakeries, a Mexican vendor selling homemade salsa and other dips along with fresh corn tortillas; and don't miss the Sunworks farm booth selling organic meats like smoked chicken, Alberta lamb, pork, beef and game. Buskers enliven the mood in summer and parking is limited, so get there as early in the morning as possible.

include the **Edmonton City Centre** (101st St and 102nd Ave.; ☎780-426-8444;www.edmontoncitycentre.com), with some 150 shops. **Commerce Place** on Jasper Avenue between 101st and 102nd streets (☎780-429-6500; www. commerceplaceedm.com) is an upscale emporium with designer shops and fine dining. **Manulife Place** (☎780-420-6236; www.manulife.com) at the corner of 101st Street and 102nd Avenue is a centre for upscale fashion, including Holt Renfrew, the elegant Toronto-based clothing store knows as "Holts." And for visitors who wish to stroll along the river, stairs lead down to the valley park from the Shaw Conference Centre, the Fairmont Hotel Macdonald and the Crowne Plaza Chateau Lacombe.

One-hour **tours** of the downtown area are offered free of charge at 1pm every Mon, Wed and Fri (Jun-Aug) by the Downtown Business Assn. (☎780-424-4085; www.edmontondowntown.com). Tours start at the DBA office (10121 Jasper Ave.); tour leaders can be identified by their bright red shirts and caps.

Art Gallery of Alberta★

Interim location: Enterprise Sq., 100, 10230 Jasper Ave. ◷Open year-round Mon–Fri 10:30am–5pm (Thu until 8pm), weekends 11am–5pm. ◷Closed major holidays. ◉$10 (free Thu 4pm–8pm). ✕&☎780-422-6223. www.artgalleryalberta.com.

At its Winston Churchill Square site of 40 years, the gallery will emerge in 2009 (or possibly 2010) housed in a new $88 million, 85,000sq ft building designed by Randall Stout Architects Inc. of Los Angeles. The gallery's future home will double the museum's exhibit space to 30,000sq ft. and permit the showing of a larger part of the 6,000-work collection. With curving lines and—if drawings are a guide—a spectacular glass atrium, the new structure will itself make a sculptural statement, as well as provide expanded education facilities, a 150-seat theatre and a high-end restaurant. The design is a radical departure from the 1969 Brutalist concrete structure by Don Bittorf, which has been demolished. The gallery, founded in 1924, changed its name from the Edmonton Art Gal-

Capital Ex

Every year in mid-July Edmonton stages a frenzied celebration called Edmonton's Capital City Exposition, or Capital Ex. This 10-day-long party takes place at the Northlands exhibition grounds on the north side of the city (Gretzky Dr. and Borden Park Rd., south of Hwy. 16). A day's gate admission ($8) gives access to plenty of excitement; grounds stay open from noon to midnight. Examples of entertainment are a circus, a midway with lots of thrilling rides, a food fair, a craft show, and in the evening, rock concerts, country-and-western concerts, aboriginal dances, Canadian Idol-type talent searches and a casino. A plethora of activities is aimed at children: concerts (with guest performers such as Barney), games, a gold-panning contest, rides and clowns. Of course, there is a parade through downtown and fireworks.

A version of the fair has taken place here for more than 125 years. For several years the fair was called the **Klondike Stampede,** recalling the days when gold prospectors came through Edmonton to begin their trek north to Dawson City, Yukon. In 2006 the name changed back to Capital Ex, the zany 19C costumes were folded away and the chuckwagon race was moved to a later date. For more information: ☎780-471-7210 or 888-800-7275. www.capitalex.ca.

lery to the Art Gallery of Alberta in 2005, when the present building project was announced.

In the interim, the gallery is housed at a former Hudson's Bay Company building on Enterprise Square; the temporary building was attractively renovated to hold the collection and has successfully staged several exhibits. Highlights of the permanent collection include contemporary works by First Nations artists and works by Canadian artists such as Emily Carr and Paul Peel, as well as contemporary international and Canadian art.

Muttart Conservatory★

9626 96A St. ○Open year-round Mon–Fri 9am–5:30pm, weekends and holidays 11am–5:30pm. ○Closed Dec 25. ☞$9. ✕♿🅿☎780-496-8755. www.muttart conservatory.ca Note: The conservatory is closed until early 2009 for expansion and renovation.

The four glass pyramids that rise from the south side of the river valley provide a striking architectural ensemble that shelters some 700 plant species. Step inside during the winter months and the contrast is striking, especially in the tropical pyramid, a steamy glass-encased space where exotic birds fly among the towering palm trees and where orchids bloom year-round. The arid pyramid offers a desert ecozone with

cactus, yucca and succulents. Another pyramid showcases plants that thrive on four different continents, although not in Edmonton's climate. The final pyramid offers a revolving array of blooms, many of them seasonal such as lilies at Easter and poinsettias at Christmas.

Behind the conservatory at riverside is the landing for the paddlewheeler *Edmonton Queen*, which offers passengers a leisurely **cruise** on the North Saskatchewan River. (✕♿🅿○Departs May–mid-Sept Thu–Sat noon, 3pm, dinner cruise 7:30pm. Sun 3:30 pm, dinner cruise 7.30pm. Round-trip 1hr. Reservations required. ☞$17.95. ☎780-424-2628, or 877-281-2428. www.edmonton queen.com).

Shaw Conference Centre

9797 Jasper Ave. ✕♿🅿○Open year-round. ☎780-421-9797. www.shawcon ferencecentre.com.

The striking architecture of the conference centre, with its total of 110,000 sq ft of exhibit space, spills in terraces down the banks of Grierson Hill on the North Saskatchewan River, surrounded by green parkland. Built in 1983, the centre was expanded in 2006, but its massive 10-storey size is not evident from the exterior because some 70 percent

©Travel Alberta

Edmonton Queen paddlewheeler

of the building is hidden underground, stretching underneath Jasper Ave. From inside, the **view**★★ over the valley through great stretches of glass is also spectacular, while the view of the interior, as the space rises under steel girders and glass over terraces connected by seemingly endless escalators, is breathtaking. A waterfall cascades down the terraces in the atrium. Interior sidewalks ("pedways") connect the conference centre to other buildings in the downtown area and to LRT stations. The entrance on Jasper Avenue gives little hint of the extraordinary space inside, so the best way to appreciate the building is to float by it on the river. The centre is used for professional and trade conferences, galas and pop concerts.

Just next to the centre, sculpted into the river bluff, is the beautiful 15ha/37acre **Louise McKinney Park,** with walking trails, benches and a garden featuring 30 varieties of roses.

Legislature Building★

Visitor centre 10820 98th Ave. Visit by guided tour (45 min) only, May–mid-Oct Mon–Fri 9am–noon hourly, weekends 12:30pm–4pm every 30min. Rest of the year Mon–Fri 9am–3pm hourly, weekends and holidays noon–4pm hourly. Closed Jan 1, Good Friday & Dec 25. 780-427-7362. www.assembly.ab.ca.

Set within 23ha/57acres of pleasant gardens overlooking the North Saskatchewan River, the five-storey, yellow granite and sandstone Alberta Legislature, completed in 1912, occupies the site of the original Fort Edmonton. The Beaux-Arts structure was designed by Allan Merrick Jeffers and Richard Blakey, who also designed the Manitoba and Saskatchewan legislature buildings. *Tours start at the Legislative Assembly Interpretive Centre just north of the main building.* The main entrance opens into a rotunda faced in granite from Vancouver Island and supported by pillars, from which a sweeping staircase rises to the

Achieving Great Heights

Edmonton's 1913 **High Level Bridge** is a striking sight as it stretches 755m /2,302 ft across the North Saskatchewan River at 109th Street, towering more than 50m/175ft above the valley. The Alberta attitude of "doing one better" is nowhere more evident than in the "The Great Divide Waterfall," created by Peter Lewis, which on summer holiday weekends cascades from the top of the bridge to the river below. From mid-May to mid-October, an old streetcar travels from Whyte Avenue in Strathcona to Government Centre and back over the bridge. The pedestrian walkway offers walkers marvelous views and a vertiginous thrill.

Alberta Legislature Building and grounds

next storeys. Upstairs is a bronze statue of Princess Louise Caroline Alberta, a daughter of Queen Victoria and the wife of Canada's governor general, for whom the province was named. The **Carillon Room,** a dome-shaped meeting space on the fifth floor features high-arched ceilings inlaid with stained glass. In a separate room sit the mechanical elements of the Alberta Carillon, an instrument similar to an electric organ with two keyboards and a pedal board that control metal alloy rods serving as the 305 bells. Every hour, the carillon rings a series of four melodies. Also on the fifth floor is a curiosity known as the **Magic Spot,** marked by a brass plate, where visitors hear the sound of water rushing past. This acoustic phenomenon occurs because the grand staircase acts as a sound tunnel for the fountain five floors below.

The **gardens** are lovely, with paths and fountains and a pool used for swimming. From the grounds, a redbrick trail leads visitors on a self-guided historical tour of old Fort Edmonton, starting at 110th Street and 99th Avenue and continuing to 97th Street.

Additional Sights

Fort Edmonton Park★★
Fox Dr. at Whitemud Dr. ○Open Jul–Aug daily 10am–6pm. Mid-May–Jun Mon–Fri 10am–4pm, weekends 10am–6pm. Sept Sun 10am–6pm and ⬥Mon–Sat guided wagon tours 11am, noon, 1pm, 2pm & 3pm. ⬥$13.25. ✖⬥🅿⬥780-496-8787. www.fortedmontonpark.com.

Kids Rambling along the ravine of the North Saskatchewan River, this park, owned and operated by the city, re-creates the history of settlement in Edmonton. The mid-19C fur-trading post itself has been reconstructed, including the Big House, a four-storey residence with a third-floor balcony from which the chief factor, or governor, could survey his domain. Quarters of the other 130 inhabitants, such as clerks, artisans, labourers and servants, have been meticulously re-created. Fort Edmonton Park also serves as a site for educational programs, day camps, festivals and special events.

From the railway station housing the visitor centre at the front entrance, board the vintage train *(free; continuous service)* to reach **Fort Edmonton,** the 1846 fur-trading post. Hop off and take a short stroll to the sprawling fort, passing along the way Indians engaged in crafts such as beading and leatherwork or in roasting bannock (Indian fry bread) on a stick. Also on view are trade and storage rooms, as well as the forge, stable and boat sheds where York boats are under construction (one floats in the river).

A streetcar *(free, continuous service)* shuttles travellers through the park's various periods in history, but explore on foot if you can. Wander past the goats and

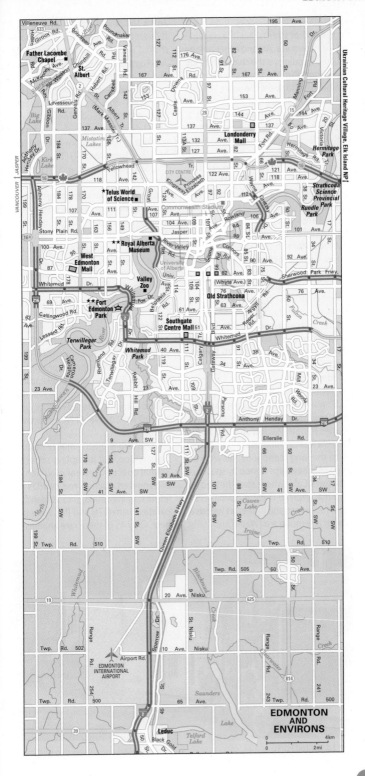

EDMONTON
AND
ENVIRONS

sheep grazing in a paddock, then head for the grid of streets, each representing a different era. Among other reconstructed buildings is the chapel built for Rev. **Robert Rundle,** the first missionary in Alberta, who spent the years 1840 to 1848 at Fort Edmonton.

The **prerailway village** contains a reconstruction of Jasper Avenue in 1885, notable for its width (so Red River carts could turn) and board walks. Along the avenue, stores sell furs, jewellery and hardware; other buildings include the North West Mounted Police post, the Dominion Land Office and the offices of the local newspaper. One original building, the 1873 McDougall Church, is the first Protestant church in Alberta built by Rev. **George McDougall** (*see Métis Crossing and Victoria Settlement below*). The 1905 Street shows Edmonton at a time of great growth. The streetcar runs down the middle of the road, along which stand penny arcades. There's also an old-fashioned candy store. Eventually 1905 Street becomes **1920 Street,** which represents a period of prosperity for Edmonton.

The rebuilt **Hotel Selkirk** (*780-496-7227; www.hotelselkirk.com*), where the 30 guest rooms are decorated with Charles Rennie Macintosh-style furniture, is a wonderful spot to relax. Stand up to the long Mahogony Bar with its shiny gold beer taps or stop by spacious Johnson's Cafe, where staff dressed as for a Masterpiece Theatre drama serve breakfast, lunch and dinner, as well as a proper afternoon tea *(Wed–Thu).*

John Janzen Nature Centre

Whitemud Dr and Fox Dr. Parking lot shared with Fort Edmonton. Open Jul–Aug weekdays 9am–6pm, weekends and holidays 11am–6pm. Mid-May–Jun weekdays 9am–4pm, weekends and holidays 11am–6pm. Sept–Dec 24 weekdays 9am–4pm weekends and holidays 1pm–4pm, Dec 26–31 daily 1pm–4pm. Rest of the year weekdays 9am–4pm, weekends and holidays 1pm–4pm. Closed Dec 25. Self-guided trails. $2. 780-496-8777. www.edmonton.ca.

Many visitors who stop at Fort Edmonton Park stroll on over to its neighbouring attraction, this nature centre. A 4km/2.5mi nature trail winds along the North Saskatchewan River valley. Local plant species are identified along the path; some weekends, nature walks are offered, but it's best to confirm by phoning ahead.

Valley Zoo

13315 Buena Vista Rd. (87th Ave.). Open Jul–Aug daily 9:30am–8pm. Mid-May–Jun daily 9:30am–6pm. Sept–mid-Oct weekdays 9:30am–4pm, weekends and holidays 9:30am–4pm. Rest of year daily 9:30am–4pm. Closed Dec 25. $9. 780-496-8777. www.valley zoo.ca.

Kids This zoo is much smaller than the Calgary Zoo, but it displays some 300 animal species, several of which are endangered, such as red pandas and lemurs. In May 2008, two Stygan's red pandas, named Tai and Pip, were born here. Only 45 of these rare animals live

Fort Edmonton Park

A Rivalry of Sports

The cities of Calgary and Edmonton, so tied by history, geography and commerce, are also intense rivals, not least in sports. The National Hockey League's **Edmonton Oilers** and **Calgary Flames** always raise the stadium rafters when they meet in either city, as do the Canadian Football League's **Calgary Stampeders** and **Edmonton Eskimos**. The Eskimos won five consecutive Grey Cups as the top CFL team from 1978 to1982, while in the seven years from 1984 to 1990, the Oilers (with hockey great Wayne Gretzky) won five Stanley Cups, the Calgary Flames taking home the 1989 Cup. Edmonton has been assigned the role of Alberta's second city, after the more populous and flashier Calgary, and a touch of resentment can cause a chip to appear on the collective Edmonton shoulder. Still, to be second in a province this rich, beautiful and dynamic is not such a bad position.

in captivity in North America, and just 2,000 to 5,000 are thought to exist in their native China. The zoo offers a variety of educational programs for adults and children, as well as day camps.

Activities for families include a petting zoo, camel rides and a mini train where small children are introduced to small animals such as prairie dogs. Among the more exotic species, whose habitats are carefully simulated, are South American porcupines that have prehensile tails so they can cling to trees; the west Caucasian tur, a small deer from the Georgian mountains; the snow leopard from the mountains of central Asia; and the bearded dragon from Australia.

West Edmonton Mall

170th to 178th Sts., 87th to 90th Aves. ⏰*Shopping hours Mon–Sat 10am–9pm, Sun 11am–5pm, holidays 10am–6pm. Hours and fees vary for waterpark and rides.* ✕ ♿ 🅿 ☎*780-444-5200. www. westedmontonmall.com.*

This 483,000sq m/5million sq ft shopping/entertainment leviathan is a destination in itself. Visitors might consider allotting a few days to the experience; two hotels (and a third on the way) are located here, so you need never leave. Among the 800 stores and services selling everything from high fashion to groceries, you can find a spa, a medical clinic, several opticians, a dental clinic, a car wash, a clinic offering minor plastic surgery and a non-denominational chapel.

🄺 Entertainment includes the **Galaxyland** amusement park, with 26 hair-raising rides and for small children, a space-themed park, and the Ice Palace skating rink, where the Edmonton Oilers sometimes practice. The newly renovated 2ha/5acre **World Waterpark** includes slides, a wave pool and a bungee jump; the Sea Life Caverns, where 200 animals such as penguins and sting rays can be viewed up close, especially if children sign up the Trainer for a Day educational program; and Sea Lion Rock, where California sea lions give daily shows. For less strenuous activity, there are two movie complexes with 21 theatres, the Palace Casino and 100 restaurants. Themed streets are **Europa Boulevard,** lined with chic shops and meant to look like Belle Epoque Paris, or Bourbon Street, which offers lively music and restaurants.

The new four-storey **Empire Club** *(open Fri, Sat and Sun evenings)* offers dancing under balloons, fireworks, confetti or simulated snowflakes, as well as six bars for refreshment. To orient yourself, it might be advisable to take a guided mall tour aboard a two-wheeled Segway personal transportation device; you can test one at the new Segway Urban Agility Course. Naturally, the mall holds the Guinness Book of Records certification for "world's largest parking lot," with 20,000 spaces.

Royal Alberta Museum★★

12845 102nd Ave. ⏰*Open year-round daily 9am–5pm.* ⏰*Closed Dec 24–25.* ☞*$10.* ✕ ♿ 🅿 ☎*780-453-9100. www. royalalbertamuseum.ca.* ✋*Galleries will remain open during a major expansion in 2009-2010.*

©Travel Alberta

Royal Alberta Museum

Located in an attractive park overlooking the river, beside the grand and gabled Government House—a conference centre that once housed Alberta's lieutenant governor—this museum is a showcase of western Canada's human and natural history. One of the most-visited museums in western Canada and one of the largest, at 18,850sq m/200,000sq ft, it is slated to undergo a $200 million expansion, with expected completion in 2010.

On the main floor, the **Wild Alberta Gallery,** formerly the Habitat Gallery, offers walk-through dioramas (including sound effects) of natural sites around the province such as a marshland where birds, fish, reptiles and mammals share space. These exhibits are constantly updated as new information and exhibit elements are developed. The **Natural History Gallery** encloses the ever-popular **Bug Room,** with its glass tanks containing live insects in their natural habitat. Trained volunteers scoop specimens out of the tanks so visitors can have a closer look. The Bird Gallery presents mounted birds from near and far, along with their eggs. Reading the Rocks explains how geologic forces have shaped the planet over the eons, while Treasures of the Earth displays minerals and gems.

A quarter of the museum's gallery space is devoted to the extraordinary **Syncrude Gallery of Aboriginal Culture,** where visitors can observe, through vivid dioramas, exhibits and first-hand testimony, as well as some 3,000 artifacts, the vast scope of aboriginal history and culture in Alberta, starting with archaeological evidence of early human migration to Alberta as the last ice sheet retreated 10,000 years ago. Tools, items of clothing, methods of artistic expression and clever adaptations to the environment are demonstrated, such as the collapsible tepee that permitted following buffalo herds. A learning tepee, a large enclosure with moving curved panels, offers an intimate sound-and-light setting for aboriginal stories. First Nations version of events, such as their arrival in Alberta and encounters with Europeans, are recounted by indigenous peoples in their own voices, and given life through dramatization.

Telus World of Science Edmonton★★

Kids *11211-142nd St. ◐Open late Jun–Labour Day daily 10am–9pm. Rest of the year Sun–Thu and holidays 10am–5pm, Fri–Sat 10am–9pm. ◐Closed Dec 25. ➥$13. ✕&P☎780-452-9100. www.telusworldofscienceedmonton.com.*

Kids Resembling a large spaceship settled into Coronation Park, the centre, which carries the name of an Alberta-based telecommunications company, was designed by renowned architect **Douglas Cardinal.** It houses an IMAX theatre and a planetarium, in addition to exhibit areas.

On Level One, the **EPCOR Environment Gallery** offers a child's-eye view of the environment as observed in the home of a family named Green. The Allard Family Gallery offers vivid carnival-style exhibits about personal health. The Hole Family Gallery, a long-time favourite, centres on a police station on a night-time avenue where a murder will soon be solved thanks to visitors' timely participation in crime-scene forensics (the police interviews are especially lively). At the **Syncrude Science Stage,** museum staff give science demonstrations *(20min–40min; hourly noon–5pm)* on topics such as extreme heat and cold, chemical explosions and comets.

On Level Two, the Trans-Canada Pipe Lines Space Place Gallery *(due to reopen in late 2008 after extensive renovation)* describes Canada's role in the latest space exploration: investigating conditions on other planets, designing vessels for interplanetary travel by humans, scanning the skies for potential collisions with meteorites, and looking for life in deep space.

On Level Three *(entrance on Level Two)*, the star-projection systems in the **Margaret Zeidler Theatre,** a 250-seat planetarium, were completely renovated in 2008 with the latest digital technology and now permit a variety of shows, including a look deep into the universe at the earliest moments of time. Housed separately, an **observatory** offers a close-up view of the stars and planets *(weather permitting, call for hours)*.

Excursions

St. Albert
19km/12mi north by Rte. 2.
In 1861 a Roman Catholic mission was founded here on the banks of the Sturgeon River by Father **Albert Lacombe** (1827-1916). The simple log **chapel,** built in 1861 by Métis craftsmen in the "post on sill" or Red River frame construction method, is the oldest building still standing in Alberta *(St. Vital Ave.; ◯open mid-May–Labour Day daily 10am–6pm; ⊗$2; ♿ 🅿 ☎780-459-7663; www.tprc. alberta.ca).* Father Lacombe, an Oblate missionary from Quebec, was a beloved

figure among the Cree, Blackfoot and Métis of Alberta, where he laboured to bring peace to the tribes and to influence government policy in their favour. White settlers across the prairies also appreciated his efforts to prevent conflict. Father Lacombe, himself part aboriginal, composed a grammar and dictionary in Cree.

The town of St. Albert, settled by Father Lacombe and a group of Métis, is the oldest unfortified town in the province. When **Vital Grandin** (1829-1902), a fellow Oblate, was named the first bishop of St. Albert in 1871, he quickly appointed Father Lacombe as vicar-general, in order to support his missionary work. The crypt of the Father Lacombe Chapel contains the tombs of Father Lacombe and Bishop Grandin, whose adjoining residence can also be visited. The chapel has been designated a provincial historic site *(👣guided tours are available: phone ahead for schedule).*

Today the pleasant city (pop. 57,719) is Alberta's seventh largest, and retains elements of its French heritage, with several French Catholic schools and French immersion programs in the English schools. The Quebec "rang" system of narrow lots perpendicular to the river can be seen along the Sturgeon River. It is worthwhile to stroll along the extensive Red Willow Urban Park trail system in the Sturgeon River Valley, or to visit the Musée Heritage Museum, located in the St. Albert Place, designed by Douglas Cardinal, whose father was Blackfoot *(5 Anne St., ◯open Tue–Sat 10am–5pm, Sun 1pm–5pm; ⊗contribution requested; ☎780-459-1528; www.artsheritage.ca/ museum).*

Elk Island National Park★
On Hwy. 16, about 35km/22mi east.
◯Open daily year-round. Hiking, camping, canoeing, cross-country skiing, golfing. ⊗$7. 🅿 ☎780-992-5790. www.pc.gc. ca. Visitor centre ♿ 🅿 ◯open May–Jun weekends only, Jul–Aug daily.
One of the smallest of Canada's national parks, the 194sqkm/75sq mi Elk Island National Park nevertheless abounds with wildlife, much of it visible to visitors. Unique in Canada, the park is completely surrounded by a 2.2m/7ft fence

©Travel Alberta

Elk Island National Park

to keep the animals from wandering into nearby suburbs, agricultural land and roadways, and to keep other animals out. Despite this restricted area and lack of natural predators such as bears or wolves, healthy herds of plains bison, woods bison, elk, mule deer and moose thrive thanks to scientific park management. Excess population is trapped and transplanted either to the wild or to other parks in Canada and the US.

Survival of the bison is due to strenuous conservation efforts launched in the late 19C, while the elk population, in steep decline in the same period, was saved by creation of a game preserve here by local citizens in 1906; the reserve became a national park in 1913. Wood bison are unique to northwestern Canada; they can be distinguished from plains bison, which once wandered over great swathes of Canada and the US, by their slightly larger size, the forward placement of the back bump, and extension of the shaggy "cape" towards the haunches. Birdwatchers also appreciate the park, where some 250 bird species have been sighted. A program to reintroduce the endangered trumpeter swan, North America's largest native bird, has slowly increased their number within the park to a few breeding pairs and several cygnets (immature swans). At the **visitor centre,** located at the park's south entrance, exhibits about the park's natural and cultural riches are extremely worthwhile; ask about the many educational programs. In the early hours of the day, herds of plains bison stand or sit in the road, while elk browse nonchalantly in meadows at dawn and dusk. Wood bison make their home in the forest and meadow on the south side of Highway 16. The park's eleven **walking trails** cross wetlands, rolling hills, aspen forests and meadows. Many sorts of wildlife can be observed and photographed, and a rich variety of birds flutter past. The easy 2.5km/1.6mi Kids **Amisk Wuche Trail** and the 150m/0.1mi **Living Waters Trail** appeal to children; floating boardwalks take hikers across ponds inhabited by wetland creatures such as waterfowl, muskrat and moose. Beavers might be seen paddling to their lodges, clenching leafy branches in their jaws.

The **Shoreline Trail** *(6km/3.8mi)* is paved and wheelchair accessible. In winter, the wildlife viewing may be even better, as foliage no longer hides animals. The park maintains ski trails, and visitors can also break their own ski or snowshoe trails.

At **Astotin Lake,** the park maintains a sandy beach and playground in summer, but the water is not suitable for swimming (skin rashes). Somewhat incongruously, the Astotin Lake amenities include a nine-hole golf course, with a pro shop offering equipment rental and meals. From a canoe or kayak (bring your own; the park does not rent boats), visitors can silently wend among the many islands in Astotin Lake to observe myriad waterfowl such as great blue herons, loons, American white pelicans and red-necked grebes. Swans, which are very shy, can sometimes be seen at Astotin Lake, particularly in autumn, when they gather to begin migration south, or in the spring, when they return. On the shores of Tawayik Lake, observable from trails and the picnic area, myriad waterfowl crowd the sky.

Also within the park lie 227 sites with evidence of aboriginal habitation, some as early as the retreat of the glaciers. This area, known as Beaver Hills, became a prime hunting ground for the Cree, who supplied beaver pelts to fur traders in such numbers that the animal became extinct here by 1830, and was reintroduced only in 1942. An interesting relic of settler days, the thatched-roof **Ukrainian Pioneer Home** is maintained as a museum.

Ukrainian Cultural Heritage Village★

On Hwy. 16, about 50km/30mi east of Edmonton. ◷*Open mid-May–Labour Day daily 10am–6pm. Rest of Sept–early Oct weekends only 10am–6pm.* ⊜ *$8.* ✕🦽🅿 ☎*780-662-3640. http://culture. alberta.ca/museums/historicsitelisting/ ukrainianvillage.*

Some 30 historic buildings have been moved to this living history site, which showcases Ukrainian settlement in east central Alberta from 1892 to 1930. Many of the towns from which these buildings have been moved have today vanished.

Settlements differed quite significantly, depending on what part of Ukraine people came from, whether they arrived in the first wave or later, and how long they had been in Canada. Immigrants travelled in groups and settled together in "blocks." In this village are homes built by settlers from Bukovyna (Catholics) and Gallicia (Orthodox), areas in the Carpathian mountains from where virtually all the early Ukrainian settlers hailed; these areas were ruled by Austria until WWI, and feudal conditions there made immigration attractive. As farmers prospered, they tended to build homes and farm buildings like those in the old country, with adaptations to Canadian conditions such as fierce winds that made south-facing doors common. Today, some 300,000 people of Ukrainian origin—just under 10 per cent of the population—live in Alberta.

Visitors can tour the grounds on foot, or take a ride on a horse-drawn wagon. Displays in the **visitor centre** provide insight into the mass migration of people from Ukraine to the Canadian Prairies. Homestead development—from early sod-covered dugout to whitewashed cottage—is explained in detail by costumed interpreters. The village includes a rural community and an early town, complete with a grain elevator, train station, provincial police post (actually the policeman's home, with a small office and jail), two churches (domed Orthodox and spired Catholic) with painted interiors, shops, a "hotel" that was a legal fiction for a village pub and of

©Travel Alberta

Orthodox church at Ukrainian Cultural Heritage Village

course a market square. Visitors should give themselves ample time to visit the interiors of the buildings, which are well restored and give an excellent idea of how families lived in houses of only one or two rooms. At the food kiosk, visitors can sample typical **Ukrainian dishes** such as the perogi (dumplings filled with cheese, potato, or sauerkraut and boiled) or sauerkraut and sausage.

Special events are held throughout the year, such as Ukrainian Day featuring traditional music, dancing and food, or the autumn celebration, where visitors can help harvest a wheat field and make sauerkraut for winter.

Reynolds-Alberta Museum ★

2km/1mi west of Hwy. 13 in Wetaskiwin, 45km/28mi south of Edmonton via Hwys. 2 and 2A. ◐*Open Jul–Aug daily 10am– 6pm. Mid-May–Jun 10am–5pm. Rest of the year Tue–Sun 10am–5pm.* ◐*Closed Jan 1, Dec 24–25.* ◉*$9. Bi-plane rides Jun–Aug.* ✕&🅿☎*780-361-1351 or 800- 661-4726. www.machinemuseum.net.*
This spacious, modern (1992) museum celebrates machines used for transport, agriculture, aviation and industry. The museum building was constructed by the Alberta government as part of a community development program.

The original collection was assembled by an owner of a Wetaskiwin car dealership, Stanley G. Reynolds, who was known to take any machine on trade-in. The collection has grown to include 350 automobiles, 70 vintage aircraft and some 1,000 pieces of agricultural equipment.

Exhibits are organized chronologically, starting from the late 19C with a horse-drawn carriage and moving forward; machines are also organized according to function, and the accompanying explanations are very helpful. Industry is represented by heavy construction and mining equipment. Rare items include a 1929 Duesenburg Phaeton Royale Model J car; a 1928 American Eagle biplane (the only surviving Canadian example), and a restored 1908 International Harvester Company gasoline traction engine. Visitors can look into the Restoration Shop where a badly treated old machine is restored, with much time and ingenuity, to mint condition.

From May to Sept, some of the vintage cars tool around the grounds and accept passengers. On afternoons from early Jun-Labour Day, weather permitting, visitors can also book 10min, 20min or 50min rides in one of two open-cock-pit biplanes (◉*$116/10min, $171/20min, $357/50min; prices may increase due to fuel costs; for times and charges, call* ☎*780-352-9689).* ◔In peak months there are long lineups for these plane rides, and no reservations are taken; it is best to show up early.

The **Canadian Aviation Hall of Fame** shares the site (◐*same hours as Reynolds-Alberta Museum*), displaying photos and memorabilia of Canada's aviation leaders.

©Travel Alberta

Victoria Settlement Provincial Historic Site

Métis Crossing Historical Park★

Take Hwy. 28 some 95km/60mi northeast of Edmonton to Smokey Lake, then south 11km/7mi on Hwy. 885 to intersection with Victoria Trail. ○*Open mid-May–Labour Day daily 11am–6pm.* ☙*Guided tours noon, 2pm &4pm.* ◌$5. ♿☎780-656-2229. www.metiscrossing.com.

This small settlement lies within a 207ha/512acre park on the south bank of the North Saskatchewan River, near the site of an early Métis settlement. This park was set up by Métis in 2005 to help celebrate and preserve their history and culture. It is being developed in stages, according to a master plan. The site is currently in phase two of a three-part expansion that will ultimately offer hotel accommodations as well as tent and RV campgrounds along the river.

The Métis, descendents of European traders and Indian women, began forming settlements and taking up farming at the urging of missionaries. Near this relatively easy ford across the river, used by aboriginal peoples for thousands of years, **George McDougall** (1821-76), a Methodist missionary from Kingston, Ontario, set up a small mission to the Cree in 1862. About 6km/4mi to the east, the Hudson's Bay Company set up a trading post (1864) that is now part of the Victoria Settlement Historic Site. Whether drawn by Methodism or trade, English-speaking Métis from Manitoba arrived, and Victoria Settlement was established. Although the Métis settlement once stretched 10km/6mi along both banks of the river, in Quebec-style strips of land, it did not endure.

Tours are a particularly good way to understand the settlement. The Historic Village Tour departs at noon, the Métis Barn Tour at 2pm, and the River's Edge Nature Trail Tour at 4pm.

At the **Métis Crossing Voyage** in late August, traditional crafts and dancing are on display; Métis are justly celebrated for their lively fiddle music.

Victoria Settlement Provincial Historic Site★

6km/4mi east of the Métis Crossing Historical Park and 10mi south of Smokey Lake on Hwy. 855. ○*Open mid-May–Labour Day daily 10am–6pm.* ◌$3.

Vegreville's Easter egg
©Travel Alberta

♿☎780-656-2333. http://culture.alberta.ca/museums.

This outdoor museum is located where the Hudson's Bay Company set up Fort Victoria in 1864. In the early 20C, Ukrainian settlers arrived in this area, while the Métis community dwindled. The nearby town of Smoky Lake was originally a Ukrainian settlement called Toporivtsi. Costumed interpreters take visitors through the 1906 Methodist chapel and the 1865 HBC clerk's house, the oldest building in Alberta still on its original foundations. The Victoria Trail, on which both historical sites lay, originally was a road for the Red River carts that travelled between Winnipeg and Edmonton.

Vegreville

103km/64mi east on Hwy 16. ☎780-632-3100. www.vegreville.com.

Should you be in the vicinity, the roadside attraction known as the world's largest **pysanka,** a festively decorated Ukrainian Easter egg, is a sure-fire photo opportunity. Built in 1974 as a tribute to the centenary of the Royal Canadian Mounted Police, the ovoid measures 8m/26ft long and weighs more than 5,000 pounds. A three-day **Ukrainian Pysanka Fair** is held annually in mid-July, with lots of music, dancing, a beer garden and authentic food (☎780-632-2777). In early August, the **Vegreville Exhibition and Country Fair** comes to town (☎780-632-3950 or 888-611-0161).

LESSER SLAVE LAKE AND VICINITY

This area of Central Alberta, an arc north of Edmonton connected by Highway 2 stretching from Athabasca through the towns of Slave Lake and Peace River to Grande Prairie in the west, offers the beauty of boreal forests of spruce, aspen and poplar, great fields of wheat swaying in the wind, broad rivers and pristine lakes. Surrounded by wide, white sand beaches, Lesser Slave Lake measures 97km/60mi long and 19km/12mi wide, covering some 1,168sq km/451sq mi; it is the eighth largest lake in Canada, the third largest in the province. Well north of the continent's population centres, pleasant communities thrive not only on forestry industries, mining and petroleum deposits, but also on agriculture and livestock raising. Wheat grows on rich glacial till deposited by the ice sheets that thousands of years ago leveled the terrain into a vast plain. The region today is sparsely settled and the biggest city, Grande Prairie, has a population of just over 50,000. Recreational opportunities such as hiking, biking, fishing, boating, hunting and golfing, as well as skiing, snowmobiling and ice-fishing in winter, abound. Forests, fields and lakes are frequented by song birds and waterfowl whose fall and spring migrations bring observers from around the world. Native animals include wolves, moose, mule deer, black bears and grizzly bears.

Extensive waterways provided trade routes for aboriginal peoples and for fur-traders and explorers heading out from Montreal as early as the 18C. **Samuel Hearne,** the Scottish explorer, crossed the Great Slave Lake north of this region (in what is now the Northwest Territories) in 1771, while **Alexander Mackenzie,** another dauntless Scot, ascended the Peace River in 1793. By the late 18C, fur-trading posts had sprung up wherever rivers provided transport. The intrepid London-born explorer **David Thompson,** then working for the Hudson's Bay Company, visited both Lesser Slave Lake and Athabasca in 1799, and shortly thereafter fur-trading posts were established in the area. The famous Athabasca Landing Trail, a 161km/100mi portage, was established by the HBC in 1875 to connect the North Saskatchewan River at Edmonton with

©Travel Alberta

Marten Mountain viewpoint, Lesser Slave Lake

Address Book

⏾For dollar-sign categories, see the Legend on the cover flap.

WHERE TO STAY

$ Best Western Slave Lake Inn & Suites – *1550 Holmes Trail SE., Slave Lake.* 🅿. ☎780-849-9400 or 800-780-7234. www.bestwesternalberta.com. *68 units.* This tidy, family-friendly inn offers popular features like fridges, microwaves, in-room jetted tubs in the guest rooms, which are basic in their decor. On-site amenities include an exercise room, hot tubs, a laundry and in the lobby, an Internet kiosk.

$ The Nest: A Boreal Hostel – *Lesser Slave Lake Provincial Park, near Slave Lake.* 🅿. ☎780-849-8240. www. borealbirdcentre.ca/media.htm. *6 rooms.* Set on the shores of Lesser Slave Lake, this log and stone hostel is open all year long. Four bunk-bed rooms and two queen-bed rooms offer overnight accommodations; guests must bring their own bedding and towels. Bathrooms must be shared, and a common kitchen comes equipped with plates, pots and cutlery. This is a bird-watcher's fantasy stay at the Boreal Centre for Bird Conservation.

$ Shaw's Point Resort – *Near Hillard's Bay Provincial Park, near HighPrairie.* 🅿✕. ☎780-751-3900. www.shaws pointresort.com. *4 cabins, 250 campsites.* This family-oriented campground spreads out over 60ha/150acres along Lesser Slave Lake. It has a sandy beach, a boat launch and two inland marinas (pontoon boat rentals), a restaurant serving three meals a day, a store, children's playground and hiking trails. **Cabins ($$)** come with bathrooms (one cabin has no shower), bed linens and towels, a BBQ and a fire pit. There are plenty of camp sites and the owners' policy is never to turn campers away.

$$ Grande Prairie Inn – *11633 Clairmont Rd., Grand Prairie.* 🅿✕ ☎780-532-5221. www.gpinn.com. *204 rooms.* Located at Highway 43 (116 Ave.) and 100 Street (Clairmont Rd.), this high-rise motor inn offers well-appointed, comfortable rooms furnished with a desk and large wardrobe, heavy draperies and free wireless Internet. Guest amenities include a sauna, and indoor pool with a Jacuzzi. The inn's **Drakes Nest Cafe ($$)** serves breakfast and lunch daily and a buffet Wednesday to Saturday evenings.

$$ Peace Valley Inn – *9609 101st St., Peace River.* 🅿✕. ☎780-624-2020 or 800-661-5897. www.peacevalleyinns. com. *90 suites.* This modern inn offers perks such as free airport shuttle, keyless entry and 60-channel cable. All suites are well-appointed and come with a fireplace, leather furniture, hydro-tubs, slate bathroom floors, plasma TVs and Internet. On-site is **Smitty's ($)**, a restaurant that serves breakfast all-day and Canadian dishes at lunch and dinner. There's also a small pub on the premises.

$$ Sawridge Inn and Conference Centre – *1200 Main St., Slave Lake.* 🅿✕ ☎780-849-4101 or www.sawridgeslave-lake.com. *175 rooms.* Part of a chain of First Nations-owned hotels in Northern Alberta, the red-roofed Sawridge on the lakeshore offers comfortable rooms plus exercise facilities, and an indoor and outdoor hot tub. There's also a billiards room and the Ridge Irish Pub plus a local shuttle service and a business centre. In-room Internet is complimentary. The Sawridge Group also an inn in Peace River.

$$ Stanford Inn – *11401 100 Ave., Grand Prairie.* 🅿✕. ☎780-539-5678 or 800-661-8160. www.stanfordinn.net. *204 rooms.* This modern hotel is well situated and with a conference centre, is suited especially for business travellers. Standard rooms come equipped with computer hookups, microwaves, coffee makers and TVs. The on-site restaurant, **Delmonica's Grill ($$)**, serves up traditional Canadian dishes at breakfast, lunch and dinner; there are also pool tables and a pub on the premises with a big-screen TV. A small fitness centre and laundry facilities round out the amenities.

$$$ Podollan Inn and Spa – *10612 99th Ave., Grande Prairie.* ✕ P Spa ☐ ☎780-830-2000 or 866-440-2080. *www.podollan.com.* 100 rooms.
This downtown hotel caters to business travellers, with high-speed Internet, ipod docking stations and flatscreen TVs. Guest rooms also come with down duvets and bathrobes; bathrooms feature walk-in showers. Amenities include a complimentary breakfast and heated underground parking. **Jax Grill and Lounge ($$$)** offers a sophisticated menu mainly of Canadian dishes enjoyed in plush leather seating around a fireplace.

WHERE TO EAT

$ The Green Spot – *4820 51st St., Athabasca.* ☎780-675-3040. **Diner.**
At this popular diner, breakfasts of pancakes and omelets are a highlight. During the summer, there are burgers, steaks and a seafood buffet at dinnertime.

$ Grassroots Bistro – *10906 102nd Ave., Fairview.* ☎780-835-2858.
Canadian. Grassroots emphasizes regional ingredients, and routinely alternates its menu of soups, gourmet sandwiches, pizza and other fare to introduce diners to new dishes. The restaurant has a great outdoor deck for summertime dining.

$ Sawridge Inn Restaurants – *9510 100th St., Peace River.* ☎780-624-3621. *www.sawridgespeaceriver.com.*
Canadian. There are three eateries at this inn: Shark's Sports Lounge is a local favourite serving up pub fare such as chicken fingers, fish and chips and burgers. The Sternwheeler Gaming Room offers a Las Vegas-style atmosphere with games galore, while **Alexander's ($$)** is an upscale alternative, featuring prime rib, pasta, pizza and other specialties of the house.

$$ Jake's Down South – *10702 108A St.* ☎780-532-5667. **Southern.**
This spacious, modern building houses a popular restaurant known for its Bayou-style dishes. Specialties include Cajun blackened catfish with spicy cranberry tomato, or jambalaya made with chicken, shrimp, chorizo sausage and garnished with mussels. Prime rib and surf and turf entrées are also served. Pizzas, burgers, sandwiches, soups, plus a large selection of appetizers are on the menu as well.

$$ The Mill Restaurant – *9703 100th St., Peace River.* ☎780-624-5588.
International. Steak, pasta and seafood dishes are the highlights of this Greek-styled restaurant that has built up a repeat clientele. Its heaping pizzas, also locally renowned, bring in those who seek a casual dining experience at moderate prices.

present-day Athabasca to the east. Arriving at Lesser Slave Lake, some travellers turned west towards the Peace River Valley, opening this fertile **Athabasca Landing Trail** area to settlement. For 40 years, until the arrival of railways in the early 20C, the trail was northern Canada's busiest route. By 1888, steamships were plying the rivers that formed a network of waterways up from Edmonton, across Lesser Slave Lake to present-day **Grouard** on the northwest end.

An interesting note to the ethnic composition of this area is the French Canadian heritage, in part the work of Oblate missionaries such as the peripatetic Albert Lacombe or Bishop **Émile Grouard** (1840-1931), for whom Grouard is named. Blocked by the expansion of English Canada to the south, Oblates and their allies in the late-19C briefly promoted a dream of a French Catholic arc of settlement across northern Canada. Following World War I, demobilized soldiers were encouraged to move up into the Peace River Valley to grow wheat.

This far north, there is no denying a certain chill during winter months, and summers are rarely hot. Average January temperatures hover around -16°C/ to -18°C/-4°F, although sometimes much, much colder. July temperatures average 18°C/64°F, although temperatures of 36°C/96.8°F have been recorded at Grande Prairie. Frost-free days total only 90 a year, with the exception of Grande Prairie, which boasts 116. However, in midsummer daylight hours total about 17 hours, 30 minutes; children play outside in sunlight until after 10pm.

Athabasca

POPULATION 2,575 – MAP OF PRINCIPAL SIGHTS

In the imagination of Albertans, the word Athabasca means "remote." The word comes from a Cree description of a place where reeds grow (Lake Athabasca is located 500km/312mi northeast of the town of Athabasca, as the crow flies). Today Athabasca is a gateway to northern riches, as huge 18-wheeler trucks rumble up and down Highway 63 leading to Fort McMurray, some 305km/190mi northeast, where petroleum is extracted from the vast Athabasca oil sands deposits. Besides oil and gas companies, major local employers are the forestry industry (Alberta Pacific pulp mill, Millar Western sawmill), agriculture, and Athabasca University. Lying 146km/91mi due north of Edmonton, the pleasant town resides on the south shore of the wide Athabasca River, which rises in the Columbia Icefield and flows 1,231km/765mi toward Lake Athabasca. It is surrounded by green boreal forest of spruce, pine and aspen on a flat terrain dotted with lakes that offer well-developed recreational amenities: Baptiste Lake and Island Lake have small communities with campgrounds and shops, and Island Lake is known for bird watching. Other popular recreational lakes nearby are Ghost, Narrow, Long, Skeleton, North Buck, Chump, Jack and Corrigal.

- **Information:** 4705 49th Ave. Open year-round Mon–Sat 9 am–7pm, Sun 9am–4pm. ☎780-675-9297 or 877-211-8669. www.athabascacountry.com. Information also available May–Sept. from the **orange caboose** on 50th Ave. along the riverfront.
- **Orient Yourself:** Athabasca can be reached in only two hours from Edmonton, 146km/91mi away. Most of the town is situated on the south bank of the Athabasca River, framed by the Tawatinaw River to the east and Muskeg Creek Valley to the west. Historic buildings are found on or near 50th Avenue along the scenic riverfront. An excellent place from which to view the town and river is the **Lions Lookout** on the far side of the river (cross the Hwy. 813 bridge, turn left and follow the road that climbs the hill).
- **Parking:** Parking is free throughout most of the town, with some meters and pay-park lots downtown.
- **Don't Miss:** At night, look up at the sky: northern lights are frequent here. NASA has set up a viewing station in conjunction with Athabasca University.

©Travel Alberta

Town of Athabasca

🕐 **Organizing Your Time:** Plan to spend a day exploring Athabasca. In midsummer, daylight lasts 17hours and 23 minutes, and it is normal to fit in a full round of golf on one of the many courses after, or even before work.

Kids **Especially for Kids:** Muskeg Creek Park.

♿ **Also See:** GREATER EDMONTON.

A Bit of History

In the late 19C and early 20C, this town was the "gateway to the north" on the Edmonton-Athabasca Landing Trail established in 1875 by Hudson's Bay Company. This trail was a jumping-off point for navigation up the Athabasca River into the vast network of waterways making up the Mackenzie River system that flows through the Great Slave Lake and into the Arctic Ocean. River trade made the town wealthy in the early 20C and imposing buildings appeared. The economy collapsed when, in short order, a 1913 fire destroyed the business district (fortunately, several buildings survived), followed by the demise of river traffic as the railway replaced boats.

Sights

The Town

The visitor centre provides a self-guided walking tour brochure. In summer, the Heritage Society offers 🐾 group tours; contact the tourism coordinator at 877-211-8669, or inquire at the tourism office (♿ see Information, above).

Athabasca welcome sign

The riverfront area, the site of the original Athabasca Landing, was rescued by a concerted local effort when, in the early 1990s, the Canadian National Railways closed the railroad yards and grain elevators it had set up there. After extensive work, the five-block area emerged as a town common, where summer festivals take place in sight of the old train station. 🖼Historical information is posted along the **boardwalk.**

Three downtown buildings have been designated provincial historic sites. The **Old Brick School** *(48th St. and 47 A Ave.),* a two-and-a-half storey brick and stone structure with a crenellated tower and gables, was built in 1913 and also served as a residence for students who lived far away. It now houses the 200-seat **Nancy Appleby Theatre of Performing Arts,** named for a local music teacher, as well as a library; a historical plaque stands near the sidewalk. The splendid Gothic revival wooden **United Church of Canada** *(4817 48th St.; services Sun 10:30am),* built in 1912 as a Methodist church and extensively restored in 1986, survived the 1913 fire that swept the downtown; it is the largest wooden building north of Edmonton. The exterior boasts two towers, gables and large Gothic windows; the interior is austere, with groined vaulting in dark wood contrasting with plain white plastering. The three-storey **Grand Union Hotel** *(4952 50th St.),* open continuously since 1914, has a colourful history, including the World War II period, when Americans building the Alaska Highway rolled up in sleeping bags in the lobby while their trucks idled outside (at minus -45°C/-50°F the engine had to run or it would freeze). The notorious 1913 fire that destroyed the downtown started in the original hotel, which also burned to the ground. The present structure was for years coated with peeling white paint which, when removed, revealed the stately architecture seen today.

Athabasca University

1 University Drive, west of downtown core, off Hwy. 2. Group tours can be reserved at ☎866-788-9041 ext. 6109. www.athabascau.ca.

This institution, an open university created by the Alberta government to provide higher education for people who don't fit the traditional university student profile, is a major employer in the area. Based on distance education, notably over the Internet, the university admits anyone over the age of 16 and tailors programs to the individual. Some 37,000 students in 50 countries are enrolled at the school, although most have never set foot in Athabasca. Tours of the campus and facilities take in the library and an art collection.

Excursion

Amber Valley

24km/15mi east of Athabasca via Hwy 55. Look for sign saying Amber Valley Hall.
Between 1909 and 1911, about 170 African-Americans, many of them Masons from Oklahoma, homesteaded a successful farming community called Pine Creek. By 1930 the village had a population of 300 and remained mostly black

---

Town Festivals

Athabasca hosts several festivals every year. **Magnificent River Rats** country music festival *(www.river-ratsfestival.com)* takes place in late June and early July, with a parade and many ancillary events. The **Old Time Fiddlers' Weekend** *(☎780-675-4828)* in late August brings out country fiddling and prompts public dancing.

---

until the 1960s. As small farms closed on the prairies due to mechanization, and as young men who served in WWII elected to live in cities, the population dwindled.

Today called Amber Valley, the town has a population of fewer than 100 people. The Amber Valley Community Hall, a cemetery and several homesteads remain. A **farmstead** occupied by Obadiah Bowen until 1996 has been designated a provincial historical resource and will be open to the public after restoration. Tours can be arranged by contacting Doug Harper at ☎780-675-4382 or LeRoy Overacker at ☎780-675-3083.

Town Trails

Athabasca is crisscrossed with trails used for walking, biking, skiing, and jogging. **Muskeg Creek Park** *(open daily year-round)*, on the west side of town, offers a variety of trails covering 17.5km/11mi, and connecting to the paved **Rotary Trail.** This latter trail winds from the Athabasca County building on the east side of town to the Ukrainian Orthodox Church on East Hill; follow the sidewalk across the bridge to find where the trail resumes along the riverfront. It leads up 55th Street to the **Muskeg Creek** trailhead on the west side of town. In addition, the **Old Landing Trail,** a gravel foot track, can be followed between Colinton and Athabasca. *Maps are available at the Athabasca Recreation office ☎780-675-2967 or from the Tourist Information Centre ☎780-675-9297. A map of Muskeg Creek trails can be downloaded at www.athabascacountry.com/maps.*

©Travel Alberta

Muskeg Creek Park

Slave Lake

POPULATION 7,031 – MAP OF PRINCIPAL SIGHTS

This town, set where the Lesser Slave River flows out from the eastern tip of Lesser Slave Lake, lies 209km/130mi north of Edmonton via Highway 2. White sand beaches stretch along a pristine lake whose temperature is quite bearable in high summer, thanks to a very shallow shoreline. Expanses of boreal forests surround the blue water and the Pelican Mountains rise to 1,020m/3,109ft above sea level on the northeastern horizon. Recreational opportunities are plentiful during the long, high-latitude summer days, when hiking, swimming, bird-watching and fishing (walleye, northern pike, perch and whitefish) are at their best. The combined Sawbridge Creek and Frontier trails, extending 28km/17mi along the lakeshore north to Marten Beach in Lesser Slave Lake Provincial Park, wind through boreal forests where songbirds flit and sing in profusion. Within the town, 16ha/40acres of parks provide expanses of green. In winter, cross-country skiing, snowmobiling and ice-fishing take people out into the sharp, invigorating cold, while the Northern Lakes Aquatics Centre and an ice-hockey arena provide indoor exercise.

- **Information:** Big Lake Country Tourism Visitor Centre, 328 2 St. NE. Open mid-May-Labour Day Sat–Thu 10am–6pm (from 9am Fri). ☎780-849-2377 or 800-261-8594. www.lesserslavelake.ca or www.slavelake.ca.
- **Orient Yourself:** Hwy. 2 runs east to west through the south end of town; it is intersected on the east side by Hwy. 88, which runs north-south. Main Street runs north to south through the town centre. Blackflies and other biting bugs are a sad fact of summer. Apply strong insect repellent, wear light-coloured clothing and consider protective gear such as mesh jackets. Even the Queen wore trousers when visiting northern Canada.
- **Parking:** On-street meters and limited free street parking can be found in most areas; there is nominal pay parking (*$2*) at Devonshire Beach.
- **Don't Miss:** The view from Marten Mountain; a visit to the Boreal Centre for Bird Conservation.
- **Organizing Your Time:** You could easily spend several days or longer exploring Lesser Slave Lake Provincial Park alone. The annual Alberta **Open Sand Sculpture Championship,** with a purse of $3,000, brings tourists and competitors in late July. A yearly Song Bird Festival is held at the end of May and plenty of fishing tournaments take place in summer.
- **Especially for Kids:** Devonshire Beach.
- **Also See:** NORTHERN ALBERTA.

A Bit of History

Originally called Sawbridge, the town grew up in the late 19C as a staging area on the Athabasca Landing Trail, although Grouard at the lake's north-western end, then called Lesser Slave Lake, was the more important community, where goods and travellers flowed to and from the Peace River Valley. Later, when the railway arrived in 1914, Sawbridge found a vocation as a lumber town, while Grouard, bypassed by the railway, declined. A flood destroyed

Slave Lake in 1936, and it was rebuilt 3.5km/2mi south at its present site. Oil and gas deposits were developed here in the 1980s, while agriculture, forest products and a commercial fishery remain principal local industries.

Although its name implies proximity, Lesser Slave Lake lies far distant from the much bigger **Great Slave Lake,** some 640km/400mi to the north in the Northwest Territories. The name comes from that of the Slavey Indians, a resourceful subarctic group speaking the Na-Dene or Athabaskan language, who roamed

©Travel Alberta

An entry for the Open Sand Sculpture Championship

near Great Slave Lake but never as far south as Lesser Slave Lake. Today, they live on reserves in the Northwest Territories. It is supposed that cartographers, focused naturally on the larger lake, simply borrowed its name for the smaller one.

Sight

Slave Lake Native Friendship Centre

416 6th Ave. NE. ⏰*open year-round weekdays 8:30am–4:30pm* ☎*780-849-3039. www.anfca.com/slavelake.html.*
This community centre primarily serves area First Nations residents with health care, social, educational and cultural programs. It was begun in the 1970s by two local women in small quarters and now is housed in a large facility. There is a small display of **handicrafts** and artifacts in the museum. Cultural programs such as family dances and traditional meals (bannock and stew) are open to the public *(phone ahead for details)*.

Additional Sight

Lesser Slave Lake Provincial Park★

15km/9mi north of Slave Lake on Hwy 88. ⏰*Open year-round, reduced hours in winter.* ♿🅿 ☎*780-849-7100. http://gateway. ce.gov.ab.ca. 113 campsites.*

Stretching 107km/66mi along the eastern shore of the lake, just north of Lesser Slave River and the town of Slave Lake, this popular park can be reached on foot along a 28km/17.5mi trail from the town or by car via Highway 88. ■
The 7km/4mi white sand **Kids** **Devonshire Beach** at the southern tip of the park, with its very shallow descent into deeper water is popular with parents of young children. The park's trails and bird observatories provide another major attraction. From the Devonshire Beach parking lot, the **Whispering Sands Trail** *(1.5km/.75mi)* leads past 1,500-year-old sand dunes along an ancient lakeshore. Devonshire Beach also provides an access point for a trail that follows the lake for 23km/14mi and is part of the Trans-Canada Trail; it can be taken on foot or by bicycle. At the park's north end, a trail leads to the summit of 938m /3,300ft **Marten Mountain,** the highest point of the Pelican Mountain uplands, where a microclimate supports alpine plants not otherwise found here, such as the lodgepole pine, running raspberry and devil's club. An easy trail *(2.5km/1.5mi)* runs from Marten Mountain viewpoint to **Lily Lake,** where brook trout can be caught.
More than 15 fish species inhabit Lesser Slave Lake; although they can be caught from shore, luck improves in a boat *(rentals available in town)*. The walleye is said to reach 9 kilograms/20 pounds, the northern walleye up to

©Travel Alberta

Trumpeter swans on the lake during migration

4 kg/10 lbs. A golf course also lies within the park. The eastern shore of the lake, between the water and Marten Mountain, forms a natural funnel for migrating birds, which avoid crossing the lake (see *Point Pelee Effect below*).

Boreal Centre for Bird Conservation
About 19km/12mi north of Slave Lake off Hwy. 88, in Lesser Slave Lake Provincial Park. Open late-May–Labour Day Mon–Fri 8am–4:30pm, weekends and holidays 10am–5pm. Rest of the year weekends 10am–4pm. ☎780-849-8240 or 866-718-2473. www.borealbird centre.ca.

Novice bird-watchers, in particular, will want to come to this centre, which provides an opportunity to learn about the many birds (more than 240 species of them), including the **tundra swan,** that gather around Lesser Slave Lake before migration to the south.

In 1994 local bird enthusiasts founded an observatory to make the most of what is known as the **Point Pelee Effect** (after the Ontario peninsula of the same name in Lake Erie that draws thousands of migratory birds): migrating birds avoid flying over the lake, a natural barrier to them, and instead head east between the lake's shoreline and Marten Mountain. During spring and fall migration season, hundreds of warblers bearing names such as the red-eyed vireo, ruby-crowned kinglet or the yellow-rumped warbler flutter through,

returning from or going to points as far away as Argentina.

The bird observatory has grown to encompass this research centre today, open since June 2006, with facilities devoted to the study of the boreal forest and the birds that make it their breeding grounds. Exhibits inside and outside educate visitors as to the area's importance globally to bird migration.

Lesser Slave Lake Bird Observatory
In Lesser Slave Lake Provincial Park, about 2km farther down the road from the Boreal Centre; follow signs toward the Lily Creek site. ☎780-849-8240 or 866-718-2473. www.lslbo.org.

At this observatory, volunteers have banded some 45,000 birds representing 243 species to determine migration patterns. On weekends, between 9am and 11am, visitors can often observe volunteers banding migrating birds. These birds are remarkably tiny to sing so loudly and to embark on such long journeys.

Excursions

Grouard
132km/82mi west of Slave Lake on Hwy. 2, then north 15km/9mi on Hwy. 750. Consider stopping at Grouard while travelling west to Peace River or Grande Prairie.

Today a village of about 300 people, Grouard was once a thriving community of more than 1,000 that aspired to regional leadership. Sights in the small town include the **St. Bernard Mission Church,** built in 1901 by Bishop **Émile Grouard** on the site of a mission founded in 1870, and still in use.

In 1913, the Edmonton, Dunvegan and British Columbia Railway chose to bypass the town. Taking many of their buildings with them, residents moved southwest to High Prairie, which lay on the railway route. For many years the village, founded as a fur-trading post named Lesser Slave Lake in 1801, had served as a staging area on the route to the Peace River Valley. Settlers, as well as gold miners on their way to the Klondike in 1897-98, disembarked here from steamboats to purchase supplies before pursuing their journeys; local stores and services flourished only as long as the steamboats did. Bishop Grouard, born in France and an accomplished artist, linguist and peacemaker among the First Nations, typified the energy and adventurousness of the Oblates of Mary Immaculate. His name also figures in the histories of Grande Prairie and the mission at Dunvegan, as well as at Fort Chipewyan on Lake Athabasca and at Lac La Biche.

The **Kapawe'no First Nation** reserve lies adjacent to the village, and a principal local attraction is the **Native Cultural Arts Museum** (*Moosehorn Lodge building of Northern Lakes College, 100 Mission St.;* ○ *open mid-May–Labour Day Mon–Sat 10am–4pm; rest of the year Tue–Thu 10am–4pm;* ☎780-751-3306). The museum contains a highly regarded **collection**★ of aboriginal and Métis crafts, placed in cultural context, as well as artifacts and photos of settlement. The **Grouard Historical Village,** a re-created 1885 Métis and aboriginal encampment, can be toured by appointment with the museum.

Just east of Grouard lies **Hilliard's Bay Provincial Park** (*13km/8mi east of Grouard via Hwy. 750;* ○ *open year-round; reduced hours in winter;* ♿️ 🅿️ ☎780-849-7124; http://gateway.cd.gov.ab.ca), offering extensive recreational facilities and delightful bird-watching: bald eagles are commonly seen, and great horned owls nest here. The park offers 189 campsites (○ *available mid-May–Labour Day*) as well as opportunities for swimming, boating, fishing, hiking and in winter, skiing.

Winigami Wildlife Provincial Park

Approximately 140km/88mi from Lesser Slave Lake via Hwy. 2 W to High Prairie then Hwy. 749 N. ○ *Open year-round; reduced hours in winter.* ☎780-523-0041. *http://gateway.cd.gov.ab.ca.*

Here, some 200 species of waterfowl and warblers have been sighted, and visitors can view ducks, grebes, sandpipers and gulls, which nest here, through **telescopes** provided at lookouts placed

©Travel Alberta

Kimiwan Bird Walk

along a lakeside trail. Bald eagles pass through on their fall migration route, feeding on ducks and gulls. The park offers the same recreational facilities as Hilliard's Bay, as well as 66 campsites (🕐*available May–mid-Oct*).

Kimiwan Bird Walk

At McLennon, 24km/15mi north of Winigami Provincial Park. Go 11km/7mi west on secondary road 679, then 13km/8mi north on Hwy. 49. 🕐*Interpreters on site May–Sept.* ☎780-324-2004. www.kimiwan birdwalk.com. *Binoculars available from the centre for on-site use.*

Perched on the south shore of Kimiwan Lake, this bird-watching mecca draws bird enthusiasts from miles around;

some 206 species of birds have been sighted. The **interpretive centre** is surrounded by boardwalks with viewing platforms and helpful signage explaining bird habitats and migration patterns. In summer, waterfowl come here to moult before heading south, and number between 5,000 to 20,000 on any given day. Migrating birds include sandpipers, long-billed dowichers, gulls, the cinnamon teal, Canada geese, and white-fronted geese. Tens of thousands of tundra and **trumpeter swans** (some 68,000 in 2006) gather here in October before migrating south. The merlin and the northern goshawk also haunt the area, preying on smaller birds.

Peace River★

POPULATION 6,240 – MAP OF PRINCIPAL SIGHTS

Set in the wide Peace River Valley, this lovely agricultural town lies at the junction of the Peace, Smokey and Heart rivers, 486km/304mi northwest of Edmonton. Peace River offers centuries of history, attractive heritage buildings and well-developed recreational facilities. From several points around the town are scenic lookouts over the river junction, the boreal forests and the hilly terrain. Hunters of big game and waterfowl as well as anglers congregate here from all over the world. Substantial oil and gas deposits nearby, as well as oil sands, have added to the town's general prosperity. Principal industries other than oil and gas are retail, as the town is a regional centre where people from a wide area come to shop; agriculture, mostly wheat and cattle; as well as services and forestry. The region's French heritage is maintained by Francophone public as well as Catholic schools. A school system serves Cree and Dene First Nations, with courses in their language. The name Peace River was applied to this area by aboriginal peoples, to mark a treaty reached between Cree and Beaver Indians near here.

- **Information:** Tourist Office, 94th Ave. on Hwy. 2 north of the town centre. Also in the railway station downtown (open May–Sept daily 10 am–6pm). ☎780-338-2364 or 800-215-4535. www.mightypeace.com.
- **Orient Yourself:** Peace River is 486km/304mi northwest of Edmonton via Hwy 2, which enters the town from the southeast and skirts downtown before crossing the river westbound; the main strip (100 Street) is a wide boulevard on the east side, and Shaftesbury Trail parallels the river on the west. The airport is 13km/8mi west of town.
- **Parking:** Meters operate in downtown Peace River and there are several pay park lots.
- **Don't Miss:** Stroll through downtown on 100 Street near the river to view the town's handsome heritage buildings.
- **Organizing Your Time:** The town itself can be explored in half a day; guided fishing and boating trips along the Peace, Heart and Smoky Rivers can add several days. For details, access www.peaceisland.ab.ca.
- **Also See:** GREATER EDMONTON

Confluence of Peace and Smoky rivers

A Bit of History

Due to the site's strategic location on aboriginal trading routes, the Scottish explorer **Alexander Mackenzie** visited as early as 1793 and set up Fort Fork for the North West Company, attracting fur traders and missionaries. He can be considered the town's founder. As people flocked to the ferry crossing, the site became known as Peace River Crossing. In the late 19C, missionaries discovered that the land was extraordinarily fertile and the growing season nearly five months long; an exhibit of Peace River wheat at the 1893 Chicago Exposition won first prize. In short order, the Peace River Valley attracted farmers from as far as the Ukraine.

Following World War I, demobilized soldiers were urged to move up into the valley, and the Edmonton, Dunvegan and BC Railway, which arrived in 1915, facilitated settlement.

Coal and oil have been extracted here since the early 20C. The Peace River oil sands deposits, estimated to contain 188 billion barrels of oil, are being developed for exploitation.

Sight

Peace River Centennial Museum
10302 99th St. ○Open mid-May–Labour Day Mon–Sat 9am–5pm. Rest of the year Mon–Fri 10am-4pm. ○Closed 25 Dec–
Jan 1. $2. ☎780-624-4261. www.peace river.govoffice.com.

Housed in a wooden building that resembles an early fur-trading fort and blockhouse, this community museum is dedicated to preserving and presenting the history of Peace River. It possesses artifacts and memorabilia dating back to the early days of the fur trade.

Exhibited in three galleries are aboriginal crafts and artifacts, historic photographs, and clothing, tools and household items donated by descendants of settlers. A few items, including a battered tin lantern, come from the site of the original Fort Fork. A gallery devoted to Scottish explorer **Alexander Mackenzie,** who camped here at Fort Fork over the winter of 1792-93, holds a permanent exhibit describing his adventures as well as displays on the fur trade; Hudson's Bay Company traps, furs, blankets and even a hat made of beaver can be viewed.

A local dentist, one Dr. **William Greene** (1874-1952), was a pioneering aviator who built some of the first aircraft in North America. Standing on the grounds is the wheel shaft of the steamboat SS *D.A. Thomas,* which plied the Peace River until 1930, when it went aground one time too many. A tiny **log cabin** stands near the museum, a reconstruction of a North West Mounted Police frontier cabin; inside are memorabilia of that heroic epoque.

Historic Dunvegan Provincial Historic Site

Just upriver is Riverfront Park, near the boat launch. A Paul Bunyanesque statue of another local hero marks the grave of **Twelve-Foot Davis,** a prospector from Vermont named Henry Fuller Davis. In 1862 Davis, who was not unusually tall, staked a claim near Barkerville, British Columbia, only 12-feet wide (hence his nickname), between much larger claims. His, however, was the only one with gold, some $15,000 worth. Davis owned a trading post in Peace River, where local people found him likable.

Excursion

Historic Dunvegan Provincial Historic Site

109km/68mi southwest of Peace River via Hwy. 2. ⏰*Open mid-May–Labour Day daily 10am–6pm.* ᴂ*$3.* ♿🅿☎*780-835-7150. http://culture.alberta.ca.*
Set on the north bank of the Peace River at a point where aboriginal peoples congregated for millennia is a re-created fur-trading post, Fort Dunvegan. Three original buildings have been restored and furnished to reflect frontier life in the latter part of the 19C.
The fort's founder, like so many early explorers, was a Scot; Archibald Norman MacLeod named the site for his ancestral castle on the Isle of Skye. Originally established by the North West Company in 1805 on the recommendation of David Thompson, the fort was taken over by the Hudson's Bay Company in 1821 and remained in operation until 1918.
An audio-visual feature *(12min)* shown in the **visitor centre** provides a good history of the site. Constructed in 1878, the Hudson Bay **factor's house,** where the factor lived with his family, evidences a basic level of comfort. The sparse **rectory** (1889) next to **St. Charles Mission Church** (1885) gives the impression that the presiding Oblate priest was ready to pack up at a moment's notice if there were souls to be saved elsewhere; Oblates were notoriously peripatetic. Father **Émile Grouard** (⏳*see Slave Lake*), when in residence, decorated the altar with some of his own paintings. Interpreters in late 19C costume populate the buildings and demonstrate how inhabitants of the fort grew their own vegetables on extensive garden plots and raised livestock.
The site is enhanced by a dramatic view of Highway 2 as it passes over the **Dunvegan Suspension Bridge,** built in 1960; at 540m/1,646ft, it is the longest suspension bridge in the province.
Adjacent to the historic site lies the **Dunvegan Provincial Park** campground *(67 sites;* ⏰*open May–Oct;* ☎*780-835-7150).* The park's Maples Day-Use Area stands on the site of an Anglican mission established in 1879, the St. Saviour's Mission; the grove of maple trees was planted by the Rev. Alfred Garrioch, whose eight-year-old daughter Agnes lies buried nearby.

Grande Prairie★

POPULATION 50,227 – MAP OF PRINCIPAL SIGHTS

Grande Prairie, set 465km/289mi northwest of Edmonton at the southern limit of the Peace River Valley, is Alberta's seventh largest city and one of its fastest-growing. Long a major retail and service centre for the surrounding agricultural country, the city has prospered over the past 25 years due to the oil and gas industry, launched in the late 1970s by discovery of the Elmworth gas field nearby. Grande Prairie offers green spaces and public gardens, especially along Bear Creek which runs north-south through the city. A huge 445ha/1,100acre park called Muskoseepi (the Cree word for Bear Creek) lies along the creek in the city's core, with tennis courts, an outdoor pool, canoe rentals for the Bear Creek Reservoir, and more than 45km/25mi of trails. A large lake to the northeast, Crystal Lake, is surrounded by a paved trail that attracts bird-watchers looking for waterfowl, especially the trumpeter swan, the city's symbol; along the path is a blind from which to stealthily view the birds.

- **Information:** Visitor Centre at the Centre 2000, 11330 106th St. on the Hwy. 43 bypass. ♿🅿☎780-7688 or 866-202-2202. www.northernvisitor.com.
- ▸ **Orient Yourself:** The city is split by Bear Creek running north-south; streets are north-south, avenues east-west. Hwy. 43, which runs through the town as 116th St., can be considered a southern extension of the Alaska Highway, which starts 135km/85mi northwest at Dawson Creek, BC, and stretches to Fairbanks, Alaska.
- 🅿 **Parking:** Meters operate in downtown Grande Prairie, as well as city and private pay-parking lots (rates vary). Most downtown hotels offer free off-street parking lots.
- **Don't Miss:** The Centre 2000 tourist information centre; parks along Bear Creek.
- 🕐 **Organizing Your Time:** The city can be easily explored in a day.
- **Especially for Kids:** Bear Creek Reservoir; the Heritage Centre in the Centre 200 building.
- **Also See:** THE CANADIAN ROCKIES

Grande Prairie Museum and Heritage Village

A Bit of History

Settlement around Grande Prairie started only in the late 19C, despite the presence of fur-traders as early as the 1770s. Hudson's Bay Company opened a post at Glace Lake in 1880, but homesteading lagged because the often muddy track called the **Edson Trail** that led here was impassable to settler wagons; a 1907 Christmas dinner attended by the entire non-aboriginal population of the district totalled exactly 11 people. Arrival of the Edmonton, Dunvegan and British Columbia Railway in 1916 changed everything, just in time for soldiers returning from World War I to come north looking for land. Another burst of population growth occurred during the drought-stricken years of the Great Depression, when farmers came north looking for watered lands. The city was named by the energetic Father (later Bishop) Émile Grouand, a French-born Oblate who strove to bring French Catholic settlers to northern Alberta.

Due to a dip in the height of the western mountains, warm air from the Pacific Coast drifts over the region, bringing generous precipitation, while the "chinook" winds warm the climate. Grande Prairie experiences 116 frost-free days annually; about 90 days can be expected elsewhere in the Lesser Slave Lake vicinity. To the north, east and west lies excellent farmland; to the south and southwest are aspen and poplar boreal forests, rising into the coniferous forests of the Rocky Mountain foothills. Wheat, canola (also known as rapeseed, a food-oil crop), barley and oats can be seen in the surrounding fields, along with cattle. Forestry industries include a major paper mill owned by Weyerhaeuser Canada.

Sights

Grande Prairie Museum and Heritage Village

102nd Ave. and 102nd St., at entrance to Muskoseepi Park. ○*Open year-round Mon–Fri 9:30am–4:30pm, Sat 10am–4:30pm, Sun noon–4:30pm.* ○*Closed major holidays.* ⌖*$5.* ♿ 🅿 ☏*780-532-5482. www.cityofgp.com*

This old-fashioned, local museum is housed in an unprepossessing red-brick building surrounded by pretty parkland. Principal exhibits centre on the area's settler history brought to life with personal memorabilia. One exhibit contains some aboriginal artifacts from archaeological digs, as well as a description of dinosaur remains found nearby. Outside, the Heritage Village is a collection of settler buildings moved here from around the area. These structures consist of log cabins, a Hudson's Bay outpost, a church and a fire hall, among others. Some vintage automobiles are on display as well.

Centre 2000★★

11330 106th St. at Bear Creek Reservoir, within Muskoseepi Park. ○*Open year-round Mon–Fri 9:30am–4:30pm, Sat 10am–4:30pm, Sun noon–4:30pm.* ○*Closed major holidays.* ♿ 🅿 ☏*780-513-0240. www.centre2000.ca.*

With its pagoda-like layers of wide roof in the classic Prairie style, this splendid building houses a tourist information centre as well as administrative offices. The 13m/40ft sculpture, looking a bit like a large roof strut, that stands in front of the building is the gnomon of the Millennium Sundial, and on Grande Prairie's many sunny days, you can tell time from it.

Downstairs is the new (opened 2004) **Kids Heritage Centre** (⌖*$5*), which fea-

Sundial, Centre 2000
©Travel Alberta

tures modern, interactive child-oriented exhibits about local history, including dioramas of the ever-popular dinosaurs and of early aboriginal inhabitants.

A stairway leads up to the **Northern Lights Lookout,** from which visitors can view much of the park but not the northern lights, due to the city's own illumination.

Grande Prairie Regional College

10726 106th Ave. Access by Hwy. 2 bypass. ♿ 🅿 ☎*780-539-2944 or 888-539-4772.* *www.gprc.ab.ca*

The dramatic campus was designed in 1974 by Douglas Cardinal (b.1934), the celebrated architect from Red Deer, whose many commissions include the Museum of Civilization in Québec and St. Mary's Church in Red Deer.

Incorporated into a bluff over Bear Creek Reservoir, the curving, organic forms typical of Cardinal's work seem to merge into the landscape and reflect the slanting rays of the sun. Some 2000 students are enrolled in full and part-time credit programs.

Forbes Homestead Provincial Historic Site

On the grounds of Queen Elizabeth II Hospital, 10409 98th St. ☎*780-532-5482. www.cityofgp.com.*

⚠The homestead is closed for restoration work until at least 2009.

Among the oldest log structures in northern Alberta, this simple cabin of squared spruce logs covered in white clapboard was constructed c.1912 by Presbyterian missionaries from Scotland.

Eager to proselytize in the settlement, not yet legally homesteaded, Alexander Forbes, and his wife, Agnes, had hauled their possessions overland in 1908 from Fort Saskatchewan near Edmonton in a "caboose," or covered cart, that could be equipped with skis in winter. On site, they first constructed a hospital (Mrs. Forbes was a trained nurse) out of spruce logs joined by a primitive slot system at the corners. They lived in the caboose for a year before constructing their own cabin. In 1917, the Forbes opened a two-storey brick schoolhouse on their prop-

Grande Prairie Regional College

Douglas J. Cardinal Theatre, Grande Prairie Regional College

erty, the largest public building north of Edmonton; it was named "Montrose" after Mrs. Forbes' home in Scotland. The whole adventure proved too much for Mrs. Forbes, who was already 60 years old when she arrived here, and she died in 1917.

Today the two-storey homestead with the original, very small hospital building attached to it, stands on the grounds of the huge modern hospital that has succeeded it.

Excursion

Grande Cache★★

See Map of Principal Sights. 182km/ 113mi south of Grande Prairie via Hwy. 40. ☎780-827-3300 or 888-827-3790. www. grandecache.ca.

In an isolated corner of the province, this town of just under 4,000 people sits within a stunning **setting**★★ on a plateau at 1,280m/4,200ft, ringed with 21 peaks of the Rockies foothills and front ranges. Bearing the moniker Gateway to **Willmore Wilderness Park,** the community edges the northern section of that vast parkland north of the Rocky Mountain Parks. Cradled on the shoulder of **Grande Mountain,** the town is a popular outdoor mecca, blessed with abundant lakes, rivers, mountains and alpine trails.

Built quickly in 1969 to accommodate the discovery of coal in the region, Grande Cache has endured a bumpy economic ride of worker layoffs, plant shutdowns and other hardships over the past 40 years as its resource-based economy (primarily coal and forestry) struggled under the weight of fluctuating world prices and wavering demand.

Today, the area's abundant wildlife and scenic beauty lure many visitors who want a mountain experience without the crowds of Banff, Canmore or Jasper National Park. Grande Cache has escaped the mad pace of resort development facing more accessible alpine towns; its wide, tree-lined boulevards and slightly outdated downtown offer a handful of mom-and-pop hotels, motels, eateries and strip malls. Many RV travellers and other road warriors drive through Grande Cache westbound on Highway 40, travelling alongside the **Smoky River** to reach Dawson Creek, BC, Mile Zero of the great **Alaska Highway.**

The town's biggest claim to fame is the annual **Canadian Death Race** (www. canadiandeathrace.com) each August,

Aerial view of Grande Cache

©Travel Alberta

Sulphur Gates, entrance to Willmore Wilderness Park

when more than 800 extreme athletes descend here to compete in a grueling, 125km/70mi, Survivor-style endurance race. The 24-hour race pushes competitors over mountain peaks, into valleys and along rivers and brings hundreds of tourists to watch the spectacle.

Grande Cache Tourism & Interpretive Centre

Hwy 40 heading into town from the east. ☎*780-827-3300. www.grandecache.ca.* Stop at this new, wood-beam visitor centre to pick up regional tourism brochures and obtain directions, perhaps, but allow an extra hour to view the nature and historical artifacts on display.

The taxidermied exhibits of local wildlife include wildcats such as lynx, bighorn sheep and other large mammals. There are also interesting dioramas and photo displays of the area's First Nations history, the town's foray into coal, and information on dinosaur tracks that have been found in ancient coal beds.

The visitor centre's staff is knowledgeable about sites and good places to view wildlife, particularly on Highway 40 at dawn and dusk.

Information about local outings such as guided horseback trips, rafting, helicopter tours, fishing, hiking and hunting can be obtained here too.

Willmore Wilderness Park

Off Hwy. 40, just 6km/3.5mi.north of the town. ☎*780-944-0313 or, www.cd.gov. ab.ca.* ◷*Open daily year-round. No facilities or services. No roads into the park. Vehicle traffic is not allowed past the Sulphur Gates Provincial Recreation Area entrance; the only access to the park is on foot or horseback, skis or snowshoes. Hiking trails are unmarked.*

This vast tract of utter wilderness stretches north from Jasper National Park to Grande Cache, running both west and south from the town. It covers an immense area of more than 460,000ha/1,137,000 acres, and is virtually bisected by the Smoky River.

Watch for the signs for a short hike near the park entrance to the **Sulphur Gate** lookout, which provides stunning **views**★★ of the sheer cliffs along the confluence of the Smoky and Sulphur rivers.

Travellers who venture into Willmore have a good chance of seeing wildlife: the park is home to black bears and grizzly bears, mountain goats, sheep, moose, caribou, wolves and cougars. The terrain is quite rugged and consists of thick stands of spruce and lodgepole pines. At the higher elevations, wide alpine meadows stretch alongside the northern Continental Divide.

NORTHERN ALBERTA

Northern Alberta presents a contrast between the roaring oil boomtown of Fort McMurray and the pristine wilderness of Wood Buffalo National Park, a UNESCO World Heritage Site that hosts one of the world's largest free-ranging herds of buffalo. At the entrance to the park, on the shores of Lake Athabasca, lies Fort Chipewyan, a boomtown when Canada's fabulously valuable natural resource was fur. Farther north, just over Alberta's boundary with the Northwest Territories, lies Fort Smith, once a fur-trading post on the banks of the Slave River that now serves as the principal entrance to the park. As well as bison, Northern Alberta has bear, moose, beaver, wolves and other wildlife, including many species of birds. It offers camping, boating and fishing for walleye and pickerel (northern pike) on its numerous lakes and rivers; dozens of fly-in fishing and hunting camps provide comfortable wilderness adventures. The Northern Lights also draw tourists. Fort McMurray, on the 65th parallel, lies within the aurora borealis zone, where night-time displays of shimmering white and green (and more rarely, red) lights are frequent from October to March, and often in August. Tourism is, indeed, an important revenue source, along with forestry, but these industries are dwarfed by the huge installations at Fort McMurray that have roared into prosperity since 2003 as oil prices have risen, and as oil companies have figured out how to recover synthetic oil economically from the bitumen lying in the Athabasca Oil Sands, the biggest known reserve of oil in the world—although it is uncertain how much can be extracted.

To the surprise of many, Northern Alberta includes, to the centre and west, some excellent prairie farmland around Fort Vermilion and High Level in the Peace River Valley, reached by Highway 35 due north from the town of Peace River. In the Fort McMurray area, however, about 40 percent of the land is covered by muskeg, a thick, peat-like buildup of decaying plants covered with vegetation that in summer is spongy and dotted with ponds veiled by clouds of blackflies. The rest of the landscape consists of boreal forests of spruce, aspen

Northern Lights, near Fort McMurray

Address Book

For dollar sign categories, see the Legend on the cover flap.

WHERE TO STAY

Be sure to reserve ahead for accommodations and restaurants in Fort McMurray, a boom town bursting at the seams.

$$ D&G's Place – *Conklin (140km/88mi south of Fort McMurray via Hwy. 881).* ☎*780-559-2928. www.dgplace.ca. 1 cabin and 2 rooms in house.* This small but modern and clean establishment offers a rest stop on the way between Edmonton and Fort McMurray, or a destination for fishing on Christina Lake or for snowmobiling vacations. On request, the owners will provide meals. Business travellers might feel a bit isolated (no Internet, only two telephone lines), but there is satellite TV and the owners will fillet and cook your walleye.

$$ Northern Lights Bed & Breakfast – *118 McDonald St., Fort Chipewyan.* ☎*780-697-3053. 5 rooms.* ☷. This modern two-storey house offers comfortable guest rooms with en suite bathrooms and satellite TV. Guests have access to a lounge, a kitchen, Internet and fax. The decor is clean-lined and Nordic, with blonde wood accents, and the owners are pleased to direct you to local sights and activities. Breakfast is included in the rate.

$$ Wah Pun Bed & Breakfast – *Fort Chipewyan.* ☎*780-697-3030. 10 rooms.* ☷. This lodging, whose name means "early morning" in Cree, lies in the midst of the boreal forest, next to Wood Bison National Park. Bright scarlet walls enliven the visitor lounge, where a small honour bar serves those craving a highball or beer. Recliners, with stacks of magazines nearby, and a pool table invite relaxation. Guest rooms are spread throughout several one- and two-storey buildings in town. In summer, tourists arrive to visit the famed park. In winter, ice-fishing and an annual February derby on frozen Lake Athabasca draw visitors. Book ahead.

$$$ Aurora Bed & Breakfast – *4143 Draper Rd., Fort McMurray.* ☎*780-799-3329. www.aurorabedandbreakfast.com.*

4 rooms. ☷. Backed into a stand of trees 8km/5mi outside of Fort McMurray, this dramatic modern log and timber inn has a cathedral ceiling in the main lounge, with windows facing north to offer excellent views of the Northern Lights (aurora borealis). Guest rooms are small but nicely decorated in rich colours. In-room fax and Internet access is provided and there's a satellite TV in the common room.

$$$ Chez Dubé Bed & Breakfast – *10102 Fraser Ave., Fort McMurray.* ☎*780-790-2367 or 800-565-0757. www.chezdube.com. 16 rooms.* ☷. Overlooking the trees and water of Borealis Park, yet right near Franklin Avenue in downtown Fort McMurray, this new chateau-like inn, with a little tower and a wrap-around veranda, offers lovely views and modern rooms with en suite bathrooms. Room decor leans to the fanciful, with chintz spreads and dried flower arrangements. The guest lounge has wood floors and big windows. For business travellers, small meeting rooms have Internet access. Breakfast is served in a pleasant dining room.

$$$ Podollan Inn and Rez – *10131 Franklin Ave,. Fort McMurray.* ☎*403-790-2000 or 888-448-2080. www.podollan.com. 100 rooms.* ✕⊡♿. This downtown hotel caters to business travellers, offering both nightly and monthly rates and across the street, a four-storey building with 36 one- and two-bedroom condo units with kitchens. Guest rooms are fairly plain but spacious and clean. Amenities include Internet service, a fitness room and coin-operated laundry. Continental breakfast is included in the rates. The **Pillar Pub ($$$)** offers a menu mainly of steaks, ribs and a fish dish or two. The chain also has a hotel in Grande Prairie.

$$$ Radisson Hotel & Suites – *435 Gregoire Dr., Fort McMurray.* ☎*780-743-2400 or 866-602-7666. www.radissonfortmcmurray.com. 134 rooms.* ✕♿⊡☷. This hotel, one of an American chain, offers complete service for the business traveller, with all the communications amenities, a fitness centre with pool, and a coin-operated laundry. Some suites have fireplaces and whirlpool baths. Families are also welcome and several vacation packages are offered. Rooms are comfortable, although the decor is standard. **PS Bistros Restaurant and Lounge ($$)** offers pub fare as well as steaks and chops. The hotel is somewhat outside of town, near the airport, so a car is necessary.

$$$ Sawridge Inn & Conference Centre – *530 McKenzie Blvd., Fort McMurray.* ☎*403-791-7900 or 888-729-7343. www.sawridgefortmcmurray.com. 188 rooms.* ✕Ⓟ☒. Situated on the south entrance to the city *(off Hwy. 63)*, the Sawridge, renovated in 2003, offers all the big-hotel amenities for business travellers. A high, wood-beam ceiling in the foyer recalls the wide western spaces, while the decor and art in the common areas and guest rooms make use of aboriginal themes. The attractive **Hearthstone Grille & Lounge ($$)**, with its stone pillars and four-sided fireplace, is one of the town's best restaurants. On the menu are pizzas, including the intriguing Canadian Hawaiian with pineapple, salads and sandwiches as well as a more elaborate menu of steaks and chops, local walleye, salmon and Arctic char and a breast of pheasant; some vegetarian choices as well. Sunday brunch *(10am–2pm)* brings in lots of locals. The fitness centre includes an indoor pool.

$$$ Stonebridge Hotel – *9713 Hardin St., Fort McMurray.* ☎*780-743-3301 or 888-419-4657. www.stonebridgefort mcmurray.com. 134 rooms.* ✕Ⓟ. Visitors find here something for everyone at this centrally-located hotel, from simple rooms to executive suites and units with kitchens. Amenities include Internet and a fitness room. Guest room decor is standard for business hotels, with an easy chair and a desk. **Smitty's Family Restaurant ($$)**, one of a Canadian chain, is adjacent to the hotel and serves simple meals.

WHERE TO EAT

$ Beirut Restaurant – *10012 Franklin Ave., Fort McMurray.* ☎*780-791-6868.* **Lebanese.** Just a few blocks north of downtown and near the river, this small eatery has great shish-kabob skewers, saffron rice and other delicacies. Some hard-to-find ingredients such as okra can be purchased at the small grocery on-site. The place is well known by locals, but the friendly owners take the time to suggest sights and offer directions to visitors passing through.

$ Tony Roma's – *8200 Franklin Ave., Fort McMurray.* ☎*780-791-3694. www. tonyromas.com.* **American.** The specialty of this popular spot is either ribs, chicken, steaks or fish plunged into a flaming grill and emerging juicy and delectable. Guests can select from a variety of sauces to personalise their choice. The menu also includes salads, soup, sandwiches and a children's menu. This American chain operates restaurants worldwide.

$$ Boston Pizza – *10202 MacDonald Ave., Fort McMurray.* ☎*780-743-5056, www.bostonpizza.com.* **Italian/Pizza.** This Canada-wide chain, which originated in Edmonton, dishes out quality pizzas, pastas, salads and sandwiches at prices higher than most pizza joints, but the quality and variety are consistently good. Try the stuffed stromboli sandwiches or the perogy pizza with sour cream, potatoes and bacon. The decor pays tribute to movie and sports history with posters and videos.

$$ Earl's – *9802 Morrison St., Fort McMurray.* ☎*780-791-3275. www. earls.ca.* **Canadian.** Located between Franklin Avenue and the Saskitawaw Trail *(Hwy. 63)*, this popular spot serves a varied menu of salads, pizzas, sandwiches and soup, as well as dishes such as Pad Thai (rice noodles with seafood, chicken and vegetables), salmon in tarragon sauce or striploin in peppercorn sauce. Part of a chain based in Richmond, British Columbia, the restaurant attracts repeat customers with reliable food and remarkable martinis.

$$ Garden Café – *9924 Biggs Ave., Fort McMurray.* ☎*780-791-6665.* **International.** Set just west of Highway 63 in downtown, this long-standing, no-frills, 7-days-a-week, late-night eatery has been dishing out its famous baked French onion soup, pasta, pizza, fajita and beef dip for more than 20 years. Its lush, plant-laden interior, even in winter, adds a splash of spring sunshine.

and poplar trees, with low-lying bushes, cut by rivers. From an airplane flying to Fort Chipewyan (accessible only by air except in winter months when the road is solid), the tar sands appear as black, watery patches scattered across the land. Most of the bitumen in the tar sands around Fort McMurray lies under a layer of sedimentary rock laid down by the Albian Boreal Sea during the Cretaceous era, some 65 million to 40 million years ago. Current thinking is that oil from Southern Alberta shifted northeast as the Rocky Mountains began to rise to the west 70 million to 40 million years ago, filtering into sand deposits left by ancient rivers that had been covered by the Cretaceous rock. Succeeding glacial ice sheets have, over the past two million years, ground down this Cretaceous shale and sandstone, but have also deposited layers of glacial till: sand, gravel, clay and boulders. Around Fort McMurray, some of these oil sands are close enough to the surface to be mined in open pits. Accessing the oil sands requires a great deal of digging with huge machinery: mechanical shovels used to scoop up the sands are the size of two-car garages.

Fort McMurray★★

POPULATION 65,400 – MAP OF PRINCIPAL SIGHTS

This former fur-trading post occupies a beautiful site at the confluence of the Athabasca and Clearwater rivers. The oil sands boom has brought a population of 56,100 in 2004—at the start of the present boom—to 65,400 in 2007, an increase of 16.5 percent in four years. As a comparison, in 1966, the population barely topped 2,000. The new arrivals are mostly Canadian, but have also included people of even more far-flung ancestry than the historically diverse Alberta ethic mix, including Europeans, South Asians and Chinese. Fort Mac, as it is called, seems in many ways a better place to live than it used to be. Young people who once migrated to more central cities now find high-paying jobs and a choice of leisure activities, and so are putting down roots here. Despite the present euphoria, locals know that, in the past, bust has followed boom, as in 1986 when oil prices slid, along with the local population. Still, with some $125 billion in oil sands investment planned for the next decade, no one is feeling too glum.

- **Information:** Regional Municipality of Wood Buffalo, 2209 Franklin Ave. ☎780-743-7000. www.woodbuffalo.ab.ca. Fort McMurray Tourism, 400 Sakitawaw Trail (Hwy. 63). Open Jun–Aug Mon–Fri 8am–6pm, weekends and holidays 9am–5pm; rest of the year Mon–Fri 8:30am–4:30pm. ☐ ♿☎780-791-4336. www.fortmcmurraytourism.com.
- ▶ **Orient Yourself:** Highway 63 is the primary route into Fort McMurray from Edmonton, but Highway 881 via Lac La Biche has been surfaced and is now a good alternative. Traffic is heavy; exercise caution. To enter town, take one of the four exits east leading to Franklin Dr., the main downtown street, running north-south. The airport is about 16km/10mi southeast of the centre. Downtown Fort McMurray boasts two shopping centres, the Peter Pond Shopping Centre (60 shops) and the River City Centre. Northeast of downtown lies MacDonald Island, with its recreational facilities (golf course, ice arena, tennis courts, squash and raquetball, with several more facilities planned) along an inlet of the Athabasca River. As golfers stroll down the green fairways, they can hear the drone of float planes taking off for sightseeing and fishing.
- ☐ **Parking:** Most of downtown parking is generally free except for a few venues like Keyano College.
- ⊚ **Don't Miss:** The Oil Sands Tour, booked with Fort McMurray Tourism well in advance (no children under age 12).

Regional Municipality of Wood Buffalo

Aerial view of Fort McMurray

🕐 **Organizing Your Time:** Allow 4-5 days to visit the area, given the driving distances, especially if you want to visit Wood Buffalo National Park. Your first stop should be the Oil Sands Discovery Centre, for an overview of the area. A bus or airplane tour (👤see Practical Information) of the oil sands will give you the scope of the huge operations. Accommodations, even campsites, are scarce due to a housing shortage, so it is essential to book well ahead.

Kids **Especially for Kids:** The Oil Sands Discovery Centre.

A Bit of History

The American explorer and fur-trader Peter Pond (👤*see sidebar)* first documented the oil sands in his journal in 1778, when he recorded seeing sticky black oil seeping from the banks of the Athabasca River. For centuries, local Cree and Chipewyan Indians used this mysterious, gooey substance to waterproof their canoes. However, it took a long time for a commercial use to develop, because bitumen—the viscous, molasses-like sort of oil found here—possesses a different chemical structure than conventional oil: a high proportion of carbon and too little hydrogen, so it must be specially treated before it can be delivered to refineries. The oil sands languished because other oil was easier and cheaper to extract.

In its natural state, bitumen's only known use, other than to caulk canoes, is to pave roads; asphalt companies exploited the sands to pave streets in Edmonton. Extracting the bitumen was hard manual labour, done with shovels and pick-axes. However, as oil prices rose and as tech-

nology improved, the tar sands (today called oil sands) attracted investment. The Great Canadian Oil Company, now Suncor, opened a modern upgrading plant in 1967, followed by Syncrude in 1978 and Albian Sands (a joint venture of Shell, Chevron and Marathon) in 2002. The upgrading process is expensive, itself using a great deal of energy as well as water, and can leave a mess behind. However, as oil prices climb, the oil sands have proven attractive.

Fort McMurray Today

One fortunate consequence of the influx of people from different parts of the world has been the opening of a handful of ethnic restaurants and stores, which in turn, has given Fort McMurray a relatively cosmopolitan atmosphere. Two shopping centres as well as office and residential developments have sprung up. **Keyano College** *(www. keyano.ca)*, with 3,000 full-time students, offers degree courses as well as technical and professional studies, many

PRACTICAL INFORMATION

AREA CODES

The Fort McMurray area has one area code (780). Local calls require the three-digit prefix. Long-distance calls to Edmonton and Northern Alberta require the 1-780 area code in advance of the number. For Calgary and Southern Alberta, dial the 403 area code. More information: www.telus.ca.

GETTING THERE

BY AIR

Fort McMurray Airport (YYM) (☎780-790-3900; www.fortmcmurray airport.com) is located southeast of Fort McMurray, 16km/11mi from city centre. **Air Canada** (☎888-247-2262) and **WestJet** (☎800-538-5696) plus these smaller airlines: First Nations-owned **Air Mikisew** (☎800-268-7112), **Corporate Express** (☎780-715-9319 or 800-661-8151) and **Northwestern Air** (☎867-872-2216) all fly into Fort McMurray's airport.

Car Rentals

Several car rental companies operate at the airport, including **Avis** (☎780-743-4773 or 800-879-2847), **Budget** (☎780-743-8215 or 800-268-8900), **Enterprise** (☎780-791-2468) and **National** (☎780-743-6393 or 800-CAR RENT).

Taxis

There are a handful of taxi companies in town (&see By Taxi below). From the airport to downtown costs about $30.

BY CAR

Be prepared for a five-hour drive from Edmonton to Fort McMurray and use cautious on Hwy. 63 (which is one-lane and two-lane each way). Traffic is heavy, especially with heavy equipment for oil sands and forestry purposes.
It is wise to drive with headlights on. There are few services on this route other than a gas station at Mariana Lakes. There is a secondary highway between Fort McMurray and Lac La Biche; Hwy. 881 was recently fully paved.

BY BUS/MOTORCOACH

Greyhound Canada (☎800-661-8747; www.greyhound.ca) serves Fort McMurray from both Calgary and Edmonton. Greyhound's depot is at 8220 Manning Ave. in Fort McMurray (☎780-791-3664).

Red Arrow (☎800-232-1958) also has service from Calgary and Edmonton. The Red Arrow depot in Fort McMurray is at 8217 Franklin Ave. (☎780-791-2990).

GETTING AROUND

BY PUBLIC TRANSPORTATION
Buses

Buses for a dozen routes depart at varying intervals from bus stops throughout the city; they run from about 6am until about 12:30am. There is no transit service on public holidays. Passes and tickets can be purchased at Municipal Hall, 9099 Franklin Ave. Adult ticket $1.25 (buses take exact fare); children under five and seniors, free. Buses are not wheelchair accessible but a specialized transportation service is offered on reduced hours; for reservations or information call ☎780-743-4157; 24-hour notice is required. ☎780-743-7090 daytime or transit@woodbuffalo.ab.ca.

BY CAR

Downtown is easy to navigate, but driving can be slow during rush hours (usually 6am-8:30am and 4pm-6pm and major plant shift changes). Road upgrades are underway.
Parking is generally free except for a few venues. Hwy. 63 swings west of downtown (main exits are Main Street, Hospital Street and Centennial Driver) and crosses the Athabasca River north of downtown, accessing several residential communities along Thickwood Blvd. The highway continues north to the Syncrude and Suncor oil sands plants and ends about 55km/35mi from Fort McMurray at a dock where barges ship goods downriver.

BY TAXI

Access Taxi ☎780-799-3333, **Sun Taxi** ☎780-743-5050, or **United Class Cabs** ☎780-743-1234.

AERIAL TOURS

Air Mikisew ☎780-743-8218; **Canadian Helicopters** ☎780-743-4888; **Highland Helicopters,** ☎780-791-0039; **McMurray Aviation,** ☎780-791-2182; **Phoenix Heli-Flight,** ☎780-799-0141; **Voyage Air,** ☎780-743-0255; **Wood Buffalo Helicopters,** ☎780-743-5588.

Most flights depart from the airport; float planes take off from an inlet of the Athabasca River called The Snye at MacDonald Island west of downtown.

GENERAL INFORMATION

VISITOR INFORMATION

Information: Regional Municipality of Wood Buffalo, 2209 Franklin Ave., Fort McMurray. ☎780-743-7000. www.woodbuffalo.ab.ca. **Fort McMurray Tourism,** 400 Sakitawaw Trail (Hwy. 63). ◷Open June–Aug Mon–Fri 8am–6pm, weekends and holidays 9am–5pm, rest of the year Mon–Fri 8:30am–4:30pm. ☎780-791-4336. www.fortmcmurraytourism.com.

ACCOMMODATION

For a selection of lodgings, ✆see the Address Book.

LOCAL PRESS

Newspapers: *Fort McMurray Today* and the **weekly** *Connect,* also the *Globe and Mail* and *National Post.*
Radio/Television: VF2182 (Aboriginal), CJOK, CKOS, CKUA, CKYX, CBXN, CHFT, CHFA (French), CFVR; CBXT-6 and CBXFT-6 (French television).

ENTERTAINMENT

Check www.fortmcmurraytourism.com, www.mymcmurray.com and the newspapers for entertainment listings. But the area is better known for outdoors activities such as kayaking, hunting, fishing and Northern Lights viewing.

USEFUL NUMBERS

Red Deer RCMP: 911 (emergency) or ☎780-799-8888 (non-emergency). **Northern Lights Regional Health Centre:** ☎780-791-6161.

AREA FESTIVALS

Jul **Rock Island Music Festival:** *MacDonald Island* www.rockislandfest.com.
Aug **InterPLAY:** *Fort McMurray* www.interplay.ca.
Early Sept **Blueberry Festival** *Fort McMurray* www.blueberryfest.ca.

RECREATION

The Regional Municipality of Wood Buffalo is an outdoor lover's paradise, especially for **boating** and **fishing (ice-fishing** in winter on Lake Athabasca). Fly-in fishing lodges and camps dot pristine lakes for pursuit of trophy-sized Northern pike, walleye and lake take.
Mikisew/Northern Sport Fishing (☎780-743-8218 or 888-268-7112, *www.mikisewsportfishing.com*) offers area fishing expeditions. Trips for groups of six or more cost about $1,200/ person.
Christina Lake Lodge (☎780-559-2224, *www.christinalakelodge.com*) offers a lakeside lodge, cabins and camping at Conklin *(south of Fort McMurray on Hwy. 881, halfway to Lac La Biche).* For other outfitters: Fort McMurray Tourism office at www.fortmcmurraytourism.com.

aimed at the oilpatch; from September to May the attractive Keyano Theatre stages drama, dance and musical performances, largely funded by oil money. The mix of locals, visitors and fortune hunters is most evident at night, when nightclubs and bars (the Oilcan Tavern is a major party spot) heat up, and the predominantly male population vies for the attention of available women. Challenges to the community include a very tight housing market (some five percent of the population lives in camp grounds, hotels or is homeless); the highest housing prices in Alberta; traffic congestion not only on roads but also at the airport; booked-up hotels and restaurants; and long lines at nearly every check-out counter.

Both Fort McMurray and Fort Chipewyan, some 450km/280mi apart as the crow flies, and farther north, the tiny community of Fort Fitzgerald (population 4) just south of Fort Smith, are part of the **Regional Municipality of Wood Buffalo,** at 68,454sq km/26,430sq mi the biggest in Canada, with a single municipal government for 11 communities and 89,167 residents (2007). Outside of Fort Mac, in the 10 other communities of Wood Buffalo municipality, a quieter rural or even wilderness life is still achievable—if one can bear the cold winters. The average temperature in January here is -19.8°C/-3.6°F. But the summers are pleasant: the average July temperature is 16.6°C/62°F.

Sights

Oil Sands Discovery Centre★★

515 McKenzie Blvd. at Hwy 63, just south of the city. ⏰Open mid-May–Labour Day daily 9am–5pm. Rest of the year Tue–Sun 10am–4pm. 👣Bus tours of the oil sands leave from this building but are booked through the tourist office. The centre offers walking tours (◎$6) of oil facilities and of the area in summer. ♿✕🅿☎780-743-7167. www.oilsandsdiscovery.com. ⏯Educational programs for the public are offered throughout the summer; inquire about the schedule the day of your visit.

Kids This modern centre, operated by the Alberta government, should be the first stop for visitors to the area: it presents an explanation of the huge projects they see all around them. Oil companies Suncor, Syncrude and Albian contribute to the exhibits, which are kept up-to-date with constant revisions. Hands-on educational displays abound and change often. Some might find the didactic emphasis on the history, science and technology of the projects a bit heavy (lots and lots of statistics), but a few facts help visitors keep some perspective on the frantic, 24hours-a-day activity out in the oilfields and the overwhelming size of every machine.

The centre also provides a live demonstration of just how the thick bitumen can be processed into synthetic crude oil. A film, **Quest for Energy** *(15min)*, gives a quick-paced version of oil sands development. On-site examples of the gigantic machines include the famous "Cyrus" bucket-wheel extractor, some six-storeys tall, weighing 850 tonnes and powered by enough electricity to supply 600 homes. Cyrus ceased its labours and was hauled to the museum in 1992; such monsters have been replaced by huge mechanical shovels and trucks, which are far more cost-efficient. ⏯For those who long to operate such a machine, an exhibit provides a virtual experience.

Heritage Park★

1 Tolen Dr. ⏰Open mid-May–Labour Day Mon–Sat 9am–5pm, Sun 9:30am–5pm. ◎$8. 👣Guided tours (◎$2) available by appointment. ♿🅿☎780-791-7575. www.fortmcmurrayhistory.com.

Established in the mid-1960s by the Fort McMurray Historical Society, this 2.6ha/6.6-acre park offers a very human insight into the rugged life in the Far North before the boom era. Maintained by the society, the park features 17 well-restored heritage buildings connected by a boardwalk and ramps that make them wheelchair accessible; flower plantings and grassy lawns add to the park-like ambiance. The society also manages an extensive archive, with historic photos and papers.

Explanatory panels describe each building, while artifacts in the Hill building are nicely displayed. Original buildings include an early 20C trapper's cabin; a

One of the giant machines used in the oil sands

Transforming Oil Sands into Oil

Alberta's three oil sands sites— Athabasca, Cold Lake and Peace River—together contain an estimated 1.7 trillion to 2.5 trillion barrels of oil, the biggest reserve in the world, but only about 175 billion barrels are recoverable with present technology, making the reserve second to Saudi Arabia's. Some 20 percent of the oil sands at Fort McMurray lie near enough to the surface to be clawed out of the ground with huge shovels. The ore extracted consists of between one to 20 percent **bitumen**, the rest being sand, gravel and clay; the mixture looks like black dirt. Ore of about eight percent and upwards of bitumen is selected for upgrading into oil. In a process developed by Dr. Karl Clark of the Alberta Research Council, this ore is then crushed, mixed with hot water to form a slurry, and delivered via pipeline to the upgrading plant where, in a separation vessel, the bitumen floats to the top and is skimmed off. The chemical structure of the viscous, heavy bitumen must then be corrected, or upgraded, breaking up the molecule so that it contains more hydrogen and less carbon, while removing sulphur and nitrogen. The end product, **called synthetic crude oil,** is sent by pipeline to refineries where it is further refined to produce gasoline, jet fuel and other products.

But what about the 80 to 90 per cent of Alberta oil sands buried too deeply for open pit mining? In a process called **Steam Assisted Gravity Drainage** (SAGO), wells are drilled into the deposit and steam is forced down, heating the bitumen so it is more liquid and rises up to the surface through the wells, leaving the sand behind or "in situ." The technology is expensive, requires a great deal of water and natural gas, and leaves behind huge tailing ponds (140,000sq km/15,444sq mi in Alberta) containing a noxious chemical brew. The environmental degradation caused by oil sands mining is widely recognized, and lease agreements require that mined areas be returned to an acceptable natural state. Today, about one-third of Canada's oil production comes from Alberta oil sands and the biggest customer is the United States.

log cabin that served as a Catholic mission in the early 20C, and white-clapboard Anglican and Presbyterian edifices; a drugstore from the 1930s, which contains a museum of artifacts such as old trapping gear; and a Royal Bank building, rather worse for the wear. The **Wop May Building,** a diminutive clapboard structure, contains a museum of bush pilot memorabilia. Most homes are log cabins while the Hill residence, although modest, would blend into a 1950s subdivision. Outside stands a **bucket-wheel excavator** that "walked" across the mine pit on caterpillar treads; the **Radium Scout,** a barge that worked the rivers; and an old railway caboose from the Northern Alberta line.

Additional Sight

The Oil Sands

Tours (2hrs) depart from the Oil Sands Discovery Centre at Hwy. 63 and McKenzie Blvd, but expect to devote 4hrs total, given traffic congestion. ◷*Tours (2hrs)* *offered mid-May–Labour Day Fri and Sat only. Availability is limited: book well in advance.* ◎*$35.* ♿ ☎*780-791-4336 or 800-565-3947. www.fortmcmurray tourism.com.* ⌂*Children must be 12 years old or older. All visitors must provide photo ID with name and birth date.*

⌂*Trips must be booked a minimum 24 hours in advance through the Fort McMurray Visitor Bureau, which deals directly with tour operators of both the Syncrude and Suncor plants. Tours for each plant generally run on separate days to curtail the heavy bus traffic on Hwy 63. Two-day hotel/plant packages can be booked for about $160. If the oil sands bus tour is not possible, consider taking an airplane tour (* ♿ *see Practical Information). Allow a half day for the oils sands tour in total.*

Hop on a tour bus and head north of Fort McMurray for a close-up look at the mining operations conducted by Syncrude and Suncor. Buses pass through the mining site for an impressive view of the incredibly big trucks and machinery. The tour may include a stop at Oil Sands Viewpoint to see Suncor's old tailing ponds, as well as a visit to a plot of land reclaimed from a Syncrude operation where 300 wood bison now roam.

Excursion

Gregoire Lake Provincial Park★

34 km/21mi southeast of Fort McMurray off Hwy 63. ○*Open daily year-round (camping May–mid-Oct).* ◻ ☎*780-334-2111. www. gateway. cd.gov.ab.ca.*
This 688ha/1,700-acre park on the northern shore of **Gregoire Lake,** some 26sq km/10sq mi in size, provides the only road-accessible recreational lake in the

region. Here the very hardy can swim in blue waters off a wide sandy beach ringed by aspen trees. The locals tend to call the lake Willow Lake, its former name. Canoes, kayaks and small motor-boats ply the waters, and anglers can try their luck for northern pike, walleye, yellow perch and stickleback. The area abuts the Gregoire Lake Natural Area. The park has three short (1-5km/.6-3mi) 🚶trails suitable for hiking, biking or skiing; bird-watchers will enjoy spotting waterfowl. The campground has 140 serviced sites. ⊘Ski trails are not maintained in winter, and snowmobiling is strictly limited.

Fort Chipewyan

POPULATION 1,007 – MAP OF PRINCIPAL SIGHTS

This historic hamlet is situated on the west shore of Lake Athabasca at an entrance to Wood Buffalo National Park. Regularly scheduled flights connect the town with the outside world; a gravel road from Fort McMurray that passes over soft muskeg, can be used for only about three months in winter, when the muskeg freezes; another winter road leads from Fort Chipewyan to Fort Smith, the principal entry to Wood Buffalo National Park. In summer a 298km/186mi boat route up the Athabasca River is also possible from Fort McMurray; experienced wilderness canoeists can finish the trip in about 6 to10 days. A tidy town with paved streets set among aspen, poplar and spruce, with a long waterfront, Fort Chipewyan possesses few amenities. Major employers locally are the government and tourism, as well as the resources industry; the town is a jumping-off point for fly-in fishing and hunting expeditions. Most inhabitants belong to Cree and Chipewyan First Nations or are Métis.

- 🛈 **Information:** Regional Municipality of Wood Buffalo, 2209 Franklin Ave., Fort McMurray. ☎780-743-7000. www.woodbuffalo.ab.ca.
- ▸ **Orient Yourself:** Fort Chipewyan lies some 280km/175 mi north of Fort McMurray, on the west bank of Lake Athabasca. A winter road from Fort McMurray is open only about three months a year, but there is scheduled air service (🕭 *see Practical Information*).
- ✎ **Don't Miss:** The Wood Buffalo Park Visitor Centre; the Catholic Church.
- ○ **Organizing Your Time:** The drive from Fort McMurray, when feasible, is adventurous. Air travel is most convenient. Allow at least 2 days here, devoting one to Wood Buffalo National Park.

A Bit of History

Fort Chipewyan was founded as a fur-trading post by the North West Company in 1788 and vies with Fort Vermilion, to the west, for the title of oldest European settlement in Alberta (much depends on definitions). For about a century, it was

a bustling regional hub, as traders, missionaries, aboriginal peoples and Métis, who plied the surrounding waterways, passed through. The arrival of the railways put an end to its importance. Most historic buildings, including the Hudson's Bay store, have been torn down. The most important heritage buildings in town are the two missionary churches, Catholic and Anglican, each demonstrating a clear architechtural style unmodified by "improvements."

Sights

Fort Chipewyan Visitor Reception Centre

Mackenzie Ave. ◷Open year-round Mon–Fri 8:30am–noon & 1pm–5pm. In addition, open intermittent weekends mid-Jun–Labour Day (call for hrs). ♿☎780-697-3662. www.pc.gc.ca.
Wood Buffalo National Park maintains this park visitor centre in Fort Chipewyan. It features educational exhibits on the park and its flora and fauna. An orientation **video** *(20min)* is shown regularly. Visitors can obtain park information, a park map and a list of outfitters and guides, as well as register for backcountry trips.

Fort Chipewyan Bicentennial Museum

109 Mackenzie Ave. ◷Open year-round Mon–Fri 9am–noon, 1pm–4pm, weekends 1pm–4:30pm. ☎780-697-3844.
Constructed to resemble a two-storey Hudson's Bay store, this locally organized museum, staffed by volunteers, opened in 1990 to commemorate the town's 200th anniversary in 1988. It boasts a fascinating array of fur-trade and First Nations artifacts, local handicrafts and clothing as well as an exhibit about the Holy Angels residential school run by the Grey Nuns. A built-to-scale **wooden replica**★ of the original fort, which was torn down in 1950, stands in the second-floor gallery.

Church of the Nativity of the Blessed Virgin Mary

269 Mackenzie Ave. ◷For entry key, inquire at the Bicentennial Museum. For information about Mass schedules, contact St. John the Baptist Church, Fort McMurray; ☎780-743-3980 or the Diocese of St. Paul, St. Paul AB. ☎780-645-3277.
This ornate wooden structure, designed in the typical Oblate Mission style, was built in 1909; it is the third church to stand on the site. The church is now a provincial historical resource, which has brought in funding for its preservation.

The first missionary, Father Taché, an energetic Oblate, arrived here in 1847. His successor, Father Faraud, cut and dressed the wood for the first church himself. Completed in 1851, it was the first Catholic mission west of St. Boniface, Manitoba. The mission grew its own food in a large garden (a lake was drained to provide soil), caught and preserved fish, and generally created a thriving community. But it was the arrival in 1862 of the dynamic Father **Émile Grouard** that set the mission on its way. He imported a printing press

Interior, Church of the Nativity of the Blessed Virgin Mary

©Susan Mate/Michelin

Peter Pond

Peter Pond (1739-1807) was the first explorer to reach Lake Athabasca and to map northwest Canada. Among his fur-trading colleagues, he was reputed for his energy, organizational skills and violent character. Born in Milford, Connecticut, he first saw military action at 16 years of age along the Quebec border. After a stint as a sailor in the West Indies, he joined his father in Detroit and never looked back. Loading up canoes with trade goods, he ventured into the wilderness to find Indians willing to trade pelts. In 1778 he led three canoes out of Cumberland Lake, Saskatchewan, to explore the Athabasca region, known only by Indian report. On the Athabasca River, near the lake, he intercepted a "vast concourse" of Cree and Chipewyan Indians heading to the Hudson's Bay Company's Prince of Wales post at Churchill. Delighted to cut their trip short, the Indians gave Pond a favourable trade, and he emerged from the region with 80,000 beaver pelts, or about 60 tons of fur; it remains a mystery how he organized the transport.

When the North West Company was formed in 1783, Pond was a founding share-holder. In subsequent trips to Athabasca, Pond gathered information from the Indi-ans, which he used to draw a famous map in 1784-85 that showed the waterways westward from the Great Lakes and Hudson Bay up to the Arctic Ocean, including Great Slave Lake and the Mackenzie River. The map inspired Alexander Mackenzie to push on to find the river that bears his name. Pond's successes were compro-mised by a reputation for violence (two murders) and by his American birth, which caused the British to mistrust him. Fellow explorer and great map-maker David Thompson said Pond was industrious and educated but "of a violent temper and unprincipled character." Pond quit trading in 1788 and returned to Milford, where he worked on maps and wrote his narrative, dying in poverty in 1807.

from his native France and rolled off prayer and hymn books in Chipewyan and Cree. Promoted to Bishop in 1873, Grouard made Fort Chipewyan his Epis-copal see and the church its cathedral. (The diocese later moved to Fort Smith, then to St. Paul, its present site.) He brought in Grey Nuns to establish the Holy Angels convent and residential school that functioned for a century, until the 1970s.

The inside of the church features large windows and a remarkable **painted interior**★. Another of Bishop Grouard's typical flourishes was to adorn the inte-rior of the church with his own paintings, at least one of which was transferred to the present church: the crucifixion is his. Later priests and nuns added their own work, using the juice of locally grown blueberries and cranberries mixed with fish oil. The **vaulted ceiling,** painted a deep blue is adorned with stars and cherubs; the murals depict scenes both divine and real, with a Virgin Mary who resembles an Indian woman and a York boat tossed in a storm on what might be the Sea of Galilee.

Church of St. Paul the Apostle★

114 Lucas St. Information about services and the key for entry are obtainable from the museum.

Consecrated in 1880, this small Anglican church, a white clapboard structure with a small steeple, dates nearly 30 years earlier than the Catholic church. The adjacent church school, constructed of squared logs in 1874, was attended by children of Hudson's Bay Company employees who were mostly Scottish from the Orkney Islands. Both church and school are built with a peculiar sys-tem of mortised joints at the corners, known as the Red River frame, which has very rarely been preserved. The church and the school, as well as the cemetery, are designated provincial historic resources.

The church edifice boasts stained glass windows with an **interior** entirely pan-elled in hand-dressed wood.

Wood Buffalo National Park★★

MAP P 272

Straddling Alberta and the Northwest Territories, Wood Buffalo National Park is one of North America's most valuable wildlife preserves. It contains both the largest free-roaming bison herd on earth—more than 5,600 strong—and the nesting grounds for the last remaining wild migratory flocks of whooping cranes. Designated a UNESCO World Heritage Site in 1983, Canada's largest park spans an area 45,000 sq km/17,400sq mi of protected land—about the size of Switzerland—approximately two-third of which lies in Alberta, and a third in the Northwest Territories. The park's headquarters and principal access are situated in Fort Smith in the Northwest Territories. Much of the park, however, is remote, explorable only by boat or plane; a labyrinth of waterways makes it easy to get lost so a stop at the park information centre is a must.

- **Information:** Wood Buffalo National Park, Fort Smith NT. ☎867-872-7960. www.pc.gc.ca.
- ▶ **Orient Yourself:** In summer, the park is accessible from Fort McMurray by river or air, and in winter, by car along a gravel road leading to Fort Chipewyan (280km/175mi); soft muskeg in summer makes the road impassable. Park headquarters and principal access are located at Fort Smith in the Northwest Territories. There is also an entrance at Fort Chipewyan. A gravel winter road leads from the Fort Chipewyan entrance through the park to Fort Smith. A maze of waterways makes it easy to get lost in the park, so a stop at the park visitor centre is a must.
- **Don't Miss:** A visit to the interpretive centre in Fort Smith or the small centre in Fort Chipewyan is a must as a first stop if you plan to explore the park in any detail.
- **Organizing Your Time:** Although there is road access to the park, it is a long way from anywhere: 1,310km/819mi from Edmonton, and 280km/175mi from Fort McMurray. You may consider flying in and renting a car in Fort Smith; alternatively drive the road from Fort McMurray (4 hours, no services en route) for an adventure. It is also possible to drive north from High Level via Highway 35 to Hay River, NWT, and then into the park on an all-weather road.
- **Especially for Kids:** The park offers hikes and canoe routes that are not strenuous for older children.

Wood Buffalo

NWT/T. Parker

Practical Information

ACCESS BY ROAD

From High Level, AB, Hwy. 35, the Mackenzie Hwy., leads to Hay River, NWT. Take Rte. 5 (near Hay River) south to the park entrance. Rte. 5, an all weather road, continues through the park to Fort Smith. From Fort Smith, an all-weather gravel road leads into Wood Buffalo's interior as far as **Peace Point Reserve** *(119km/74mi)*. From Fort Vermilion on the west side, a winter road leads to Garden Creek within the park, but this is not a maintained entrance. There is no all-weather road to Fort Chipewyan, although, for three months in the winter, a road links Fort Smith, Fort Chipewyan and Fort McMurray.

ACCESS BY AIR

Northwestern Air Lease operates scheduled flights from Edmonton and Yellowknife. ☎867-872-2216. Charter flights to Fort Smith and Fort Chipewyan available. First Nations-owned **Air Mikisew** offers regular flights between Fort McMurray and Edmonton to Fort Chipewayn *(☎780-743-8218)*. A sibling company called **Mikisew Sport Fishing** offers a range of wilderness fishing trips.
For more flight options, see ⒼPractical Information. Car rentals available in Fort Smith and Fort McMurray (winter) but not in Fort Chipewyan.

A Bit of Geology

The park offers visitors a subtle, tantalizing beauty that exemplifies the northern boreal plain, as well as an opportunity to view abundant wildlife: bears, wolves, moose, lynx, marten, wolverines and other fur-bearing animals that attracted traders two centuries ago, as well as the rare whooping crane and peregrine falcon.

The boreal plain, consisting of glacial till overlying porous sedimentary bedrock almost uniformly saturated with water, offers a vista of muskeg, meandering streams, lakes, ponds and boreal forest, interspersed with salt flats and sinkholes.

The Peace/Athabasca Delta, at the west end of Lake Athabasca at Fort Chipewyan, where the two rivers flow into the Slave River, is one of the largest inland deltas in the world and a vitally important wetland; many waterfowl nest or congregate here before migration.

Four North American flyways pass over the park. Whooping cranes gather here before heading 3,500km/2,188mi south to the Arkansas National Wildlife Refuge to pass the winter. Many rivers drain into this delta. **Lake Claire,** Alberta's largest lake at 1,436sq km/554sq mi, lies entirely within the park.

A Bit of History

Wood Buffalo was established in 1922 to protect the 500 wood bison that still existed, and the herd increased rapidly. In 1925, a group of plains buffalo was released in the park, a decision that almost turned to disaster as the two herds intermingled (it had been thought the park was so vast they'd never meet). The plains variety infected the local bison with bovine tuberculosis and brucellosis. However, in 1959 a herd of healthy semi-pure wood buffalo was found in a remote corner of the park, and these animals served to re-introduce the wood buffalo not only here, but also at Elk Island National Park near Edmonton. As a result of 1925 experiment, the

Whooping crane

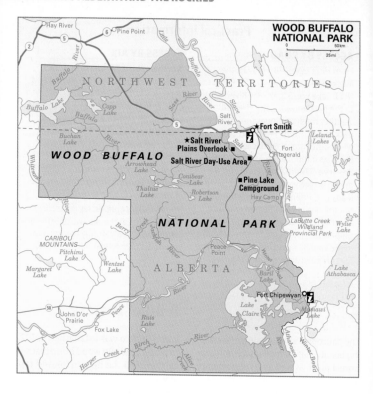

park's herd, described as wood bison, often exhibit distinctly plains characteristics. **Wood bison** tend to be slightly larger (over 2,000kg/4,400lbs) and darker than **plains bison,** as well as generally less shaggy. The wood bison's "cape" extends back over the haunches; its beard is discrete and pointed, and its hump is farther forward than that of a plains buffalo. The two subspecies are genetically distinct, although no scientific evidence indicates which is more attractive.

Visit

⊙*Open year-round. Hiking, camping, boating, fishing. Limited accommodations in Fort Chipewyan and Fort Smith. Park map and list of licensed guides and outfitters available at the two park visitor centres: Fort Chipewyan (MacKenzie Ave.; open year-round Mon–Fri 8:30am–noon & 1pm–5pm; in summer, open most weekends 1pm–5pm; ☎780-697-3662).* ⊙*No entry or gate fees. Park administration*

☎*867-872-7960. Visitor centre at Fort Smith (126 McDougal Rd. at Portage Ave.;* ⊙*open 3rd weekend in May–Labour Day Mon–Fri 9am–noon & 1pm–5pm, weekends 1pm–5pm; rest of the year closed weekends. ☎867-872-7960). Website for both: www.pc.gc.ca.*

Route 5

The approach to the park along Highway 5 from the vicinity of Hay River, NWT, is a pretty **drive** through boreal spruce and aspen forest. Bison can often be seen grazing by the roadside closer to Fort Smith. At the Angus Fire Tower, a **sinkhole** typifies the region's *karst* (limestone) topography; hundreds of these sinkholes are scattered through the region ranging from 3m/10ft wide to nearly 100m/300ft in width.

A short side road *(30km/19mi west of Fort Smith)* leads to the Salt River Plains **overlook★**, which provides an intriguing vista of a salt flat. This broad plain of the Salt River shimmers white in the summer sun, the river winding sinuously through scattered patches of forest and meadow,

Wilderness by Water

Exploring Wood Buffalo National Park by its waterways offers a peaceful encounter with nature, reminiscent of the way aboriginal inhabitants travelled centuries ago. Wilderness **canoe trips** along the park's two major rivers, the Peace and the Slave, require back-country experience, considerable planning and a park permit. Canoe trips along smaller rivers into the park's backcountry are also possible *(rentals available in Fort Smith)*. Guided canoe tours into the park are offered by several local outfitters *(contact the park visitor centre)*. Boating on Pine Lake is confined to its northern section. Motorboats are allowed on major rivers. *Contact park authorities regarding natural hazards within the park's river systems.* ⊘*Use of personal watercraft is not permitted in the park.*

as well as beds of salt. The salt plains are a product of underground deposits laid down by an ancient ocean.

Fort Smith★

Once the major town in the Territories, Fort Smith is yet another of the historic fur-trading sites that dot Canada's North. At the park visitor centre, a multimedia **presentation** *(18min)* offers an excellent grounding in the national park's history and ecology. Just a few blocks away, **Northern Life Museum** *(McDougal Rd. and King St.; call for hours; ☎867-872-2859)* and **Fort Smith Mission Historic Park**★ offer insight into the area's history *(Breynat St. & Mercredi Ave.; ⏰open daily; ☎867-874-6702)*. The city's Slave River boardwalk *(end of Simpson St.)* affords a view of the **rapids,** where a party of early explorers perished.

For accommodations, contact Visitor Infocentre in Fort Smith; ☎867-872-3065; www.fortsmithtourism.ca.

Fort Smith to Pine Lake★★

The all-weather gravel road into the heart of the park affords access to several notable sights and the opportunity to see bison anywhere along the road. The Salt River day-use area *(25km/15.5mi south of Fort Smith)* provides a short hiking path, the **Karstland Trail,** through the park's unusual broken topography. At 31km/19mi the South Loop trailhead initiates a pleasant *(4km/2.5mi)* hike through beautiful boreal forest down to **Grosbeak Lake,** an otherworldly salt flat dotted with boulders dropped by retreating glaciers.

Pine Lake Campground, at 60km/37mi, is an attractive facility overlooking a turquoise lake with a sandy beach, a spot long used by aboriginal peoples as a summer retreat. The lake is a particularly good place for swimming.

Lily pads, Wood Buffalo National Park

©Travel Alberta

A

B

C

INDEX

INDEX

INDEX

WHERE TO STAY

INDEX

WHERE TO EAT

MAPS AND PLANS

LIST OF MAPS

COMPANION PUBLICATIONS

MAP 583 NORTHEASTERN USA AND EASTERN CANADA

MAP 585 WESTERN USA AND WESTERN CANADA

- ◆ Large-format maps providing detailed road systems; includes driving distances, interstate rest stops, border crossings and interchanges.
- ◆ Comprehensive city and town index
- ◆ Scale 1:2,400,000 (1 inch = approx. 38 miles)

NORTH AMERICA ROAD ATLAS

- ◆ A geographically organized atlas with extensive detailed coverage of the USA, Canada and Mexico. Includes 246 city maps, distance chart, state and provincial driving requirements and a climate chart
- ◆ Comprehensive city and town index
- ◆ Easy to follow "Go-to" pointers

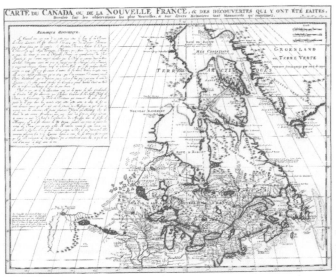

Historic Urban Plans

Canada (1719)

LEGEND

★★★ **Highly recommended**
★★ **Recommended**
★ **Interesting**

Sight symbols

Recommended itineraries with departure point

🏛️ ⛪	Church, chapel – Synagogue		Building described
○	Town described		Other building
AZ B	Map co-ordinates locating sights	■	Small building, statue
■ ▲	Other points of interest	● ⚜	Fountain – Ruins
⚒ ⌒	Mine – Cave	🛈	Visitor information
🌬️ 🗼	Windmill – Lighthouse		Ship – Shipwreck
☆ ⛪	Fort – Mission	🌟 ☙	Panorama – View

Other symbols

🛡️	Interstate highway (USA)	🛡️	US highway	180	Other route
🍁	Trans-Canada highway	401	Canadian highway		Mexican federal highway

	Highway, bridge		Major city thoroughfare
	Toll highway, interchange		City street with median
	Divided highway		One-way street
	Major, minor route		Pedestrian Street
15 (21)	Distance in miles (kilometers)	➦	Tunnel
2149/655	Pass, elevation *(feet/meters)*		Steps – Gate
△6288(1917)	Mtn. peak, elevation *(feet/meters)*	△ ⛲	Drawbridge - Water tower
✈ ✈	Airport – Airfield	P ✉	Parking – Main post office
	Ferry: Cars and passengers		University – Hospital
	Ferry: Passengers only	🚂 🚌	Train station – Bus station
	Waterfall – Lock – Dam	●	Subway station
	International boundary	❶	Digressions – Observatory
	State boundary, provincial boundary		Cemetery – Swamp
🍇	Winery	‖‖‖	Long lines

Recreation

	Gondola, chairlift		Stadium – Golf course
🚂	Tourist or steam railway		Park, garden
⚓	Harbor, lake cruise – Marina		Wildlife reserve
🏄	Surfing – Windsurfing		Wildlife/Safari park, zoo
🤿 🛶	Diving – Kayaking		Walking path, trail
⛷️ 🎿	Ski area – Cross-country skiing	🚶	Hiking trail

🔅 Sight of special interest for children

Abbreviations and special symbols

MP	Marine Park	NP	National Park	NF	National Forest
NHS	National Historic Site			PP	Provincial Park

Visitor centre : Local - 🛈 Provincial - 🛈

16 Yellowhead Highway ⊘ Subway station (Montreal)

All maps are oriented north, unless otherwise indicated by a directional arrow

Little Red Riding Hood

But Little Red Riding Hood had her regional map with her, and so she did not fall into the trap. She did not take the path through the wood and she did not meet the big bad wolf. Instead, she chose the picturesque touring route straight to Grandmother's house, and arrived safely with her cake and her little pot of butter.

The End

With Michelin maps, go your own way.

Michelin Apa Publications Ltd

A joint venture between Michelin and Langenscheidt

Suite 6, Tulip House, 70 Borough High Street, London SE1 1XF, United Kingdom

© 2009 Michelin Apa Publications Ltd
ISBN 978-1-906261-55-9
Printed: August 2008
Printed and bound: Himmer, Germany